P9-BZR-034

The Municipal
Year Book
2013

The authoritative source book of local government data and developments

The Municipal
Year Book
2013

Washington, DC

ICMA *Leaders at the Core of Better Communities*

Volume 80, 2013

ISBN: 978-0-87326-778-6

ISSN: 0077-2186

43676

Library of Congress Catalog Card Number: 34-27121

Design and composition: Erika Abrams, Charles E. Mountain

Contents

Acknowledgments viii

Inside the *Year Book* ix

Management Trends and Survey Research ix

Directories xi

Organization of Data xi

Uses of Statistical Data xiv

Limitations of the Data xvi

Types of Statistics xvii

Summary xviii

Management Trends and Survey Research

1 Growing Income Disparity and the Implications for Local Government 3

Ron Carlee

The State of Income Disparity 4

The Consequences of Income Disparity 7

Political Polarization and the Unlikelihood of a Consensus Approach to Income Equality 9

The Special Challenge for City/County Managers 11

Practical Tools for Addressing Income Disparity at the Local Level 12

Conclusion 14

2 Perspectives on Changes in City Government Structure 17

James H. Svara   Jennifer Claire Auer

Survey Methodology 17

Definitions and Findings 18

Summary 32

3 Local Government Support for Food System Development: An Initial Scan of the Landscape 35

Laura Goddeeris   Michael W. Hamm

Methods 36

Policies and Regulations Supporting Food Access and Production 37

Community Projects and Programs 38

Food as a Topic in Local Plans 40

Responsibility, Collaboration, and Councils 41

Federal Support for Food System Development 43

Conclusions and Recommendations 44

4 Building Child- and Age-Friendly Communities in Tight Fiscal Times 47
Mildred E. Warner   Lydia J. Morken
   Changes in America's Demographic Profile 47
   Economic Development and the Need for Public Investment 48
   Multigenerational Planning Opportunities 51
   Demographic and Fiscal Challenges 53
   Conclusion 55

5 Collaborative Governance and Leadership: A 2012 Survey of Local Government Collaboration 57
Rosemary O'Leary   Catherine M. Gerard
   Survey Methodology 58
   Use of Collaboration as a Management Strategy 58
   Recent Collaborative Experiences 60
   What Makes Collaboration Work? 62
   Consequences of Collaboration 63
   Challenges to Collaboration 65
   The Skill Sets of the Successful Local Government Collaborator 65
   Conclusion 69

6 Electronic Democracy at the Grass Roots 71
Donald F. Norris   Christopher G. Reddick
   Method 72
   E-Democracy Activities 73
   Planning for E-Democracy 75
   Management of E-Democracy 75
   Impacts of E-Democracy on Local Government 75
   Barriers to E-Democracy 77
   Conclusion 78

7 Volunteer Use in Local Government Service Delivery 79
Rebecca Nesbit   Jeffrey L. Brudney
   Background 79
   Survey Response and Methodology 81
   Methods of Analysis 81
   Findings 84
   Summary 87

8 Recurrent Themes in Local Government Innovation 89
Karen Thoreson   James H. Svara
   Improving the Economic Environment 90
   Sustainability Initiatives 91
   Innovative Infrastructure 92
   Engaging Citizens for Community Development 93
   Organizational Design 94
   Lessons Learned 95
   Conclusion 97

9 CAO Salary and Compensation: Stability Is the Trend 99

Evelina R. Moulder   Ron Carlee

  Survey Methodology   100

  Base Salary   100

  Compensation beyond Base Salary   103

  Salary and Performance Review   103

  Pay Decreases and Furlough Days   105

  Benefits   105

  Employment Contracts/Agreements   106

  Severance Benefits   106

  Summary   106

  Appendix Table 9-A1: City Salaries by Population Group within States   110

  Appendix Table 9-A2: County Salaries by Population Group within States   120

10 Police and Fire Personnel, Salaries, and Expenditures for 2012 125

Evelina R. Moulder

  Methodology   125

  Administration   126

  Personnel   126

  Staffing Requirements for Fire Personnel   130

  Hours Worked per Shift   130

  Salary and Longevity Pay   130

  Expenditures   134

  Conclusion   139

Directories

1 Directory Tables 145

  U.S. State Municipal Leagues   146

  Provincial and Territorial Associations and Unions in Canada   148

  State Agencies for Community Affairs   149

  Provincial and Territorial Agencies for Local Affairs in Canada   152

  U.S. Municipal Management Associations   153

  International Municipal Management Associations   155

  U.S. State Associations of Counties   156

  U.S. Councils of Governments Recognized by ICMA   158

2 Professional, Special Assistance, and Educational Organizations Serving Local and State Governments 161

Authors and Contributors 177

Cumulative Index, 2009-2013 183

Acknowledgments

The Municipal Year Book, which provides local government officials with information on local government management, represents an important part of ICMA's extensive research program. Each year, ICMA surveys local officials on a variety of topics, and the data derived from their responses constitute the primary information source for the *Year Book.* Authors from local, state, and federal government agencies; universities; and public interest groups as well as ICMA staff prepare articles that describe the data collected and examine trends and developments affecting local government.

We would like to express our appreciation to the thousands of city and county managers, clerks, finance officers, personnel directors, police chiefs, fire chiefs, and other officials who patiently and conscientiously responded to ICMA questionnaires. It is only because of their time-consuming efforts that we are able to provide the information in this volume.

In addition, I would like to thank the ICMA staff who have devoted countless hours to making the *Year Book* so valuable. Ann I. Mahoney is the director of publishing and Jane C. Cotnoir is the *Year Book* editor. Other ICMA staff members who contributed to this publication are Evelina Moulder, director of survey research and information management; Erik Sundvall, director of creative services; Erika Abrams, graphic designer; Sebia Clark, program analyst; and Nedra James, executive assistant. Finally, thanks go to Sandra F. Chizinsky, ICMA consulting editor.

Robert J. O'Neill Jr.
Executive Director
ICMA

Inside the *Year Book*

Local government concerns are increasingly complex and sophisticated, and the need for familiarity with a broad range of issues is unsurpassed. Furthering the knowledge base needed to better manage local government is one of ICMA's top goals.

Management Trends and Survey Research

1 Growing Income Disparity and the Implications for Local Government

Since the Great Recession began, ICMA has been trying to understand its impact on local government. Among the six drivers consistently identified as affecting local government is the increasing gap between the haves and have-nots. Negative social impacts, including violence, have been shown to be the result not of poverty per se, but of growing income disparity, particularly in high-income countries. Many see this disparity as primarily a federal or state issue, but because the federal and state governments are largely deadlocked politically and financially, the responsibility for dealing with this issue has largely devolved to local governments. To examine the implications of this devolution, this article begins with the data, translates them into human terms, and examines the challenges confronting local governments that have both the will and the ability to grapple with the complexities inherent in economic disparity.

2 Perspectives on Changes in City Government Structure

ICMA has been conducting a survey on municipal form of government for many years. The survey provides a snapshot of the responding governments, and it collects data from each about any structural changes that have been considered in the five-year period since the previous survey. This article, which presents an analysis of the results of the 2011 survey, adds another set of data, a long-term perspective, and supplemental historical and census data to extend the picture of current conditions and developing trends—an undertaking that is particularly relevant now that the use of the council-manager form has moved into its second century.

3 Local Government Support for Food System Development: An Initial Scan of the Landscape

Local government awareness of local and regional food systems and the opportunities they present has been increasing dramatically. Compelled by a variety of concerns, including inequitable food access (or so-called food deserts), preservation of local agricultural heritage, and even calls to action from professional organizations and the White House, communities across the country have introduced plans, policies, programs, and partnerships to support food system development. In 2012, ICMA partnered with the Michigan State University Center to conduct a national survey to assess local government support for food system development. Using data and findings from that survey, this article presents the first analysis of local governments' overall awareness of and involvement in food system support; it also identifies possible motivations for and perspectives on such involvement.

4 Building Child- and Age-Friendly Communities in Tight Fiscal Times

America is aging. By 2040, the number of U.S. residents over age 65 will have doubled from 40 million in 2010 to over 80 million. At the same time,

America's birthrate is declining while its younger population is changing. In 2011, for the first time ever, minority births outnumbered white births in the United States, and young families with children are growing fastest among the Hispanic population. This leaves municipalities facing a dual challenge: how to meet the needs of both a rapidly aging population and families with young children. Rather than viewing this as a trade-off between older adults and children, communities that strive for generational balance in their demographic composition and service delivery will have stronger economic development and fiscal health. After reviewing America's changing demographics, this article explores the complementarities between seniors and young children, the need for economic development that invests in both groups, and the demographic and fiscal challenges that impede such investment.

5 Collaborative Governance and Leadership: A 2012 Survey of Local Government Collaboration

Today's local government managers are working in a landscape in which efforts to improve the efficiency and effectiveness of service delivery require new approaches. One such approach is collaboration. In 2010 members of the U.S. Senior Executive Service were surveyed on their use of collaboration as a management strategy. In 2012 that survey was tailored to local government managers to learn more about their use of collaboration. In addition to the fact that 97% of all surveyed local government managers reported using collaboration as a management strategy, this article highlights the preliminary findings from that survey, including managers' reasons for using collaboration, factors that make collaboration work, consequences of and challenges to collaboration, and the skill sets needed by the successful local government collaborator.

6 Electronic Democracy at the Grass Roots

Public participation in local government in the United States is typically very low, whether measured by voting in local elections; by attendance at city council meetings, county board meetings, or public hearings; or by other means. For some time now, proponents of electronic government (e-government) have argued that one outcome of e-government would almost inevitably be e-democracy, which would be a tool to improve the otherwise low rate of citizen participation in government. However, few if any systematic studies have been undertaken to ascertain whether and to what extent e-democracy is being practiced among governments anywhere in the world. Using data collected from a survey conducted in 2011, this article begins to address

that gap in the literature vis-à-vis local governments in the United States.

7 Volunteer Use in Local Government Service Delivery

The first decade of the 21st century witnessed repeated calls for volunteers to assist with public sector service delivery. At the local level, fiscal stringency led officials to advocate the use of volunteers to shore up public services and even compensate for cutbacks in paid personnel. This article first reviews data on volunteer use derived from ICMA's alternative service delivery (ASD) surveys, undertaken every five years since 1982. It then briefly describes the relevant data from ICMA's 2007 ASD survey and analyzes those data according to several variables of interest to assess local government use of volunteers in seven main areas of service: public works/transportation, public utilities, public safety, health and human services, parks and recreation, cultural and arts programs, and support functions.

8 Recurrent Themes in Local Government Innovation

Sharing information about creative problem solving and innovative solutions is an important service that any jurisdiction can provide to the entire local government community. This article highlights 26 noteworthy approaches to making local government more effective in addressing community problems and addressing the needs of citizens. These approaches, which have been implemented by communities of all different sizes and from all different regions of the country, fall into five broad categories: the economic environment, sustainability initiatives, innovative infrastructure, engaging citizens for community development, and organizational design. The article then examines key features of the highlighted cases and reviews lessons learned from them.

9 CAO Salary and Compensation: Stability Is the Trend

Compensation of public employees is often a topic of media coverage, especially when the occasional outlier in benefits and compensation makes the news. But what are the norms? What is typical in salary and benefits for a city or county manager or chief appointed official? "ICMA Guidelines for Compensation" state that the compensation of local government managers should be "fair, reasonable, transparent, and based on comparable public salaries nationally and regionally." But what is fair and reasonable? They further state that "compensation should be based on the position requirements, the complexity of the job reflected in the composition of the organization and community, the leadership needed, labor market conditions, cost of living in the community, and the organization's ability to pay." Examining new data from a 2012 national survey of local government executives, this article looks at compensation issues for city, county, and town managers and administrators within the context of the ICMA guidelines.

10 Police and Fire Personnel, Salaries, and Expenditures for 2012

Continuing the trend identified in 2010 when police and fire departments, like other local government departments, saw their budgets reduced, police and fire expenditures in 2012 continue to be a concern in some communities. There is hope that as the housing market continues to strengthen, property tax revenues may slowly increase, and that this increase in revenue for municipal budgets may eventually bring a halt to staffing reductions. This article, a longtime staple of *The Municipal Year Book*, is based on the results of an annual survey that is meant to provide a general picture of police and fire personnel and expenditures for each year. It presents the following information for both police and fire departments in tabular form: total personnel, the number of uniformed personnel, minimum crew per fire apparatus, entrance and maximum salaries, information on longevity pay, and a breakdown of departmental expenditures. Data from the 2012 survey are compared with those from 2011.

Directories

Directory 1 consists of eight lists providing the names and websites of U.S. state municipal leagues; provincial and territorial associations and unions in Canada; state agencies for community affairs; provincial and territorial agencies for local affairs in Canada; U.S. municipal management associations; international municipal management associations; state associations of counties; and U.S. councils of governments recognized by ICMA.

Directory 2 presents "Professional, Special Assistance, and Educational Organizations Serving Local and State Governments." The 79 organizations that are included provide educational and research services to members and others, strengthening professionalism in government administration.

Organization of Data

Most of the tabular data for *The Municipal Year Book 2013* were obtained from public officials through questionnaires developed and administered by ICMA. ICMA maintains databases with the results of these surveys. All survey responses are reviewed for errors. Extreme values are identified and investigated; logic checks are applied in the analysis of the results.

Government Definitions

A municipality, by census definition, is a "political subdivision within which a municipal corporation has been established to provide general local government for a specific population concentration in a defined area." This definition includes all active governmental units officially designated as cities, boroughs (except in Alaska), villages, or towns (except in New England, Minnesota, New York, and Wisconsin), and it generally includes all places incorporated under the procedures established by the several states.

Counties are the primary political administrative divisions of the state. In Louisiana these units are called parishes. Alaska has county-type governments called boroughs. There are certain unorganized areas of some states that are not included in the *Year Book* database and that have a county designation from the Census Bureau for strictly administrative purposes. These comprise 11 areas in Alaska, 5 areas in Rhode Island, 8 areas in Connecticut, and 7 areas in Massachusetts.[1]

According to the U.S. Bureau of the Census, in January 2007 there were 89,476 governments in the United States (Table 1).

Table 1 U.S. Local Governments, 2007

Local governments	89,476
County	3,033
Municipal	19,492
Town or township	16,519
School district	13,051
Special district	37,381

Municipality Classification

Table 2 details the distribution of all municipalities of 2,500 and over in population by population, geographic region and division, metro status, and form of government.

Population This edition of the *Year Book* generally uses the 2000 Census Bureau figures for placing local governments in the United States into population groups for tabular presentation. The population categories are self-explanatory.

Geographic Classification Nine geographic divisions and four regions are used by the Bureau of the Census (Figure 1). The nine divisions are *New England:* Connecticut, Maine, Massachusetts, New

Table 2 Cumulative Distribution of U.S. Municipalities with a Population of 2,500 and Over

Classification	2,500 and over	5,000 and over	10,000 and over	25,000 and over	50,000 and over	100,000 and over	250,000 and over	500,000 and over	Over 1,000,000
Total, all cities	7,524	5,531	3,597	1,658	770	284	76	34	9
Population group									
Over 1,000,000	9	9	9	9	9	9	9	9	9
500,000-1,000,000	25	25	25	25	25	25	25	25	...[1]
250,000-499,999	42	42	42	42	42	42	42	...	...
100,000-249,999	208	208	208	208	208	208	...	...	...
50,000-99,999	486	486	486	486	486	...	...	...	...
25,000-49,999	888	888	888	888	...	...	...	...	...
10,000-24,999	1,939	1,939	1,939	...	...	...	...	...	...
5,000-9,999	1,934	1,934	...	...	...	...	...	...	...
2,500-4,999	1,993	...	...	...	...	...	...	...	...
Geographic region									
Northeast	2,013	1,505	925	355	125	33	8	4	2
North-Central	2,176	1,552	1,005	413	163	48	16	5	1
South	2,204	1,524	963	439	216	94	26	14	3
West	1,131	950	704	451	266	109	26	11	3
Geographic division									
New England	753	570	364	143	51	12	1	1	...
Mid-Atlantic	1,261	936	561	212	74	21	7	3	2
East North-Central	1,457	1,087	723	302	108	29	9	5	1
West North-Central	719	465	283	112	55	19	7	...	...
South Atlantic	976	673	441	210	107	43	10	4	...
East South-Central	458	325	190	73	26	13	4	3	...
West South-Central	771	525	331	155	83	38	12	7	3
Mountain	416	321	203	122	63	31	9	5	1
Pacific Coast	713	629	501	329	203	78	17	6	2
Metro status									
Metropolitan Statistical Area	4,418	3,459	2,415	1,323	699	272	74	33	9
Micropolitan Statistical Area	1,062	766	520	98	2	...	...	...	...
New England City and Town Area	521	413	258	67	11	...	...	...	...
Undesignated	1,523	893	404	170	58	12	2	1	...
Form of government									
Mayor-council	3,291	2,187	1,324	566	268	104	43	22	6
Council-manager	3,671	2,931	2,040	1,037	485	175	31	11	3
Commission	142	109	70	28	12	5	2	1	...
Town meeting	353	247	117	6	...	...	...	...	...
Rep. town meeting	67	57	46	21	5	...	...	...	...

Note: This table comprises *only* city-type local governments with populations of 2,500 and above.

1 (...) indicates data not applicable or not reported.

Hampshire, Rhode Island, and Vermont; *Mid-Atlantic:* New Jersey, New York, and Pennsylvania; *East North-Central:* Illinois, Indiana, Michigan, Ohio, and Wisconsin; *West North-Central:* Iowa, Kansas, Minnesota, Missouri, Nebraska, North Dakota, and South Dakota; *South Atlantic:* Delaware, the District of Columbia, Florida, Georgia, Maryland, North Carolina, South Carolina, Virginia, and West Virginia; *East South-Central:* Alabama, Kentucky, Mississippi, and Tennessee; *West South-Central:* Arkansas, Louisiana, Oklahoma, and Texas; *Mountain:* Arizona, Colorado, Idaho, Montana, Nevada, New Mexico, Utah, and Wyoming; and *Pacific Coast:* Alaska, California, Hawaii, Oregon, and Washington.

The geographic regions are consolidations of states in divisions: *Northeast:* Connecticut, Maine, Massachusetts, New Hampshire, New Jersey, New York, Pennsylvania, Rhode Island, and Vermont; *North Central:* Illinois, Indiana, Iowa, Kansas, Michigan, Minnesota, Missouri, Nebraska, North Dakota, Ohio, South Dakota, and Wisconsin; *South:* Alabama, Arkansas, Delaware, the District of Columbia, Florida, Georgia, Kentucky,

Louisiana, Maryland, Mississippi, North Carolina, Oklahoma, South Carolina, Tennessee, Texas, Virginia, and West Virginia; and *West:* Alaska, Arizona, California, Colorado, Hawaii, Idaho, Montana, Nevada, New Mexico, Oregon, Utah, Washington, and Wyoming.

Metro Status   Metro status refers to the status of a municipality within the context of the U.S. Office of Management and Budget (OMB) definition of a statistical area. The OMB has redefined metropolitan statistical areas, metropolitan divisions, micropolitan statistical areas, combined statistical areas, and New England city and town areas in the United States. ICMA is in the process of updating its local government records to correspond to these new definitions, but the updates are not available at this time.

Form of Government   Form of government relates primarily to the organization of the legislative and executive branches of municipalities and townships.

In the *mayor-council* form, an elected council or board serves as the legislative body. The head of government is the chief elected official, who is generally

Figure 1   U.S. Bureau of the Census Geographic Regions and Divisions

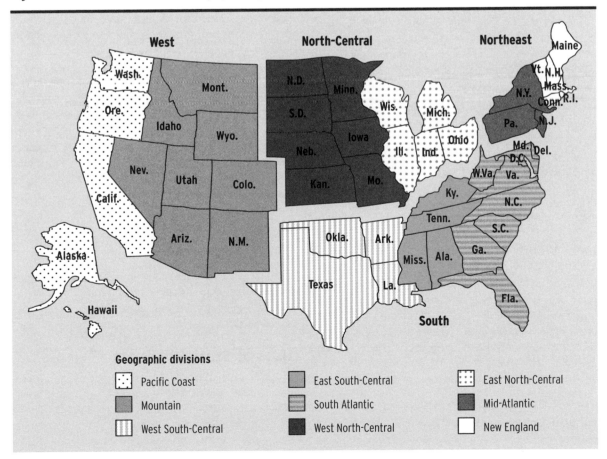

elected separately from the council and has significant administrative authority.

Many cities with a mayor-council form of government have a city administrator who is appointed by the elected representatives (council) and/or the chief elected official and is responsible to the elected officials. Appointed city administrators in mayor-council governments have limited administrative authority: they often do not directly appoint department heads or other key city personnel, and their responsibility for budget preparation and administration, although significant, is subordinate to that of the elected officials.

Under the *council-manager* form, the elected council or board and chief elected official (e.g., the mayor) are responsible for making policy. A professional administrator appointed by the council or board has full responsibility for the day-to-day operations of the government.

The *commission* form of government operates with an elected commission performing both legislative and executive functions, generally with departmental administration divided among the commissioners.

The *town meeting* form of government is a system in which all qualified voters of a municipality meet to make basic policy and elect officials to carry out the policies.

Under the representative town meeting form of government, the voters select a large number of citizens to represent them at the town meeting(s). All citizens can participate in the meeting(s), but only the representatives may vote.

County Classification

Counties are the primary political administrative divisions of the states. The county-type governments in Alaska are called boroughs. Table 3 details the distribution of counties throughout the nation, using the same geographic and population categories as Table 2.

Metro Status Metro status refers to the status of a municipality within the context of the OMB definition of a statistical area. The OMB has redefined metropolitan statistical areas, metropolitan divisions, micropolitan statistical areas, combined statistical areas, and New England city and town areas in the United States. ICMA is in the process of updating its local government records to correspond to these new definitions, but the updates are not available at this time.

Form of Government For counties, form of government relates to the structural organization of the legislative and executive branches of counties;

counties are classified as being with or without an administrator. There are three basic forms of county government: commission, council-administrator, and council–elected executive.

The *commission* form of government is characterized by a governing board that shares the administrative and, to an extent, legislative responsibilities with several independently elected functional officials.

In counties with the *council-administrator* form, an administrator is appointed by, and responsible to, the elected council to carry out directives.

The *council–elected executive* form features two branches of government: the executive and the legislative. The independently elected executive is considered the formal head of the county.

The use of varying types of local government is an institutional response to the needs, requirements, and articulated demands of citizens at the local level. Within each type of local government, structures are developed to provide adequate services. These structural adaptations are a partial result of the geographic location, population, metropolitan status, and form of government of the jurisdiction involved.

Consolidated Governments

The Bureau of the Census defines a consolidated government as a unit of local government in which the functions of a primary incorporated place and its county or minor civil division have merged.[2] There are several categories of consolidations: city-county consolidations that operate primarily as cities (Table 4), metropolitan governments operating primarily as cities (Table 5), and areas that maintain certain types of county offices but as part of another city or township government (Table 6). In addition, the District of Columbia is counted by the Census Bureau as a city, a separate county area, and a separate state area. To avoid double counting in survey results, ICMA counts the District of Columbia only as a city.

The Census Bureau defines independent cities as those operating outside of a county area and administering functions commonly performed by counties (Table 7). The bureau counts independent cities as counties. For survey research purposes, ICMA counts independent cities as municipal, not county governments.

Uses of Statistical Data

The *Municipal Year Book* uses primary and secondary data sources. ICMA collects and publishes the primary source data. Secondary source data are data collected by another organization. Most of the primary source data are collected through survey research. ICMA develops questionnaires on a variety of subjects

Table 3 Cumulative Distribution of U.S. Counties

Classification	All counties	Population								
		2,500 and over	5,000 and over	10,000 and over	25,000 and over	50,000 and over	100,000 and over	250,000 and over	500,000 and over	Over 1,000,000
Total, all counties	3,031	2,901	2,737	2,358	1,530	916	526	230	106	33
Population group										
Over 1,000,000	33	33	33	33	33	33	33	33	33	33
500,000-1,000,000	73	73	73	73	73	73	73	73	73	...[1]
250,000-499,999	124	124	124	124	124	124	124	124	...	...
100,000-249,999	296	296	296	296	296	296	296	...	...	...
50,000-99,999	390	390	390	390	390	390	...	...	...	...
25,000-49,999	614	614	614	614	614	...	...	...	...	...
10,000-24,999	828	828	828	828	...	...	...	...	...	...
5,000-9,999	379	379	379	...	...	...	...	...	...	...
2,500-4,999	164	164	...	...	...	...	...	...	...	...
Under 2,500	130	...	...	...	...	...	...	...	...	...
Geographic region										
Northeast	189	189	188	183	175	132	86	45	21	3
North-Central	1,051	991	902	730	447	238	133	47	21	6
South	1,366	1,337	1,295	1,152	707	402	212	83	35	11
West	425	384	352	293	201	144	95	55	29	13
Geographic division										
New England	45	45	45	43	40	24	14	6	2	...
Mid-Atlantic	144	144	143	140	135	108	72	39	19	3
East North-Central	436	435	430	403	293	169	98	34	15	5
West North-Central	615	556	472	327	154	69	35	13	6	1
South Atlantic	541	539	533	484	331	209	120	50	21	6
East South-Central	359	357	354	321	179	83	32	7	2	...
West South-Central	466	441	408	347	197	110	60	26	12	5
Mountain	276	244	217	167	97	59	38	18	9	3
Pacific Coast	149	140	135	126	104	85	57	37	20	10
Metro status										
Metropolitan Statistical Area	975	973	970	932	789	653	475	225	104	33
Micropolitan Statistical Area	646	637	631	595	483	206	31	...	...	...
Undesignated	1,410	1,291	1,136	831	258	57	20	5	2	...
Form of government										
County commission	1,724	1,621	1,493	1,210	685	329	151	54	20	6
Council-manager/ administrator	818	803	784	736	558	381	236	103	49	18
Council-elected executive	489	477	460	412	287	206	139	73	37	9

1 (...) indicates data not applicable or not reported.

Table 4 Legally Designated Consolidated City-County Governments Operating Primarily as Cities, 2007

State	Consolidated government
Alaska	City and Borough of Anchorage
	City and Borough of Juneau
	City and Borough of Sitka
California	City and County of San Francisco
Colorado	City and County of Broomfield
	City and County of Denver
Hawaii	City and County of Honolulu
Kansas	Kansas City and Wyandotte County
Montana	Anaconda-Deer Lodge
	Butte-Silver Bow

Table 5 Metropolitan Governments, 2007

State	Consolidated city
Tennessee	Hartsville-Trousdale County
	Lynchburg-Moore County
	Nashville-Davidson

Note: The Census Bureau treats these as consolidated cities.

during a given year and then pretests and refines them to increase the validity of each survey instrument. Once completed, the surveys are sent to officials in all cities above a given population level (e.g., 2,500 and above, 10,000 and above, etc.). For example, the city managers or chief administrative officers receive the *ICMA Economic Development Survey*, and finance officers receive the *Police and Fire Personnel, Salaries, and Expenditures* survey.

ICMA conducts the *Police and Fire Personnel, Salaries, and Expenditures* survey every year. Other research projects are conducted every five years, and some are one-time efforts to provide information on subjects of current interest.

Limitations of the Data

Regardless of the subject or type of data presented, data should be read cautiously. All policy, political, and social data have strengths and limitations. These factors should be considered in any analysis and application. Statistics are no magic guide to perfect understanding and decision making, but they can shed light on particular subjects and questions in lieu of haphazard and subjective information. They can clarify trends in policy expenditures, processes, and impacts and thus

Table 6 Areas That Maintain Certain Types of County Offices but as Part of Another Government, 2007

State	County	Other government
Florida	Duval	City of Jacksonville
Georgia	Chattahoochee	Cusseta-Chattahoochee County unified
	Clarke	Athens-Clarke County unified
	Georgetown-Quitman County	Georgetown-Quitman County unified
	Muscogee	City of Columbus
	Richmond	City of Augusta
	Webster and cities of Preston and Weston	Webster County unified
Hawaii	Kalawao	State of Hawaii
Indiana	Marion	City of Indianapolis
Kentucky	Lexington-Fayette Urban County	Lexington-Fayette
	Louisville-Jefferson County	Louisville-Jefferson
Louisiana	Parish of East Baton Rouge	City of Baton Rouge
	Parish of Lafayette	City of Lafayette
	Parish of Orleans	City of New Orleans
	Terrebonne Parish	Terrebonne Parish consolidated
Massachusetts	County of Nantucket	Town of Nantucket
	County of Suffolk	City of Boston
New York	County of Bronx	New York City
	County of Kings	New York City
	County of New York	New York City
	County of Queens	New York City
	County of Richmond	New York City
Pennsylvania	County of Philadelphia	City of Philadelphia

Table 7 Independent Cities

State	Independent city
Maryland	Baltimore City
Missouri	St. Louis
Nevada	Carson City
Virginia	Alexandria
Virginia	Bedford
Virginia	Bristol
Virginia	Buena Vista
Virginia	Charlottesville
Virginia	Chesapeake
Virginia	Colonial Heights
Virginia	Covington
Virginia	Danville
Virginia	Emporia
Virginia	Fairfax
Virginia	Falls Church
Virginia	Franklin
Virginia	Fredericksburg
Virginia	Galax
Virginia	Hampton
Virginia	Harrisonburg
Virginia	Hopewell
Virginia	Lexington
Virginia	Lynchburg
Virginia	Manassas
Virginia	Manassas Park
Virginia	Martinsville
Virginia	Newport News
Virginia	Norfolk
Virginia	Norton
Virginia	Petersburg
Virginia	Poquoson
Virginia	Portsmouth
Virginia	Radford
Virginia	Richmond
Virginia	Roanoke
Virginia	Salem
Virginia	Staunton
Virginia	Suffolk
Virginia	Virginia Beach
Virginia	Waynesboro
Virginia	Williamsburg
Virginia	Winchester

assist in evaluating the equity and efficiency of alternative courses of action. Statistical data are most valuable when one remembers their imperfections, both actual and potential, while drawing conclusions.

For example, readers should examine the response bias for each survey. Surveys may be sent to all municipalities above a certain population threshold, but not all of those surveys are necessarily returned. Jurisdictions that do not respond are rarely mirror images of those that do. ICMA reduces the severity of this problem by maximizing the opportunities to respond through second and (sometimes) third requests. But although this practice mitigates the problem, response bias invariably appears. Consequently, ICMA always includes a "Survey Response" table in each article that analyzes the results of a particular survey. This allows the reader to examine the patterns and degrees of response bias through a variety of demographic and structural variables.

Other possible problems can occur with survey data. Local governments have a variety of record-keeping systems. Therefore, some of the data (particularly those on expenditures) may lack uniformity. In addition, no matter how carefully a questionnaire is refined, problems such as divergent interpretations of directions, definitions, and specific questions invariably arise. However, when inconsistencies or apparently extreme data are reported, every attempt is made to verify these responses through follow-up telephone calls.

Types of Statistics

There are basically two types of statistics: descriptive and inferential.

Descriptive

Most of the data presented in this volume are purely descriptive. Descriptive statistics summarize some characteristics of a group of numbers. A few numbers represent many. If someone wants to find out something about the age of a city's workforce, for example, it would be quite cumbersome to read a list of several hundred numbers (each representing the age of individual employees). It would be much easier to have a few summary descriptive statistics, such as the mean (average) or the range (the highest value minus the lowest value). These two "pieces" of information would not convey all the details of the entire data set, but they can help and are much more useful and understandable than complete numerical lists.

There are essentially two types of descriptive statistics: measures of central tendency and measures of dispersion.

Measures of Central Tendency These types of statistics indicate the most common or typical value of a data set. The most popular examples are the mean and median. The mean is simply the arithmetic average. It is calculated by summing the items in a data set and dividing by the total number of items. For example, given the salaries of $15,000, $20,000, $25,000, $30,000, and $35,000, the mean is $25,000 ($125,000 divided by 5).

The mean is the most widely used and intuitively obvious measure of central tendency. However, it is sensitive to extreme values. A few large or small numbers in a data set can produce a mean that is not representative of the "typical" value. Consider the example of the five salaries above. Suppose the highest value was not $35,000 but $135,000. The mean of the data set would now be $45,000 ($225,000 divided by 5). This figure, however, is not representative of this group of numbers because it is substantially greater than four of the five values and is $90,000 below the high score. A data set such as this is "positively skewed" (i.e., it has one or more extremely high scores). Under these circumstances (or when the data set is "negatively skewed" with extremely low scores), it is more appropriate to use the median as a measure of central tendency.

The median is the middle score of a data set that is arranged in order of increasing magnitude. Theoretically, it represents the point that is equivalent to the 50th percentile. For a data set with an odd number of items, the median has the same number of observations above and below it (e.g., the third value in a data set of 5 or the eighth value in a data set of 15). With an even number of cases, the median is the average of the middle two scores (e.g., the seventh and eighth values in a data set of 14). In the example of the five salaries used above, the median is $25,000 regardless of whether the largest score is $35,000 or $135,000. When the mean exceeds the median, the data set is positively skewed. If the median exceeds the mean, it is negatively skewed.

Measures of Dispersion   This form of descriptive statistics indicates how widely scattered or spread out the numbers are in a data set. Some common measures of dispersion are the range and the interquartile range. The range is simply the highest value minus the lowest value. For the numbers 3, 7, 50, 80, and 100, the range is 97 (100 – 3 = 97). For the numbers 3, 7, 50, 80, and 1,000, it is 997 (1,000 – 3 = 997). Quartiles divide a data set into four equal parts similar to the way percentiles divide a data set into 100 equal parts. Consequently, the third quartile is equivalent to the 75th percentile, and the first quartile is equivalent to the 25th percentile. The interquartile range is the value of the third quartile minus the value of the first quartile.

Inferential

Inferential statistics permit the social and policy researcher to make inferences about whether a cor-

relation exists between two (or more) variables in a population based on data from a sample. Specifically, inferential statistics provide the probability that the sample results could have occurred by chance if there were really no relationship between the variables in the population as a whole. If the probability of random occurrence is sufficiently low (below the researcher's preestablished significance level), then the null hypothesis—that there is no association between the variables—is rejected. This lends indirect support to the research hypothesis that a correlation does exist. If they can rule out chance factors (the null hypothesis), researchers conclude that they have found a "statistically significant" relationship between the two variables under examination.

Significance tests are those statistics that permit inferences about whether variables are correlated but provide nothing directly about the strength of such correlations. Measures of association, on the other hand, indicate how strong relationships are between variables. These statistics range from a high of + 1.0 (for a perfect positive correlation), to zero (indicating no correlation), to a low of –1.0 (for a perfect negative correlation).

Some common significance tests are the chi square and difference-of-means tests. Some common measures of association are Yule's Q, Sommer's Gamma, Lambda, Cramer's V, Pearson's C, and the correlation coefficient. Anyone seeking further information on these tests and measures should consult any major statistics textbook.[3]

Inferential statistics are used less frequently in this volume than descriptive statistics. However, whenever possible, the data have been presented so that the user can calculate inferential statistics whenever appropriate.

Summary

All social, political, and economic data are collected with imperfect techniques in an imperfect world. Therefore, users of such data should be continuously cognizant of the strengths and weaknesses of the information from which they are attempting to draw conclusions. Readers should note the limitations of the data published in this volume. Particular attention should be paid to the process of data collection and potential problems such as response bias.

Notes

1. The terms *city* and *cities*, as used in this volume, refer to cities, villages, towns, townships, and boroughs.

2. See U.S. Census Bureau, *Consolidated Federal Funds Report for Fiscal Year 2009: State and County Areas* (August 2010), Appendix A, census.gov/prod/2010pubs/cffr-09.pdf.

3. For additional information on statistics, see Tari Renner's *Statistics Unraveled: A Practical Guide to Using Data in Decision Making* (Washington, D.C.: ICMA, 1988).

Management Trends and Survey Research

1 Growing Income Disparity and the Implications for Local Government

2 Perspectives on Changes in City Government Structure

3 Local Government Support for Food System Development: An Initial Scan of the Landscape

4 Building Child- and Age-Friendly Communities in Tight Fiscal Times

5 Collaborative Governance and Leadership: A 2012 Survey of Local Government Collaboration

6 Electronic Democracy at the Grass Roots

7 Volunteer Use in Local Government Service Delivery

8 Recurrent Themes in Local Government Innovation

9 CAO Salary and Compensation: Stability Is the Trend

10 Police and Fire Personnel, Salaries, and Expenditures for 2012

1

Growing Income Disparity and the Implications for Local Government

Ron Carlee
ICMA

Since the advent of the Great Recession, ICMA has been trying to understand the implications for local government. The association has held a series of conversations with its members and others interested in local government in order to track major trends in society. Six drivers are consistently identified as pervasively affecting local government: the economy and the public fiscal crisis, demographic changes, increasingly polarized politics, technology, the environment, and the increasing gap between the haves and have-nots.[1] This article explores the last of these drivers.

Although many people see economic disparity as primarily a federal or state issue, the federal and state governments are, in fact, largely deadlocked politically and financially, leaving most major issues at the doorstep of local governments. To examine the implications of this devolution of responsibility, this article begins with the data, translates them into human terms, and examines the challenges confronting local governments that seek to grapple with the complexities inherent in economic disparity. Specifically, this article explores the following issues:

- The state of economic disparity across the United States and relative to other countries
- The consequences of income disparity and the potential for a new era of social unrest

SELECTED FINDINGS

Negative social impacts, including violence, are the result not of poverty per se, but of growing income disparity, particularly in high-income countries. According to the Census Bureau's analysis in 2011, the top 20% of the U.S. population had 51% of the income, whereas the lowest 20% had only 3.2%, and the Pew Research Center found that the majority of Americans believe this growing income gap to be a bad thing. Pew also found that the percentage of upper-income households living in predominantly upper-income census tracts doubled from 9% in 1980 to 18% in 2010. Residential segregation can only make the situation worse.

With political polarization and financial impasses hindering state and federal action, it is up to the will and capacity of local governments to tackle economic disparity in their communities. However, when asked in a 2010 ICMA survey to assess their communities' priorities, 20% of local government managers said that social justice was *not* a priority whereas 9% said that it was a high priority, and 14% considered housing for all income groups to be a high priority while 15% said it was not a priority at all.

3

- The challenges posed by political polarization in addressing income disparity
- Special challenges to city/county managers, who are mostly white, male, and upper income
- Practical tools that local governments can use to mitigate income disparity.

The State of Income Disparity

Income disparity is typically considered in terms of two measures: total wealth (i.e., net worth, assets minus liabilities) and annual income (receipts from wages, dividends, assistance, etc.). Disparity is commonly analyzed for both measures by dividing population groups into quintiles, each containing 20% of the population. If there were equal distribution of wealth, each quintile would control 20% of the wealth or income. This is neither possible, however, nor expected. Disparity can also be analyzed comparatively, such as between counties, states, or countries. This is accomplished through the creation of an index, the most common being the Gini index, named after the Italian who created it. An index score of zero indicates equal distribution, while an index score of 1.0 signifies perfect inequality (one group has all the money).

By all measures, economic disparity is increasing in the United States. The level of disparity in this country is greater than people perceive it to be and substantially greater than what they think it *should* be. The vaulted middle class is shrinking, and the lower class is growing. The following sections discuss income disparity using four different approaches:

- People's perceptions of disparity
- National calculations of disparity
- International comparisons of disparity
- Trends affecting the "middle class."

People's Perceptions of Disparity

There is a perception that income disparity in this country is less than it really is. In 2011, researchers Michael I. Norton and Dan Ariely asked people in the United States how much wealth they thought was fair for each 20% to control.[2] According to their findings, people thought that the top 20% should control about 32% of the wealth and the bottom 20% should control just a little more than 10% (Figure 1–1).

Despite this tolerance for a certain level of inequality, what is striking about the study is how much wealth people "thought" each 20% controlled versus the actual amounts: "respondents vastly underestimated the actual level of wealth inequality in the United States, believing that the wealthiest quintile held about 59% of the wealth when the actual number is closer to 84%."[3]

Figure 1-1 Actual U.S. Wealth Distribution in 2011, Plotted against the Estimated and Ideal Distributions

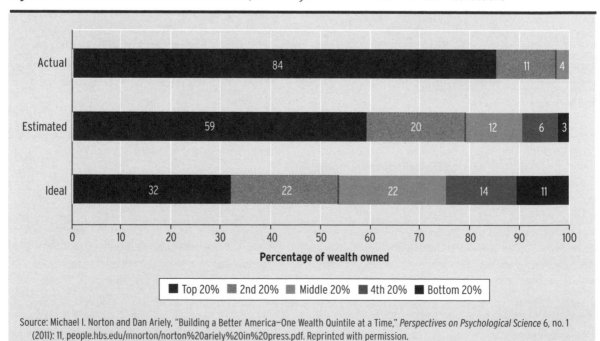

Source: Michael I. Norton and Dan Ariely, "Building a Better America—One Wealth Quintile at a Time," *Perspectives on Psychological Science* 6, no. 1 (2011): 11, people.hbs.edu/mnorton/norton%20ariely%20in%20press.pdf. Reprinted with permission.

National Calculations of Income Disparity

The Census Bureau's income analysis establishes the national "median household income," meaning that half the households make more than this amount and the other half make less.[4] In 2011, the median household income was $50,054, down 1.5% from 2010, 8.1% lower than in 2007, and 8.9% lower than in 1999. Households are losing ground.[5] In this calculation of income (not wealth), the top 20% had 51% of the income, compared to the lowest 20%, which had only 3.2% of the income (see Figure 1–2, in which each segment represents 20% of the population). The top 5% had 22.3% of the income.[6]

The following are the actual income amounts by quintile:[7]

- Bottom quintile: $20,262 a year or less
- 2nd quintile: $20,263 to $38,520
- Middle quintile: $38,521 to $62,434
- 4th quintile: $62,435 to $101,582
- Top quintile: $101,583 and over
- Top 5%: $186,000 and over.

Note that people in the bottom 20% of the population are living on incomes of less than $20,000 a year; the top 5% begins at $186,000, which is less than half of the top income level of $400,000 that had tax breaks permanently extended by Congress at the beginning of 2013.[8]

The Census Bureau also calculates household income on the basis of other demographic factors, and found the following disparities among race and culture in 2011 (Figure 1–3):

Figure 1-2 Income Distributions by Quintiles

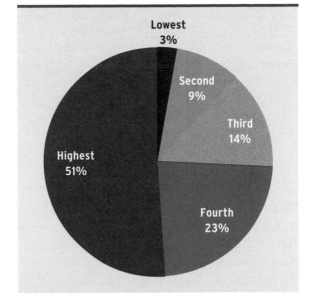

Source: Data extracted from Carmen DeNavas-Walt, Bernadette D. Proctor, and Jessica C. Smith, *Income, Poverty, and Health Insurance Coverage in the United States: 2011*, U.S. Census Bureau Current Population Reports, P60-243 (Washington, D.C.: U.S. Government Printing Office, September 2012), census.gov/prod/2012pubs/p60-243.pdf.

- Asian households: 30% above the median income
- White households: 11% above the median income
- Hispanic households: 23% below the median income
- Black households: 36% below the median income.[9]

And women earned 77% of what men earned.[10]

Figure 1-3 Variance from Median Income, by Race, 2011

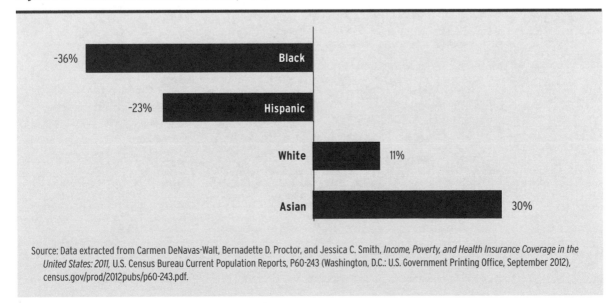

Source: Data extracted from Carmen DeNavas-Walt, Bernadette D. Proctor, and Jessica C. Smith, *Income, Poverty, and Health Insurance Coverage in the United States: 2011*, U.S. Census Bureau Current Population Reports, P60-243 (Washington, D.C.: U.S. Government Printing Office, September 2012), census.gov/prod/2012pubs/p60-243.pdf.

Like all social issues, income inequality will occur in and affect different local governments in very different ways. Using the five-year 2006–2010 Gini index to measure income disparity, the Census Bureau reported in 2012 that the scores across U.S. counties ranged from a low of 0.207 (less disparity) to a high 0.645 (more disparity); for the nation overall, the index was 0.467.[11] This report, unsurprisingly, shows that the greatest income disparity is in the more populous counties. Figure 1–4 gives an indication of how widespread the differences are across the United States.

International Comparisons of Income Disparity

Internationally, the United States is a leader in income disparity. To make international comparisons, the Organisation for Economic Co-operation and Development (OECD) compiles data using the Gini index. Among the 34 countries for which the OECD does research, the United States ranked 31st in income equality; according to data from 2008, only Turkey, Mexico, and Chile had greater income disparity.[12] The United Kingdom ranked 28th and Canada ranked 23rd. In the Norton and Ariely study noted above, U.S. residents were shown three unlabeled depictions of income distribution: one equally distributed, one showing actual distribution in the United States, and one showing Sweden, which is ranked 7th in the OECD report. Respondents chose the unlabeled Sweden distribution as the distribution of choice by an overwhelming 90%.[13] Figure 1–5 shows the Gini index for the top ten countries in income disparity, along with the United States and Sweden. A higher index number means greater disparity. Canada, France, Germany, and Japan have less disparity and do not make the top ten. Data are not available for China and Russia.[14]

The Dwindling Middle Class

The United States has always been proud of the middle class, viewing it as an example of economic success in a nonhierarchical, democratic society. According to a 2012 Pew Research Center report, median middle-class income fell 5% and median middle-class wealth (assets minus debt) declined by 28% during the past decade. This assessment is based on people earning incomes between $39,418 and $118,255 in 2011 dollars.[15]

Figure 1-4 Gini Index of Income Disparity in the United States by County, 2006-2010

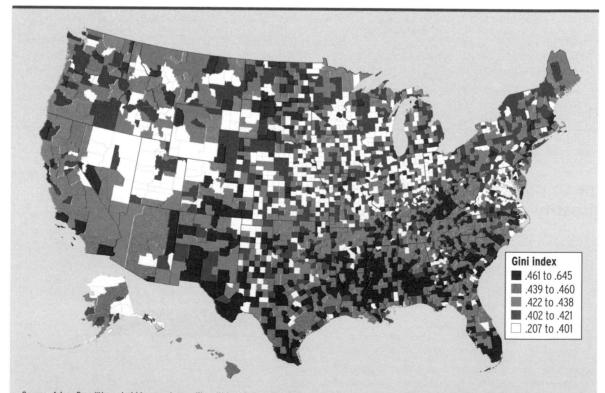

Gini index
- ■ .461 to .645
- ■ .439 to .460
- ■ .422 to .438
- ■ .402 to .421
- □ .207 to .401

Source: Adam Bee, "Household Income Inequality within U.S. Counties 2006-2012," *American Community Survey Briefs* (Washington, D.C.: U.S. Census Bureau, February 2012), 2, census.gov/prod/2012pubs/acsbr10-18.pdf.

Figure 1-5   Gini Index for the Top Ten Countries in Income Disparity and Sweden

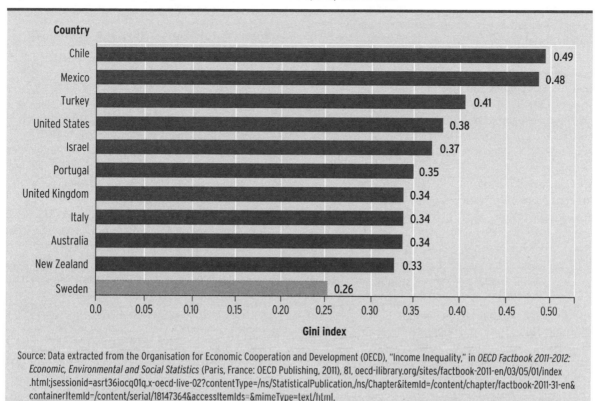

Source: Data extracted from the Organisation for Economic Cooperation and Development (OECD), "Income Inequality," in *OECD Factbook 2011-2012: Economic, Environmental and Social Statistics* (Paris, France: OECD Publishing, 2011), 81, oecd-ilibrary.org/sites/factbook-2011-en/03/05/01/index .html;jsessionid=asrt36iocq01q.x-oecd-live-02?contentType=/ns/StatisticalPublication,/ns/Chapter&itemId=/content/chapter/factbook-2011-31-en& containerItemId=/content/serial/18147364&accessItemIds=&mimeType=text/html.

That same Pew report noted that in 2012, 49% of the population self-identified as middle class, a drop from 53% in 2008, while the proportion who see themselves as lower class rose from 25% in 2008 to 32% in 2012.[16] For the increasing numbers of people who see themselves falling from the "middle" class to the "lower" class, their perception is supported by reality. At the same time, the most well-off are controlling more and more of the wealth.

The Consequences of Income Disparity

"There is nothing either good or bad, but thinking makes it so."

So wrote Shakespeare (*Hamlet*, 2.1). The question is, do people think that income disparity is good or bad? How do people "feel" about the distribution? This answer: not so good. In another 2012 report, the Pew Research Center found that 65% of respondents believe that the income gap between the rich and the poor has gotten larger in the past 10 years, and 57% of the people who believe this think that it is a "bad thing."[17] According to 76% of those respondents,

"Today it's really true that the rich just get richer while the poor get poorer." And 58% believe that the rich are also not paying their fair share in taxes.[18]

Why we think income disparity is bad can vary. François Nielsen, a sociologist at the University of North Carolina in Chapel Hill, wrote,

How does the degree of inequality in the social environment affect individuals in that environment? There are many issues involved here, including how can we distinguish an effect of inequality per se from the "absolute" effects of environmental characteristics, such as hunger or poverty? E.g., Is the young man moved to break into the rich mansion because he is poor in absolute terms, or because he cannot stand the contrast between the luxurious lifestyle of the rich and his own modest circumstances? Am I depressed because I have no money, or is my depression aggravated because I know Bill Gates has too much of it?[19]

These perceptions are leading toward an increased sense of "conflict" between the rich and the poor, as indicated by 66% of respondents to yet another recent Pew survey.[20] This perception was up 19% points from

47% in 2009. Respondents said that there was more conflict between rich and poor than between immigrants and native born, between blacks and whites, and between the young and the old.

But will these perceptions of conflict result in outright conflict? If so, what would that conflict look like? What are the implications for leaders at the local level? These are the troubling questions about the larger economic trend of income inequality. Will the have-nots become increasingly frustrated in ways that will spill out into social disruption? Will growing numbers of people find their dreams deferred, and will those dreams dry up, like Langston Hughes's raisin in the sun, or will they explode? Large-scale urban unrest has not occurred in the United States since the 1960s—especially 1967, when there were eight major incidents of urban violence and damage. Could such an explosion of urban unrest occur today?[21] The Occupy Movement that emerged in 2011 was based on issues of economic inequality; however, it was mostly benign, notwithstanding some publicized clashes with police. The difference between these two examples of urban unrest is that the Occupy Movement was a "movement" seeking policy change, albeit

change not well defined. The riots, on the other hand, were outbursts of violence intent on destruction.

Shame, Humiliation, Envy, and Jealousy

James Gilligan's research indicates that a major cause of violence is the feeling of shame or humiliation. Closely related feelings, according to Gilligan, are envy and jealousy: "People feel inferior to those whom they envy, or of whom they are jealous, with respect to whatever it is that they feel envious or jealous about." He goes on to say, "People resort to violence when they feel that they can wipe out shame only by shaming those who they feel shamed them. The most powerful way to shame anyone is by means of violence."[22]

Will the growing sense and growing reality of income disparity result in feelings of shame and envy that could manifest in violence? We know from surveys that the recent recession has been viewed and experienced very differently by people in upper-income groups than by those in lower-income groups (Figure 1–6).

As noted earlier, an increasing number of people self-identify as lower class: approximately one-third of respondents (32%) to another Pew survey in 2012 compared with 25% in 2008.[23] The biggest increase

Figure 1-6 Effects of Recession on Upper-Income vs. Lower-Income Adults

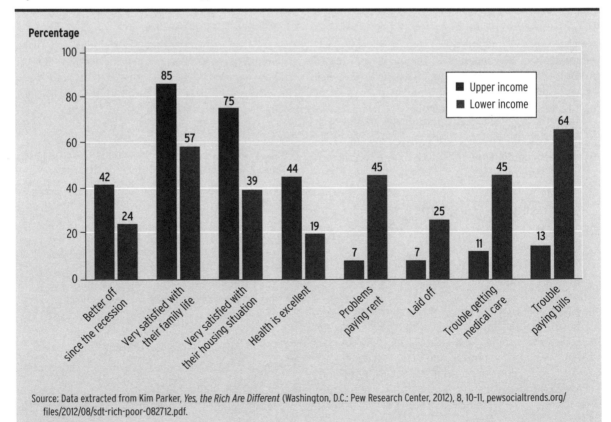

Source: Data extracted from Kim Parker, *Yes, the Rich Are Different* (Washington, D.C.: Pew Research Center, 2012), 8, 10-11, pewsocialtrends.org/files/2012/08/sdt-rich-poor-082712.pdf.

was among 18- to 29-year-olds, 39% of whom self-identified as lower class compared with 25% four years earlier. Since younger people commit most of the violence, the fact that young people increasingly see themselves as lower class is alarming. The percentages of blacks and whites who see themselves as lower class are about the same (33% and 31%, respectively); among Hispanics, however, it is 40%, the largest proportion of any demographic.

Economic Segregation

As disparity has increased, so has housing segregation: In 1980, in 27 of the nation's 30 largest metropolitan areas, 23% of lower-income households lived in census tracts that were majority lower income, compared with 28% in 2010.[24] Not only are poor people living in segregated neighborhoods, but so, too, are the rich—cutting themselves off from the reality of poverty. The percentage of upper-income households living in census tracts where the majority of households are also upper income doubled from 9% in 1980 to 18% in 2010.

Should these developments—a physical concentration of poverty and isolation of the wealthy—raise concerns of local government leaders? Could housing segregation lead to more people living in communities that cause them to feel shame? And if we create even larger concentrations of people living in humiliating conditions and perceiving no chance to escape, does urban America risk a resurgence of social disruption? According to Richard Wilkinson, a public health professor at the University of Nottingham,

> The most well-established environmental determinant of levels of violence is the scale of income differences between rich and poor. More unequal societies tend to be more violent. . . . [T]he tendency for rates of violent crime and homicide to be higher where there is more inequality is part of a more general tendency for the quality of social relations to be poorer in more hierarchical societies.[25]

Professor Wilkinson, writing later with Kate Pickett, asserts that violence is only one consequence of income disparity. In their book *The Spirit Level*, they correlate income disparity with the following conditions in addition to the rate of homicide:

- Level of trust
- Mental illness (including drug and alcohol addiction)
- Life expectancy and infant mortality
- Obesity

- Children's educational performance
- Teenage births
- Imprisonment rates
- Social mobility.[26]

Using readily available data from other parties, such as the international data cited earlier in this article, they plotted each of the above factors against income disparity for 21 "rich countries" against income disparity in the 50 U.S. states (Figure 1–7).

The major point in all these data is that negative social impacts are not the result of poverty in an absolute sense, but a result of growing income disparity, particularly in high-income countries—an area in which the United States leads the way. Residential segregation can only make the situation worse.

Political Polarization and the Unlikelihood of a Consensus Approach to Income Equality

Many think that the 2012 U.S. presidential election was a referendum on income disparity, with the winning candidate running a campaign to raise taxes on the wealthy. However, one can hardly say that the reelected president has an unqualified mandate. The losing candidate still got more than 47% of the vote, garnering support from over 60 million people; he carried 24 states. Of the ten states with the largest margins of victory, Obama carried five and Romney carried five, with the margin for each ranging from a low of 62% to a high of 72% (excluding the District of Columbia, which Obama carried by 91%).[27]

Especially striking are the results at the substate level: Romney carried 2,423 counties compared with 690 counties carried by the reelected president—a ratio among counties (i.e., local governments) of 3.5 to 1. The overall vote, while relatively close, was actually quite lopsided among different demographics as well (Table 1–1): Romney carried 59% of the white vote—the demographic that holds most of the money and power.

Exit polls reveal deeper polarizing differences, reinforcing the findings of earlier surveys, such as the 2012 Pew Research Center study on trends in American values. Pew studied partisan differences across 48 "values" areas and found that overall differences between Democrats and Republicans from 1987 to 2012 almost doubled—from a difference of 10% points to a difference of 18% points.[28] The individual issue area on which partisans differed the most was social safety net programs: a difference of 23 percentage points in 1987 compared with a difference of 41 percentage points

Figure 1-7 Health and Social Problems in 21 Countries, by Income Inequality

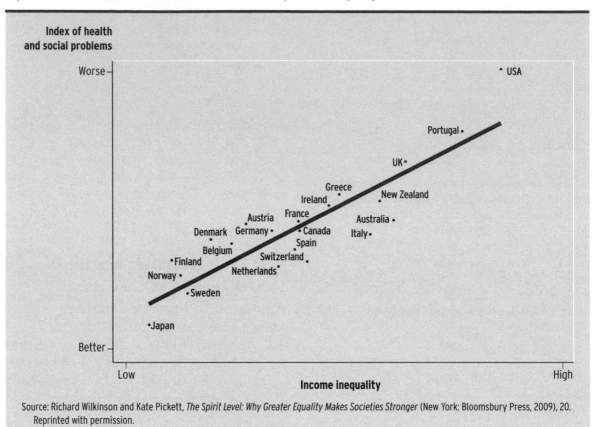

Source: Richard Wilkinson and Kate Pickett, *The Spirit Level: Why Greater Equality Makes Societies Stronger* (New York: Bloomsbury Press, 2009), 20. Reprinted with permission.

Table 1-1 Demographic Trends in the 2012 Presidential Election, Based on Exit Polls

Obama's large majorities	Romney's large majorities
Race/culture	
93% African Americans	59% Whites
73% Asians	
71% Latinos	
Sex/race	
55% Women	52% Men
96% Black women	62% White men
Age	
60% 18- to 29-year-olds	56% 65 years old or greater
Political orientation	
86% Liberals	82% Conservatives
Religion	
62% Never attend services	63% Attend services weekly
69% Jewish	57% Protestant
70% None	78% Born-again Christian
Income	
60% < $50,000	53% ≥ $50,000

Source: CNN Politics, "President: Full Results," at cnn.com/election/2012/results/race/president#exit-polls.

in 2012, amounting to an increase of 18 percentage points.[29]

The 2012 election exit polls bring into sharp focus the differences on issues such as abortion, health care, immigration, same-sex marriage, and, especially, the role of government (Table 1–2). Among Romney voters, 74% believed that government is doing too much compared with 81% of Obama voters who said that government should do more. These differences continue to play out nationally in the post-election period, especially with regard to taxes and spending priorities. While everyone says compromise is needed, they usually mean that the other side needs to compromise. Thus, political will—the critical element to alter the direction of increasing income disparity—appears lacking for the foreseeable future at the national level.

The same is true in a number of states, as indicated by their willingness (or lack thereof) to exercise their options under the Patient Protection and Affordable Care Act to expand Medicaid coverage. As with most social issues, assuming that the will and capacity are there, it will be left up to local governments to deal with the effects of economic disparity.

Table 1-2 Social Issues in the 2012 Presidential Election, based on Exit Polls

Issue	Obama voters	Romney voters
Abortion	67% Keep legal	77% Make illegal
Health care law	92% Expand	93% Repeal completely
Taxes	70% Increase $250k+	75% No increases
Immigration	61% Offer legal status	73% Deport
Government	81% Do more	74% Is doing too much
Same-sex marriage	73% Yes	74% No

Source: CNN Politics, "President: Full Results," at cnn.com/election/2012/results/race/president#exit-polls.

Note: The percentages shown are for the Obama and Romney voters who responded to the question as indicated. For example, on the abortion question, 59% of all voters said that it should be legal and 36% said it should be illegal. Among the 59% who said abortion should be legal, 67% of them voted for Obama. Among the 36% who said that abortion should be illegal, 77% voted for Romney.

The Special Challenge for City/County Managers

Just as the extent to which income disparity differs from one community to another, even more so does a community's awareness of it and willingness and ability to respond to it. In a 2010 survey on local government sustainability policies and programs, ICMA asked local government managers to what extent social equity was a priority in their communities. Twice as many respondents said that social justice was *not* a priority (20%) as said that it was a high priority (9%).[30] There are many very "red" local governments in the United States: remember, in the 2012 presidential election, Romney carried 78% of the counties. Given the practical realities at the local level, the question is whether people at that level can rise above partisanship and accompanying political rhetoric to create healthy, safe, and economically sustainable communities. Do local governments have the political will to address economic disparity, and if so, do they also have the resources? This poses a special challenge to city/county managers, who are overwhelmingly part of the upper-income, white male demographic.

In the 1970s, researcher Robert L. Lineberry was examining equity in services delivery in urban communities, and he became concerned about professional local government managers. He found that city managers were predominantly white men with middle-class values, values that were perpetuated throughout the local government bureaucracy. The demographics of the profession is, in fact, largely the same 35 years later. ICMA's current membership is over 75% male and over 80% white.[31] More than 51% of managers earn incomes in the top 20% (above $101,583), and 7% of managers have incomes in the top 5% (above $186,000).[32]

Here is the paradox: professional city management was created at the turn of the 20th century as part of a reform movement. At that time, reform focused on incompetence and corruption in cities. As it happened, however, the "reformers" tended to be relatively conservative, upper-income white men, and the paradigm for professional city managers was established. This led Lineberry to question whether those managers would be able to bring an adequate policy perspective to address the issues of non-white, low-income city residents. He went so far as to claim that "urban reformism . . . represents one of those cases where one generation's reforms are the next generation's problems."[33] Members of the profession are still debating this issue a generation after Lineberry's work. In a recent ICMA article, Robert O'Neill, executive director of ICMA, writes about the "increasing gap between the haves and have nots" as one of six drivers affecting local government. Reflecting on conversations he has had with ICMA members, O'Neill notes that today's set of challenges "raises some interesting questions for the future of the profession of local government management. Among the most important is: Will professional managers be the reformers or are they to be reformed?"[34]

The issue is to what extent the demographic characteristics of professional managers adversely affect—consciously or unconsciously—social equity in the ways they make administrative decisions. While elected officials actually set policy and approve the budget allocations, many of these service allocation decisions are made in the bureaucracy led by the professional manager. According to Lineberry, these "myriads of little [administrative] decisions" determine the service allocation patterns: "Made once, a decision is an exercise of discretion; made twice, it is precedential; made ad infinitum, it is a decision rule for the treatment of all cases."[35]

Lineberry discusses five ways in which local government bureaucracies make allocation decisions administratively:

- Demand, such as a service request
- Need, such as a response to high crime
- Equality: simply give everyone the same thing
- Pressure: the squeaky wheel
- Professional norms, such as the *Manual on Uniform Traffic Control Devices*.

None of these determinants is inherently bad, but each has a potential downside. It is the responsibility of the city/county manager to establish these internal decision-making rules in the pursuit of efficiency and effectiveness. The question is to what extent equity is also a value.

Lineberry acknowledges that there are trade-offs in how services are delivered and that these trade-offs are "better made consciously than unconsciously; as decisions rather than non-decisions."[36] This requires a conscious recognition by local government leaders of their own class values and possible prejudices. The fact that the profession itself continues to debate these issues internally is a positive sign of self-awareness. In the words of ICMA's official vision statement, the profession exists to "build sustainable communities to improve lives worldwide." Similarly, the fourth tenet of the ICMA Code of Ethics is to "recognize that the chief function of local government at all times is to serve the best interests of *all* people" (italics mine).

Practical Tools for Addressing Income Disparity at the Local Level

If there is a willingness to address income disparity at the local level, practical tools are available. The approaches fall into two categories:

1. Mitigating the "shame" of economic disparity by ensuring equity in service delivery and inclusion in government participation

2. Directly reducing disparity through income assistance.

The first approach need not have partisan overtones as it is rooted in founding U.S. principles related to equality. In fact, the alternative is at best merely regressive and at worst overtly discriminatory. Equity in service delivery and civic enfranchisement do not require additional resources or an expansion of government.

The second approach is more controversial and will likely generate policy and partisan debate. At its extreme, direct intervention will be viewed as socialistic in a society committed to the free market, the pioneer spirit of perseverance, and lifting one's self up by the bootstraps. The question is whether the combination of free market and government policies (or lack thereof) have created an environment whereby some people cannot realistically lift themselves up through their own hard work. A related question is whether failure to address this issue could create threats to all residents of a community. Asked differently, can communities of great disparity ultimately afford *not* to address the issue?

Equity in Basic Functions of Local Government In the normal course of exercising its powers, a local government can mitigate or exacerbate the affects of income disparity. Specifically, it can promote greater equity among people of different income levels in the way it (1) delivers and allocates services, (2) engages the public, (3) regulates the creation of neighborhoods through zoning and land use, and (4) raises revenue.

Service Delivery/Allocation. On the issue of service delivery there should be little debate. Service delivery is important for addressing economic disparity because local government services constitute a real economic benefit to the people who receive them.

In fact, the idea of equity in local government service delivery is generally taken for granted today. It is easy to forget that in the not-so-distant past, some local governments proactively promoted inequality, toward the preservation of a racially segregated society of privilege and inferiority. Lineberry, noted above, wrote:

> The problems I discuss—service allocation and discrimination, the relationship between power structure and policy, the legal and operative standards for equality in urban policy, and bureaucratic monopoly in service delivery—are generalized issues in city politics. . . . There is more to urban policy than a budget.[37]

Lineberry sets the stage for his study with this description: "In the tiny town of Shaw, Mississippi, 97 percent of the homes without sanitary sewers were in black dwelling units; 98 percent of the town's houses not fronting on paved streets were black-occupied; all of the city's new mercury vapor street lighting went to all-white neighborhoods."[38] Society today has largely moved beyond such overt demonstrations of discrimination in the allocation of local services; however, to what extent has service equity really been achieved and what is the evidence that it has been?

Without question there is economic value in a low-income person having access to a library that provides free broadband Internet services on current-generation digital equipment. Access to a parks, open space, and community gardens is of real value to a family who is living in a 700-square-foot apartment and will never own a home on a quarter-acre lot. But, as Lineberry notes, local public services are not a logical vehicle for redistribution of income on the scale that would alter the trend toward increasing income disparity. Thus, the questions posed here are: Can the allocation of local public services be used to at least mitigate the impacts of income disparity and, if so, should it? And if the answer to either question is yes, which services and in what ways? Are the public services and facilities in economically segregated communities so poor as to further degrade and isolate residents, or are they sufficient to provide a better quality of life and, by doing so, help lift people up and promote opportunities to escape from poverty?[39]

Civic Enfranchisement. In the context of income disparity, the question is whether the economic disenfranchisement of low-income households leads to their political disenfranchisement. If, as noted in the previous section, quality public services and facilities can mitigate the effects of income disparity, why not actually engage directly with low-income residents, especially those living in economically segregated communities, to determine what services and facilities would be most helpful and in what ways? This will involve going into the neighborhoods where people live and at times when they are available. Engagement requires communicating with people in jargon-free language they can understand. It also requires the ability to genuinely listen.

Much has been written about civic engagement, so a long discussion is not required here.[40] Suffice it to say that public hearings are not civic engagement. Three minutes at a microphone in the council chamber may be an essential and even valuable part of the deliberative process of local government bodies, but hearings do not constitute actual engagement: they draw from a very small segment of the community, and they do not provide for informed dialogue. Fortunately, there are numerous other approaches that have been tested and documented, from simple neighborhood forums to sophisticated polling.

Neighborhood Creation through Land Use Planning and Zoning. Notwithstanding libertarian philosophies that would remove government completely from land use planning and zoning, most local governments—even those that are ultraconservative—see land use planning and zoning as a legitimate and prudent local government function to provide order and protect private investments. While there may be vociferous arguments in specific cases, the general value of land use planning and regulations is widely acknowledged.

With regard to ameliorating the effects of income disparity, there are several ways to use land use planning and zoning:

- *Inclusive zoning.* Requiring low- and moderate-income housing in new residential developments is one way to avoid creating economically segregated communities.
- *Access to jobs.* While access to jobs can be facilitated partially through mixed-use development so

that jobs and residences are co-located, this is not a panacea and cannot be accomplished quickly. More critical is providing the transportation links—especially public transportation—between low- and moderate-income residential areas to job centers.

- *Access to recreation and open space.* As already noted, many low-income people will never have their own backyards. In dense urban areas they will live in walk-up, deteriorating apartment buildings, and in more suburban or rural areas, they may live in small, mostly cheaply made houses or in manufactured housing (typically demeaned as "trailers"). The availability of convenient and safe open space for passive and active recreation is critical to quality of life and requires thoughtful land use planning.
- *Regulation of gated communities.* There are few more visible signs of economic hierarchy than a heavily fortified gated residential community. The clear message is "we are better than anyone else, and you are not wanted here!" Clustered, high-end residential developments are inevitable, but do they have to be impenetrable fortresses? And if they are open, will they be welcoming to others, or will residents be on the lookout for a Trayvon Martin passing through.[41]

This is obviously not an exhaustive list. Again, the point is to raise the question: how can land use planning and zoning exacerbate or mitigate income disparity and economic segregation?

Regressive Local Government Revenues. As local governments confront post-recession downsizing, there will obviously be an impact on services: what services do residents get, which residents get the services, and how much do they get. What will the impacts be on people of different income levels? Similarly, as local governments scramble to make up for lost revenues, on whom will the revenue burden fall? Given the debates on the relative progressivity and regressivity of local tax and revenue structures and ways to increase fairness, this is clearly a large subject worthy of a more complete discussion beyond the scope of this report.

Nevertheless, an issue of concern that should be raised here is the impact of funding public services through fees rather than general tax dollars. Many local governments are compelled to consider fees, largely because of constraints that states have imposed on them regarding taxes they are permitted to impose and caps on those taxes. Rather than being able to obtain needed revenues through progressive tax sources such as income and wealth taxes, which could have a substantial impact on income disparity, local governments are left with the most regressive approach of charging fees—in essence, requiring everyone to pay a market price for essential services that are provided by a publicly created monopoly (whether it be the government itself, a contractor, or a franchisee). Even on discretionary services, such as recreation centers, the imposition of partial expense-recovery fees to access the service may have a discriminatory affect on low-income residents even though their property taxes (paid indirectly by landlords) and sales taxes may be subsidizing the service.

As with service delivery, there are trade-offs in how revenues are raised, and decisions are better made consciously than unconsciously, with consideration given to the consequences for all populations within the community. Income-based sliding fee schedules, exemptions, and "scholarships" are tools that local governments have used to mitigate the impacts of fees on lower-income households.

Direct Income Assistance to Reduce Income Disparity Few local governments have the capacity or legal authority to provide direct income subsidies such as those provided by the federal government. The most common area for local action is affordable housing for lower-income households.

Nationally, the primary method for subsidizing housing has been through the federal Section 8 housing program, administered through local housing authorities. Indisputably, the federal government program does not come close to meeting the need. And despite long waiting lists for Section 8 vouchers, there is no chance that the federal government, in this era of deficit reduction, will be expanding housing programs any time soon.

This brings the issue back to the local level. In the 2010 ICMA survey referenced above, local government managers were asked whether "housing for all income groups" was a priority, and their answers were split, with 14% saying it was a high priority and 15% saying that it was not a priority at all.[42] They were also asked which of the following actions to promote social inclusion have been adopted by their communities (shown in parentheses are the percentages of communities that provide the action):

- Financial support/incentives for affordable housing (33%)
- Supportive housing to people with disabilities (15%)
- Housing options for the elderly (27%)
- Housing to homeless persons (10%).[43]

These survey results raise a number of questions about the interest, willingness, and ability of local governments to engage in local affordable housing strate-

gies. For the one-third of respondents that reported adopting financial support and incentives, the tools they have used include the traditional approach: the creation of dedicated, publicly owned and operated housing for low-income households. Although more complicated legally, some local governments impose rent controls on private real estate owners through ordinances.

Many other approaches have emerged, however, that address issues of affordable housing without contributing to economic segregation. Among the options are (1) portable direct subsidies to individual households and (2) subsidies to create mixed-income housing. The following examples from Arlington County, Virginia, illustrate how such programs can work:

- *Direct rental subsidy.* Arlington manages a local voucher program called Housing Grants. The program is patterned after the federal Section 8 program, but it has stricter eligibility requirements (available only to working families with children, the elderly, or people who are permanently disabled) and provides lower subsidies. Housing grants provide support to over 1,000 households scattered throughout the community.[44]

- *Mixed-income subsidy.* Using general fund dollars and developer contributions, Arlington provides long-term low- or no-interest loans mostly to nonprofit housing providers for the acquisition and/or rehabilitation of rental housing. There is a heavy emphasis on mixed-income housing, so Arlington's subsidy is used to write down the rents for a certain number of units in a market-rate residential development. Arlington has approximately 14% of its rental housing under these long-term (typically 30-year) subsidy commitments.[45]

These two examples and variations of them in other communities provide practical approaches to income assistance at the local level. For low-income homeowners, various income-based tax abatement tools have been used. The strategies employed in any given jurisdiction will vary according to the jurisdiction's legal authority, political will, tradition, and fiscal capacity. An extensive list of strategies and tools can be obtained from The National Housing Institute (nhi.org). Although the capacity to subsidize income at the local level will never match that of the federal and state governments, local assistance can make a meaningful difference.

Conclusion

This article is not intended to be alarmist; there is no evidence that U.S. communities are tinderboxes waiting to explode. Instead, this compilation of research is provided as a cautionary alert. The data are unambiguous. An increasing share of the wealth in this country is becoming concentrated in a much smaller percentage of the population, the middle class is shrinking, and the lower classes and people who perceive themselves as lower class are growing. Neighborhoods are becoming increasingly segregated on the basis of income. Research shows that income disparity correlates with a host of social problems, particularly violence. And the public is deeply polarized on a wide range of social values.

While federal and state intervention may be needed to achieve a marked change in economic disparity, the stalemate at these levels of government leaves the challenge to local governments and their

communities, for whom the consequences of a divided society will be tangible. The challenge for local leaders—appointed and elected—is first to understand the conditions in their communities and the impacts those conditions have on the lives of people at the bottom of the economic and social continuum. With a clear understanding of local conditions and a conscious recognition of their own societal views, local leaders can then explore the options available to them, formulate a vision and direction that fits their local conditions, and act with thought and intent. The alternative is to sit back, wait, and react to whatever may happen: perhaps an easier approach in the short term, but one fraught with risk.

Notes

1 Bob O'Neill, "Leadership and the Profession: Where To from Here?" *Public Management (PM)* 95 (March 2013): 21–23.

2 Michael I. Norton and Dan Ariely, "Building a Better America—One Wealth Quintile at a Time," *Perspectives on Psychological Science* 6, no. 1 (2011): 10, people.hbs .edu/mnorton/norton%20ariely%20in%20press.pdf.

3 Ibid.

4 Carmen DeNavas-Walt, Bernadette D. Proctor, and Jessica C. Smith, *Income, Poverty, and Health Insurance Coverage in the United States: 2011*, U.S. Census Bureau Current Population Reports, P60-243 (Washington, D.C.: U.S. Government Printing Office, September 2012), census.gov/prod/2012pubs/p60-243.pdf. The income and poverty estimates in the Census Bureau study "are based solely on money income before taxes and do not include the value of noncash benefits, such as those provided by the Supplemental Nutrition Assistance Program (SNAP), Medicare, Medicaid, public housing, and employer-provided fringe benefits" (3).

5 Ibid., 7.

6 Ibid., 8, Table 2.

7 Ibid., 10.

8 Karen Weise, "The Fiscal-Cliff Deal and Taxes: We'll All Pay More," *BloombergBusinessweek*, January 2, 2013, businessweek.com/articles/2013-01-02/the-fiscal-cliff-deal-and-taxes-well-all-pay-more (accessed January 4, 2013).

9 Ibid., 5.

10 Ibid., 9.

11 Adam Bee, "Household Income Inequality within U.S. Counties: 2006–2012," *American Community Survey Briefs* (Washington, D.C.: U.S. Census Bureau, February 2012), 1, census.gov/prod/2012pubs/acsbr10-18.pdf. This calculation only includes income, not total wealth or transfer payments.

12 Organisation for Economic Cooperation and Development (OECD), "Income Inequality," in *OECD Factbook 2011–2012: Economic, Environmental and Social Statistics* (Paris, France: OECD Publishing, 2011), 81, oecd-ilibrary.org/sites/factbook-2011-en/03/05/01/ index.html;jsessionid = asrt36iocq01q.x-oecd-live-

02?contentType = /ns/StatisticalPublication,/ns/ Chapter&itemId = /content/chapter/factbook-2011-31-en&containerItemId = /content/serial/18147364&access ItemIds = &mimeType = text/html.

13 Norton and Ariely, "Building a Better America," 10.

14 For a more academic discussion of the math and the applicability, see Wikipedia's article on the Gini index. See also the World Bank at data.worldbank.org/indicator/ SI.POV.GINI; Paul Allison, "Measures of Inequality," *American Sociological Review* 43 (December 1978): 865–880, stanford.edu/group/scspi/_media/pdf/Classic_ Media/Allison_1978_Measurement.pdf; and François Nielsen, "Income Inequality & Dualism" (February 21, 2008), unc.edu/~nielsen/special/s2/s2.htm. Comparative Gini calculations can be found in the OECD *Factbook 2011–2012* and in the Central Intelligence Agency, *The World Factbook* (updated weekly), cia.gov/library/ publications/the-world-factbook/ fields/2172.html.

15 Pew Research Center, *The Lost Decade of the Middle Class* (Washington, D.C., August 2012), 2, pewsocialtrends .org/files/2012/08/pew-social-trends-lost-decade-of-the-middle-class.pdf.

16 Ibid., 3–4.

17 Kim Parker, *Yes, the Rich Are Different* (Washington, D.C.: Pew Research Center, 2012), 6, pewsocialtrends .org/files/2012/08/sdt-rich-poor-082712.pdf.

18 Ibid., 4.

19 Nielsen, "Income Inequality & Dualism" (see note 14).

20 Rich Morin, *Rising Share of Americans See Conflict between Rich and Poor* (Washington, D.C.: Pew Research Center, January 2012), 4, pewsocialtrends.org/ files/2012/01/Rich-vs-Poor.pdf.

21 The Kerner Commission studied 164 disorders reported during the first nine months of 1967. Eight of those disorders (5%) were major in terms of violence and damage, 33 (20%) were serious but not major, and the remaining 123 (75%) were minor. In the 75 disorders studied by a Senate subcommittee, 83 deaths were reported; 82% of those deaths and more than half of the injuries occurred in Newark and Detroit. About 10% of the dead and 38% of the injured were public employees, primarily law officers and firemen. The overwhelming

majority of persons killed or injured in all the disorders were African American civilians. See the *Report of the National Advisory Commission on Civil Disorders* (The Kerner Report), 1968. For a listing of urban riots in the United States and other countries since the early 1900s, see Wikipedia at en.wikipedia .org/wiki/Urban_riots.

22 James Gilligan, "Shame, Guilt, and Violence," *Social Research* 70, no. 4 (Winter 2003): 1149–1189, accessible at internationalpsychoanalysis.net/wp-content/uploads/2009/02/shamegilligan.pdf.

23 Rich Morin and Seth Motel, *A Third of Americans Now Say They Are in the Lower Classes* (Washington, D.C.: Pew Research Center, 2012), 1, pewsocialtrends.org/files/2012/09/the-lower-classes-final.pdf.

24 Richard Fry and *Paul Taylor, The Rise of Residential Segregation by Income* (Washington, D.C.: Pew Research Center, August 2012), 12, pewsocialtrends.org/files/2012/08/Rise-of-Residential-Income-Segregation-2012.2 .pdf. As interactive maps developed by Pew reveal, this is not just an inner-city problem, but one that spills into the suburbs. See "Residential Segregation by Income: Philadelphia," pewsocialtrends.org/income-segregation/philadelphia/.

25 Richard Wilkinson, "Why Is Violence More Common Where Inequality Is Greater?," *Annals of the New York Academy of Sciences* 1036, no. 1 (December 2004): 1.

26 Richard Wilkinson and Kate Pickett, *The Spirit Level: Why Greater Equality Makes Societies Stronger* (New York: Bloomsbury Press, 2009), 19.

27 Dave Leip's Atlas of U.S. Presidential Elections, uselectionatlas.org.

28 Pew Research Center, *Partisan Polarization Surges in Bush, Obama Years: Trends in American Values: 1987–2012* (Washington, D.C., June 2012), 19, people-press .org/files/legacy-pdf/06-04-12%20Values%20Release.pdf.

29 Ibid., 4, 20.

30 James Svara, "The Early Stage of Local Government Action to Promote Sustainability," in *The Municipal Year Book 2011* (Washington, D.C.: ICMA, 2011), 47. Survey results can also be found on the ICMA website at icma.org/en/results/home/surveying/survey_research/survey_results.

31 Interestingly, ICMA has no statistics on the number of women members until 1989, when women were 11.5% of the membership; as of 2012 women made up 24%

of the membership. In 1989, blacks were 3.5% of the membership, increasing to only 5% by 2012. The ICMA Board has adopted a number of strategies to increase women and minorities, but with mixed results.

32 Evelina Moulder and Ron Carlee, "CAO Salary and Compensation: Stability Is the Trend," in *The Municipal Year Book 2013* (Washington, D.C.: ICMA Press, 2013), 99–109.

33 Robert L. Lineberry, *Equality and Urban Policy: The Distribution of Municipal Public Services,* Vol. 39, Sage Library of Social Research (Beverly Hills, Calif.: Sage, 1977), 149.

34 O'Neill, "Leadership and the Profession," 21–22.

35 Lineberry, *Equality and Urban Policy,* 153.

36 Ibid., 197.

37 Lineberry, *Equality and Urban Policy,* 7.

38 Ibid., 9.

39 I vividly remember visiting the social services office of a suburban community in the mid-1990s. It was located in a low-income section of the community in what appeared to be a converted school building surrounded by a parking lot. A 12-foot chain-link fence topped with razor wire enclosed the entire site. When one entered the front of the building, the "greeting" came from an armed guard. The message of distrust to the neighborhood and to anyone entering the building was unambiguous.

40 James H. Svara and Janet Denhardt, eds., *The Connected Community: Local Governments as Partners in Citizen Engagement and Community Building,* a White Paper for the Alliance for Innovation, Arizona State University, October 15, 2010.

41 Trayvon Martin was an unarmed 17-year-old African American killed on February 26, 2012, by a "neighborhood watch coordinator" for the gated community in Sanford, Florida. See the *Orlando Sentinel* and other news sources for details.

42 Svara, "Early Stage of Local Government Action," 47.

43 Ibid., 60.

44 For a summary of Arlington's Housing Grants program, see arlingtonva.us/departments/HumanServices/services/eid/file86576.pdf.

45 Department of Community Planning, Housing and Development, *Meeting the Affordable Housing Challenge: Annual Affordable Housing Targets Report for FY 2011* (Arlington County, Va., n.d.), arlingtonva.us/departments/CPHD/housing/pdf/file85030.pdf.

2

Perspectives on Changes in City Government Structure

James H. Svara
Arizona State University

Jennifer Claire Auer
Arizona State University

ICMA has been conducting a survey on municipal form of government for many years, and it maintains a comprehensive database of local governments with information about the form of government used. The survey provides a snapshot of the responding governments and collects data from each about any structural changes that have been considered in the five-year period since the previous survey. This year ICMA adds another set of data to extend the picture of current conditions and developing trends, and because the council-manager form has moved into its second century since the last form-of-government survey was conducted, this analysis adds a long-term perspective supplemented with historical and census data.

Survey Methodology

The *Municipal Form of Government, 2011* survey was mailed in the fall of 2011 to all municipalities with a population of 2,500 and over and to those 1,316 municipalities with populations under 2,500 that are in the ICMA database, generally because an ICMA member is the chief appointed official (CAO). A second mailing was sent to those municipalities that did not respond to the first one. The final response rate for all cities surveyed was 41% (Table 2–1).

There are two issues related to the characteristics of survey respondents that affect how results

SELECTED FINDINGS

Population increases since 2000 have resulted in 35 additional cities with populations over 100,000. For all cities over 100,000, 64% use the council-manager form of government. The expansion in the number of council-manager governments as a result of the growing population, together with the fact that the council-manager form has been retained in most cities in which it was challenged, indicates that use of this form will continue to expand among cities of 100,000 and over in population.

At least half of all cities have the position of chief appointed official (CAO). This reflects a substantial increase since the 1991 form-of-government survey, when 35% of the responding mayor-council cities reported having a CAO.

The proportion of city councils that use standing committees to consider specific policy matters rose from 54% in 2006 to 66% in 2011.

are reported. First, the 1,316 cities with a population under 2,500 in the ICMA database represent just over one-tenth of the more than 12,700 incorporated

Table 2-1 Survey Response

Classification	No. of municipalities surveyed[a] (A)	Respondents No.	Respondents % of (A)
Total respondents	8,813	3,566	41
Population group			
Over 1,000,000	9	2	22
500,000-1,000,000	23	9	39
250,000-499,999	36	17	47
100,000-249,999	180	86	48
50,000-99,999	421	199	47
25,000-49,999	786	366	47
10,000-24,999	1,850	769	42
5,000-9,999	1,939	760	39
2,500-4,999	2,253	807	36
Under 2,500	1,316	551	42
Geographic region			
Northeast	2,217	716	32
North-Central	2,581	1,124	44
South	2,623	1,072	41
West	1,392	654	47
Geographic division			
New England	865	373	43
Mid-Atlantic	1,352	343	25
East North-Central	1,643	678	41
West North-Central	947	453	48
South Atlantic	1,216	570	47
East South-Central	522	159	31
West South-Central	883	342	39
Mountain	496	231	47
Pacific Coast	889	417	47
Metro status			
Metropolitan Statistical Area	4,884	2,040	42
Micropolitan Statistical Area	1,308	523	40
NECTA[b]	539	244	45
Undesignated	2,082	759	37

a   For a definition of terms, please see "Inside the *Year Book*," xi–xiv.

b   New England City and Town Area.

localities with this population identified by the Census Bureau; of those 1,316 cities, 551 cities responded to the survey, which amounts to only about 4% of those identified by the bureau. Thus, it is not possible to generalize from those 551 respondents to all very small cities in the United States.[1] At the same time, the inclusion of these cities in calculations can affect the overall proportions. In some instances in the text, we indicate that we are reporting percentages only for cities of 2,500 and above in population, although all results are included in most tables.

Second, the response rate to the *Municipal Form of Government* survey has dropped in each succeeding survey since 1991, when the rate for cities of 2,500 and above in population was 71% compared to 40% for cities of this size in 2011. It is likely that cities with a connection to the purpose of ICMA—either those using the council-manager form or those having an appointed administrator—are more likely to respond.[2] Since it is potentially misleading to compare characteristics over time that could be affected by changing response rates, this discussion supplements the survey responses with additional data.

Definitions and Findings

The *Municipal Form of Government, 2011* survey used the following definitions for the five forms of government:

- *Mayor-council:* Elected council or board serves as the legislative body. The chief elected official is the head of government, with significant administrative authority, generally elected separately from the council.

- *Council-manager:* Elected council or board and chief elected official (e.g., mayor) are responsible for making policy with advice of the chief appointed official. A professional administrator appointed by the board or council has full responsibility for the day-to-day operations of the government.

- *Commission:* Members of a board of elected commissioners serve as heads of specific departments and collectively sit as the legislative body of the government.

- *Town meeting:* Qualified voters convene to make basic policy and to choose a board of selectmen. The selectmen and elected officers carry out the policies established by the government.

- *Representative town meeting:* Voters select citizens to represent them at the town meeting. All citizens may attend and participate in debate, but only representatives may vote.

The United States is rare among countries in the widespread use of two major forms of government that are based on different constitutional principles. The council-manager form was first adopted as an experiment in 1908 in Staunton, Virginia. It attracted widespread attention after being endorsed by the National Municipal League in the league's second Model City Charter, adopted in 1915, and it spread to almost 400 cities by the early 1930s. Although there were few new adoptions during the Depression, the use of the council-manager form exploded after World War II and continues to grow. As indicated in Figure 2–1, which is based on the ICMA database reported over time in *The Municipal Year Book*, the form is currently used in 10 times more cities than in 1933, and its use has continued to expand in all population size categories.

According to the ICMA database,[3] the proportion of cities 2,500 and over that use the council-manager form is now 49%, compared with 44% that use the mayor-council form. The shift to the council-manager form has been somewhat lower in smaller communities. Only 38% of cities between 2,500 and 4,999 in population use that form, compared with 47% of cities between 5,000 and 9,999. In cities of 10,000 and above, 57% use the council-manager form and 37% use the mayor-council form.[4]

In addition, a small proportion of cities use the other forms of government. In this breakdown, for which the 2011 form-of-government survey is the source of the data, the town meeting and representative town meeting forms were reported by 7% overall and by 60% of New England municipalities (Table 2–2). The town meeting is used predominantly in cities under 10,000 in population, whereas the representative town meeting is used in cities between 10,000 and 100,000. Just over 1% of all cities reported using the commission form of government.

Because it is commonly held that the council-manager form is predominantly found in smaller cities (although, as already noted, it is used somewhat less in the smallest cities), there is special interest in seeing how the use of this form breaks down in cities of 100,000 and above in population. Table 2–3 provides a breakdown in the use of all forms for all large cities based on a separate data collection.

With population increases, particularly in cities in the Sunbelt, there were 274 cities with populations over 100,000 in the 2010 Census compared with 239 in 2000.[5] Two-thirds of the cities with a million or more in population use the mayor-council form of government, although Dallas, Phoenix, and San Antonio exemplify the effective use of the council-manager form in very large cities (and San José will be joining their ranks in this decade). For all cities of 100,000 and above, 35% use the mayor-council form, 64% use the council-manager form, and one city uses the commission form.

Figure 2-1 Growth in Number of Council-Manager Governments Overall and by Size of City, 1933-2012

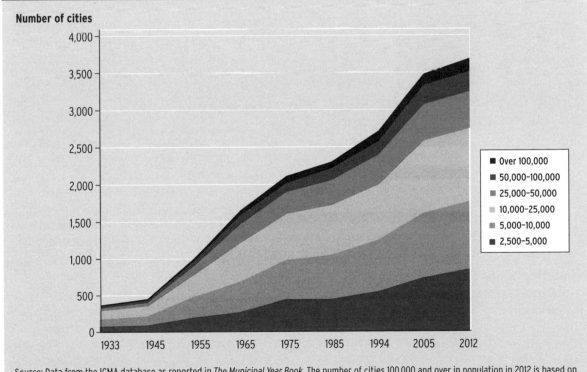

Source: Data from the ICMA database as reported in *The Municipal Year Book.* The number of cities 100,000 and over in population in 2012 is based on 2010 Census data.

Table 2-2 Municipal Form of Government, 2011

Classification	No. reporting (A)	Mayor-council		Council-manager		Commission		Town meeting		Representative town meeting	
		No.	% of (A)	No.	% of (A)	No.	% of (A)	No.	% of (A)	No.	% of (A)
Total respondents	3,566	1,182	33	2,098	59	49	1	216	6	21	1
Population group											
Over 1,000,000	2	1	50	1	50	0	0	0	0	0	0
500,000–1,000,000	9	5	56	4	44	0	0	0	0	0	0
250,000–499,999	17	10	59	7	41	0	0	0	0	0	0
100,000–249,999	86	20	23	66	77	0	0	0	0	0	0
50,000–99,999	199	43	22	148	74	3	2	0	0	5	3
25,000–49,999	366	104	28	253	69	2	1	3	1	4	1
10,000–24,999	769	204	27	496	65	15	2	48	6	6	1
5,000–9,999	760	238	31	443	58	9	1	67	9	3	*
2,500–4,999	807	340	42	403	50	6	1	57	7	1	*
Under 2,500	551	219	40	277	50	13	2	40	7	2	*
Geographic division											
New England	373	42	11	108	29	0	0	209	56	14	4
Mid-Atlantic	343	150	44	173	50	16	5	0	0	3	1
East North-Central	678	274	40	385	57	11	2	5	1	3	*
West North-Central	453	224	49	218	48	10	2	0	0	1	*
South Atlantic	570	115	20	446	78	9	2	0	0	0	0
East South-Central	159	106	67	50	31	3	2	0	0	0	0
West South-Central	342	101	30	241	71	0	0	0	0	0	0
Mountain	231	72	31	159	69	0	0	0	0	0	0
Pacific Coast	417	99	24	318	76	0	0	0	0	0	0
Metro status											
Metropolitan Statistical Area	2,040	695	34	1,321	65	22	1	2	*	–	0
Micropolitan Statistical Area	523	200	38	319	61	4	1	–	0	–	0
NECTA[a]	244	8	7	62	25	–	0	151	62	13	5
Undesignated	759	269	35	396	52	23	3	63	8	8	1

a   New England City and Town Area.

* = Less than 0.5%.

Despite the impression conveyed in the media that large cities, by referenda, are abandoning the council-manager form, the record is actually mixed. Since 1990, the mayor-council form has replaced the council-manager form in 9 cities with 100,000 or more in population, but the council-manager form has replaced the mayor-council or commission form in 4 other cities.[6] During the same period, 9 large cities rejected abandonment of the council-manager form while 2 other cities rejected adoption of the strong mayor form. One city voted down a shift from mayor-council to council-manager form. There is no clear trend in the changes, although the strong mayor-council option has been replaced or rejected in 14 of the 24 cities in which it was considered. Thus, the retention of the council-manager form in most cities where it is challenged, together with the growing number of large council-manager governments that has resulted from the growing population, indicates that use of this form will continue to expand among cities 100,000 and above in population.

Of the cities responding to the 2011 survey, 95 cities of all sizes reported an effort to change the form of

Table 2-3 Form of Government Used in Large Cities

Form of government	Total		1 million+		500-999k		250-499k		100-249k	
	No.	%	No.	%	No.	%	No.	%	No.	%
Council-manager	176	64	3	33	8	33	20	49	145	73
Mayor-council	97	35	6	67	15	63	21	51	55	28
Commission	1	*	0	0	1	4	0	0	0	0
Total	274	100	9	100	24	100	41	100	200	100

Source: Population is based on the 2010 Census. Form-of-government classification is from a dataset of all cities over 10,000 in population, prepared by Kimberly Nelson at North Illinois University. The preparation of the dataset is described in Kimberly Nelson and James Svara, "Adaptation of Models Versus Variations in Form: Classifying Structures of City Government," *Urban Affairs Review* 45, no. 4 (2010): 544-562.

Note: Percentages may not add to 100% because of rounding.

* = Less than 0.5%.

government in the past five years and provided information about the outcome. As shown in Table 2–4, changes to the council-manager form were approved in 42 cases and to the mayor-council form in 5 cases, and one change was approved to the town meeting form. Similar patterns had been reported in 2006: during the five years preceding that survey, 35 of 70 proposed changes to the council-manager form were approved, along with 5 of 23 proposed changes to the mayor-council form.[7]

Legal Basis of Form of Government

Regarding the establishment of the municipality's structure or form of government, a majority of respondents overall (56%) reported that the legal basis for their form of government is established in the city charter rather than by state law or local ordinance (not shown). However, legal bases differ substantially by form of government, population size, and region. The council-manager form, for example, is much more likely to be incorporated in the city charter (64%), indicating an intentional choice and long-term commitment by local officials and citizens. More cities with the mayor-council form, on the other hand, rely on state law (29%) or on a local ordinance (24%) that can be changed by a subsequent council. The town meeting form is also likely to be based on state law (39%) or charter (38%). For cities of 2,500 and above in population, the larger the city, the more likely it is that its form of government is stipulated in the charter. Geographically, the South Atlantic division leads in the use of charters (93%) as the legal basis for the form of government, followed by West South-Central (66%) and New England (60%) divisions.

Position of Chief Appointed Official

Along with an expansion in the use of the council-manager form of government, there has been a dramatic increase in the proportion of cities that have a CAO. By definition, this position is found in council-

Table 2-4 Changes in Form of Government, 2007-2011

From	To	Approved	Not approved
Mayor-council	Council-manager	34	17
Mayor-council	Commission, town meeting (TM), or unknown	0	6
Council-manager	Mayor-council	5	17
Council-manager	Town meeting	1	2
Commission	Council-manager	7	1
Commission	Mayor-council	0	1
Town meeting	Mayor-council	0	1
Town meeting	Council-manager	1	0
Town meeting	Representative IM	0	1
Representative TM	Town meeting	0	1
		48	47

manager cities; in addition, among respondents to the 2011 form-of-government survey, over three in five mayor-council cities have a CAO, as do over three-quarters of cities that use other forms of government (Table 2–5). However, a 2010 study of all cities over 10,000 in population found that mayor-council cities are evenly divided in the use and nonuse of the CAO position.[8] Although the current estimates vary, they reflect a substantial increase since the 1991 form-of-government survey, when 35% of the responding mayor-council cities reported having a CAO.

Legal Basis for Position The 2011 survey shows that the legal basis of the CAO position differs greatly by form of government. Whereas 63% of the CAO positions in council-manager cities are based on charter or state law, 69% of the CAO positions in mayor-council cities are based on ordinance, resolution, or action by the mayor (not shown).

Table 2-5 Presence of a Chief Appointed Official in Municipality

Classification	No. reporting (A)	Yes No.	Yes % of (A)
Total respondents	3,554	3,025	85
Population group			
Over 1,000,000	2	2	100
500,000-1,000,000	9	5	56
250,000-499,999	17	13	77
100,000-249,999	85	76	89
50,000-99,999	198	179	90
25,000-49,999	364	309	85
10,000-24,999	765	679	89
5,000-9,999	759	656	86
2,500-4,999	804	647	81
Under 2,500	551	459	83
Geographic division			
New England	370	299	81
Mid-Atlantic	342	284	83
East North-Central	674	528	78
West North-Central	451	404	90
South Atlantic	569	533	94
East South-Central	158	97	61
West South-Central	342	293	86
Mountain	231	199	86
Pacific Coast	417	388	93
Metro status			
Metropolitan Statistical Area	2,035	1,771	87
Micropolitan Statistical Area	521	428	82
NECTA[a]	241	196	81
Undesignated	757	630	83
Form of government			
Mayor-council	1,174	717	61
Council-manager	2,096	2,080	99
Commission	48	37	77
Town meeting	216	176	82
Representative town meeting	20	15	75

a New England City and Town Area.

Appointment The method of appointing the CAO is difficult to track in detail over time, but there are substantial differences based on form of government (Table 2–6). In 95% of the council-manager cities, the council (77%) or the council and mayor (18%) appoint the city manager. In 5% of the council-manager cities (all under 50,000 in population), the respondents reported that either the mayor nominates the manager and the council approves, or the mayor alone appoints the manager, but these responses may be reporting informal practices rather than formal provisions.[9]

In mayor-council cities, there is substantial variation. Although it is common to assume mayoral control of the appointment, this happens in only 14% of the cities (Table 2–6). It is more common for the council (39%) or the council and mayor acting together (21%) to appoint the CAO. In almost another quarter of the mayor-council cities (24%), the mayor nominates the CAO and the council approves, although the actual use of this method is higher in larger cities.[10] There is evidence to indicate that the council's involvement in appointing the CAO contributes to a greater sense of accountability in the CAO to both the mayor and the council. In cities where the mayor and council jointly choose the CAO, the relationship between the CAO and elected officials can approximate the conditions in council-manager cities. This relationship is not as close when the mayor's nominee must be confirmed by the council, but even then, CAOs report that they have a greater sense of accountability to the council than when they are appointed by the mayor alone.[11]

Changes in the Position of CAO During the past five years, among cities proposing a change in the CAO position, eight mayor-council cities (27%) added the position of CAO, as did five commission and town meeting cities (50%) (not shown). On the other hand, the position was eliminated in four mayor-council cities (29%) and in one commission and one town meeting city (14%).

The Chief Elected Official

The chief elected official (CEO) is the mayor in most cities (85%) or a council president or chair (15%) in the remaining cities (not shown). Approximately 90% of town meeting and representative town meeting cities, as well as 14% of council-manager cities, have a council president but not a mayor. Almost one in three mayor-council cities has both a mayor and a council president compared with only one in eight council-manager cities (not shown). Survey respondents were instructed to answer the questions that followed on the basis of the position of mayor, if they have one, or the position of council president or chair if they do not have a mayor.

Election It is common to think of the mayor's office as an elected position, although this is not true in most counties and was not originally the case in most

Table 2-6   Appointment of Chief Appointed Official

Classification	No. reporting (A)	CEO No.	CEO % of (A)	Council No.	Council % of (A)	Combination of CEO and council No.	Combination of CEO and council % of (A)	Nominated by mayor/ approved by council No.	Nominated by mayor/ approved by council % of (A)	Nominated by council/ approved by mayor No.	Nominated by council/ approved by mayor % of (A)	Other No.	Other % of (A)
Total respondents	2,870	123	4	1,946	68	509	18	259	9	6	*	27	1
Population group													
Over 1,000,000	2	1	50	1	50	0	0	0	0	0	0	0	0
500,000-1,000,000	5	0	0	1	20	3	60	1	20	0	0	0	0
250,000-499,999	12	4	33	3	25	2	17	2	17	0	0	1	8
100,000-249,999	76	3	4	52	68	18	24	3	4	0	0	0	0
50,000-99,999	175	7	4	118	67	38	22	12	7	0	0	0	0
25,000-49,999	293	10	3	197	67	58	20	27	9	0	0	1	*
10,000-24,999	641	34	5	440	69	114	18	49	8	0	0	4	1
5,000-9,999	627	26	4	439	70	89	14	65	10	1	*	7	1
2,500-4,999	610	25	4	400	66	107	18	67	11	4	1	7	1
Under 2,500	429	13	3	295	69	80	19	33	8	1	*	7	2
Geographic division													
New England	290	18	6	247	85	16	6	3	1	0	0	6	2
Mid-Atlantic	271	10	4	189	70	43	16	27	10	2	1	0	0
East North-Central	495	40	8	269	54	100	20	80	16	2	*	4	1
West North-Central	385	12	3	232	60	86	22	51	13	1	*	3	1
South Atlantic	498	10	2	350	70	112	23	24	5	0	0	2	*
East South-Central	88	8	9	51	58	18	21	8	9	0	0	3	3
West South-Central	277	6	2	202	73	46	17	20	7	1	*	2	1
Mountain	192	3	2	109	57	52	27	26	14	0	0	2	1
Pacific Coast	374	16	4	297	79	36	10	20	5	0	0	5	1
Metro status													
Metropolitan Statistical Area	1,680	74	4	1,087	65	326	19	173	10	5	*	15	1
Micropolitan Statistical Area	403	18	5	269	67	75	19	36	9	1	*	4	1
NECTA[a]	190	15	8	156	82	12	6	2	1	0	0	5	3
Undesignated	597	16	3	434	73	96	16	48	8	0	0	3	1
Form of government													
Mayor-council	677	92	14	266	39	142	21	161	24	2	*	14	2
Council-manager	1,973	15	1	1,509	77	346	18	92	5	4	*	7	*
Commission	36	0	0	25	69	7	19	4	11	0	0	0	0
Town meeting	169	15	9	136	81	12	7	1	1	0	0	5	3
Representative town meeting	15	1	7	10	67	2	13	1	7	0	0	1	7

Note: Percentages may not total 100% because of rounding.

a   New England City and Town Area.

* = Less than 0.5%.

council-manager cities. Over time, the use of direct election has increased to 69% in council-manager cities; it is nearly universal in mayor-council cities and is used in all cities of 250,000 and over in population (Table 2–7). A substantial minority of council-manager cities use selection from among members of the council, designation of the highest vote getter, or rotation,[12] methods that are commonly used in commission and town meeting cities.

The CEO is far more likely to be a full-time position in mayor-council (30%) than council-manager (6%) cities, but most mayors in cities with 250,000 or more residents have full-time mayors (not shown).

Terms of Office Regarding the CEO's term of office, the highest percentage of respondents (46%) reported a four-year term, followed by a two-year term (33%) (not shown). Four-year terms were generally reported by higher percentages of larger cities than smaller cities, and by 87% of cities in the East South-Central division followed by 69% of cities in the Mountain division. In contrast, the greatest use of the two-year term is in the West South-Central division (52%). Many cities in New England (42%) use a one-year term, presumably in combination with their greater use of the town meeting form and their practice of choosing the CEO from among council members. Council-manager cities show the highest percentage reporting two-year terms (38%), and mayor-council cities show the highest percentage reporting four-year terms (69%).

The use of a legal limit on the number of terms allowed for the CEO is rare. The vast majority (91%) of cities reported that such limits are not in place (not shown); those cities that do have term limits, however, generally have larger populations. Where term limits are imposed, the majority (56%) of cities have a limit of two terms, followed by 25% with a limit of three terms.

Responsibilities and Authority CEOs have varying degrees of responsibility and authority, depending on the form of government, and there is widespread variation among specific cities that use the same form.

Serving on the Council and Voting in Meetings The mayor-council form of government is based on the principle of separation of powers that divides the executive from the legislature. Despite this expectation, the CEO serves on the council in 45% of mayor-council cities (not shown). In contrast, over 90% of mayors in council-manager cities of 25,000 and over in population serve on the council, and the proportion stays above three-quarters for smaller cities.

Signifying their active involvement in the council, 70% of mayors in council-manager cities and more than 85% of mayors in commission, town meeting, and representative town meeting governments can vote on all issues before the council (Table 2–8). In contrast, the CEO has this authority in only 23% of mayor-council cities. Still, among mayor-council cities, 57% permit the CEO to vote to break a tie while 16% never permit the CEO to vote.

Mayors in a majority of mayor-council cities (56%) have the authority to veto actions of the council (not shown), but there is great variation by the size of the city. Whereas virtually all mayors in large and medium-sized mayor-council cities have the veto, that proportion drops below 70% in cities below 25,000 in population and to less than half in cities under 5,000. Overall, 14% of council-manager mayors have the veto, and there is little variation by city size. Veto power is less common in other forms of government.

Developing the Budget The authority for developing the budget submitted to the council is typically given to the mayor in larger mayor-council cities. But among responding mayor-council cities below 25,000 in population, fewer than half reported that the mayor is responsible—either alone or in combination with the CAO—for preparing the budget (not shown); in those cases, the CAO (and the chief financial officer) is more likely to have that responsibility. In council-manager cities of all sizes, on the other hand, developing the budget is usually a responsibility of the CAO.

Appointing Department Directors The authority for appointing department heads is generally assigned to the executive in city government, although other officials share the responsibility or exercise it directly. The sharing of appointment authority increases as city size declines. Among responding mayor-council cities of 25,000 and over in population, the mayor either fills appointed department director positions alone (36%) or shares this authority with others (27%). Among smaller mayor-council cities, 19% of mayors have this authority alone while 35% of mayors share it (Table 2–9).

In council-manager cities, by comparison, there is greater concentration of appointment power, as well as somewhat greater uniformity, in the CAO's position: in larger cities, 59% of CAOs have this authority alone and 26% share it, compared with 45% and 31%, respectively, in smaller cities (Table 2–9). In almost half of the commission cities, however, the council makes appointments, whereas over 60% of the town meeting cities directly elect some or all department heads (not shown).

Other Areas of Authority The CEO can have several other areas of authority. Most CEOs can assign council

Table 2-7 Method of Selecting Chief Elected Official

Classification	No. reporting (A)	Voters elect directly		Council selects from among its members		The council member receiving the most votes in the general election is selected		Council members rotate into the position of chief elected official		Other	
		No.	% of (A)	No.	% of (A)	No.	% of (A)	No.	% of (A)	No.	% of (A)
Total respondents	3,395	2,591	76	704	21	12	*	65	2	23	1
Population group											
Over 1,000,000	2	2	100	0	0	0	0	0	0	0	0
500,000–1,000,000	9	9	100	0	0	0	0	0	0	0	0
250,000–499,999	16	16	100	0	0	0	0	0	0	0	0
100,000–249,999	82	70	85	10	12	0	0	2	2	0	0
50,000–99,999	194	145	75	40	21	3	2	5	3	1	1
25,000–49,999	353	260	74	81	23	3	1	8	2	1	0
10,000–24,999	725	521	72	178	25	5	1	16	2	5	1
5,000–9,999	729	550	75	160	22	0	0	16	2	3	0
2,500–4,999	764	615	80	132	17	1	0	10	1	6	1
Under 2,500	521	403	77	103	20	0	0	8	2	7	1
Geographic division											
New England	323	130	40	160	50	3	1	25	8	5	2
Mid-Atlantic	331	212	64	107	32	0	0	8	2	4	1
East North-Central	652	542	83	101	15	2	0	3	0	4	1
West North-Central	434	398	92	35	8	1	0	0	0	0	0
South Atlantic	550	462	84	80	15	3	1	4	1	1	0
East South-Central	151	132	87	18	12	0	0	0	0	1	1
West South-Central	325	289	89	33	10	0	0	0	0	3	1
Mountain	224	195	87	29	13	0	0	0	0	0	0
Pacific Coast	405	231	57	141	35	3	1	25	6	5	1
Metro status											
Metropolitan Statistical Area	1,962	1,600	82	315	16	9	0	29	1	9	0
Micropolitan Statistical Area	501	419	84	78	16	1	0	0	0	3	1
NECTA[a]	208	84	40	102	49	2	1	18	9	2	1
Undesignated	724	488	67	209	29	0	0	18	2	9	1
Form of government											
Mayor-council	1,143	1,093	96	40	3	0	0	1	0	9	1
Council-manager	2,004	1,390	69	555	28	12	1	40	2	7	0
Commission	45	23	51	19	42	0	0	1	2	2	4
Town meeting	182	73	40	82	45	0	0	22	12	5	3
Representative town meeting	21	12	57	8	38	0	0	1	5	0	0

a New England City and Town Area.

* = Less than 0.5%.

Table 2-8 Voting Authority of the Chief Elected Official in Council Meetings

Classification	No. reporting (A)	On all issues		Only to break a tie		Never		Other	
		No.	% of (A)	No.	% of (A)	No.	% of (A)	No.	% of (A)
Total respondents	3,372	1,874	56	1,191	35	230	7	77	2
Population group									
Over 1,000,000	2	1	50	0	0	1	50	0	0
500,000–1,000,000	9	4	44	0	0	5	56	0	0
250,000–499,999	16	4	25	2	13	8	50	2	13
100,000–249,999	83	62	75	12	14	8	10	1	1
50,000–99,999	192	135	70	29	15	22	11	6	3
25,000–49,999	350	222	63	83	24	38	11	7	2
10,000–24,999	721	442	61	201	28	56	8	22	3
5,000–9,999	719	398	55	272	38	33	5	16	2
2,500–4,999	757	348	46	367	48	29	4	13	2
Under 2,500	523	258	49	225	43	30	6	10	2
Geographic division									
New England	321	267	83	23	7	28	9	3	1
Mid-Atlantic	327	180	55	122	37	16	5	9	3
East North-Central	644	327	51	230	36	62	10	25	4
West North-Central	434	169	39	187	43	63	15	15	3
South Atlantic	550	278	51	248	45	18	3	6	1
East South-Central	147	70	48	58	39	17	12	2	1
West South-Central	327	156	48	153	47	13	4	5	2
Mountain	220	124	56	87	40	5	2	4	2
Pacific Coast	402	303	75	83	21	8	2	8	2
Metro status									
Metropolitan Statistical Area	1,953	1,071	55	689	35	141	7	52	3
Micropolitan Statistical Area	498	225	45	223	45	39	8	11	2
NECTA[a]	206	185	90	9	4	11	5	1	0
Undesignated	715	393	55	270	38	39	5	13	2
Form of government									
Mayor-council	1,124	256	23	644	57	180	16	44	4
Council-manager	2,004	1,395	70	533	27	44	2	32	2
Commission	44	39	89	5	11	0	0	0	0
Town meeting	180	167	93	8	4	4	2	1	1
Representative town meeting	20	17	85	1	5	2	10	0	0

a New England City and Town Area.

members to chair or serve on committees and can appoint citizens to serve on advisory or quasi-judicial authorities, boards, or commissions (Table 2–10). Making an annual report to the council and citizens is a common practice in mayor-council, town meeting, and representative town meeting cities but is found less often in council-manager and commission cities. Still, in council-manager cities, the use of an annual report has increased from 32% in 2006 to 42% in 2011 (not shown). A majority of mayor-council cities and 18% of

Table 2-9 Who Appoints Department Directors, by Form and Population Size

| Appointer | Mayor-council | | Council-manager | |
	25,000 and over, %	Under 25,000, %	25,000 and over, %	Under 25,000, %
Chief elected official (CEO)	36	19	2	3
Chief administrative officer (CAO)	2	4	59	45
CEO/CAO	2	4	1	4
CAO/council	8	9	14	17
CEO/council approves	24	26	2	4
Council	10	25	5	14
CAO with council consent	5	6	9	8
CEO/CAO/council	2	4	2	2
Other	11	3	6	3
Total	100	100	100	100
	(173)	(958)	(466)	(1,553)

council-manager cities report that the CEO receives the annual budget developed by the CAO or chief financial officer.[13]

Changes in Authority In the five years since the 2006 form-of-government survey was conducted, proposals to increase the powers and authorities of the CEO have been made in 17 mayor-council cities with five approvals (29% acceptance); in 29 council-manager cities with eight approvals (28%); and in 7 town meeting cities with three approvals (43%). There was one proposal in a commission city and one in a representative town meeting city with no approvals (not shown).

On the other hand, proposals to decrease the powers and authorities of the CEO have been made in 19 mayor-council cities with seven approvals (37%), in 31 council-manager cities with six approvals (19%), and in 3 town meeting cities with one approval (33%).

Election and Terms of Council Members

One of the central features of the urban reform movement and the second Model City Charter was the removal of a council candidate's political party from the ballot. The 2011 form-of-government survey results show that while political party is on the ballot in only 21% of cities reporting, it is twice as likely to be found in mayor-council cities than in council-manager cities (not shown). The major exception is in the Mid-Atlantic division, which has largely retained the use of partisan elections (91%). In no other geographic division does the proportion of partisan elections exceed 25%.

At-Large and Ward/District Elections Two-thirds of all local government respondents (66%) reported that all council members are elected at large, rather than some or all being elected by ward or district (Table 2-11).[14] Not unexpectedly, ward/district-based elections significantly increase with city population. Of the 27 large cities with a population of 250,000 and above, only 2 use at-large elections exclusively, but over half have a combination of at-large and district seats. In cities under 25,000, on the other hand, 69% use at-large elections. Just 54% of mayor-council governments use at-large elections, while 70% or more of the other government forms do. There are also some marked geographic differences. The highest use of at-large elections is found in the Pacific Coast (89%) and New England (81%) division cities. Only 47% of cities in the West North-Central division reported using at-large elections, but this division has the highest

Table 2-10 Other Authorities of Chief Elected Officials, by Form

Authorities	Mayor-council, %	Council-manager, %	Commission, %	Town meeting, %	Representative town meeting, %
Assign council members to chair or serve on committees and make assignments to those committees.	66	72	52	43	69
Appoint citizens to serve on advisory or quasi-judicial authorities, boards, or commissions.	78	62	76	45	46
Make an annual report to the council and citizens on the state of the community.	61	43	30	60	69
Receive the annual budget developed by the chief appointed official and present the budget to the council.	55	18	49	44	31

Table 2-11 Method of Electing Council Members

Classification	No. reporting (A)	All at-large		All by ward/district		Combination of at-large and ward/ district	
		No.	% of (A)	No.	% of (A)	No.	% of (A)
Total respondents	3,450	2,287	66	569	17	594	17
Population group							
Over 1,000,000	2	0	0	1	50	1	50
500,000-1,000,000	9	2	22	2	22	5	56
250,000-499,999	16	0	0	8	50	8	50
100,000-249,999	83	37	45	13	16	33	40
50,000-99,999	193	109	57	18	9	66	34
25,000-49,999	356	207	58	59	17	90	25
10,000-24,999	740	468	63	120	16	152	21
5,000-9,999	736	468	64	137	19	131	18
2,500-4,999	779	548	70	146	19	85	11
Under 2,500	536	448	84	65	12	23	4
Geographic division							
New England	349	283	81	21	6	45	12
Mid-Atlantic	336	232	69	70	21	34	10
East North-Central	653	392	60	124	19	137	21
West North-Central	442	207	47	138	31	97	22
South Atlantic	552	384	70	69	13	99	18
East South-Central	151	88	58	35	23	28	19
West South-Central	335	182	54	54	16	99	30
Mountain	225	159	71	33	15	33	15
Pacific Coast	407	360	89	25	6	22	5
Metro status							
Metropolitan Statistical Area	1,979	1,301	66	303	15	375	19
Micropolitan Statistical Area	513	289	56	113	22	111	22
NECTA[a]	223	199	89	5	2	19	9
Undesignated	735	498	68	148	20	89	12
Form of government							
Mayor-council	1,144	615	54	293	26	236	21
Council-manager	2,041	1,432	70	255	13	354	17
Commission	48	36	75	9	19	3	6
Town meeting	198	185	93	12	6	1	1
Representative town meeting	19	19	100	0	0	0	0

a   New England City and Town Area.

percentage of cities that elect all council members from districts (31%).

Among the responding cities 2,500 and over in population, half use at-large and nonpartisan elections as originally advocated by the municipal reform movement, and only 5% use the traditional pairing of district and partisan elections (not shown). The reform model has been reconceived as more cities have recognized the importance of minority and geographic representation, and 15% of all cities of 2,500 and over have a combination of at-large and district seats with nonpartisan elections (not shown). Another 5% use a combination approach with partisan elections. The remaining cities use partisan and at-large elections (12%) and nonpartisan district elections (12%).

In large cities of 100,000 and over in population, the mix of practices is more evenly balanced. The largest category is nonpartisan with a combination of district and at-large (39%), followed by nonpartisan at-large elections (31%) and nonpartisan district elections (16%). Partisan elections are used in only 15% of these cities, and of these, only 7% use the partisan elections with districts. Thus, there are a variety of contexts that influence the selection and representational orientation of council members in large cities.

Council Member Work Status The vast majority of city councils have part-time members. Only 260 cities (8%) reported having full-time members and another 45 have a combination of full- and part-time members (not shown). This proportion of 1 in 12 cities with full-time members is fairly consistent across city population sizes, and 40% of councils with full-time members are in mayor-council cities.

Council Terms of Office Regardless of how council members are elected, almost two-thirds of respondents reported four-year terms (not shown). Nearly the entire remaining third reported two- or three-year terms, with a small minority of cities (mostly council-manager) using terms longer than four years. The most variation in term length occurs by geography, as cities in the New England and the West South-Central divisions reported much lower percentages of four-year terms than cities in the other divisions.

A recent effort to change election practices—viewed by proponents as a reform of city councils—has focused on term limits. Since it gained prominence in 1992, the movement has not had great impact on council composition.[15] Only 10% of respondents overall reported a limit on the number of terms that a council member may serve (not shown). Limits are most common in the Mountain division cities (32%) and, to a lesser degree, in cities in the West South-Central division (18%). Otherwise, it is more often a big-city practice. About half the cities with 250,000 or more residents reported using term limits for council members, as did 24% of the cities between 50,000 and 249,999 in population. Term limits are more common in council-manager cities (13%) than in mayor-council (5%) or commission (8%) cities. They are almost never used in the town meeting cities. There

has been no systematic change in the use of term limits since 2006.

Eighty-five percent of respondents indicated that terms of office are staggered, a practice that provides some continuity. Staggered terms are more often a medium- and small-city practice, reported by just half of the large cities (not shown). Noticeable variations in term limits and continuity exist according to form of government. Cities with the council-manager form are more likely than those with any other form to report staggered terms (92%) (not shown).

Changes in Elections A small percentage of cities (101, or 3% of respondents) attempted to make one or more changes in council elections to or from an at-large, district/ward, or combination system (not shown). Such attempts were equally likely among the different forms of government and most likely among larger cities, but approval was relatively infrequent in all cases. Twenty-seven cities realized a change in council elections in the five-year period since the last survey. Regarding the CEO, just 20% of the 55 cities that proposed election changes for that position were approved. In addition to election method changes, 107 cities proposed more or fewer council/board seats or a change in the proportion of council members being elected by district/ward, and almost a third of these proposals found approval.

Committees and Citizen Boards

An increasing number of city councils use standing committees—permanent bodies with set memberships and regularly scheduled meetings—to consider specific policy matters. The proportion rose from 54% in 2006 to 66% in 2011 (not shown).

Ninety-five percent of municipalities reported using citizen authorities, boards, or commissions, and they almost all appoint (rather than elect) a portion of the citizen members. Although only 7% of respondents use elections to determine their citizen board membership, the proportion that does so is much higher in New England cities (47%) (not shown). This may be a function of the town meeting and representative town meeting forms of government, both of which show much higher percentages with elected members of citizen groups (60% and 44%, respectively) than the other forms.

The citizen boards or commissions typically serve multiple functions. The vast majority (89%) serve in an advisory role, usually in zoning and planning decisions, but some local governments also reported a decision-making (39%) and a quasi-judicial role (33%)—for example, hearing zoning appeals—for their citizen boards and commissions (not shown). New England cities with town meeting and representative town meeting forms of government show percentages well above 'average reporting a decision-making role for these groups. Figure 2–2 shows the functional areas in which citizen groups are used. The most common is zoning (86%) and the least common is ethics (8%)—the same proportions found in 2006.

Provisions for Initiative, Referenda, and Recall

There are various provisions that allow citizens or the council to introduce items on a ballot. In order of the most common to least common method used, these provisions are legislative referendum, recall, initiative, and popular referendum (Figure 2–3).

Legislative Referendum Legislative referendum allows the council to send the vote directly to citizens by placing any question on the ballot for approval or rejection. The results may be binding or nonbinding. About 70% of municipalities reported a provision for legislative referenda (Figure 2–3). Cities with a mayor-council form of government (along with commission cities) were the least likely to report using this type of provision, particularly compared with town meeting and representative town meeting governments, where nearly 80% reported using it (not shown). Among geographic divisions, close to 62% of cities in the East South-Central division do not provide for legislative referendum, compared with 31% overall.

Figure 2-2   Areas of Committee Use

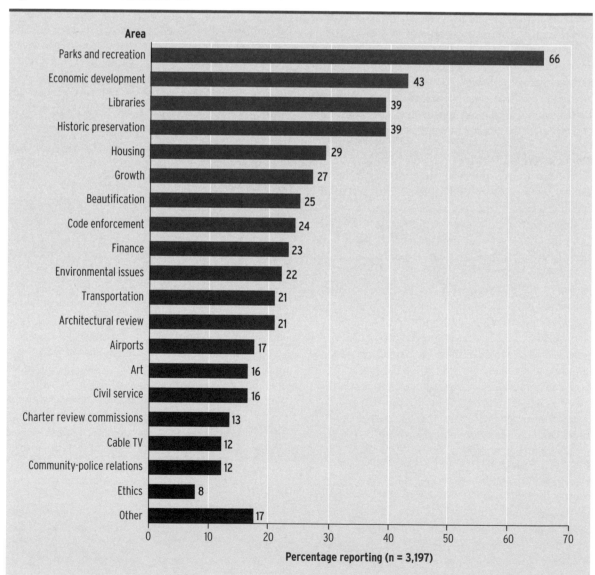

Figure 2-3 Provisions for Referenda, Initiative, and Recall

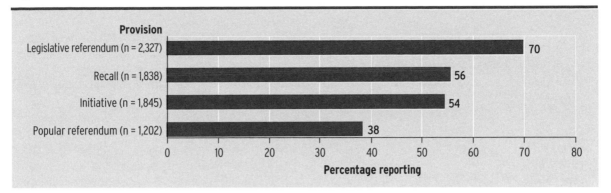

For those municipalities that reported providing for a legislative referendum, the survey included a follow-up question to determine which items must be placed on the ballot for voter approval. Bond measures and charter amendments were reported by the highest percentages (64% and 56%, respectively) (not shown), while proposed ordinances, home rule changes, and other items were required less frequently. There is more variation by population and geographic division regarding charter amendments, with no discernible pattern emerging. For the most part, mayor-council and council-manager governments have similar referendum requirements.

Recall Recall allows citizens to collect signatures for a petition to place on the ballot a question of whether an elected official should be removed from office before his or her term has expired. It was reported in more than half the reporting municipalities (56%), and 5% of respondents with this provision filed recall petitions in 2011 (not shown). The highest percentages are found among larger local governments, but no fewer than half the municipalities in any size category provide for a recall. Among the geographic divisions, Pacific Coast cities show the highest percentage reporting this provision (82%), followed by the Mountain and West South-Central divisions at 78% and 77%, respectively (not shown). Its use among different forms of government varies slightly, with fewer mayor-council localities than council-manager localities providing recall rights (50% compared to 61%).

Initiative A majority of municipalities (54%) reported providing for an initiative, through which citizens can place charter, ordinance, or home rule changes on the ballot by collecting the required number of signatures on a petition. There are three types of initiative: indirect, direct, and nonbinding. The *indirect* provision requires that before any charter,

ordinance, or home rule change proposed by citizens through a petition process can be placed on the ballot, the council must consider it. Vote results are then binding on the local government. In contrast, the *direct* initiative requires that any change petitioned by citizens be placed directly on the ballot for a vote. The direct initiative can be *nonbinding*, in which case voters can approve or reject it, but implementation of the initiative is not binding on the local government. According to survey respondents, indirect and direct initiatives are about equally likely (51% vs. 48%), but nonbinding initiatives are relatively uncommon, reported by only 17% of respondents (not shown).

Here, too, the highest percentages of initiative users are seen among larger local governments (Table 2–12). Almost all cities with a population of 250,000 and above offer citizens this opportunity. The proportion drops precipitously with population until, among cities reporting with a population under 5,000, less than 50% offer the initiative option. The percentages vary even more by geographic division, as the highest percentages providing for an initiative are in cities in the Mountain (80%), New England (77%), and Pacific Coast (77%) divisions, and the lowest are in East South-Central division cities (20%), followed by cities in the South Atlantic and Mid-Atlantic divisions (31% and 39%, respectively).

As with the legislative referendum and recall provisions, mayor-council governments are less likely than council-manager governments to have an initiative provision—and by a fairly wide margin. Forty-four percent of the former and 59% of the latter provide for initiatives.

Popular Referendum Popular referendum is similar to the initiative process. It allows citizens to collect signatures on a petition to place on the ballot any charter, ordinance, or home rule change that has been adopted by the local government before the change can take

Table 2-12   Provision for Initiative and Type of Initiative Process

Classification	No. reporting (A)	Has provision for initiative		Type of initiative process			
		No.	% of (A)	No. reporting (B)	Indirect % of (B)	Direct % of (B)	Nonbinding initiative % of B
Total respondents	3,392	1,845	54	1,714	50	48	16
Population group							
Over 1,000,000	2	2	100	2	100	0	0
500,000-1,000,000	9	9	100	8	50	38	13
250,000-499,999	16	14	88	14	36	71	7
100,000-249,999	81	61	75	58	48	55	12
50,000-99,999	195	151	77	139	60	37	20
25,000-49,999	350	226	65	205	53	48	16
10,000-24,999	730	458	63	421	52	44	19
5,000-9,999	729	364	50	343	45	55	17
2,500-4,999	759	334	44	314	50	47	13
Under 2,500	521	226	43	210	45	49	15
Geographic division							
New England	358	276	77	264	50	45	29
Mid-Atlantic	323	127	39	116	43	41	40
East North-Central	634	369	58	344	44	54	20
West North-Central	428	180	42	168	65	36	7
South Atlantic	544	168	31	151	64	34	11
East South-Central	154	31	20	31	36	58	10
West South-Central	329	211	64	194	44	55	6
Mountain	222	177	80	169	50	49	11
Pacific Coast	400	306	77	277	49	53	11
Form of government							
Mayor-council	1,107	482	44	443	46	48	21
Council-manager	2,011	1,183	59	1,106	52	48	12
Commission	45	19	42	17	41	29	41
Town meeting	208	149	72	138	44	47	33
Representative town meeting	21	12	57	10	50	20	40

effect. Approximately 39% of municipalities reported this option for citizens, with cities in larger population groups showing higher percentages than smaller cities. Council-manager and mayor-council cities use the referendum at approximately the same rate, while town meeting and representative town meeting cities show slightly higher percentages, and commissions show slightly lower ones. Among geographic divisions, the popular referendum is used by a majority of cities in the Mountain (58%) and Pacific Coast (54%) division cities, and it is also widely used in New England (46%) and West South-Central (43%) divisions cities. The least use is found in the Mid-Atlantic (27%), East South-Central (22%), and South Atlantic (20%) divisions (not shown).

Summary

The 2011 survey results show a continuation of trends that have been evolving over extended periods of time. The council-manager form itself has evolved over the past 100 years from being an atypical constitutional framework usually found in small and moderate-sized cities to being the predominant form in cities of all sizes except the very small and the very large, and the number of cities using the form continues to grow. The commission form is now rarely used, and the town meeting and representative town meeting forms are largely confined to New England.

The use of the CAO position in mayor-council cities has also expanded, and the formal provisions for appointing the position create the likelihood of a range of working relationships with elected officials. The CAO may be the agent of the mayor and council, much like in the council-manager form, when appointed jointly by the mayor and council, or may act primarily as the agent of a strong executive mayor when appointed by the mayor alone. Council approval of a mayoral nomi-

nation is likely to reinforce higher CAO accountability to the council but not equal to that shown to the mayor.

The electoral context of the council is determined by whether candidates are identified on the ballot by party affiliation and whether the constituency is based on wards/districts, the city at-large, or a combination of both. Most cities have nonpartisan ballots and at least some at-large members of the council. Provisions for direct democracy are widely used.

For structural features that define authority and assign responsibilities, the recurring theme is variety. Despite broad differences between the major forms of government, officials and citizens must be sensitive to local nuances in structure and practice.

Notes

1 For example, survey respondents from very small cities are more likely to have the council-manager form or an appointed administrator than are nonrespondents.

2 The response rate to the *Municipal Form of Government, 2011* survey was 50% from council-manager cities of 2,500 and over in population and 29% from mayor-council cities.

3 "Inside the Year Book," in *The Municipal Year Book 2012* (Washington, D.C.: ICMA Press, 2012), xiii.

4 In the *Municipal Form of Government, 2011* survey, the proportion of cities 2,500 and over in population reporting use of the council-manager form is 60%, and the proportion of cities over 10,000 indicating use of the council-manager form is 67%. These figures indicate that respondents to the survey overrepresented the actual use of the council-manager form to some extent.

5 U.S. Census Bureau, *County and City Data Book: 2000*, Table C-1, census.gov/prod/2002pubs/00ccdb/cc00_tabC1 .pdf.

6 James Svara and Douglas Watson, *More than Mayor or Manager: Campaigns to Change Form of Government in America's Large Cities* (Washington: Georgetown University Press, 2010), 12–13, with supplemental information from the *Municipal Form of Government, 2011* survey, identify these cities in each category: (1) changed from council-manager to mayor-council (Fresno, Oakland, and San Diego, California; Hartford, Connecticut; Miami and St. Petersburg, Florida; Toledo, Ohio; Richmond, Virginia; and Spokane, Washington); (2) changed from mayor-council to council-manager (Topeka, Kansas; and El Paso, Texas); (3) changed from commission to council-manager form (Cedar Rapids, Iowa); (4) rejected change from council-manager to mayor-council (Little Rock, Arkansas; Des Moines, Iowa; Grand Rapids, Michigan; Kansas City, Missouri; Cincinnati, Ohio; Tulsa, Oklahoma; Corpus Christi and Dallas, Texas; and Worcester, Massachusetts); and (5) rejected change from commission (Portland, Oregon) and weak mayor-council (St. Louis, Missouri) to mayor-council. Centennial, Colorado, a new city with over 100,000 in population that was incorporated in 2001, adopted a home rule charter in 2008 with the council-manager form of government.

7 Evelina R. Moulder, "Municipal Form of Government: Trends in Structure, Responsibility, and Composition," in *The Municipal Year Book 2008* (Washington, D.C.: ICMA Press, 2008), 31.

8 Kimberly Nelson and James Svara, "Adaptation of Models versus Variations in Form: Classifying Structures of City Government," *Urban Affairs Review* 45, no. 4 (2010): 544–562, Table 2. The *Municipal Form of Government, 2011* survey shows little variation by population size in the percentage of mayor-council cities that have a CAO.

9 Nelson and Svara, "Adaptation of Models," Table 2, found only 22 (0.7%) council-manager cities over 10,000 in population in which the mayor nominates the city manager to the council and no cases of mayoral appointment. Of the 92 council-manager cities in the *Municipal Form of Government, 2011* survey that reported that method of appointing the manager, only 21 indicated later in the survey that the mayor has the authority to nominate the manager.

10 When cities of 10,000 and above responding to the *Municipal Form of Government, 2011* survey are considered, 22% of the CAOs are appointed by mayors, 49% by the council or the mayor and council, and 24% by the mayor nominating and the council approving. These figures are closer to Nelson and Svara, "Adaptation of Models," Table 2, findings for all cities of this size: mayor appoints, 25%; mayor and council appoint, 32%; and mayor nominates and council approves, 43%. Thus, either the survey respondents overrepresented the joint and shared appointment approach, or there was confusion in distinguishing joint appointment by the mayor and council from mayoral nomination and council approval.

11 James Svara, "Do We Still Need Model Charters? The Meaning and Relevance of Reform in the Twenty-First Century," *National Civic Review* 90 (Spring 2001): 19–33.

12 There are 12 states in which half or more of council-manager cities use selection by council members, designation of the highest vote getter, or rotation: California, 69%; Connecticut, 86%; Idaho, 75%; Indiana, 91%; Massachusetts, 83%; Minnesota, 85%; New Jersey, 69%; New Mexico, 50%; Oklahoma, 50%; Pennsylvania, 56%; Rhode Island, 92%; and Vermont, 78%. Surveys of council members indicate that directly elected mayors are

more likely to be viewed as visionaries than those who are selected by other methods. See James H. Svara, *The Facilitative Leader in City Hall: Reexamining the Scope and Contributions* (Boca Raton, Fla.: CRC Press, 2008), 14.

13 More research is needed to determine whether the mayor simply transmits the budget to the council or recommends changes in the budget. The survey refers to "present[ing] the budget with comments and suggestions to the council for consideration."

14 When very small cities (those with 2,500 or fewer residents) are excluded from the results, 63% of respondents reported using at-large elections.

15 John Clayton Thomas, "The Term Limitations Movement," *National Civic Review* 81, no. 2 (1992): 155–173. In the survey results, 8% of cities reported term limits for both the mayor and council positions, and an additional 2% reported limits for only the mayor or only the council members.

3

Local Government Support for Food System Development: An Initial Scan of the Landscape

Laura Goddeeris
Michigan State University

Michael W. Hamm
Michigan State University

In the five years since the Oxford English Dictionary proclaimed *locavore* (a person who is interested in eating locally produced food) the word of the year, there has been an undeniable increase in local government awareness of local and regional food systems and the opportunities they present.

Compelled by a variety of concerns, including inequitable food access (or so-called food deserts), preservation of local agricultural heritage, and even calls to action from professional organizations and the White House,[1] communities of all sizes and in all regions of the country have introduced plans, policies, programs, and partnerships to support food system development.[2]

As used in this article, the term *food system* encompasses the stakeholders, processes, and linkages involved in taking food from its point of production to its point of consumption and/or disposal. In communities across the United States, public, private, and nonprofit entities facilitate this progression on a local or regional scale, primarily to leverage associated economic development, community development, or environmental benefits.

Recent surveys of local governments have identified moderate to high levels of activity associated with farmers' markets and community gardening.[3]

SELECTED FINDINGS

Among food-related programs, the two most commonly recognized by local governments are farmers' markets (75%) and emergency food provision (61%).

The U.S. Department of Housing and Urban Development's Community Development Block Grant (CDBG) program is the federal program most commonly used by local governments (42%) for food system development.

While there is a high incidence of local government–supported programs specifically related to ensuring that vulnerable populations have access to food, such programs tend to be oriented toward emergencies; programs designed to generally improve equitable food access are less common.

Supporting such activities may serve as an entry point for local governments that wish to engage in food system development. Some communities, however, have

This project was funded through the Food & Community program of the W. K. Kellogg Foundation (wkkf.org/what-we-support/healthy-kids/food-and-community.aspx).

taken a more active role. Several large cities, for example, have created positions devoted to the coordination of food policy or programming across departments and agencies—an approach that is less common, and probably less feasible, for smaller communities.

In 2012, in partnership with the Michigan State University (MSU) Center for Regional Food Systems, ICMA conducted a national survey to investigate the landscape of local governments' food-related policies, programs, and plans. The survey represents the most comprehensive effort to date to assess the status of local government support for food system development. In this first analysis of the data, we consider local governments' overall awareness of and involvement in food system support; we also identify possible motivations for and perspectives on such involvement.

In addition to querying local governments about their specific activities in the realm of food system development, we asked about their awareness and use of various programs offered by federal departments and agencies. The results show that local governments in general—across all population sizes, geographic regions, and types—are indeed using a diverse range of federal programs to fund food system development; however, usage varies significantly among agencies (some agencies' programs are used at higher rates than others) and programs (some agencies have many programs—and of those, some are more likely to be used than others). This finding suggests that additional resources and technical assistance could help local governments more effectively support food system development; it also indicates the far-reaching nature of and the potential for innovation in food system support.

Methods

The survey instrument was designed to present a wide array of potential strategies that can be used to develop local and regional food systems and to capture the nature of local government support for those strategies. For instance, if a farmers' market is present in a community, does the local government permit it as a use by right? And does the local government devote staff to the management of the market, or does the market operate completely independently?

Many of the examples of food-related policies, programs, and plans were culled from case study research on food systems.[4] The examples were categorized under broad headings, including food access and production; land use and planning; and community

and economic development and public health. The instrument's content and design were also informed by recent local government surveys and ICMA staff expertise. Our colleagues at MSU and on the staff of the U.S. Department of Agriculture (USDA) provided additional input on content and analysis.*

The survey was distributed to all counties, and to all municipalities with populations over 2,500, for a total of 10,575 communities. Hard copies were distributed twice—in May and in August of 2012. (The hard copy included a URL to an online response option.) Nearly 2,000 communities across 50 states responded to the survey, for a total response rate of 19%. Table 3–1 summarizes the responses, and Figure 3–1

Table 3-1 Survey Response

Classification	No. of municipalities/ counties[a] surveyed (A)	Respondents No.	% of (A)
Total	10,575	1,957	19
Population group			
100,000 and above	811	172	21
50,000–99,999	875	147	17
25,000–49,999	1,499	261	17
10,000–24,999	2,762	486	18
5,000–9,999	2,304	440	19
4,999 and under	2,324	451	19
Geographic division			
New England	799	141	18
Mid-Atlantic	1,416	173	12
East North-Central	1,903	406	21
West North-Central	1,341	298	22
South Atlantic	1,496	331	22
East South-Central	827	93	11
West South-Central	1,246	184	15
Mountain	691	145	21
Pacific Coast	856	186	22
Metro type			
Municipalities	7,537	1,490	20
Counties	3,038	467	15

a For a definition of terms, please see "Inside the *Year Book*," xi–xiv.

* We wish to express our appreciation for comments and suggestions from Tad McGalliard and Evelina Moulder, ICMA; Kathryn Colasanti, John Goddeeris, and Mark Skidmore, Michigan State University; Jill Auburn, Luanne Lohr, and the Know Your Farmer, Know Your Food data subcommittee, U.S. Department of Agriculture.

Figure 3-1 Distribution of Responses by State and Geographic Division

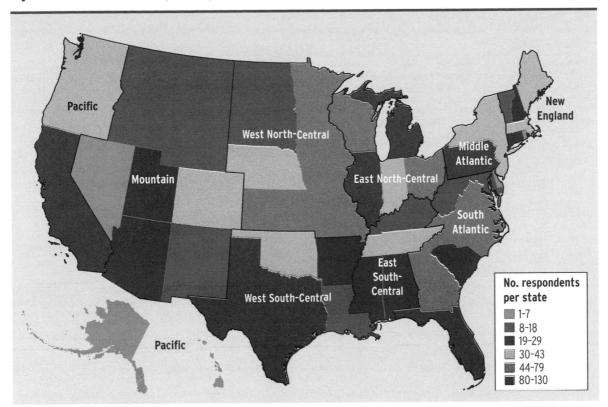

illustrates the distribution by state and geographic division. With respect to population size, geographic location, and type of place, the distribution of responses generally follow that of the communities surveyed. With respect to form of government, council-manager communities account for the largest share of responses (45%, not shown).

Policies and Regulations Supporting Food Access and Production

The survey offered 14 examples (and an option to add additional examples) of food access and production practices that could be affected by local policies or regulations. The list included items such as the location of farmers' markets or other retail food sources, mobile food vending, access to land and water for community gardens, strategies for ensuring that vulnerable populations have access to food, and "buy local" requirements.

Figure 3–2 lists the food-related issues that local government policies, ordinances, or other regulations are most likely to address. The issue that heads the list is the permitting of farmers' markets (nearly 60%); and about half the respondents cited the related but distinct issue of allowing produce sales at locations other than farmers' markets, such as farm stands (or from community or residential gardens, an activity that is not always permitted).

Local governments are supporting a range of activities often regarded as components of "urban agriculture." Community gardening, for example, receives support through policies ensuring access to land and water. Policies that allow the keeping of chickens, goats, bees, or other animals in non-traditional (e.g., residential) zones were reported by 38% of respondents. Green roofs or other sources of edible landscaping are permitted in residential or commercial areas by 40% of responding communities. Respondents also reported support for backyard (33%) and municipal (23%) composting of food and other organic waste.

Whether purveying tacos, ice cream, the latest sandwich trend, or even groceries, mobile food vending has grown in popularity in recent years,[5] and 45% of responding communities regulate where mobile food vendors can locate. Although the survey instrument did not ask respondents how restrictive such policies are, the existence of regulations for mobile food vending indicates some awareness, on the part of local governments, of a potentially complex food access issue.

Figure 3-2 Food-related Issues Most Likely to Be Addressed by Local Government Policies, Ordinances, or Regulations

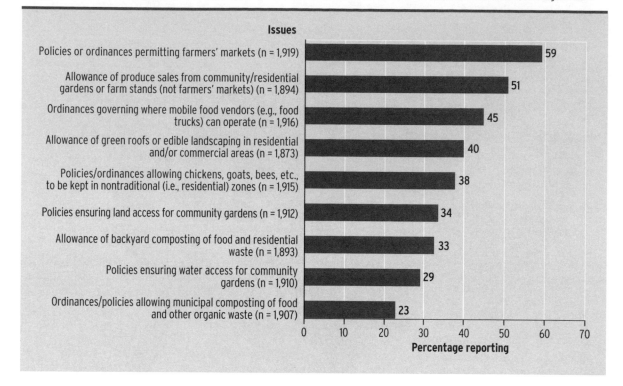

For the policy topics listed in Figure 3–2, about 80% of the affirmative responses came from municipalities and about 20% from counties (not shown). For other issues not listed (e.g., requirements that farmers' market vendors accept electronic benefit transfers, or taxes or regulations related to "unhealthy food"[6]), the rates of affirmative responses were similar between municipalities and counties but much lower in number (fewer than 100 total cases per topic).

To determine how many food-related policies are in place in each community, we treated *all* policies as equal in significance. Some respondents left some or all policy questions blank. For counting purposes, we excluded the 16 respondents who left all policy questions unanswered. For respondents who answered some but not all policy questions, we treated a missing value as a no response. As a result, the counts can be considered somewhat conservative.

The average community (based on 1,941) has 3.6 food-related policies in place (not shown). This number is higher for municipalities (4) and lower for counties (2.4). The average increases with population size: for communities with populations below 10,000, the number of policies is lower than the national average, while the largest communities reported the greatest number of policies (5 on average). Finally, the average number of policies in the Pacific Coast (5.2), Moun-

tain (4), and New England (4.3) geographic divisions exceeds the national average (not shown).

The survey also captured comments related to food access and production policies. A few county respondents noted that their level of government has no responsibility for food-related policies—a perspective that seems to have been confirmed by the fact that, overall, municipalities are more likely than counties to have food-related policies. Nevertheless, we did find examples of county-level policies for each issue listed. Some respondents also noted that although their communities do not have policies that support the activities listed and that such activities are not actively encouraged, neither are they explicitly restricted.

Community Projects and Programs

We were interested in tracking the availability of food-related projects or programs in (1) land use and planning and (2) community and economic development and public health. We were also interested in the extent of local government involvement in these projects or programs. For each program type, the survey offered respondents three options for describing how the program is provided: by the local government alone, by the local government in partnership with another entity, or with no local government involvement.

What, How, and Where: A Slice of the Results

The survey on which this article is based revealed a range of policies, programs, plans, and partnerships in communities of all sizes and types and in all regions of the country. Some respondents described more comprehensive approaches to food system development. Select examples include the following:

Cabarrus County, North Carolina (est. 2011 pop. 181,468)

The Cabarrus County Board of Commissioners established a food policy council to advise the board on policies that would promote a sustainable local food economy and the health of county residents. The board appointed the council's members and hired a staff coordinator. The county also commissioned consultants to conduct a food system assessment to summarize current conditions and opportunities and to recommend further development of the food system.

In partnership with the North Carolina Cooperative Extension, the county established an incubator farm, where new farmers receive classroom and hands-on training to help them establish farm businesses. The county uses funds reserved for farmland preservation and agricultural development to support the incubator's infrastructure and operating expenses.

Finally, to further its objectives for the local food economy, the county supported the development of a local harvest facility offering meat slaughter and processing services.

Middleton, Wisconsin (est. 2011 pop. 17,729)

The Middleton Sustainable City Plan, which emerged from a process led by a team of elected officials, city staff, and community residents, includes a section on food, the economy, and fair trade. Adopted by the city council in 2010, it calls on the Middleton city government to monitor statistics on family food security (e.g., the number of families that qualify for free or reduced-cost school meals) and encourages preference for local and/or fair trade products for government purchasing.

Through its zoning ordinance, Middleton supports community gardening and urban agriculture, including the keeping of bees and chickens. The city has started one community garden and orchard on city land and is starting another on school district land.

Finally, Middleton has collaborated with two surrounding communities on a food waste study and is working on a compost program, under which residents are currently permitted to drop off yard waste at a composting facility free of charge.

Story County, Iowa (est. 2011 pop. 89,663)

Following an investigation and report undertaken by the planning and zoning department on local and regional food system issues and opportunities, the Story County Board of Supervisors established the Grow Story County Committee and formally adopted food system planning as part of the planning and zoning department's scope of work.

The board subsequently adopted a five-year strategic plan, Local Food and Farms: Growing Story County's Citizens and Economy, which had been developed by the Grow Story County Committee; the plan focuses on food production, markets, infrastructure, and coordination. The board is responsible for determining the priority of the implementation steps outlined in the plan.

Where programs were available, about 80% of respondents supplied detailed information on their provision (not shown). We calculated the rate of *any* (i.e., all or partial) local government involvement in the program versus no local government involvement. We then characterized the likelihood of local government involvement as low, medium, or high.[7] For the various programs included in the survey, Figure 3–3 indicates their availability among responding jurisdictions and the likelihood of local government involvement.

Farmers' markets top the list of available programs (75%)—which is probably not surprising since the number of markets nationwide has grown steadily since 1994, when USDA started compiling a national directory.[8] Programs related to emergency food provision and donations of surplus food also have high incidence rates (61% and 59%, respectively). The top five most frequently

Figure 3-3   Food-related Projects and Programs

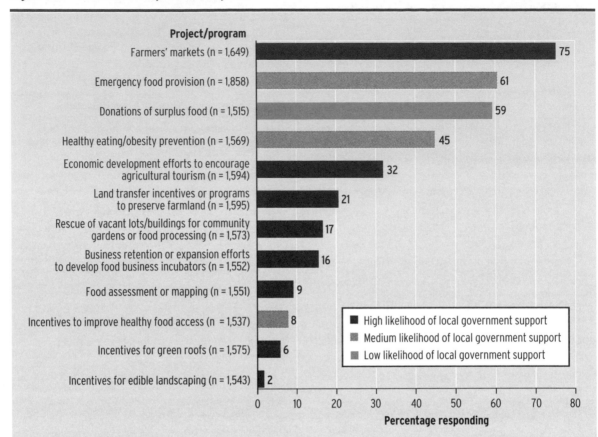

cited programs also include healthy eating or obesity prevention initiatives (45%) and economic development efforts to encourage agricultural tourism (32%).

In addition to calculating program availability and local government involvement, we developed program counts, again assigning equal significance to all programs.[9] The average number of programs per community (based on 1,926) is 3 (not shown). The average is higher for communities with a population of 10,000 or more and continues to rise with population. Average program counts are also higher in the Pacific Coast, Mountain, New England, and South Atlantic geographic divisions. For all averages calculated, the level of local government involvement hovers around 50%.

Food as a Topic in Local Plans

We asked respondents to indicate whether their communities have any of the following types of plans in place:

- Comprehensive plan
- Sustainability plan
- Climate change plan
- Economic development plan

- Land use plan
- Transportation plan
- Housing plan
- Community development plan.

We also asked whether these or any other plans address issues related to food production, processing, distribution, access, or disposal.

Of the 1,603 local governments that reported having one or more of the types of plans listed, 306 (19%) reported that one or more types of planning documents address food issues (not shown). Among counties and municipalities with these types of plans, counties are more likely to address food issues (24% and 18%, respectively). Among communities with populations of 25,000 or more that have at least one of the types of plans specified, the percentage whose plans address food issues is higher than the average of 19%, increasing to a high of 46% among communities with populations of at least 100,000. Communities located in the Mountain, New England, South Atlantic, and especially Pacific Coast geographic divisions are more likely to address food-related issues in their plans.

Table 3-2   Influence of Planning Documents on Incidence of Food-related Policies and Programs

	Total reporting[a]	Average no. of policies or programs reported	Food-related issues addressed by at least one plan (average no. of policies or programs)	
			Yes	No
Policies	1,601	3.9	5.4	3.6
Programs	1,596	3.2	4.7	2.9
Programs with local government involvement	1,596	1.6	2.8	1.3

Note: The sample used for this table includes only those respondents who indicated that they have any of the eight types of plans in place. It excludes those who (1) left all the plan-related questions blank or who (2) partially completed the section on plans but did not affirmatively indicate the presence of any plans. We also ran the analyses excluding only those who skipped this section entirely (1) and observed little variance in the results.

a   The number of respondents varies because respondents had to answer more than one set of questions to be included in the analyses.

Responses indicate that food-related issues are addressed by all types of plans presented in the survey—and more. Nearly one-third (29%) of all climate change plans and one-quarter of all sustainability plans address food topics—133 planning documents in total (not shown). Among comprehensive plans, 173 address food topics, representing 13% of all communities with such plans. Comprehensive plans for larger communities, as well as for communities in the Pacific Coast and New England divisions, are more likely to address food topics than those in smaller communities and other divisions. Given the shelf life of such documents and the fact that food systems planning is a relatively new area of emphasis,[10] these modest numbers seem very significant.

As summarized in Table 3-2, having any sort of plan that deals with food is positively correlated with both the number of food-related policies and the number of food-related programs reported by communities.

Responsibility, Collaboration, and Councils

Food systems intersect with virtually all other systems in a community, yet government departments devoted exclusively to food issues are rare.[11] Therefore, we asked communities to indicate whether food systems fall within the scope of responsibility for various departments. Among the 1,268 respondents who reported that food issues fall under the scope of responsibility for at least one department, departments of public health or environmental health were cited most frequently (58% of all respondents) (Figure 3–4). Among counties, health departments were by far the most commonly cited (88%).

In addition to the options offered in the survey, other departments frequently mentioned include human or social services, human resources, administration, and zoning or code enforcement. Some communities pointed to other levels of government, both larger and smaller, as well. On average, municipalities and counties indicated that 1.6 departments deal with food-related issues (not shown). Variation in the mean is fairly limited across geographic divisions and population groups.

While food systems can be thought of as existing in nested levels (i.e., local, regional, national, and global), they are not always aligned with political or administrative boundaries. Some researchers and practitioners have suggested that a regional approach is the ideal level for developing food systems that benefit local communities and the stakeholders within them.[12] (For example, planning for food distribution at a regional scale could help link densely populated urban areas—potential markets—with small- and medium-scale producers in surrounding rural communities.) Thus, we asked respondents whether any of their food-related projects or programs had been undertaken in collaboration or coordination with nearby communities or surrounding regions. Of 1,888 respondents, 22% indicated that they are engaged in efforts spanning political jurisdictions (not shown). Asked to elaborate on the nature of these collaborations, respondents mentioned issues such as emergency food provision, "locally grown" campaigns, agritourism promotion, and "healthy community" initiatives.

Food policy councils initially emerged, in part, because of the absence of a single government agency or department charged with comprehensive oversight of food system issues. These bodies, which may be organized at the local, regional, or state level, have grown in number in recent years[13] and offer another means of collaborating across jurisdictions—an observation that was confirmed by survey results: 313 respondents (16%) indicated that government staff participate in some type of food council (not shown). Few communities indicated that such councils are official government bodies, however; the vast majority described them as ad hoc committees, public-private partnerships, and the like.[14]

As indicated in Tables 3–3 and 3–4, participation in food policy councils and collaboration with other

Figure 3-4 Department Responsible for Food Issues

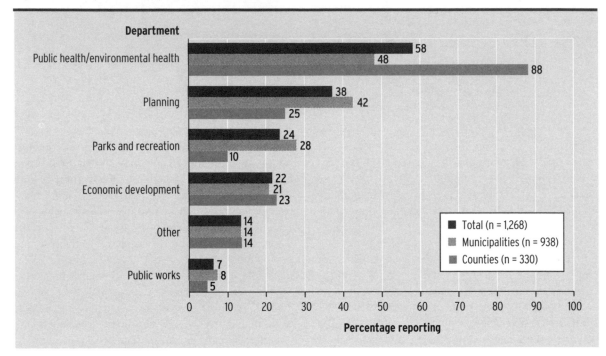

Table 3-3 Influence of Participation in a Food Policy Council on Incidence of Food-related Policies and Programs

	Total reporting[a]	Average no. of policies or programs reported	Local government participates in a food policy council or similar group (average no. of policies or programs)	
			Yes	No
Policies	1,913	3.7	5.0	3.4
Programs	1,903	3.0	4.7	2.6
Programs with local government involvement	1,903	1.5	2.9	1.2

a   The number of respondents varies because respondents had to answer more than one set of questions to be included in the analyses.

Table 3-4 Influence of Collaboration with Other Communities or Regions on Incidence of Food-related Policies and Programs

	Total reporting[a]	Average no. of policies or programs reported	Local government collaborates with other communities or regions (average no. of policies or programs)	
			Yes	No
Policies	1,886	3.6	4.5	3.4
Programs	1,876	3.0	4.5	2.5
Programs with local government involvement	1,876	1.5	2.5	1.2

a   The number of respondents varies because respondents had to answer more than one set of questions to be included in the analyses.

jurisdictions, respectively, are positively correlated with the average number of policies and programs reported.

Federal Support for Food System Development

Respondents were asked about their awareness of, interest in, and use of various federal programs available to support food system development. The programs listed in the survey represent a range of departments and agencies, including USDA, the Department of Housing and Urban Development (HUD), the Department of Transportation (DOT), the Department of Health and Human Services, and the Environmental Protection Agency (EPA). Figure 3–5 summarizes the results.

USDA is perhaps the most obvious source of potential federal support for food system development. In 2009, USDA launched the Know Your Farmer, Know Your Food (KYF2) initiative to increase awareness, accessibility, and coordination of USDA programs that could be used to support the development of local and regional food systems.[15] Under the KYF2 initiative, local governments are eligible for several types of support;

Figure 3-5 Awareness of, Use of, and Interest in Federal Programs

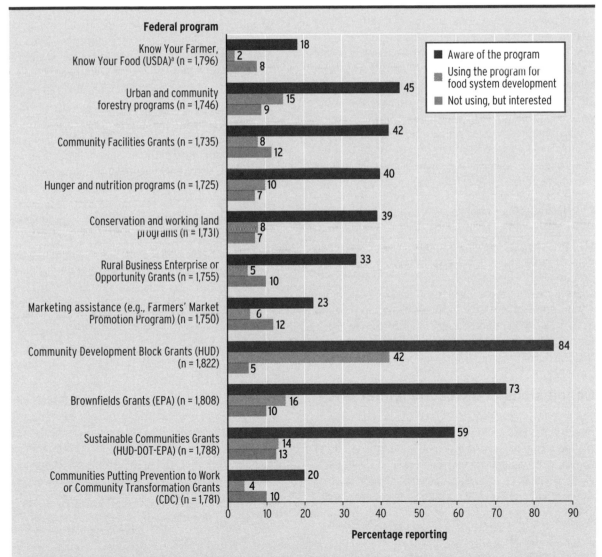

Note: Programs vary widely with respect to number and frequency of grants awarded, total amount awarded, maximum size of individual awards, and eligibility criteria.

a The six types of programs below, from "Urban and community forestry programs" through "Marketing assistance," are examples of specific USDA programs encompassed by the "Know Your Farmer, Know Your Food" initiative.

other forms of assistance focus on other stakeholder groups, including producers, nonprofits, and academic institutions. The survey inquired about the KYF2 initiative overall, as well as about specific programs for which local governments may be eligible. While familiarity with the KYF2 initiative as such is low, respondents are more aware of individual programs and report higher rates of usage for food system development.

USDA is not the only department that can fund food-related programs,[16] and its resources may not be as accessible to urban as to rural communities. The program most likely to be used is HUD's Community Development Block Grant (CDBG) program: 765 respondents (42%) indicated the use of CDBG funding (Figure 3–5). This is a particularly interesting finding because food is not an explicit priority for HUD programming. And although our results indicate that community development plans, such as HUD-required housing plans and Consolidated Plans, are unlikely to address food issues, local government efforts or initiatives in support of gardening or food gathering (gleaning), farmers' markets, and other programs to improve food access may be eligible for CDBG funding. A final caveat: although the survey explicitly asked whether each program is being used to fund food system development, some respondents may have indicated instead whether they are using the program at all.

The second-highest level of use (16%) reported is for EPA's Brownfields Grants, which provide funding that can be used for the assessment or cleanup of potential food production sites (Figure 3–5). The highest level of interest for any federal program (13%) was reported for the Sustainable Communities Grants, a joint effort of HUD, EPA, and DOT. Recent grantees have incorporated food access and distribution issues into broader strategies that are designed to promote livable, thriving communities and regions.[17]

Conclusions and Recommendations

The survey elicited national data that can be used as preliminary indicators of local government support for food system development in communities across America. In general, we found a great deal of activity in a range of communities, which suggests that as local governments learn from one another, there may be an opportunity for accelerated growth in this arena. Among the specific areas in which this might occur are the following:

- *Food and security.* Communities are thinking about food from the perspective of security. The high use of CDBGs to support food systems is in keeping with this finding, as food-related efforts funded through the program are likely to be part of broad antipoverty initiatives. Respondents often categorized food as a social service issue, and there is a high incidence of programs—many of which are supported by local governments—specifically related to ensuring that vulnerable populations have access to food. However, such programs tend to be oriented toward emergencies; programs designed to generally improve equitable food access are less common.

- *Food and health.* Local governments, particularly at the county level, see a clear connection between food and health and are most likely to identify county health departments as government stakeholders with food-related responsibilities, such as the inspection of dining establishments. But some local governments also view food from a broader public health perspective and are engaged in prevention (of obesity, in particular) and planning efforts designed to improve community health.

- *Food versus agriculture.* Respondents often distinguished between food and agriculture; for example, those from rural areas indicated that they plan for the latter, but not the former. The fact that few respondents used the words *food* and *agriculture* in tandem suggests that local governments tend not to view food as a system and may lack awareness of the connection between food production and consumption.

- *Food as essential, inevitable, . . . or irrelevant.* Respondents from all types of communities commented on the relevance of the food system to development. Some respondents, such as those from rural communities, indicated that agriculture is essential to the economic viability of their community or region. Others described food production as part of the community fabric, and suggested that there is little need to develop specific policies or programs to encourage it or to facilitate food access. Some communities are completely devoid of commercial zones for food retail or open space for food production. Interestingly, both municipalities and counties pointed to each other and suggested that food issues could be more appropriately handled by other levels of government.

- *Food as comprehensive.* The survey results suggest that few communities have embraced local and regional food system development in a comprehensive way, but the small percentage of communities that have done so are diverse in size, geographic location, and type of locality.[18]

The survey on which this article is based was designed to identify food-related policies, programs, and plans; departmental associations; collaborations; and use of federal programs among municipalities and counties. The findings certainly suggest the need for further research to identify the most appropriate practices for local governments that are considering (perhaps at the urging of constituents) expanding their stake in food system development; the findings should also encourage innovation. Somewhere across America there is a local government entity of similar size, similar constituency, or similar type that has identified ways to use food system development as a lever for community development, economic development, or general improvements in residents' quality of life. We hope that the survey and this article will be the first step in publicizing quantitative data on a wide range of examples so that all local governments can all learn from the experiences of their peer organizations.

Notes

1. See, for example, American Planning Association (APA), *Policy Guide on Community and Regional Food Planning* (Chicago: APA, 2007), planning.org/policy/guides/pdf/foodplanning.pdf; and Let's Move!, "A Call to Action for Mayors and Local Elected Officials," letsmove.gov/become-lets-move-city-or-town.

2. For additional information on how and where this has occurred, see Harvard Law School Food Law and Policy Clinic, *Good Laws, Good Food: Putting Local Food Policy to Work for Our Communities* (Cambridge: Harvard Food Law and Policy Clinic, 2012), law.harvard.edu/academics/clinical/lsc/documents/FINAL_LOCAL_TOOLKIT2.pdf.

3. See, for example, ICMA, "ICMA 2010 Sustainability Survey Results," icma.org/en/icma/knowledge_network/documents/kn/Document/301646/ICMA_2010_Sustainability_Survey_Results; and National Association of Counties (NACo), "2010 County Sustainability Strategies," naco.org/programs/csd/Documents/Green%20Government/2010%20County%20Sustainability%20Strategies.pdf.

4. See, for example, Kailee Neuner, Sylvia Kelly, and Samina Raja, *Planning to Eat? Innovative Local Government Plans and Policies to Build Healthy Food Systems in the United States* (Buffalo: Food Systems Planning and Healthy Communities Lab, State University of New York at Buffalo, 2011), farmlandinfo.org/documents/39040/Planning_to_eat_SUNYBuffalo.pdf.

5. See, for example, Jane Black, "Green Carts Put Fresh Produce Where the People Are," *Washington Post*, April 17, 2012, articles.washingtonpost.com/2012-04-17/lifestyle/35451714_1_green-carts-fruit-and-vegetable-carts-tisch-illumination-fund; and Alfonso Morales and Gregg Kettles, "Healthy Food Outside: Farmers' Markets, Taco Trucks, and Sidewalk Fruit Vendors," *Journal of Contemporary Health Law and Policy* 26 (2009): 20–48.

6. The survey instrument offered examples of taxes on junk food or restrictions on fast-food locations but ultimately left "unhealthy food" to the interpretation of respondents.

7. To make this characterization, we divided the total instances of any local government involvement by the total number of respondents providing details on provision (for each type of program). We then categorized those percentages as low (0–33%), medium (34–66%), or high (67–100%).

8. For more on farmers' market data, see USDA Agricultural Marketing Service, "Farmers Markets and Local Food Marketing," ams.usda.gov/AMSv1.0/FARMERSMARKETS.

9. Some respondents left some or all of the program questions blank. We excluded the 31 respondents who left all program questions unanswered. If a respondent answered some but not all of the questions, a missing value was treated as a no response—which probably somewhat inflated the no responses. Thus, the counts can be considered somewhat conservative.

10. For a sense of how interest in food systems planning has evolved in recent years, see APA, *Policy Guide*.

11. The few jurisdictions that have created positions devoted to the coordination of food issues tend to be larger cities. See, for example, City and County of San Francisco, "San Francisco Food," sfgov3.org/index.aspx?page=753; Baltimore Department of Planning, "Planning/Baltimore Food Policy Initiative," baltimorecity.gov/Government/AgenciesDepartments/Planning/BaltimoreFoodPolicyInitiative.aspx; and New York City Center for Economic Opportunity, "Office of the Food Policy Coordinator," nyc.gov/html/ceo/html/programs/food_policy.shtml. See also Karen Thoreson and James Svara, "Recurrent Themes in Local Government Innovation," in *The Municipal Year Book 2013* (Washington, D.C.: ICMA Press, 2013), 91–92.

12. Kate Clancy and Kathryn Ruhf, "Is Local Enough? Some Arguments for Regional Food Systems," *Choices* 25, no. 1 (2010), choicesmagazine.org/magazine/article.php?article=114; and Delaware Valley Regional Planning Commission (DVRPC), *Greater Philadelphia Food System Study* (Philadelphia: DVRPC, 2010), dvrpc.org/asp/pubs/publicationabstract.asp?pub_id=09066A.

13. Community Food Security Coalition, "List of Food Policy Councils in North America," April 2012, foodsecurity.org/programs/food-policy-councils/list-of-food-policy-councils-in-north-america/.

14. For more information on food policy councils, see Planning and Community Health Research Center, *Food Policy Councils: Helping Local, Regional, and State Governments Address Food System Challenges* (Chicago: APA, 2011), planning.org/nationalcenters/health/briefingpapers/pdf/foodcouncils.pdf.

15. For more information on this initiative, see USDA, "Know Your Farmer, Know Your Food," usda.gov/wps/portal/usda/knowyourfarmer?navid=KNOWYOURFARMER.

16. For more discussion of this topic, see Maggie Gosselin, *Beyond the USDA: How Other Government Agencies Can Support a Healthier, More Sustainable Food System* (Minneapolis, Minn.: Institute for Agriculture and Trade Policy, 2010), iatp.org/files/258_2_107172.pdf.

17. For summaries of recently funded projects, see U.S. Department of Housing and Urban Development (HUD), "HUD FY2011 Sustainable Communities Grantees," portal.hud.gov/hudportal/documents/huddoc?id = SUM_OF_FY11COMCHALGRANTS.PDF; and HUD, "HUD FY2010 Community Challenge Planning Grants Summaries," portal.hud.gov/hudportal/documents/huddoc?id = FY10_ComChallPlanGrantSum.pdf.

18. To reach this conclusion, we selected the records where (1) the total number of policies and programs exceeded the overall means (3.6 and 3, respectively), (2) the total number of local government–supported programs exceeded 1.5, (3) food issues were addressed by at least one type of plan, and (4) the local government was participating in a food policy council and/or collaborating with other jurisdictions. The result was a total of 112 records.

4

Building Child- and Age-Friendly Communities in Tight Fiscal Times

Mildred E. Warner
Cornell University

Lydia J. Morken
Cornell University

Municipalities face a dual challenge: how to meet the needs of both a rapidly aging population and families with young children. Rather than viewing this challenge as a tradeoff between older adults and children, communities that strive for generational balance in their demographic composition and service delivery will find they have stronger economic development and fiscal health. After reviewing the changing demographic profile of America, this article explores the complementarities between seniors and young children, the need for economic development that invests in these two groups, and the demographic and fiscal challenges that impede such investment.

Changes in America's Demographic Profile

America is aging. By 2030, nearly one in five U.S. residents will be over age 65, and the number of these residents will double from 40 million in 2010 to over 80 million by 2040.[1] The largest growth will be in the over-85 age group. This increase in the proportion of the oldest Americans will raise new challenges for cities in terms of urban design, service delivery, and finance. Because the current generation of seniors relies more

SELECTED FINDINGS

The percentage of elders in society is rising, but communities with balanced demographic profiles—those that seek to attract and retain families with children—experience more economic growth.

While public investment in seniors is primarily the responsibility of the federal government, investment in our children's future is primarily the responsibility of our state and local governments. Yet public spending on children is only one-third the spending on seniors.

Integrated service delivery and planning can help communities meet the needs of both children and seniors, but rural and suburban communities lag in service delivery.

on the private automobile for transportation than any generation before it, mobility will become an enormous challenge when elders can no longer drive themselves. Yet more of these seniors will be living alone, and declining birthrates over the past several decades,

Research was made possible by the USDA National Institute for Food and Agriculture research grant #2011-68006-30793.

combined with a steady rise in the number of women working full-time, mean that fewer adult children will be available to provide care for older parents or other aging family members. As a consequence, many seniors will not have access to family support.

At the same time, the birthrate in America is declining while America's younger population is changing. In 2011, for the first time ever, minority births outnumbered white births in the United States.[2] The U.S. Census projects that by 2040, half the U.S. population will be people of color. Immigrants tend to be younger—in their prime working-age years—and young families with children are growing fastest among the Hispanic population.[3] This more diverse young population stands in stark contrast to the senior population, which is primarily white (Figure 4–1).

In Europe, both birthrates and immigration rates are lower than those in the United States and thus cannot counteract that continent's rapidly aging population. Figure 4–2 shows, for example, the hollowing out of the population pyramid in Spain. By contrast, U.S. communities are lucky; immigration creates a "demographic dividend" that mitigates our declining birthrate, renews our population, and provides a robust foundation of younger people on which the future of the country rests. But we need more investment in the young if we are to reap this demographic dividend.

Currently, government spending on seniors in the United States is about two-and-a-half times government spending on children ($8,942 per child compared to $21,904 per senior).[4] And while the federal government provides 97% of public support for seniors, it provides only 32% of public support for children.[5] Investment in our children's future is primarily the responsibility of our state and local governments. A 2010 National Bureau of Economics Research study shows that while federal spending on citizens begins to rise after age 50 (owing primarily to Medicare and Social Security), state and local spending spikes during two periods in the life cycle: for school-aged children (primarily for K-12 schooling) and for seniors over 75 (for local support services to help seniors remain independent or to cover the costs of nursing homes) (Figure 4–3).[6]

And even then, school-age children exact a state and local expense averaging around $11,200 per child, whereas state and local costs for seniors over 75 are higher ($12,000 per elder on average) and rise steeply.[7]

Economic Development and the Need for Public Investment

In order to fund quality local services, local governments need economic development. Two popular economic development strategies focus on attracting

Figure 4-1 U.S. Population by Age and Race/Ethnicity

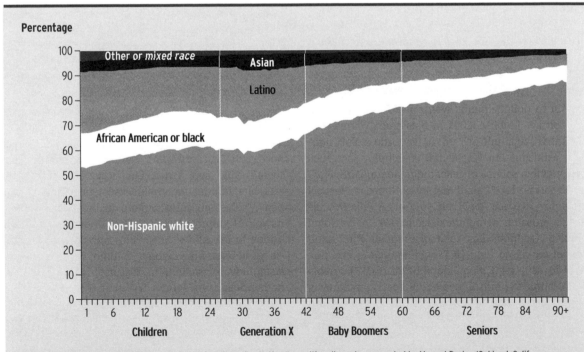

Source: PolicyLink, "America's Tomorrow: Equity in a Changing Nation," a multimedia series presented by Manuel Pastor (Oakland, Calif.: PolicyLink, 2011), based on 2005-2009 Public Use Microdata.

Figure 4-2   Population Distribution by Age and Gender, Spain and the United States (2010)

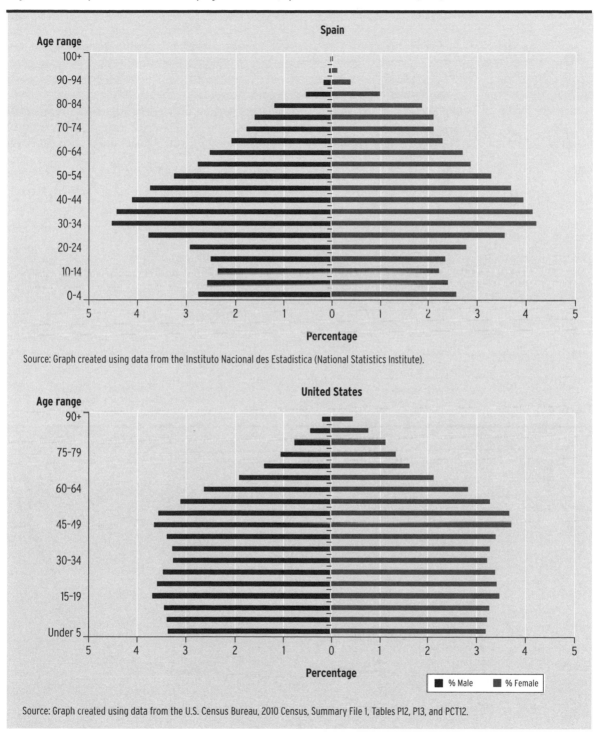

Source: Graph created using data from the Instituto Nacional des Estadistica (National Statistics Institute).

Source: Graph created using data from the U.S. Census Bureau, 2010 Census, Summary File 1, Tables P12, P13, and PCT12.

young professionals and empty nesters. The first is the "creative class" strategy, promoted by Richard Florida; this approach has led to investments in recreational and environmental amenities as well as to reinvestment in downtowns for single living.[8] The second is the attraction of retirees as "gray gold" for the pension income and talents they can bring to a community.[9]

But economic development leaders today recognize the equally critical need for a balanced strategy, one that also seeks to maintain and nurture workers as they form families. A recent study of 233 U.S. cities found that despite the strength of some of the variables inherent in Florida's creative class (e.g., college education and diversity), the most significant factors in economic growth include investment in public infrastructure (schools, parks, and recreation) and in such demographic variables as married adults with children and high school graduation rates.[10]

The economic development concern is that we are not investing enough in our children and youth to secure our future. Noted demographer Dowell Myers points to the important generational social compact between babies and boomers: this young generation will be the workforce, care providers, and tax payers of the future.[11] As a society we need to invest in the education, skills, and family supports to ensure that this generation grows up to be productive citizens who can step into the roles vacated by retiring boomers. Such investment is especially important in communities with large percentages of young families of color for whom educational and employment opportunities are especially critical if we are to fill positions vacated by retiring baby boomers. Cities need to give more attention to multifamily housing, multilingual programming, and services that integrate newcomers into the fabric of community life.

Yet underinvestment is particularly acute for children from birth to age 5, when nutrition, health care, and early education are especially critical to long-term brain development and future economic success.[12] Indeed, Figure 4–3 shows that public investment in the youngest children is the lowest of any age group (under $3,000 per child). This is the human capital investment challenge that economists now recognize. With this issue in mind, economic and business leaders formed ReadyNation (readynation.org/), a think tank and lobby group created to promote business community advocacy for increased investment in early care and education.

Families with children are often perceived as a cost to the local economy because of high levels of school spending. In a 2008 survey conducted by the American Planning Association (APA), just over half of the responding planners agreed with the statement that "most families do not generate sufficient tax revenue to cover the cost of services they demand" (Table 4–1).[13] Some communities try to restrict affordable family housing as a way to reduce local service delivery costs. This is shortsighted, however, as it ignores the increasing importance of human capital investment as a critical economic development strategy for state

Figure 4-3 Government Spending (in Thousands) by Age in 2004

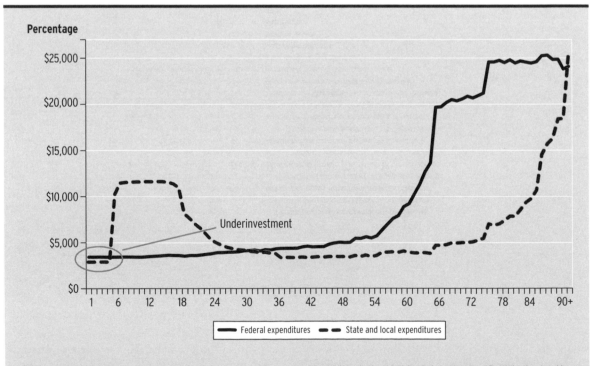

Source: Adapted from Ryan D. Edwards, *Forecasting Government Revenue and Expenditure in the U.S. Using Data on Age-Specific Utilization* (working paper WP10-01, National Transfer Accounts Project, February 15, 2010), graph calculated from Table B-7, qcpages.qc.edu/~redwards/Papers/edwards-forecasting-0210.pdf.

Table 4-1 Planners' Attitudes toward Families

Statement	Total respondents (A)	Agree with statement No.	% of (A)
Families are important to community growth, sustainability, and diversity.	884	856	97
Families are the most likely population group to reinvest in their community through time, money, and other forms of civic engagement.	884	687	78
Most families do not generate sufficient tax revenue to cover the cost of services they demand.	881	464	53
Families represent a valuable consumer population.	877	848	97
Communities that keep people for the whole life cycle (children, single adults, parents, elderly) are more vibrant.	884	797	90
The needs of families are similar to the needs of the elderly with regards to the physical environment (e.g. parks, transportation, affordable housing).	884	566	64

Source: *APA Family Friendly Planning Survey, 2008.* See Evelyn Israel and Mildred Warner, "Planning for Family Friendly Communities," *PAS Memo* (November/December 2008), planning.org/pas/memo/open/nov2008/index.htm.

and local governments. It also ignores the possibility of shared services between schools and local government to better meet the needs of both children and the elderly. Indeed, the APA survey found that 64% of planners agreed that the needs of the elderly and children are similar with respect to transportation, affordable housing, and services.[14]

The future requires a more balanced approach. In the same APA survey, 97% of responding planners agreed that families with children are important to community growth, sustainability, and diversity, and 90% agreed that communities that keep residents for the whole life cycle are more vibrant (Table 4–1).[15] Thus, while popular strategies for economic development have targeted young professionals and empty nesters, it is time to give more attention to meeting the needs of families with young children. Why? Because families contribute significantly to the local economy through their spending on local services.[16] As demographic transformation leads to a smaller and more diverse pool of young people, communities must find ways to balance the needs of an increasingly heterogeneous population to be sustainable. Keys to achieving this are attention to universal design, affordable housing development, transportation, and services that integrate the needs of residents across the life cycle.[17]

Multigenerational Planning Opportunities

In light of the country's changing demographic profile, fiscal exigencies, and shifting service demands, a more thoughtful, more comprehensive approach is called for. To that end, planning across generations is becoming increasingly important as a way to address the needs of both seniors and children. The features that seniors need to age in place successfully are similar to those that children need for healthy development. The World Health Organization (WHO) has outlined these principles for age-friendly communities,[18] and UNICEF has done the same for child-friendly cities.[19] Both lists share a focus on walkability, affordable housing, nearby services, accessible transportation, parks and recreation, and opportunities for social and civic engagement. As our population diversifies, meeting the needs of all residents, regardless of age, ethnicity, and income, requires new planning strategies, the integration of services, and intergenerational coalition building to build the political will to raise taxes to pay for needed services.

Development Strategies

According to the 2010 *Maturing of America* survey, conducted by ICMA with the National Association of Area Agencies on Aging to assess local-level service delivery for seniors, fewer than half the responding communities are using planning tools to meet the needs of their changing populations.[20] However, the same survey reports that two-thirds of urban communities, 44% of suburbs, and 35% of rural communities have developed intergenerational programming.[21] Zoning for affordable housing, accessory units, child care in residential units, and density bonuses—as well as mandated sidewalks, conveniently located services, improved street lighting, and accessible parks—all are planning tools that can be used to promote a child- and age-friendly community.

One tool that can be used to promote the development of needed infrastructure is impact fees. Impact fees enable cities to augment traditional sources of government funding for community services with supplemental funds from private developers. Specifically, they enable communities to build needed parks, community centers, and child care facilities while children are still young. This is especially important in poor cities where market demand may not be strong enough to signal a supply response, and in cities where rapid growth has outstripped service delivery. A recent study of 349 cities across the country found that municipalities that use developer impact fees to provide community facilities, parks, and child care had lower crime rates than those that do not use such fees.[22] This shows that providing services to meet the needs of the current generation of youth also has a wider community benefit. As part of a mixed-use zoning strategy, cities throughout California have included incentives in developer agreements to incorporate child care into new housing, transit, and industrial park projects.[23]

A 2010 AARP survey found that 88% of those 65 and older agreed or strongly agreed that they desire to age in place in their home communities and neighborhoods, near family and friend support networks.[24] Meeting this goal requires attention to universal design in housing, mixed-use development to ensure access to nearby services, new approaches to mobility, and opportunities for social and civic engagement. While cities such as New York have been championing age-friendly policies, such policies are also possible in sprawling cities and suburbs. According to the *Maturing of America* survey, a higher percentage of suburbs than of metro or rural communities has zoning requirements to support aging in place and "complete streets."[25] Lifelong Communities, led by the Atlanta Regional Commission, helps municipalities with plans, designs, and funding to meet the needs of a rapidly aging population in a mostly low-density suburban context.[26]

Service Integration

Service integration—across agencies and age groups—can promote more efficient use of resources and more effective programming. Neighborhood-based schools are important community resources to provide accessible intergenerational programming;[27] across the country, schools and cities are collaborating to share recreational facilities and other amenities. This may involve the school using a public park or pool, or the broader community using the school gym, playing fields, and auditorium. Such shared use promotes better coordination of community resources and integration across the generations—integration that builds community connections.

However, implementation of joint use is not without its challenges, one of which is concerns over liability and security. At a 2012 ICMA focus group on prospects for multigenerational planning, city managers noted that schools are closing themselves off from the broader community because of liability and security concerns.[28] But liability, security, and the different needs of different age groups can be accommodated in integrated programs. While schools have focused primarily on the 5- to 18-year-old population and often think their liability covers only this age group, city governments have experience designing services for residents of all ages.

Also of concern in service integration are the allocation of maintenance costs and the coordination of different funding streams and time lines, but these can be resolved through collaborative planning.[29] Charlotte-Mecklenburg, North Carolina, for example, coordinates capital projects and facility planning between local governments and school districts. Schools have donated land to build transportation hubs next to elementary schools—complete with school playfields atop parking decks. Rather than building senior centers, many communities are now building community centers for all ages. But it takes vision, collaborative spirit, and openness to new ideas and innovation as well as regulatory flexibility. For example, the city of Emeryville, California, is building a new school/community center/park that will house all services—from child care to senior services—under one roof. It is pursuing an integrated approach because the city wants to attract and retain residents for the entire life cycle—especially young families with children, whom it views as critical to the city's future.

Political Coalitions in the Planning Process

Cities can help to build political will for multigenerational planning and shared services through broadening the participatory planning process to include both youth and the elderly. The *Maturing of America* survey found that two-thirds of communities engage older adults in comprehensive planning regarding their needs,[30] while the Center for Cities and Schools has developed a curriculum for use in schools to promote youth involvement in planning.[31] Civic participation is a key principle in both the WHO and UNICEF approaches to building age- and child-friendly cities. Durham, North Carolina, earned a Local Government Innovation Award in 2012 for its efforts to involve neighborhood residents in community redesign to better meet the needs of *all* residents in a distressed urban neighborhood.

As cities face more limited budgets, new approaches to service delivery must be identified. The 2008 American Planning Association survey identified NIMBY-ism as the top barrier to planning for the needs of young families.[32] While NIMBY attitudes among residents can block family services and affordable housing, communities can overcome such resistance by promoting family and youth participation in the planning process, increasing awareness of the benefits of family-friendly elements (e.g., child care by right, which allows child care in residential neighborhoods, and accessory flats) for the entire community, and addressing pedestrian needs in their site planning and zoning.[33] Conflict and competition over resources need to be replaced with approaches that combine resources and services. Elders have many skills to share from a lifetime of experience, and youth can provide important insights and help to seniors. Communities that come together across cultural, ethnic, and age differences will recognize new

opportunities that can promote new investment and long-term sustainability.

Demographic and Fiscal Challenges

The sprawling design of U.S. communities creates special challenges to intergenerational planning, especially in suburban and rural areas. According to the *Maturing of America* survey, rural and suburban communities lag behind their metro core counterparts in every category of service delivery measured[34] (Figure 4–4). Of the 43 services measured on the survey, an average of 56% are available in rural communities compared with 58% in suburban communities and 75% in metro core communities.[35] Mobility is an especially important

Figure 4-4 Average Number of Services Provided, by Metro Status

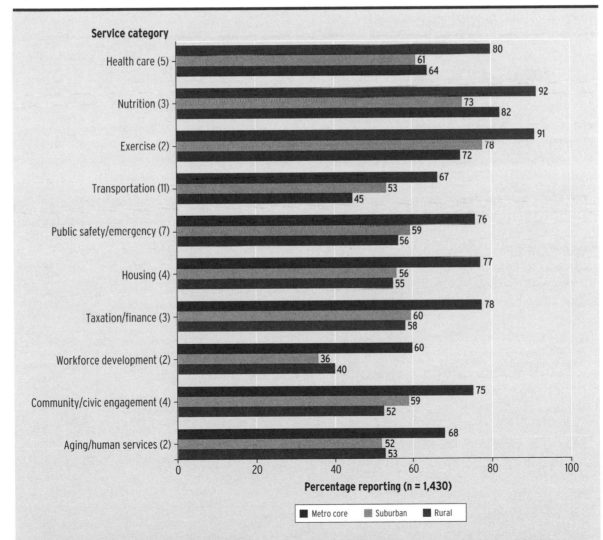

Source: Data from the *Maturing of America* survey 2010, reported in Lydia Morken and Mildred Warner, *Planning for the Aging Population: Rural Responses to the Challenge* (issue brief, Department of City and Regional Planning, Cornell University, October 2012), 2, mildredwarner.org/p/146.

Note: Numbers in parentheses reflect the number of questions in each category on the survey.

problem for these communities. Only 43% of rural and 56% of suburban communities offer paratransit services, compared to 74% of urban communities, and public transit is even less common in rural (33%) and suburban (48%) communities (not shown).[36] Walkability is also a challenge, as sidewalk systems linking residential areas to services are available in only half of rural communities compared to two-thirds of suburbs and urban communities (not shown).[37]

Compounding the problem, a look at Table 4–2 shows that suburbs and rural areas that responded to the *Maturing of America* survey have higher proportions of elder residents than do urban communities. Rural communities show the highest percentage of elders as well as lower household income and higher

poverty rates. This means an increased need for local government services. Suburbs, by contrast, have higher household income and lower poverty rates, but their senior populations grew by 36% from 2000 to 2010, a rate that is 50% higher than the rate of general population growth (23%). As suburbs and rural areas age, they need to identify ways to meet the needs of their changing populations.

As for fiscal challenges, while all governments are stressed in tight fiscal times, the challenges for rural communities are especially acute. Using Census of Government Finance data from 2007, we determined that rural communities responding to the *Maturing of America* survey have lower property tax revenues than suburbs but higher expenditures. Their costs of

Table 4-2 Demographic and Fiscal Challenges

	Metro core	Suburban	Rural
Maturing of America survey respondents (total = 1,430)	180	712	538
Demographic overview			
Percentage 65 and older[a]	12.6%	13.9%	16.8%
Percentage < 18 years old[a]	23.4%	24.5%	23.3%
Percentage change in population, 2000-2010[a,b]	15.2%	23.0%	5.7%
Percentage change in population of 65 and older, 2000-2010[a,b]	19.7%	36.1%	12.1%
Median household income (in 2010 dollars)[c]	$51,325	$67,116	$41,610
Poverty rate[c]	15.2%	9.2%	16.9%
Poverty rate among 65 and older living independently[c]	8.8%	7.3%	11.3%
Revenue and expenditure[d]			
Property tax per capita, 2007	$494.72	$542.10	$397.93
State aid per capita, 2007	$421.93	$230.81	$372.79
Total local government expenditures per capita, 2007	$2,179.90	$1,624.18	$1,722.05
Maturing of America survey highlights[e]			
Services available for older adults (percentage of 43 services included in survey)	74.9%	58.5%	55.4%
Places with zoning requirements that support aging in place	42.2%	48.9%	31.4%
Places with zoning requirements that support "complete streets"	49.4%	55.5%	43.9%
Places with a strategic plan that specifically reflects the needs and potential contributions of older adults	23.3%	15.4%	13.4%
Places with programs specifically developed to provide intergenerational activities	66.7%	44.1%	34.8%

Note: All values reflect U.S. Census averages for the 1,430 survey respondents to 2010 *Maturing of America* survey.

a   Raw data from U.S. Census 2010.

b   Raw data from U.S. Census 2000.

c   *American Community Survey 2006-2010,* census.gov/acs/www/data_documentation/2010_release/.

d   Data from U.S. Census of Governments 2007, *State and Local Government Finances, Individual Unit File,* http://harvester.census.gov/filedownload/2007cog_finance_individual_units.zip.

e   Lydia Morken and Mildred E. Warner, "Planning for the Aging Population: Rural Responses to the Challenge" (issue brief, Department of City and Regional Planning, Cornell University, October 2012), mildredwarner.org/p/146.

service delivery are higher because of sparse settlement patterns. Whereas suburban residents can benefit from access to nearby urban services, such service spillovers are not available to rural residents. Suburbs, however, receive less state aid than either rural or urban communities, primarily because of their lower poverty and higher income.

Conclusion

Cities across the United States face the dual challenges of fiscal stress and demographic change. In essence, communities will face more demand for public services in the future as baby boomers age. Can local planning help address the challenge?

Fewer than half of surveyed communities have addressed the needs of children or older adults in their strategic and comprehensive plans.[38] Clearly, future strategic planning must incorporate the needs of both seniors and children. Cities are increasingly recognizing that the needs of both populations are similar. If attention to the needs of seniors can be coupled with attention to the needs of children and young families, we can design communities that mobilize local resources to meet the needs of all residents across the entire life course. Investing more in services for children and youth now not only supports parents and builds the workforce of the future but also helps communities realize new ways to promote development, integrate services, and build political support for new approaches to service delivery. City managers can help bring long-term economic stability to their communities by encouraging family-friendly policies in physical design, promoting service integration across age groups, and broadening the net of public participation. In this way, cities can create vibrant, resilient communities for residents across the life cycle.

Notes

1 U.S. Census Bureau, "An Older and More Diverse Nation by Midcentury," August 14, 2008, census.gov/newsroom/releases/archives/population/cb08-123.html.

2 Jeffrey Passel, Gretchen Livingston, and D'Vera Cohn, "Explaining Why Minority Births Now Outnumber White Births" (Washington, D.C.: Pew Research Center, May 17, 2012), pewsocialtrends.org/2012/05/17/explaining-why-minority-births-now-outnumber-white-births/.

3 Ibid.

4 Julia B. Isaacs, *How Much Do We Spend on Children and the Elderly?* (Washington, D.C.: The Brookings Institution), 1, brookings.edu/reports/2009/ ~ /media/68F7781F1612493E8AD0F419F7A35E65.pdf.

5 Ibid., 8, Table 2.

6 Ryan D. Edwards, *Forecasting Government Revenue and Expenditure in the U.S. Using Data on Age-Specific Utilization* (working paper WP10-01, National Transfer Accounts Project, February 15, 2010), 32, qcpages.qc.edu/ ~ redwards/Papers/edwards-forecasting-0210.pdf.

7 Authors' calculation based on 2004 data from Edwards, *Forecasting Government Revenue and Expenditure,* Table B7.

8 Richard Florida, *The Rise of the Creative Class* (New York: Basic Books, 2002).

9 David L. Brown and Nina Glasgow, "Are Older In-Migrants to Rural Communities 'Grey Gold'?" *Rural New York Minute* (Community and Rural Development Institute), Issue 14 (February 2008), devsoc.cals.cornell.edu/cals/devsoc/outreach/cardi/publications/loader.cfm?csModule = security/getfile&PageID = 219025.

10 Laura Reese, "Creative Class or Procreative Class: Implications for Local Economic Development," *Theoretical and Empirical Research in Urban Management* 7, no. 1 (February 2012): 5–26, um.ase.ro/no71/1.pdf.

11 Dowell Myers, *Immigrants and Boomers: Forging a New Social Contract for the Future of America* (New York: Russell Sage Foundation, 2007).

12 Jack P. Shonkoff and Deborah A. Phillips, eds., *From Neurons to Neighborhoods: The Science of Early Childhood Development* (Washington D.C.: National Academies Press, 2000).

13 Evelyn Israel and Mildred Warner, "Planning for Family Friendly Communities," *PAS Memo* (November/December 2008), planning.org/pas/memo/open/nov2008/ index.htm.

14 Ibid.

15 Ibid.

16 Mildred Warner and Rebecca Baran-Rees, "The Economic Importance of Families with Children" (issue brief, Department of City and Regional Planning, Cornell University, March 2012), mildredwarner.org/p/129.

17 Mildred Warner, George Homsy, and Esther Greenhouse, "Multi-generational Community Planning: Linking the Needs of Children and Older Adults" (issue brief, Department of City and Regional Planning, Cornell University, April 2010), mildredwarner.org/p/130.

18 World Health Organization (WHO), *Global Age-Friendly Cities: A Guide* (Geneva, Switzerland: WHO Press, 2007), who.int/ageing/publications/Global_age_friendly_cities_Guide_English.pdf.

19 UNICEF, *Building Child Friendly Cities: A Framework for Action* (Florence, Italy: UNICEF Innocenti Research Centre, International Secretariat for Child Friendly Cities, 2004), unicef-irc.org/publications/416.

20 National Association of Area Agencies on Aging (n4a), *The Maturing of America: Communities Moving Forward for an Aging Population* (Washington, D.C.: n4a, June 2011), 22, n4a.org/files/MOA_FINAL_Rpt.pdf.

21 Lydia Morken and Mildred E. Warner, "Planning for the Aging Population: Rural Responses to the Challenge" (issue brief, Department of City and Regional Planning, Cornell University, October 2012), 6, mildredwarner.org/p/146.

22 Joseph Rukus and Mildred E. Warner, "Crime Rates and Collective Efficacy: The Role of Family Friendly Planning," *Cities* (forthcoming), doi.org/10.1016/j.cities.2012.09.006.

23 Kristen Anderson and Ellen Dektar, *Child Care and Community Development* (briefing paper, Planning for Family Friendly Communities, April 2010), mildredwarner.org/p/131.

24 Teresa A. Keenan, *Home and Community Preferences of the 45+ Population* (Washington, D.C.: AARP, 2010), 4, assets.aarp.org/rgcenter/general/home-community-services-10.pdf.

25 Morken and Warner, "Planning for the Aging Population," 7.

26 Lydia Morken, "Cities Plan for the Aging Population: Lessons from New York City and Atlanta" (issue brief, Department of City and Regional Planning, Cornell University, August 2012), mildredwarner.org/p/134.

27 Mary Filardo et al., *Joint Use of Public Schools: A Framework for a New Social Contract* (Washington, D.C.: 21st Century School Fund and Center for Cities and Schools, April 2010), citiesandschools.berkeley.edu/reports/Joint-Use-Concept-Paper.pdf.

28 ICMA, "Focus Group on Multi-Generational Planning" (ICMA 98th Annual Conference, Phoenix, Arizona, October 7–10, 2012).

29 Lydia Morken and Rebecca Baran-Rees, "Joint Use: School Community Collaboration" (issue brief, Department of City and Regional Planning, Cornell University, November 2012), mildredwarner.org/p/147.

30 n4a, *Maturing of America*, 19.

31 Deborah L. McKoy et al., *YPlan Handbook* (Berkeley, Calif.: Center for Communities and Schools, 2010), citiesandschools.berkeley.edu/yplan.html.

32 Israel and Warner, "Planning for Family Friendly Communities."

33 Mildred E. Warner and Joseph Rukus, "Planners' Role in Creating Family Friendly Communities: Action, Participation and Resistance," *Journal of Urban Affairs* (forthcoming), mildredwarner.org/p/145.

34 Morken and Warner, "Planning for the Aging Population," 2.

35 Ibid., 2.

36 Ibid., 3.

37 Ibid.

38 Morken and Warner, "Planning for the Aging Population"; Israel and Warner, "Planning for Family Friendly Communities."

5

Collaborative Governance and Leadership: A 2012 Survey of Local Government Collaboration

Rosemary O'Leary
University of Kansas

Catherine M. Gerard
The Maxwell School, Syracuse University

In today's local government, efforts to improve the efficiency and effectiveness of service delivery require new approaches to addressing public issues. One such approach is collaboration—and for several reasons. First, most public challenges require a response that exceeds the capabilities and resources of any one department, organization, or jurisdiction, and collaboration, including multijurisdictional partnerships, provides a way to stretch resources and accomplish more with less. Second, technology is enabling local governments to share information in ways that are integrative and interoperable, with one outcome being a greater emphasis on collaborative governance. Finally, citizens are seeking more avenues for engaging in governance, which can mean new and different forms of collaborative problem solving and decision making.

In 2010, we surveyed members of the U.S. Senior Executive Service on their use of collaboration as a management strategy. In 2012, to learn about the use of collaboration in local government, we tailored that survey to local government managers. On the survey we used the following definition:

> Collaboration means to work across boundaries with two or more organizations to solve

SELECTED FINDINGS

Nearly all surveyed local government managers (97%) reported that they use collaboration as a management strategy; 86% reported doing so because it is the "right thing to do."

Of all the positive results of collaboration, the one cited most often was better performance outcomes—specifically, economic benefits such as efficiencies achieved through pooled resources, lower costs, and economies of scale.

When asked to identify the skill set of the collaborative manager, 74% of respondents cited individual attributes such as having an open mind, as well as being unselfish, patient, trustworthy, self-confident, and risk oriented.

problems that cannot be solved or easily solved by single organizations. Collaboration can include the public."

This article highlights our preliminary findings.

The authors wish to express their deep gratitude to Maxwell graduate students Joe Ralbovsky, Jessica Rubin, Ben Wilhelm, Amy Johnson, and Tian Tang, as well as to Maxwell staff member Xueyi Chen and Professor Yujin Choi of Florida International University, for their expert assistance with survey development, coding, and analysis.

Survey Methodology

In the spring of 2012, after a pretest and adjustments to the 2010 survey, we mailed postcards to all U.S. cities with a population of 2,500 and above, as well as to all U.S. counties, alerting them that the survey was coming. We then sent surveys to each of these jurisdictions with a stamped, self-addressed return envelope. We mailed a second round of surveys two weeks later, followed by a reminder postcard and a third and final round of surveys two weeks after the second round, making the length of the survey process six weeks. Respondents had the option of mailing the completed surveys back to us or entering their responses online. Of the 10,500 surveys that were sent out, 1,417 usable responses were returned for a response rate of 13.5%. Completed surveys totaled 1,042. The demographic and professional distributions of responding communities and local government managers are shown in Table 5–1.

We analyzed answers to closed-ended questions using standard statistical analytical techniques. For the purpose of this article, only descriptive statistics were generated. The responses to the few open-ended survey questions were analyzed using ATLAS.ti, a qualitative analysis software package (atlasti.com/), and coded by a team of five researchers. Intersubjective coding tests were performed weekly during the 10 weeks of coding and analysis.

We were initially disappointed with the 13.5% response rate. Yet after we started reading, coding, and analyzing the 1,417 responses, we realized that, for the most part, we had attracted the "believers" in collaboration, as these respondents offered example after example about how they use collaboration as a management strategy. This left us with a treasure trove of insights about collaboration from local government managers who see it as an essential tool in their tool boxes.

Use of Collaboration as a Management Strategy

> "Collaboration is my leadership style. It empowers staff and builds trust and buy-in. In all major projects, collaboration is used."
>
> — *Comments of a village manager*

At the top of the questionnaire, we asked respondents whether collaboration is one of their management strategies, and an overwhelming 97% of 1,042 responding local government managers said that it is (not shown). They were then presented with a list of eight reasons for choosing collaboration as a management strategy. Their answers fell into five main groups:

Table 5-1   Survey Response

Classification	Respondents No.	%
Jurisdictions		
Population (n = 1,043)		
More than 1,000,000	7	1
500,001–1,000,000	13	1
100,001–500,000	76	7
25,001–100,000	254	24
25,000 and under	693	66
Geographic region[a] (n = 875)		
Northeast	213	24
Southeast	166	19
Southwest	104	12
Midwest	379	43
West	13	2
Respondents		
Sex (n = 1,016)		
Male	766	75
Female	250	25
Age (n = 1,043)		
22–35	101	10
36–45	162	16
46–55	336	32
55–64	376	36
65+	68	7
Level of education (n = 1,060)		
Not college graduate	110	11
College graduate	250	24
Advanced degree	700	66
Type of position (n = 993)		
Appointed	758	76
Elected	107	11
Career public servant	117	12
Other	11	1
Time with organization (years) (n = 1,043)		
0–1	143	14
2–3	171	16
4–5	131	13
6–7	104	10
8–9	72	7
10+	422	41
Time in position (years) (n = 1,043)		
0–1	173	17
2–3	194	19
4–5	151	15
6–7	126	12
8–9	73	7
10+	326	31

a   Many respondents did not designate a geographic area as they wanted to remain truly anonymous. Those who did selected the area of the country they thought they were from. Geographic designations were taken from previous ICMA surveys and were not defined.

1. Collaboration is implicitly mandated.
2. Collaboration improves outcomes.
3. Collaboration improves the problem-solving process.
4. Collaboration builds relationships and credibility.
5. Collaboration is explicitly mandated.

Figure 5–1 shows the percentage of survey respondents who selected each of the eight reasons shown on the survey instrument (multiple responses were permitted), and the accompanying sidebar locates those and other reasons (i.e., the coded open-ended responses) that were cited within each of the five main groups identified above.

Collaboration Is Implicitly Mandated

Asked why they use collaboration as a management strategy, sizable majority of local government officials (86%) answered that collaboration is the "right thing to do" (Figure 5–1). Their open-ended responses reveal that they consider collaboration to be in keeping with community values regarding how public problems should be solved, how public work should be done, how the public should be served, and how taxpayers' money should be spent.

As well as being congruent with community values, a collaborative approach is also perceived as being congruent with the organizational or jurisdictional culture within which these managers work. Culture

is to organizations what character and personality are to individuals. The term *organizational culture* refers to the organization's values and beliefs that drive behavior. Thus, to be a successful and accepted member of an organization means behaving in ways that are consistent with that organization's culture, which is passed on to those who enter the organization through formal and informal socialization. The finding that local government managers regard collaboration with other organizations and jurisdictions as part of the culture of their communities and organizations contrasts notably with the stereotype of public bureaucracies as excessively hierarchical and protective of their turf.

Collaboration Improves Outcomes

In light of the changing nature of local government—the complexity of public problems, the interdependence of missions, and the need for stakeholder perspectives in decision making—local government managers regard collaboration as a highly effective approach to increasing performance. Among the specific advantages of collaboration, respondents identified goal and mission achievement, better results, greater effectiveness, increased capacity building, better service delivery, more efficiency, and more sustainable solutions.

Moreover, collaboration is seen as an important mechanism for leveraging or coordinating scarce

Figure 5-1 Reasons for Choosing Collaboration as a Management Strategy

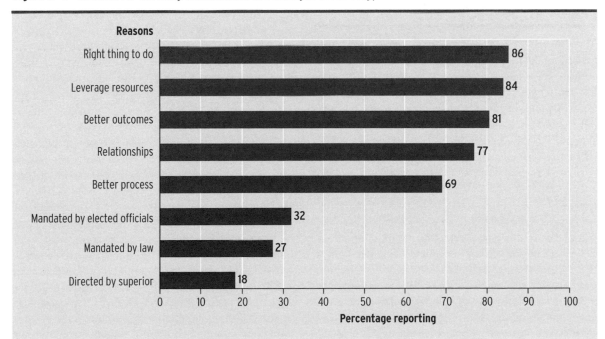

Reasons for Choosing Collaboration as a Management Strategy

1. It is implicitly mandated
   - "Right thing to do"
   - Consistent with community values
2. To improve outcomes
   - Leveraged resources
   - Goal and mission achievement
   - Better results
   - Greater effectiveness
   - Increased capacity building
   - Better service delivery
   - More efficiency
   - More sustainable solutions
3. To improve the problem-solving process
   - Achieve consensus
   - Achieve integration
   - Achieve teamwork
   - Bring in a diversity of ideas
   - Broaden options
   - Catalyze boundary spanning
4. To build relationships and credibility
   - Build alliances
   - Build credibility with others
5. It is explicitly mandated
   - By elected officials
   - By law
   - By superiors
   - By other levels of government

---

teamwork. The collaborative process builds ownership of ideas and commitment to implementation, thus yielding more durable and sustainable results. A significant by-product of the process is that employees learn about their organization and about other organizations with which they interact.

Collaboration Builds Relationships and Credibility

In an operating environment where local government organizations are increasingly interdependent, resources are scarce, and demands for solutions are high, local government managers use collaboration to build alliances and relationships that will help them and their agencies. They believe that successful collaboration builds the credibility of the players.

Collaboration Is Explicitly Mandated

Explicitly mandated collaboration, which was cited by the smallest percentages of respondents, manifests itself in different ways. In this context, the most common mandates come from legislation, policy, others levels of government, or directive by an elected official.

Recent Collaborative Experiences

"It was long . . . drawn out . . . frustrating, and worth it."

— *Comments of a city manager*

Nearly all survey respondents (86% of 1,042) (not shown) said that they had been involved in a recent collaboration. Asked to describe their experience in terms of type and purpose, 827 managers gave examples of a rich array of collaborations: intergovernmental, intersectoral, and those involving the public.

Only 30 (or 4%) of 827 descriptive responses discussed internal collaboration—that is, the collaboration of agencies or units within the home organization (not shown). Instead, the majority of collaborations described (75%) were intergovernmental—with other municipalities, community agencies, federal agencies, businesses, state and county organizations, and, in one case, another country—while intersectoral collaboration (i.e., with private or nonprofit organizations) made up 18% of responses. Collaboration with citizens constituted only 3% of the responses.

Local managers collaborate on many substantive issues: fire and emergency response, economic development, infrastructure planning and development, and housing, to name a few (Figure 5–2; responses coded as "other" are not included). They are also involved in collaborations of various types. As one individual commented, "We collaborate on anything

resources, such as funds, time, staff, and expertise, as well as knowledge, new perspectives, and networks. For some managers, the need for more sophisticated, innovative products leads them to collaborate because developing such products requires multiple actors, shared information, ongoing idea generation, and collaborative problem solving.

Collaboration Improves the Problem-Solving Process

Another reason local government managers use collaboration as a management strategy is that it builds a richer process for working together and solving problems. Respondents noted that collaboration improves problem solving by focusing on needs, bringing in a diversity of ideas, catalyzing boundary spanning, and broadening options. They described it as a way to achieve consensus, compromise, integration, and

Figure 5-2 Policy and Service Areas of Collaboration

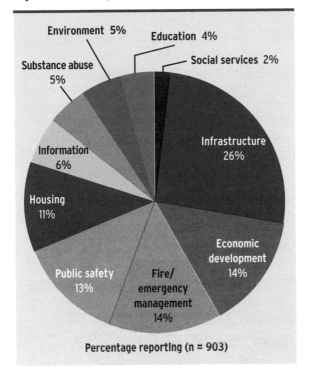

Percentage reporting (n = 903)

we can." While not all collaborations are successful, and some respondents described efforts that failed, many more offered stories of successes or works in progress. What follows are examples of collaborations, organized by purpose.

Need to Stretch Resources

Respondents pointed to budgetary concerns and described how collaboration offers the opportunity to take advantage of economies of scale. For example, some jurisdictions have formed intermunicipal (and city-county) health benefits consortia to reduce employee and retiree health benefit costs. Many jurisdictions share police, fire, facilities, and information services; deliver health care to adjoining jurisdictions; and collaborate on purchasing decisions. For example, in Michigan, the cities of Kalamazoo and Portage have developed shared purchasing agreements with Kalamazoo County; in Pennsylvania, the boroughs of Harmony and Zelienople have a shared services plan that covers contracted police services, equipment, and materials. Respondents also reported a county and city sharing purchasing, as well as many jurisdictions sharing police, fire, facilities, and information services. Collaborating on bids and grant proposals was another theme; for example, six villages prepared a joint bid for road resurfacing, and several counties are developing a joint grant proposal for federal disaster funds. The

need for Federal Emergency Management Agency certification of a shared levee system prompted cities and a county to collaborate on a special project.

Need for Structural Changes

A second purpose of collaboration is to create new structures for better and more efficient services. Often this entails mergers and consolidations—some mandated, some voluntary—but some local governments are creating new structures, such as consolidations of fire departments, police forces, emergency dispatch units, and forensic centers; and of housing and economic development agencies. An interesting trend is the creation of regional authorities for transportation planning and facilities, water, sewage treatment, ambulance services, and power. The municipalities of Albany County, New York, for example, formed a public benefit corporation to jointly administer storm-water permits issued by the state environmental agency. Another example is Illinois Enterprise Zone 52, a shared area of development joining four jurisdictions in the state in order to increase employment and decrease poverty.

Need for Process Improvement

Some respondents collaborate for process improvement. One city and county reported working together on a process to educate citizens about a sales tax to benefit law enforcement. Others jurisdictions are working to coordinate emergency management processes and standards for fire-rescue service delivery. For example, in Kootenai County, Idaho, the cities of Coeur d'Alene, Rathdrum, and Hayden have developed a unified land use code. Elsewhere, another city brought together all relevant departments to create a new grass-mowing process that reduces travel and other costs and improves consistency and quality. Several respondents reported that their jurisdictions had introduced collaborative budgeting processes; many others collaborated to redesign their bidding processes. Planning is another area for collaboration: in Colorado, La Plata County is working on a joint planning agreement with the city of Durango to improve transportation infrastructure and thereby attract new business.

Need for Better Service

Improving service to the public is at the heart of many local government collaborations. An enhanced telephone system to warn citizens about severe weather resulted from a collaboration of Calhoun, Chicksaw, Itawambu, Lafayette, Lee, Monroe, Pontocos, and Union Counties in Mississippi. In California, the local United Way and the regional planning agency joined with Maricose County to develop a 10-year plan to reduce homelessness; the plan has resulted in new veteran housing and the renovation of 1,000 of housing units. In one village, where a highway left citizens with no safe way to cross the village, the municipality is working with the school district to obtain a state transportation grant for a bridge and walkway. In California, the Transportation Authority CALTRAN, Contra Costa County, and East Bay Regional Parks have joined to complete a public/private recreational complex for the community. Elsewhere, a city effort to build a farmers' market involved hospitals, businesses, governments, nonprofits, and faith-based organizations. Another city partnered with civic groups to raise private funds for a LEED (Leadership in Energy and Environmental Design)-certified community meeting space.

What Makes Collaboration Work?

In light of the many challenges to collaboration, respondents were shown a list of 20 possible factors and asked to identify those that they believed make collaboration work. Again, we coded and grouped their responses, including their open-ended answers to "Others, please specify," into five major themes: (1) people and their relationships, (2) the need to achieve results, (3) a sense of urgency, (4) directives from the top, and (5) organizational supports. Figure 5–3 shows the percentage of survey respondents who selected each of the 20 factors presented on the survey instrument (multiple responses were permitted), and the accompanying sidebar locates those and other

Figure 5-3   Factors That Make Collaboration Work

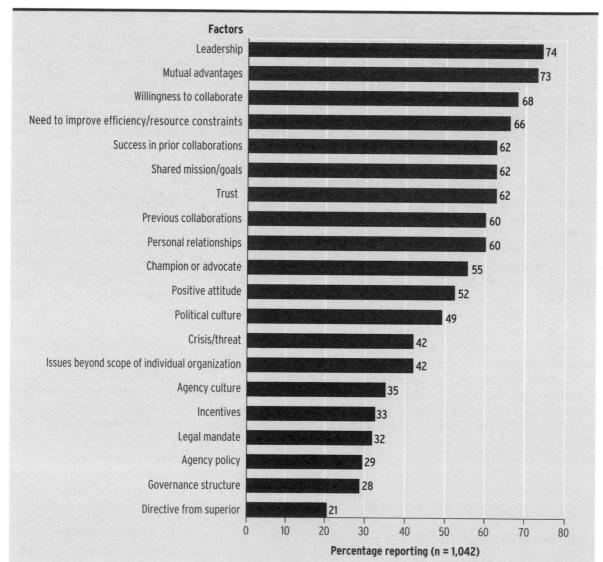

Percentage reporting (n = 1,042)

Factors for Collaboration

1. People and their relationships
   - Leadership
   - Champions
   - Past positive experience with partners
   - Personal desire
2. The need to achieve results
   - Scarce resources
   - Cross-jurisdictional challenges
   - Mutual advantages
3. A sense of urgency
   - Crisis
   - Threat
   - Pressures
   - Needed services not being delivered
4. Directives from the top
   - Community values
   - Elected officials
   - Federal or state mandates
5. Organizational supports
   - Government structure
   - Culture and incentives

---

reasons (i.e., the coded open-ended responses) that were cited within each of the five main groups identified above.

People and Their Relationships

Local government managers consider leadership to be a strong factor for collaboration. Such leadership may be embodied in a dynamic new local government manager with a vision for innovative thinking or in a political leader who is on board with that thinking. Potential partners—those with shared missions who seek mutually beneficial solutions—may also be a positive force for collaboration; the attitude of the collaborators, described as openness, trust, willingness, frankness, belief in shared interests, and a desire to serve the greater good, is seen as motivational. For some, past successes and positive experiences with collaboration contribute to the desire to collaborate again. Still others pointed to a personal desire to learn from others and expand their networks.

The Need to Achieve Results

Respondents reported that collaboration is motivated by the need to achieve results with scarce resources and to develop integrative solutions to complex issues. They see it as an opportunity for local governments to leverage resources, eliminate duplication, and coordinate efforts. The nature of the public problems they face—complex, cross-organizational, and cross-sectoral—also prompts a collaborative approach. Further, the fact that collaboration yields benefits for all parties is seen as a powerful incentive.

A Sense of Urgency

For some local government managers, a strong sense of urgency, a current crisis, or a threat from external forces catalyzes collaboration. Other managers decide to collaborate when needed services are not being delivered. And whereas some managers are motivated by past success with collaboration, others are motivated by the failure of other approaches to accomplish their goals.

Directives from the Top

Respondents described mandates, legislation, and directives from elected officials as catalysts for collaboration. Inferred directives, including community values, organizational culture, and personal values, were again mentioned, but this time as motivators rather than reasons for collaboration.

Organizational Supports

The fifth category of factors for collaboration concerns the organization. Leadership has already been mentioned as a significant factor here, but sometimes leadership is not enough. Respondents noted that a local government's structure—its organizational design, distributed governance (i.e., people other than those in government handling government services), and work dispersal (i.e., functions that require a collaborative approach)—can be conducive to collaborative efforts, as can the dissemination of research findings and other information about the benefits of such efforts in local government work. And, of course, incentives for those participating in collaboration are crucial motivators.

Consequences of Collaboration

Governments have increasingly used collaborative strategies with multiple organizations to address complex problems in diverse policy areas. From the popularity of collaboration, we can assume that most local government managers see it as a highly beneficial management strategy, but some survey respondents identified downsides to collaboration as well.

The Positive Results of Collaboration

When asked to identify the positive results of collaboration and shown a list of nine possible options, nearly all the surveyed managers selected at least one indicator of positive results. Figure 5–4 shows the percentage of respondents who selected each of the nine options (multiple responses were permitted), and the accompanying sidebar locates those and other reasons (i.e., the coded open-ended responses) within three major groups: better performance outcomes, better relationship-focused outcomes, and better process outcomes.

Of the three groups of positive results of collaboration, the one cited most often was better performance outcomes. In this context, *performance* usually refers to economic benefits, such as efficiencies achieved through pooled resources, lower costs, and economies of scale. Improved quality of work product or decisions, including sustainability, timeliness, and better public service, were also cited. Other responses described performance outcomes in terms of learning and synergy; in the latter case, respondents focused on the collaborative results that trump what a single organization could have done by itself.

The second major group of positive results involves better relationship-focused outcomes, including greater buy-in and ownership of solutions by—as well as less resistance from—the collaborators. Inherent in the idea of collaboration as building relationships are a greater willingness to collaborate in the future, more interaction among local government public servants, and alliance building. Human resource benefits such as empowerment, improved job satisfaction, leveraged

---

The Positive Results of Collaboration

1. Better performance outcomes
   - Economic benefits
   - Economies of scale
   - Better public service
   - Higher quality work
   - Mission accomplishment
   - Quality decisions
   - Sustainability
   - Timeliness
2. Better relationship-focused outcomes
   - Buy-in of parties
   - Ownership of solutions
   - Alliances
   - Learning
3. Better process outcomes
   - More efficient and less cumbersome practices

---

capability, stronger alignment of individual skills, and less stress were also noted.

The third major group concerns better process outcomes. Here, local government managers gave examples of two or more departments or jurisdictions needing to work together to implement a program and, through purposeful collaboration, initiating a less cumbersome and more efficient process.

Figure 5-4   The Positive Results of Collaboration

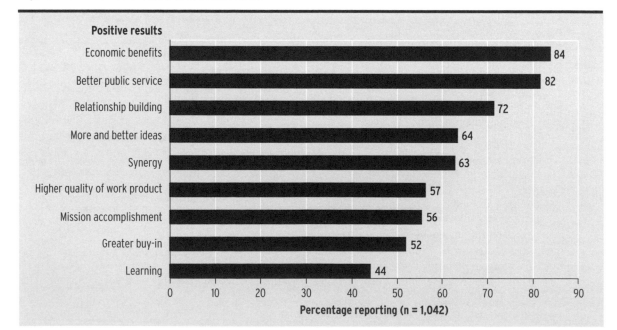

The Negative Results of Collaboration

Shown a list of nine possible negative results of collaboration, 66% of respondents noted that it is time-consuming, 58% cited conflict (between collaborating organizations, with the public), and 45% mentioned stress (Figure 5–5). Also checked was the jurisdiction's loss of power and the fact that collaborative efforts may lead to no results. Other negatives include free riders, suboptimal outcomes, loss of resources (such as staff, funding, and political support), and personal loss (of reputation and power).

Challenges to Collaboration

Public managers who engage in collaboration face significant obstacles. Some challenges have to do with a lack of resources or skills, but the most demanding ones relate to the complex political environment in which these managers collaborate and the people with whom they must work. We showed respondents a list of 13 possible challenges (gleaned from prior work and research) and asked them to select those they believe to be important. Turf wars (79%), political culture (75%), and reaching consensus (73%) were the most commonly cited challenges (Figure 5–6), while at least half the respondents identified relational challenges such as lack of mutual trust, lack of communication, and difficult personalities. One-third or more of the respondents said that their ability to successfully collaborate was hampered by a lack of shared mission, of leadership, and of perceived benefits, as well as by agency culture, time, regulations, and logistics.

The Skill Sets of the Successful Local Government Collaborator

The survey asked local government managers to identify the skill set of the successful collaborator. In our previous work with federal managers, responses to this question surprised us the most. Our predictions, based on the public management and leadership literature, were that their answers would fall into three groups: first, strategic management and visioning; second, facilitation and collaborative problem solving; and third, interpersonal skills. Instead, the most frequently mentioned answers dealt with individual attributes and interpersonal skills, followed by group process skills, strategic leadership, and substantive/technical knowledge (in that order).

For this survey, we replicated the question exactly to see if the responses would be the same, and for the most part, they were—with a minor shift in order: individual attributes (74%), followed by interpersonal skills (21%), strategic leadership (13%), group process skills (12%), and substantive/technical knowledge (4%) (not shown). In fact, the emphasis on individual attributes was even more pronounced than expected. Previous studies have discussed collaborative competencies, including specific skills for collaborators, but

Figure 5-5   The Negative Results of Collaboration

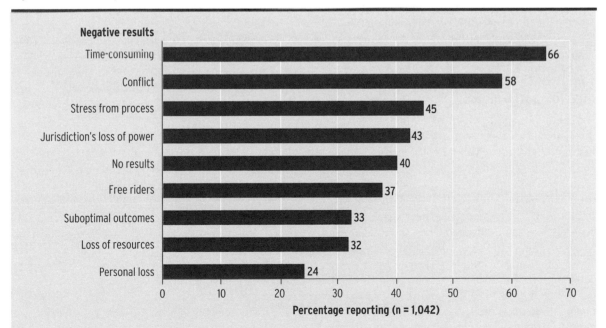

Figure 5-6 Challenges to Collaboration

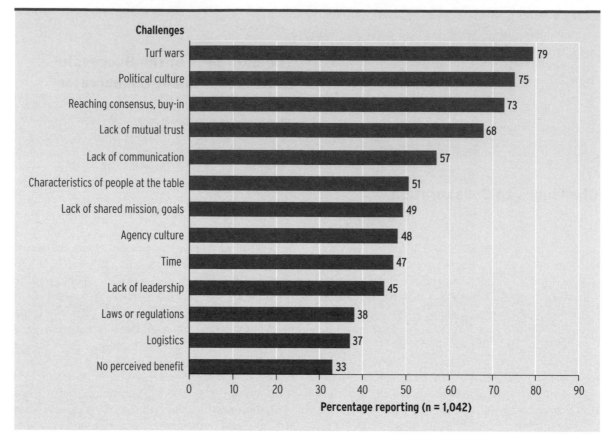

the individual attributes that leaders possess have not been emphasized in the literature and have been mentioned by only a few authors.[1] In analyzing this part of our survey, we find ourselves in the middle of a debate about whether effective collaborators are born or made and, more importantly, whether the individual attributes needed by collaborative leaders can be acquired.

Individual Attributes

For these local government managers, as well as for the federal managers in the earlier survey, the primary skill set for successful collaborators is defined by individual attributes, the most important of which is an open mind (Figure 5–7). Respondents cited the need for collaborators to be open to new ideas, to the ideas of others, to change, and to helping others succeed. Being unselfish, often described as having a low ego and letting go, was the attribute with the second-highest percentage. Beyond that, successful collaborators are seen as patient and trustworthy, yet self-confident and risk oriented. They need to be flexible, demonstrate honesty and integrity, operate with persistence and diligence, and be goal oriented.

Other mentioned attributes include being empathetic, respectful, and diplomatic.

Interpersonal Skills

The second most important skill set among survey respondents is interpersonal skills. Specifically, respondents indicated that a collaborator must be a good communicator, an excellent listener, and adept at working with people through interpersonal communication and relationship building (Figure 5–8).

Strategic Leadership

Strategic leadership, defined as creating vision, is currently championed by many public administration scholars who study networks and collaboration. Survey respondents agreed that strategic leadership skills are important but ranked them third as a skill set. Primary within this skill set is leadership (Figure 5–9), which they described as managing the process, providing coordination, and, at times, using authority. Beyond that, the successful collaborator is perceived as a skilled visionary who has the ability to see the big picture and can develop the goals, structures, inputs, and actions to achieve that

Figure 5-7 Skill Set #1: Individual Attributes

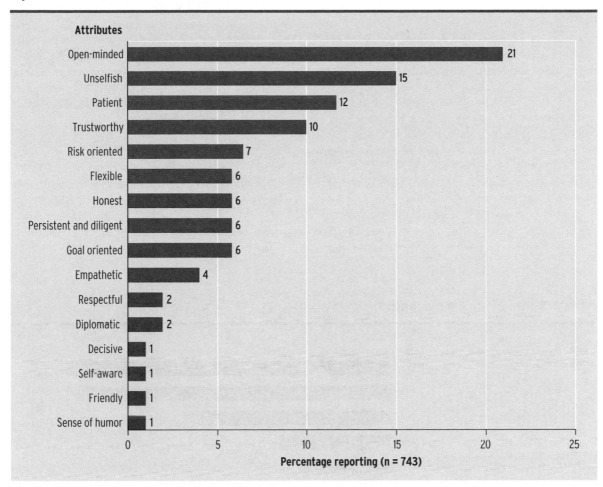

Percentage reporting (n = 743)

Figure 5-7 Skill Set #2: Interpersonal Skills

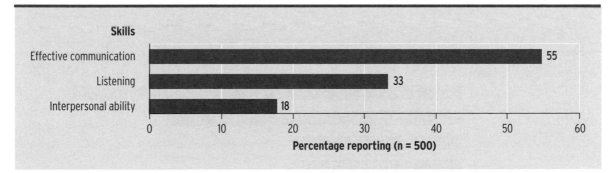

Percentage reporting (n = 500)

vision. This manager exercises facilitative leadership and uses creative approaches to problem solving. Of lesser importance but interesting nevertheless is the collaborative manager's ability to share leadership, power, goals, and credit. The last attribute identified within this skill set is strategic thinking.

Group Process Skills

The fourth skill set identified as most important for the successful collaborator is group process skills. Respondents emphasized that a successful collaborator needs to be adept at compromise, interest-based or collaborative problem solving, and negotiation

(Figure 5–10). Other important skills in this category are facilitation, consensus building, conflict management, and mediation.

As a group process skill, the topic of conflict management in collaboration came up repeatedly throughout survey responses. A majority of respondents (71%) said that collaboration is positively linked to conflict (not shown). When asked in what ways, almost half the respondents said that it leverages conflict for better outcomes, almost 20% said that it solves conflict, and about 17% said that it prevents conflict (not shown). Only 8% think that collaboration causes or worsens conflict, while 6% believe that there is no relationship.

To better understand how local government managers handle conflict within collaborations, we provided a list of nine conflict management strategies and asked respondents to indicate which they used and the importance of each. Over 50% indicated that compromise, listening to all sides, identifying common ground, focusing on the outcome, giving voice to everyone, negotiating, and interest-based problem solving were most used and important strategies (Figure 5–11). Other, less commonly cited methods of managing conflict in collaboration include mediation and allowing conflict to happen.

Substantive/Technical Knowledge

The fifth important skill set of the successful collaborator was identified as substantive/technical knowledge. Implicit within this skill set are expert technical knowledge or subject expertise, organizational and project management skills, and time management (Figure 5–12).

Figure 5-9   Skill Set #3: Strategic Leadership

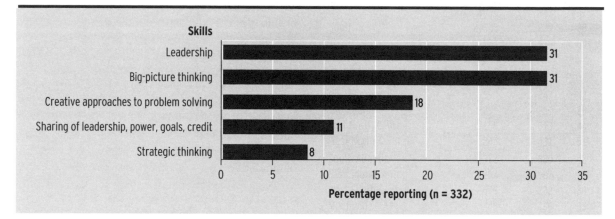

Figure 5-10   Skill Set #4: Group Process Skills

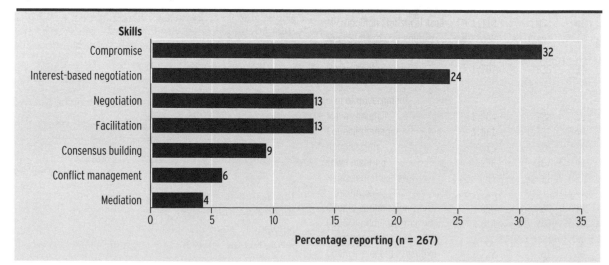

Figure 5-11 Conflict Management Strategies

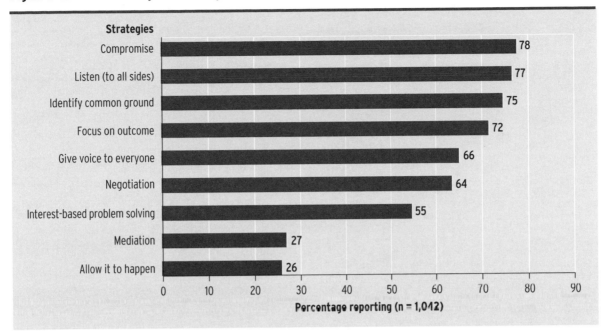

Strategies

Percentage reporting (n = 1,042)

Figure 5-12 Skill Set #5: Substantive/Technical Knowledge

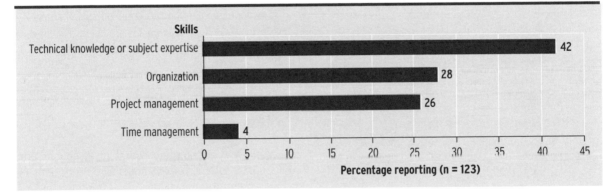

Skills

Percentage reporting (n = 123)

Conclusion

Among the most interesting and important findings from our survey of local government managers and their use of collaboration was the certainty expressed by so many that, in an environment of scarce resources, collaboration is often the way to get things done. Also significant was a strong sense of community values that implicitly mandates a collaborative approach to serving the public. And we were struck as well by the variety of collaborative experiences and participants involved. Describing those experiences and participants, respondents characterized collaboration as long, messy, and conflictual. At the same time, however, they see themselves as possessing the requisite skills and attributes to manage conflict, build relationships, and get results.

We are still gathering data to understand collaborative governance and leadership at the local government level. We ask that any local government manager who would be willing to be interviewed for this ongoing project or would like to offer additional data contact Rosemary O'Leary at oleary@ku.edu.

Notes

1 See, for example, Russell M. Linden, *Working across Boundaries: Making Collaboration Work in Government and Nonprofit Organizations* (San Francisco: Jossey-Bass, 2002); Barbara C. Crosby and John M. Bryson, *Leadership for the Common Good: Tackling Public Problems in a Shared-Power World* (San-Francisco: Jossey-Bass, 2005); and Ricardo S. Morse, "Developing Public Leaders in an Age of Collaborative Governance," in *Innovations in Public Leadership Development*, ed. Ricardo S. Morse and Terry F. Buss (Washington D.C.: National Academy of Public Administration, 2008).

6

Electronic Democracy at the Grass Roots

Donald F. Norris
University of Maryland, Baltimore County

Christopher G. Reddick
University of Texas at San Antonio

Public participation in local government in the United States is typically very low, whether measured by voting in local elections, attendance at city council or county board meetings, attendance at public hearings or meetings, or other means. For some time now, proponents of electronic government (e-government) have argued that one outcome of e-government would almost inevitably be e-democracy, which would be a tool to improve the otherwise low rate of citizen participation in government. However, few if any systematic studies have been undertaken to date to ascertain whether and to what extent e-democracy is being practiced among governments anywhere in the world. Using data collected from a survey conducted in 2011, this study begins to address that gap in the literature vis-à-vis local governments in the United States.

Although definitions of *e-democracy* vary, most writers use the term to mean something akin to a significantly expanded degree of citizen participation in government via the Internet or other electronic means. For our purposes, *e-democracy* means

> the use of electronic means, principally although not solely through local government web sites and the Internet, to promote and enhance citizen engagement with and participation in governmental activities, programs and decision-making.

SELECTED FINDINGS

Adoption of e-democracy by U.S. local governments has been quite low. In the 12 months preceding the survey, only one activity–enabling citizens to view a public hearing or meeting–was adopted by more than half of responding local governments (57%).

Of those local governments that have adopted e-participation, 69% characterize it as mostly government to citizens, which does not suggest meaningful citizen participation.

The barriers to e-participation reported by the largest percentages of governments mostly fall into two categories: those directly or indirectly related to a lack of funding and those indicative of a lack of demand from citizens and local officials.

This is the definition we used in our survey. Please note that we consider the terms *e-democracy* and *e-participation* synonymous, and we use them interchangeably in this article.

Method

This survey was based in part on a similar survey conducted by ICMA in 2006.[1] Recognizing that much has changed in the world of e-government and e-democracy since then, we needed to update the 2006 instrument at least somewhat to capture recent e-democracy issues and trends. Therefore, prior to developing the 2011 instrument, we asked a sample of local information technology (IT) directors and chief information officers with expert knowledge of the subject area to review the 2006 instrument and recommend changes to reflect developments in local e-democracy over the intervening five years.*

Armed with these expert practitioners' suggestions, we worked cooperatively with the ICMA survey research staff to write the 2011 questionnaire. While many of the questions are identical to those in the 2006 survey, we added a number of new questions, deleting a nearly equal number to keep the length of the survey manageable. Respondents were advised that, for our purposes, the terms *e-participation* and *e-democracy* were being used synonymously and that, to simplify things for the questionnaire, we used the term *e-participation* to mean both.

ICMA mailed the surveys in the spring of 2011 to all municipal governments with populations of 2,500 and greater and to all county governments of the same size that have either elected executives or appointed managers. ICMA also provided an online option for completing the survey. Nearly 8 in 10 respondents (79%) returned paper surveys, while the balance completed the online version. ICMA sent a second mailing to local governments that had not responded to the first one. (A copy of the 2011 survey instrument and results can be found on the ICMA website at icma.org/en/results/home/surveying/survey_research/survey_results.) For our purposes, we limited our analyses to all municipal and county governments with populations of 10,000 and above. For this reason, our percentages differ from those reported by ICMA.

Of the 4,456 surveys mailed to municipalities and counties of 10,000 and above, 1,233 were returned for a response rate of 28% (Table 6–1). This response rate is consistent with that of other surveys recently conducted by the ICMA (around 30%), although it is lower than the response rate of 37% to the 2006 survey. ICMA has noticed a decline in responses to its surveys in recent years, which it attributes, in part, to

the impact of the Great Recession on local staff cutbacks: local governments understandably have fewer resources to devote to completing surveys.[2]

As seen in Table 6–1, local governments over 1 million in population and those between 10,000 and 24,999

Table 6-1 Survey Response

Classification	No. of municipalities/ counties[a] surveyed (A)	Respondents No.	Respondents % of (A)
Total respondents	4,456	1,233	28
Population group			
Over 1,000,000	33	7	21
500,000–1,000,000	73	35	34
250,000–499,999	117	24	29
100,000–249,999	370	115	31
50,000–99,999	630	206	33
25,000–49,999	1,064	297	28
10,000–24,999	2,169	549	25
Geographic region			
Northeast	1,000	187	19
North-Central	1,237	372	30
South	1,417	399	28
West	802	275	34
Metro status			
Central	858	323	38
Suburban	2,318	685	30
Independent	1,276	318	25
Form of government			
Municipal			
Mayor-council	1,201	213	18
Council-manager	1,883	683	36
Other	222	45	20
County			
Council-administrator (manager)	735	221	30
Council-elected executive	415	71	17

a For a definition of terms, please see "Inside the *Year Book*," xi–xiv.

---

* We wish to acknowledge and express our appreciation to the following local government officials who reviewed the 2006 survey instrument and provided comments and suggestions that we then used in developing the 2011 instrument: Michael Cannon, chief information officer (CIO), Rockville, Maryland; Ira Levy, director of technology and communication services, Howard County, Maryland; David Molchany, deputy county executive (previously CIO), Fairfax County, Virginia; Elliot Schlanger, CIO, State of Maryland (previously CIO, Baltimore, Maryland); and Paul Thorn, information technology manager, Annapolis, Maryland. Any errors or omissions are those of the authors and in no way reflect on these officials or their advice.

were underrepresented in the sample while those between 500,000 and 1,000,000 were overrepresented. Local governments in the Northeast were underrepresented while those in the West were overrepresented. Among municipalities, the mayor-council form of government was substantially underrepresented, as was the council–elected executive form of government among counties.

E-Democracy Activities

Local governments were asked whether, during the 12 months prior to the survey, they had engaged in one or more of several e-participation activities. The results suggest the underwhelming adoption of e-democracy by U.S. local governments. Only one activity—enabling citizens to view a public hearing or meeting—has been adopted by more than half of local governments (57%) (Table 6–2). Only two more show substantial adoption rates: enabling citizens to post comments (45%) and enabling citizens to participate in a poll or survey (44%). One activity, conducting electronic public consultations, has been adopted by a quarter (27%) of local governments. Of the remaining seven activities, three have been adopted by between 12% and 17% of local governments, while four have been adopted by no more than 7%.

If current adoption rates for e-democracy are low, rates for plans to adopt in the future are even lower. The survey asked about concrete plans to undertake any of the listed e-participation activities within the coming 12 months, and only one activity—enabling citizens to view a hearing or meeting—was reported by as many as 11% of respondents (Table 6–2). Two other activities—enabling citizens to participate in a poll or survey and enabling citizens to post comments—were reported by about 9% and 8%, respectively. All others were reported by 5% or fewer of the responding governments. We discuss possible reasons for these low adoption rates later in this article.

When the governments that adopted e-democracy were asked why they did so, the great majority of respondents checked "it is the right thing to do" (81%) (Figure 6–1). Other responses include "demanded or required by top administrators" (41%); "demanded or required by elected officials" (40%); "to keep up with other governments" (32%); and "demanded by citizens" (29%). Asked the most important reason, a majority (61%) of the 356 respondents who answered the question said "the right thing to do" (not shown).

We wanted to know whether local e-participation projects and activities are mostly government to citizen or citizen to government. This is important because if those projects and activities are mainly a matter of governments providing information, etc., to citizens, that leaves little opportunity for meaningful citizen participation. Of the 899 local governments that responded to this question, nearly 7 in 10 said mostly government to citizens (69%) and about a quarter (27%) said about half and half; only 4% said mostly citizens to government (not shown).

Table 6-2 E-Participation Activities by Local Government

Activities	No. responding (A)	Activities undertaken in past 12 months Yes		Concrete plans to undertake activities in next 12 months Yes	
		No.	% of (A)	No.	% of (A)
Enabled citizens to view a hearing or meeting	1,146	650	57	121	11
Enabled citizens to post comments	1,141	519	45	96	8
Enabled citizens to participate in a poll or survey	1,139	499	44	103	9
Conducted public consultations, e.g., engaged public in the budget process	1,143	305	27	59	5
Enabled citizens to participate in a hearing or meeting	1,149	196	17	48	4
Conducted one or more non-narrated or guided discussion forums about important local issues	1,152	161	14	27	2
Conducted one or more narrated or guided discussion forums about important local issues	1,151	137	12	46	4
Enabled citizens to vote in an election or referendum	1,161	83	7	18	2
Permitted or facilitated electronic citizen petitions	1,156	56	5	14	1
Conducted electronic town halls	955	44	5	22	3
Facilitated or operated chat rooms	1,156	51	4	18	2
Other	303	62	21	14	5

These responses, together with the data in Table 6–2, strongly suggest not just that few local governments have adopted e-democracy activities, but that fewer still have enabled meaningful citizen participation through those activities. Nevertheless, when asked the extent to which their local governments take seriously and act upon the results of e-participation projects and activities in their decisions and actions, most (67%) of the 881 respondents who answered the question said that their governments take it seriously, whereas fewer than 8% (one in 12) said that their governments do not take it seriously and a quarter (26%) assessed it to be about half and half (not shown).

As to whether local officials actively promote or give attention to e-democracy, the respondents reported that 44% of appointed officials do provide such support while only 28% of elected officials do so

(Figure 6–2). Conversely, 26% of appointed officials and 42% of elected officials reportedly do *not* actively promote or give attention to e-participation. These data do not suggest overwhelming support among local officials for e-democracy, but they do indicate that appointed officials are more likely to promote e-democracy than elected officials.

Might citizen demand provide the impetus that is not being provided by local officials? It would not appear so. When asked whether citizen grassroots groups or organizations are actively pushing for e-participation opportunities within the local government, just over three quarters of respondents (78% of 1,145) reported little or no citizen demand for e-participation in their communities, while 16% noted some demand and only 6% reported significant demand (not shown). Lack of citizen demand combined with lack of much support from local

Figure 6-1   Reasons for Local Government Engagement in E-Participation Projects and Activities

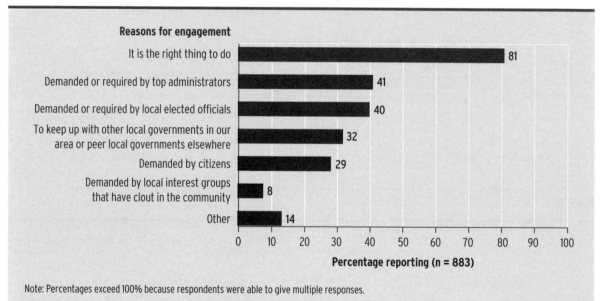

Reasons for engagement

It is the right thing to do	81
Demanded or required by top administrators	41
Demanded or required by local elected officials	40
To keep up with other local governments in our area or peer local governments elsewhere	32
Demanded by citizens	29
Demanded by local interest groups that have clout in the community	8
Other	14

Percentage reporting (n = 883)

Note: Percentages exceed 100% because respondents were able to give multiple responses.

Figure 6-2   Local Government Officials' Promotion/Attention to E-Participation

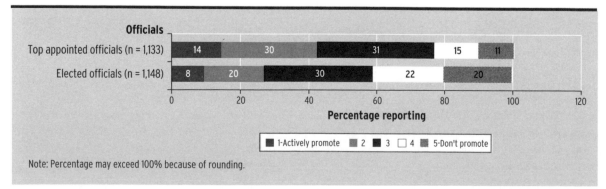

Officials

Top appointed officials (n = 1,133): 14 | 30 | 31 | 15 | 11
Elected officials (n = 1,148): 8 | 20 | 30 | 22 | 20

Percentage reporting

■ 1-Actively promote ■ 2 ■ 3 □ 4 ■ 5-Don't promote

Note: Percentage may exceed 100% because of rounding.

officials may help to explain why these governments have adopted so few e-participation activities. We discuss this issue further on under "Barriers to E-Democracy."

Planning for E-Democracy

One of the standard recommendations regarding IT in government is that it should be well planned. As this applies to e-government as well, we asked several questions about planning for e-participation. First, we asked whether the local governments conduct formal planning for e-participation projects or efforts, and nearly three-quarters (72% of 903 respondents) said that they do not (not shown). Among the 255 that do engage in formal planning, slightly over half (54%) said that they do so as part of planning for local IT and about the same proportion (55%) reported doing so as part of planning for local e-government (55%); only a quarter (25%) said that they engage in formal planning for e-participation only (not shown). (These percentages exceed 100% because respondents could choose all the responses that applied.)

We then asked whether responding governments had conducted surveys within the previous three years to learn what types of online information, services, or participation their residents wanted available on the local government website. Three-quarters (75% of 1,178 respondents) reported that they had not conducted such a survey within the past three years (not shown). Among the 286 respondents that had, however, 50% reported that the focus of their surveys was on online information, services, and participation; 47% said that it was on online information and services; and 4% said it was on online participation only (not shown). Respondents were also asked about their intent to conduct such a survey within the next 12 months, and the great majority (84%) reported no such plans.

Management of E-Democracy

When asked which local government office was responsible for e-participation, 41% of respondents said the city/county manager/administrator's office, while one in five said the IT department (21%) or public information office (21%) (Figure 6–3). As to how they develop applications for their e-participation projects and activities, respondents reported using a variety of means, including in-house development (80%), in-house staff working with consultants (38%), programs purchased from vendors (29%), and outsourcing (21%) (Figure 6–4). Asked to identify the most common method, 62% of 835 respondents cited in-house development (not shown).

Since part of managing e-participation might include pre- and postanalyses of any e-participation activities that local governments have implemented,

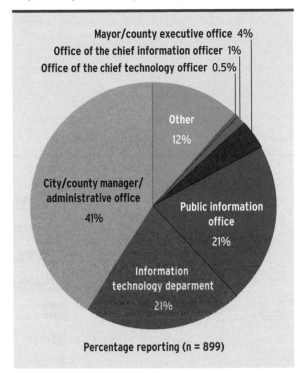

Figure 6-3 Local Government Organization with Principal Responsibility for E-Participation Projects and Activities

we asked respondents whether they had conducted cost-benefit or other formal analyses before implementing e-participation activities. Only a small minority (15% of 898 respondents) reported having done so (not shown). We also asked whether they had conducted formal impact or effectiveness analyses of e-participation activities after such activities were implemented, and again, only a small minority (14% of 897 respondents) said that they had (not shown).

Impacts of E-Democracy on Local Government

We showed respondents a list of eight possible impacts on local government as a result of e-participation and asked them which, if any, they had observed. About 6 in 10 of the responding governments reported three impacts: an increase in workload or time demands on technology personnel (62%), an increase in the quantity of information available to local officials for decision making (61%), and an increase in the quantity of citizen participation (61%) (Table 6–3). Just over half of the respondents reported an increase in workload demands on line and staff personnel (51%) and an increase in the quality of information available to local officials for decision making (51%). About a third of the responding governments reporting the remaining three impacts: a higher quality of citizen participation

(36%), greater citizen trust in government (35%), and better decision making by local officials (35%). At least two of these impacts (increased workload and time demands on technology personnel and on line and staff personnel) should be considered negative.

As for the most significant positive and negative impacts, respondents cited quantity of citizen participation and citizen trust in government as the most significant positive impacts (24% and 20%, respec-

tively, of 873 respondents). The most significant negative impact was workload and time demands on technology personnel, followed by workload and time demands on line and staff personnel (42% and 37%, respectively, of 877 respondents) (not shown).

One of the claims often made by proponents of e-government and e-democracy is that these capabilities will fundamentally improve relationships between citizens and their governments. Accordingly,

Figure 6-4   How E-Government Projects and Activities Are Developed

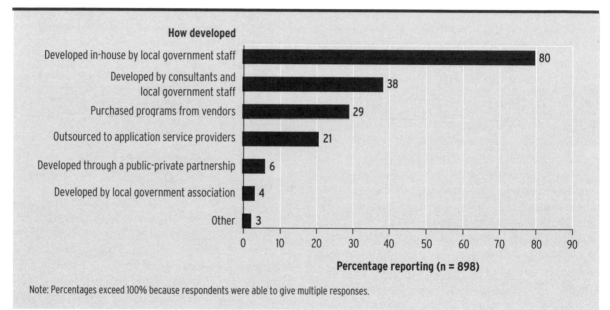

Note: Percentages exceed 100% because respondents were able to give multiple responses.

Table 6-3   Impacts Experienced as a Result of E-Participation

Activities	No. responding (A)	Increased No.	Increased % of (A)	No difference No.	No difference % of (A)	Decreased No.	Decreased % of (A)	Do not know No.	Do not know % of (A)
Workload or time demands on local government technology personnel	873	541	62	232	27	20	2	80	9
Quantity of information available to local officials for decision making	867	529	61	249	29	1	*	88	10
Quantity of citizen participation	873	529	61	245	28	4	1	95	11
Workload or time demands on local government line and staff personnel	877	449	51	270	31	72	8	86	10
Quality of information available to local officials for decision making	868	440	51	321	37	5	1	102	12
Quality of citizen participation	868	314	36	394	46	21	2	139	16
Citizen trust in government	868	306	35	287	33	12	1	263	30
Better decision making by local officials	867	304	35	386	45	1	*	176	20
Other	88	17	19	22	25	0	0	49	56

Note: Percentages may not total 100% because of rounding.

* = Less than 0.5%.

we asked respondents whether they had observed any changes between citizens and elected officials or between citizens and appointed administrators due to e-participation. For the most part, respondents said that e-participation has not changed the relationship between citizens and elected officials (58%) or between citizens and local administrators (55%) (not shown). But sizeable minorities did feel that e-participation has improved relations between citizens and elected officials (40%) or between citizens and local administrators (43%). Hardly any respondents reported that those relationships have deteriorated.

The impact data are somewhat puzzling given how few governments have adopted e-participation activities. We suspect that something akin to a halo

effect may have occurred. That is, local governments have adopted at least some e-participation activities and have reportedly done so mainly because they think it is the right thing to do. And if adoption of e-participation is the right thing to do, the impacts of e-participation must be positive. Unfortunately, the survey data alone are insufficient to help us understand this apparent contradiction: while few e-participation activities have been adopted, sizeable fractions of governments report positive impacts, including in the relationship between citizens and their governments.

Barriers to E-Democracy

It is logical to assume that there are reasons for why local governments have adopted so few e-participation

Figure 6-5 Barriers Encountered to Providing E-Participation

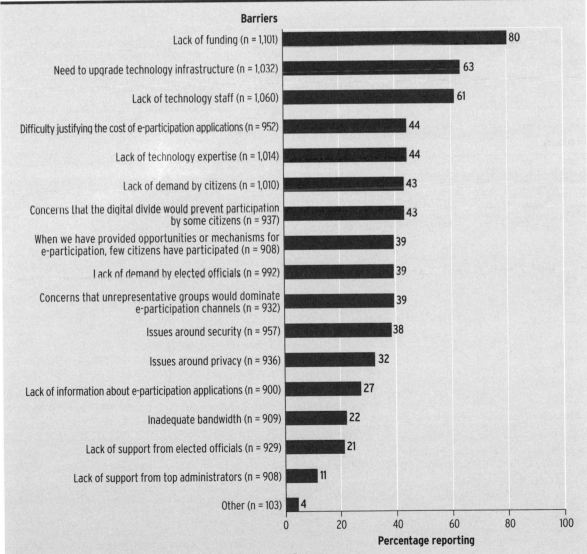

Note: Percentages exceed 100% because respondents were able to give multiple responses.

activities. We presented respondents with a list of 16 possible barriers to adoption and asked which, if any, their governments have encountered. The barrier reported by the largest percentage of governments is lack of funding (80%), followed by three barriers that are directly or indirectly related to it: need to upgrade technology (63%), lack of technology staff (61%), and difficulty justifying the cost of e-participation activities (44%) (Figure 6–5). Lack of technology expertise (44%) might also be a funding issue because few local governments can match the salaries offered in the private sector for technologists.

Other notable barriers reported in the survey are lack of citizen demand (43%), lack of citizen participation in e-democracy opportunities (39%), and lack of demand by elected officials (39%). These findings are important because they reveal that, in the absence of demand and participation, local governments will not be likely to expand e-participation activities.

Substantial numbers of governments also reported concerns that the digital divide would prevent some citizen e-participation (43%), concerns that unrepresentative groups would dominate e-participation (39%), security issues (38%), and privacy issues (32%). Less than a third of governments reported any of the remaining barriers.

Notes

1. Donald F. Norris, "E-democracy among U.S. Local Governments" (paper presented at the International Symposium on E-Participation and Local E-Democracy, Budapest, Hungary, July 26–28, and Baltimore, Maryland, August 3, 2006).

Conclusion

Perhaps the most important finding of this survey is that, contrary to the claims made by proponents, few U.S. local governments seem to have embraced e-democracy. This is clear from the data in Table 6–2, which show that only one e-participation activity has been adopted by more than half of local governments and that most activities allow only passive citizen participation. Moreover, hardly any governments have plans to implement e-participation activities in the near future, few governments plan for e-democracy, and fewer still have surveyed their residents about a desire for online information, services, or participation.

The low rates of adoption are almost certainly explained, at least in part, by the barriers identified—particularly, lack of funding (and barriers directly or indirectly associated with it) and lack of demand from citizens and elected officials. Again, without strong citizen demand for and official promotion of opportunities to facilitate e-democracy, local governments are not likely to expand e-participation activities. Further studies will be needed to determine whether funding limitations can be overcome, whether demand will increase, and whether a combination of the two might improve e-participation adoption at the grass roots.

2. Evelina Moulder, director of survey research, ICMA, personal communication with author, November 7, 2011.

7

Volunteer Use in Local Government Service Delivery

Rebecca Nesbit
University of Kansas

Jeffrey L. Brudney
University of North Carolina at Wilmington

The first decade of the 21st century witnessed repeated calls for volunteers to assist with public sector service delivery. At the local level, fiscal stringency led both elected and appointed officials to advocate the use of volunteers to shore up public services and even to compensate for cutbacks in paid personnel.

This article assesses volunteer involvement in local government as of 2007. After reviewing the relevant scholarly literature, we briefly describe the data set from ICMA's 2007 *Alternative Service Delivery* (ASD) survey, which includes data on volunteers. We then present findings concerning local government use of volunteers across a range of public service domains.

Because the data were developed as part of ICMA's periodic ASD surveys, we cannot address volunteer involvement throughout the U.S. federal system. However, the data do provide systematic information on volunteer involvement in municipalities and counties—the public organizations closest to the populace and offering the most opportunities for volunteerism. Local governments are also the only level of government for which samples of volunteer use can be systematically obtained.

Background

The first major study to focus on volunteer involvement in government agencies was probably

SELECTED FINDINGS

Overall, 27% of local governments use volunteers to provide some type of service.

The area with the greatest volunteer use is culture and the arts: 21.5% of municipalities and 15.1% of counties use volunteers in such programs.

Population size is related to volunteer use: smaller jurisdictions are more likely to use volunteers in public safety, and larger jurisdictions are more likely to use them in health and human services and cultural and arts programs.

Fostering Volunteer Programs in the Public Sector.[1] On the basis of available research,[2] Jeffrey Brudney, one of the coauthors of this article, estimated that "a significant amount of volunteer labor is directed to public agencies: U.S. government agencies operate as many as 20 to 30% of all organized volunteer programs, and perhaps another 20 to 30% of these programs are associated with the public sector."[3] Subsequent research has not contradicted those estimates; they are still regarded as defining the broad outlines of government-based volunteerism.

Twice each decade, beginning in the 1980s, ICMA has administered surveys focusing on local government approaches to service delivery. According to the first of these surveys, which was conducted in 1982, about one-third (31%) of reporting municipalities and counties used volunteers for cultural and arts programming, making it the most common area for volunteer participation. The second-most-common area was museum operations (20%), followed by recreation services (19%), programs for the elderly (18%), and several categories of public safety services: fire prevention/suppression (17%), emergency medical service (EMS) (15%), and ambulance service (14%).[4]

ICMA's 1988 ASD survey showed that volunteer use had become more established: there were marked increases in volunteer involvement in the service domains where it had been most prevalent in 1982. For example, 41% of responding municipalities and counties used citizen volunteers in cultural and arts programming, 34% in museum operations, 26% in recreation services, and 25% in programs for the elderly. In other areas, the rate of volunteer involvement nearly doubled over 1982 levels: volunteer use in drug and alcohol treatment increased from 6% to 10%; in child welfare programs, from 6% to 11%, and in crime prevention, from 9% to 16%. Volunteer use also remained strong in the public safety arena: 19% of responding municipalities and counties used volunteers in fire prevention/suppression, 18% in EMS, and 17% in ambulance service.[5] Finally, by 1988, volunteers had begun to play a significant role in local government efforts to address homelessness: of the more than one-quarter of municipalities and counties reporting problems with homelessness, 26% reported that volunteers assisted at homeless shelters, and 37% stated that volunteers served in food programs for homeless people.[6]

During the 1990s, the ASD surveys continued to explore local government use of volunteers. On the basis of the 1992 survey, *The Municipal Year Book 1994* reported, surprisingly, that local government use of volunteers, particularly in cultural and arts programming and in programs for the elderly, had declined relative to 1982 levels. According to Rowan Miranda and Karlyn Andersen, "while use of volunteers is likely to continue, a downward trend is apparent. Significant decreases in the use of volunteers have occurred in almost all service areas reported on by survey respondents."[7] Given the levels of volunteer involvement in local government that were established by earlier ICMA ASD surveys, as well as the general promotion of volunteerism during the previous decade, this decline was unexpected.

ICMA's 1997 ASD survey showed that volunteer involvement continued to be most prevalent in cultural and arts programming (21% of municipalities and counties); museum operations (20%); health and human services, such as homeless shelters (9%) and programs for the elderly (14%); and public safety, including fire prevention/suppression (15%), EMS (11%), and ambulance service (11%).[8] Although local government use of volunteers remained relatively stable in the 1992 and 1997 surveys, the downward trend revealed by the 1992 survey continued, with "some fairly substantial decreases in the use of volunteers between 1988 and 1997."[9] Moreover, "although volunteers were used in almost every service category in 1997, fewer than 1% of governments report[ed] their use for many of these services."[10]

Writing in *The Municipal Year Book 1999*, Elaine Morley proposed several possible reasons for these trends, including the following:

- Possible changes over time in municipalities' and counties' rates of response to the ASD surveys

- Failure to account, in survey administration, for volunteer involvement in nonprofit and for-profit organizations with which local governments contract for services

- The omission from ICMA surveys of some service domains, such as public education, where volunteer involvement is likely pronounced

- Issues that might have inhibited local governments from using volunteers (e.g., difficulty obtaining enough volunteers to sustain reliable service provision, liability and insurance problems, and the necessity of screening volunteers to ensure public safety).[11]

These speculations call for further research.

Using data from a new administration of ICMA's ASD survey completed in 2002, Mildred Warner and Amir Hefetz observed in the *The Municipal Year Book 2004* that volunteers, franchises, and subsidies were the least common approaches to service delivery, collectively accounting for less than 4% of service delivery overall.[12] As in previous ICMA surveys, volunteer involvement was most common in museum operations (31% of municipalities and counties), cultural and arts programming (27%), and programs for the elderly (17%); in addition, more than 10% of local governments used volunteers in fire prevention/suppression, EMS, and ambulance service.

The results of ICMA's 2007 ASD survey, as reported by Warner and Hefetz in the *The Municipal Year Book 2009*, suggest further declines in local government use of volunteers.[13] In 2002, volunteer involvement averaged 3% across all services but had dropped to 2% by 2007.[14] Service domains that had historically had high levels of volunteer involvement also showed declines; for example, use of volunteers in museum operations dropped from 31% of local government in 2002 to 19% in 2007; cultural and arts programs dropped from 27% to 21%; homeless shelters from 9% to 5%; and programs for the elderly from 17% to 11%. In the public safety arena, volunteer involvement was more stable overall than in other areas but still reflected decreases. Fire prevention/suppression remained steady (13% of municipalities and counties in both 2002 and 2007), but volunteer use in EMS dropped from 10% in 2002 to 8% in 2007, and in ambulance service from 11% to 8%. Warner and Hefetz observed that the decline in local government volunteer use "could become more of a challenge as baby boomers age and public financing for the arts falters."[15]

This review of the ICMA's survey-based literature on volunteer participation in local government service delivery paints a broad picture, highlighting the areas in which volunteer use has been most prominent over time. The remainder of this article offers a more in-depth portrait of how and where volunteers are involved in local government service delivery.

Survey Response and Methodology

To provide an overview of volunteer involvement in the delivery of local government services, we used ICMA's 2007 ASD survey. The survey assessed local government use of a variety of service options to deliver 67 local public services. Surveys were mailed to chief administrative officers in municipalities with populations of 10,000 and over; in counties with populations of 25,000 and over; and to a random sample of one in eight municipalities with populations between 2,500 and 9,999 and one in eight counties with populations between 2,500 and 24,999.[16] The response rate for the 2007 survey was 26.2%, and the data set included 1,599 usable responses: 1,244 from municipalities and 355 from counties.

Table 7–1 shows survey response rates broken down by demographic classifications. As with past ASD surveys, the response rate was higher among municipalities than counties. Responses were highest from the Pacific Coast, Mountain, South Atlantic, and West North-Central divisions, and lowest from the East South-Central and Mid-Atlantic divisions. Suburban localities represented more than half the sample, and independent (rural) localities represented a larger proportion than central (core metro) cities.[17]

Table 7-1 Response Rates, 2007 Alternative Service Delivery Survey

Classification	No. jurisdictions surveyed (A)	Respondents No.	Respondents % of (A)
All	6,095	1,599	26
Municipalities[a]	4,241	1,244	29
Counties[a]	1,854	355	19
Population			
Over 1,000,000	37	9	24
500,000–1,000,000	86	18	21
250,000–499,999	146	39	27
100,000–249,999	454	157	35
50,000–99,999	793	190	24
25,000–49,999	1,420	350	25
10,000–24,999	2,032	525	26
5,000–9,999	599	156	26
2,500–4,999	528	155	29
Region			
New England	485	111	23
Mid-Atlantic	849	153	18
East North-Central	1,181	327	28
West North-Central	613	190	31
South Atlantic	875	287	33
East South-Central	459	63	14
West South-Central	654	141	22
Mountain	349	114	33
Pacific Coast	630	213	34
Metro status			
Central	993	274	28
Suburban	2,932	841	29
Independent	2,170	484	22

Source: Mildred E. Warner and Amir Hefetz, "Cooperative Competition: Alternative Service Delivery, 2002-2007," in *The Municipal Year Book 2009* (Washington, D.C.: ICMA, 2009), 12.

a   For a definition of terms, please see "Inside the *Year Book*," xi-xiv.

Methods of Analysis

For each service addressed in the survey, respondents were asked to indicate whether their local governments provided the service—and if so, what the method of delivery was: employees, another government, private for-profits, private nonprofits, franchises/concessions, subsidies, or volunteers. Table 7–2 depicts the distribution of volunteer use among local governments that indicated a particular service delivery method for a given service (as a result, the sample size for each service is different). The results presented in the table are comparable to those of the ASD surveys reviewed in the first section of this article.

For simplicity, the rest of this article presents findings on volunteer use in seven main service areas defined by ICMA: public works/transportation, public utilities, public safety, health and human services, parks and recreation, cultural and arts programs, and support functions. These areas are designated in Table 7–2, which also identifies the constituent services.

Table 7-2 Local Government Use of Volunteers for Service Delivery

Service area	Sample size (A)	Municipalities, % of (A)	Counties, % of (A)	All local governments, % of (A)
Public works/transportation				
Residential solid-waste collection	932	0.1	0.9	0.2
Commercial solid-waste collection	699	0.0	0.0	0.0
Solid-waste disposal	851	0.0	0.6	0.1
Street repair	1,180	0.0	0.0	0.0
Street/parking lot cleaning	1,035	0.3	0.0	0.3
Snow plowing/sanding	917	0.0	0.0	0.0
Traffic sign/signal installation/maintenance	1,070	0.0	0.6	0.1
Parking meter maintenance and collection	279	0.0	0.0	0.0
Tree trimming and planting on public rights-of-way	1,066	3.7	1.4	3.4
Maintenance and administration of cemeteries	55	2.2	14.6	3.5
Inspection/code enforcement	1,146	0.1	0.0	0.1
Operation of parking lots and garages	454	0.3	0.0	0.2
Operation/maintenance of bus transit system	403	0.3	0.0	0.2
Operation/maintenance of paratransit	366	1.0	0.0	0.8
Operation of airports	422	0.9	1.0	1.0
Water distribution	908	0.0	0.0	0.0
Water treatment	851	0.0	0.0	0.0
Sewage collection and treatment	942	0.0	0.0	0.0
Disposal of sludge	782	0.3	0.0	0.3
Disposal of hazardous materials	615	1.4	5.0	2.0
Public utilities				
Electric utility operation and management	387	0.0	0.0	0.0
Gas utility operation and management	315	0.0	0.0	0.0
Utility meter reading	794	0.0	0.0	0.0
Utility billing	818	0.0	0.0	0.0
Public safety				
Crime prevention/patrol	1,206	2.3	4.3	2.7
Police/fire communications	1,157	2.1	1.7	2.0
Fire prevention/suppression	1,044	11.4	22.9	13.0
Emergency medical service	940	7.5	13.2	8.4
Ambulance service	860	7.2	12.8	8.1
Traffic control/parking enforcement	1,028	0.9	3.1	1.2
Vehicle towing and storage	422	0.0	0.0	0.0

Table 7-2 Local Government Use of Volunteers for Service Delivery

Service area	Sample size (A)	Municipalities, % of (A)	Counties, % of (A)	All local governments, % of (A)
Health and human services				
Sanitary inspection	731	0.2	0.0	0.1
Insect/rodent control	597	0.0	0.0	0.0
Animal control	1,022	0.6	3.3	1.1
Operation of animal shelters	722	2.9	6.3	3.6
Operation of day care facilities	320	1.8	0.0	1.6
Child welfare programs	411	3.4	1.4	2.7
Programs for the elderly	799	10.7	13.7	11.4
Operation/management of hospitals	253	0.5	0.0	0.4
Public health programs	512	2.5	1.6	2.1
Drug and alcohol treatment programs	395	2.0	2.1	2.0
Operation of mental health programs and facilities	369	1.4	1.3	1.4
Prisons/jails	648	0.0	0.9	0.3
Operation of homeless shelters	288	4.9	3.2	4.5
Workforce development/job-training programs	409	0.7	0.7	0.7
Intake/eligibility determination for welfare programs	388	0.4	0.0	0.3
Parks and recreation				
Operation and maintenance of recreation facilities	1,130	4.7	8.3	5.3
Parks landscaping and maintenance	1,141	3.4	5.6	3.8
Operation of convention centers and auditoriums	381	1.2	3.7	1.6
Cultural and arts programs				
Operation of cultural and arts programs	567	21.5	15.1	20.6
Operation of libraries	792	6.9	11.1	7.7
Operation of museums	433	19.1	20.5	19.4
Support functions				
Buildings and grounds maintenance	1,222	0.8	3.3	1.3
Building security	958	0.4	0.0	0.3
Fleet management/vehicle maintenance: heavy equipment	1,140	0.1	0.0	0.1
Fleet management/vehicle maintenance: emergency vehicles	1,085	0.5	0.5	0.5
Fleet management/vehicle maintenance: all other vehicles	1,152	0.1	0.0	0.1
Payroll	1,288	0.0	0.0	0.0
Tax bill processing	903	0.0	0.0	0.0
Tax assessing	821	0.0	0.0	0.0
Data processing	1,090	0.1	0.0	0.1
Collection of delinquent taxes	890	0.0	0.0	0.0
Title records/plat map maintenance	797	0.0	0.0	0.0
Legal services	1,042	0.1	0.0	0.1
Secretarial services	1,107	0.2	0.0	0.2
Personnel services	898	0.0	0.0	0.0
Public relations/public information	1,116	0.6	0.0	0.5

The descriptive analyses indicate the percentage of local governments using volunteers in each of the seven service areas, categorized by several variables of interest. For each of the aggregated volunteering variables[18] and for volunteering overall, we also present the results of a one-way analysis of variance, a statistical procedure that allowed us to test whether differences in mean or average scores on a variable across categories (e.g., difference in volunteer use by local governments across seven service areas) were sufficiently large or robust to allow us to reject the "null hypothesis," which holds that the observed differences could be attributable to chance or random fluctuations alone.

Findings

Table 7–2 shows the distribution of volunteer use by municipalities and counties in delivering local public services. In keeping with findings from previous surveys, the area with the greatest volunteer use was culture and the arts: as of 2007, 21.5% of municipalities and 15.1% of counties used volunteers in such programs. Volunteer use was nearly as high in museums (19.1% of municipalities and 20.5% of counties) and less high in libraries (6.9% and 11.1%, respectively). By contrast, no municipalities or counties reported using volunteers in public utilities. In all, 19 services had no volunteer involvement.

In public works/transportation, the most common use of volunteers was in the maintenance and administration of cemeteries (2.2% of municipalities and 14.6% of counties), followed by tree trimming and planting (3.7% of municipalities and 1.4% of counties). In public safety, volunteers were used most in fire prevention/suppression (11.4% of municipalities and 22.9% of counties), although they were also used for EMS (7.5% of municipalities and 13.2% of counties) and ambulance services (7.2% of municipalities and 12.8% of counties). In health and human services, volunteers were most commonly used to run programs for the elderly (10.7% of municipalities and 13.7% of counties), homeless shelters (4.9% of municipalities and 3.2% of counties), animal shelters (2.9% of municipalities and 6.3% of counties), and child welfare programs (3.4% of municipalities and 1.4% of counties). With respect to other health and human services, few localities (3.3% or less) use volunteers.

In parks and recreation, volunteers helped to maintain recreation facilities (4.7% of municipalities and 8.3% of counties) and to provide park landscaping (3.4% of municipalities and 5.6% of counties); they were not commonly used in the operation of convention centers and auditoriums. Nor was volunteer use common in support functions, but of all the support functions, building and grounds maintenance was the one most likely to use volunteers (0.8% of municipalities and 3.3% of counties). Overall, Table 7–2 shows great variety in the areas where volunteers were used—but, with the exception of culture and the arts, shows little depth in volunteer use for any individual service.

Table 7–3 shows local government volunteer use in relation to population. It is important to note that because of the way in which the aggregated variables were constructed, the percentage of local governments using volunteers is lower in Tables 7–3 through 7–7 than in Table 7–2. (Because no local governments in 2007 used volunteers in public utilities [see Table 7–2], we omitted this service area from further consideration in this article.) According to the analysis of variance statistical test, population size is related to the percentage of localities using volunteers in the areas of public works/transportation ($p < .05$), public safety ($p < .001$), health and human services ($p < .001$), and cultural and arts programs ($p < .05$).[19] Interestingly, the pattern of the size-based relationships is not consistent: for public works/transportation, smaller localities appear to use volunteers more than larger ones do. For health and human services and cultural and arts programs, the pattern is reversed, with larger localities more likely to use volunteers. These relationships may reflect different needs among smaller and larger local governments.

Table 7–4 depicts local government volunteer use in various regions. Regional effects are most pronounced in public safety ($p < .001$). In particular, 26% of localities in the Northeast and 14% in the South used volunteers for at least one public safety–related service. By contrast, just 7% of localities in the North-Central and West regions did so. The percentage of local governments that used volunteers for service delivery did not differ significantly by region for any other service area.

We also found that volunteer use differs by form of government (see Table 7–5). Among municipalities, 20% of commission/town meeting governments used volunteers in health and human services, compared with 6% of mayor-council governments and 8% of council-manager governments ($p < .01$). Form of government also matters for volunteer use in cultural and arts programs ($p < .01$), in which 28% of municipalities with commission or town meeting governments used volunteers, compared with 10% of mayor-council municipalities and 12% of council-manager municipalities.

In counties, form of government is related to volunteer use in public works/transportation ($p < .05$) and public safety ($p < .05$): 8% of counties with the

Table 7-3 Local Government Use of Volunteers, by Population, 2007

Population	Total (A)	Public works/ transportation	Public safety	Health and human services	Parks and recreation	Cultural and arts programs	Support functions	Any service area
Total respondents	1,599	78	194	136	80	187	29	426
		% of (A)	% of (A)	% of (A)	% of (A)	% of (A)	% of (A)	% of (A)
250,000 and over	66	3	9	17	8	18	3	27
100,00-249,999	157	4	6	15	7	17	2	30
50,000-99,999	190	2	10	12	4	14	2	29
25,000-49,999	350	5	11	7	4	10	1	25
10,000-24,999	525	6	12	7	4	10	2	24
5,000-9,999	156	8	21	4	6	13	3	35
2,500-4,999	155	5	17	6	6	8	2	25
Total	1,599	5	12	9	5	12	2	27
F test statistic[a]		4.13*	14.33***	20.14***	0.14	6.04*	0.05	0.19

a The F test statistic represents the results of a one-way analysis of variance. If the F test statistic is greater than the threshold value (which varies for each column, depending on the number of observations), the test is statistically significant.

*$p < .05$.

***$p < .001$.

Table 7-4 Local Government Use of Volunteers, by Region, 2007

Population	Total (A)	Public works/ transportation	Public safety	Health and human services	Parks and recreation	Cultural and arts programs	Support functions	Any service area
Total respondents	1,599	78	194	136	80	187	29	426
		% of (A)	% of (A)	% of (A)	% of (A)	% of (A)	% of (A)	% of (A)
Northeast	264	6	26	10	8	14	4	38
North-Central	517	5	7	7	4	9	1	21
South	491	4	14	8	4	11	1	27
West	327	4	7	10	6	16	2	27
Total	1,599	5	124	9	5	12	2	27
F test statistic[a]		1.96	21.59***	0.21	0.49	1.37	0.32	2.68

a See note on Table 7-3.

***$p < .001$.

commission form of government used volunteers in public works/transportation, compared with 1% of council-administrator and 2% of council–elected executive counties. In public safety, 21% of council-administrator counties use volunteers, compared with 16% of counties with council–elected executive governments and 9% of counties with commissions.

When analyzed by type of jurisdiction (Table 7-6), local government use of volunteers is found in the area of public safety ($p < .001$) as well as in any service ($p < .01$). Forty-one percent of both townships and boroughs used volunteers in public safety. In all other types of jurisdictions, volunteer use was much lower (18% or less). With respect to volunteer use overall, townships and boroughs appear more likely to use volunteers than other types of jurisdictions. (It should be noted, however, that some of the subsamples are very small.)

Table 7-5 Local Government Use of Volunteers, by Form of Government, 2007

Population	Total (A)	Public works/ transportation	Public safety	Health and human services	Parks and recreation	Cultural and arts programs	Support functions	Any service area
Total respondents	1,599	78	194	136	80	187	29	426
		% of (A)	% of (A)	% of (A)	% of (A)	% of (A)	% of (A)	% of (A)
Municipalities								
Mayor-council	327	5	12	6	6	10	1	25
Council-manager	856	5	11	8	4	12	2	25
Commission or town meeting	61	8	21	20	10	28	5	41
Subtotal	1,244	5	12	8	5	12	2	26
F test statistic[a]		0.07	0.47	8.50**	0.00	8.51**	2.05	2.14
Counties								
Commission	179	8	9	7	5	9	2	25
Council- administrator	95	1	21	14	8	18	4	40
Council-elected executive	81	2	16	12	4	4	1	27
Subtotal	355	5	14	10	5	10	3	30
Total	1,599	5	12	9	5	12	2	27
F test statistic[a]		5.07*	4.02*	2.27	0.01	0.44	0.05	0.74

a See note on Table 7-3.

*$p < .05$.

**$p < .01$.

Table 7-6 Local Government Use of Volunteers, by Type of Local Government, 2007

Type of local government	Total (A)	Public works/ transportation	Public safety	Health and human services	Parks and recreation	Cultural and arts programs	Support functions	Any service area
Total respondents	1,599	78	194	136	80	187	29	426
		% of (A)	% of (A)	% of (A)	% of (A)	% of (A)	% of (A)	% of (A)
City	885	5	7	7	4	12	1	22
Town	153	9	18	12	8	18	2	32
Village	100	4	11	7	6	13	3	27
Township	70	1	41	11	11	7	4	44
Borough	37	5	41	3	5	5	3	46
District	2	0	0	0	0	50	0	50
County	350	5	14	14	5	10	3	30
Total	1,587	5	12	9	5	12	2	27
F test statistic[a]		0.02	19.87***	1.74	1.09	1.15	3.58	10.27**

a See note on Table 7-3.

**$p < .01$.

***$p < .001$.

Table 7-7 Local Government Use of Volunteers, by Metropolitan Status, 2007

Metropolitan status	Total (A)	Public works/ transportation	Public safety	Health and human services	Parks and recreation	Cultural and arts programs	Support functions	Any service area
Total respondents	1,599	78	194	136	80	187	29	426
		% of (A)	% of (A)	% of (A)	% of (A)	% of (A)	% of (A)	% of (A)
Central	274	4	8	11	7	14	1	27
Suburban	841	4	12	8	5	12	2	27
Independent	484	6	15	7	4	10	2	26
Total	1,599	5	12	9	5	12	2	27
F test statistic[a]		2.81	7.75**	3.89*	2.08	2.81	0.11	0.01

a See note on Table 7-3.

*$p < .05$.

**$p < .01$.

Table 7–7 shows that metropolitan status is most relevant to volunteer use in the areas of public safety ($p < .01$) and health and human services ($p < .05$). Among independent municipalities, 15% used volunteers for public safety services, compared with 12% of suburban municipalities and 8% of central municipalities. In health and human services, central municipalities were somewhat more likely to use volunteers (11%) than suburban (8%) or independent (7%) municipalities.

Summary

ICMA's 2007 ASD survey indicates that local government use of volunteers is greatest in cultural and arts programs, public safety, and health and human services. Overall, 27% of localities used volunteers to provide some kind of service; 12% use volunteers to deliver cultural and arts programming and public safety services, and 9% used them to deliver health and human services (Tables 7–3 through 7–7). To a lesser degree, local governments used volunteers in public works/transportation (5%) and parks and recreation (5%). Few local governments used volunteers for support functions (2%), and none used volunteers in the area of public utilities. In general, these patterns confirm those established in earlier ICMA ASD surveys.

Certain local government characteristics are related to volunteer use. Population size, for example, is related to volunteer use in interesting ways: smaller jurisdictions are more likely to use volunteers in public safety, and larger jurisdictions are more likely to do so in health and human services and cultural and arts programs. Although population may affect the service domains where volunteers are used, region is not strongly related

to volunteer use: the one regional pattern is that jurisdictions in the Northeast are more likely to use volunteers in public safety. Form of government also appears to have limited impact on volunteer use. Among municipalities, the commission or town meeting form is related to the use of volunteers in human services and in cultural and arts programs. Among counties, the council-administrator form is related to overall use of volunteers and to the use of volunteers in public safety. Counties with the commission form of government are more likely than counties with other forms of government to use volunteers for public works.

On the basis of volunteer involvement in particular services, earlier ICMA ASD studies suggested that, since the 1990s, local governments have been making rather limited use of volunteers. However, when one considers volunteer use in general, and in broader service areas rather than in specific services, a somewhat different picture emerges: according to the 2007 ICMA ASD survey, more than one-quarter of local governments used volunteers to deliver public services, and the rate was even higher in certain population groups, regions of the country, and types of government. Moreover, many local governments rely on volunteers in ways that are not addressed in the ICMA survey, such as in the provision of education; through contracting relationships with nonprofit organizations; and through participation on public boards, committees, and councils.

Given these findings, volunteer involvement in local government merits greater attention. At most, we may know the aggregate patterns of involvement, as reflected in the findings of this research. Despite their importance as human resources, however, we do not know precisely how local governments use or manage volunteers, or how to motivate and retain this resource.[20] Such information is likely to become crucial

in the years ahead, as local governments weigh alternative methods for delivering public services.

Notes

1 Jeffrey L. Brudney, *Fostering Volunteer Programs in the Public Sector: Planning, Initiating, and Managing Voluntary Activities* (San Francisco: Jossey-Bass, 1990).

2 Available research included ICMA's previous ASD surveys and sources such as National Association of Counties (NACo), *The Volunteer Tool Box: Visions for Improving the Service of America's Counties* (Washington, D.C.: NACo, 1990).

3 Brudney, *Fostering Volunteer Programs*, 2.

4 Elaine Morley, "Patterns in the Use of Alternative Service Delivery Approaches," in *The Municipal Year Book 1989* (Washington, D.C.: International City/County Management Association [ICMA], 1989), 40.

5 Ibid.

6. Ibid., 39.

7 Rowan Miranda and Karlyn Andersen, "Alternative Service Delivery in Local Government, 1982–1992," in *The Municipal Year Book 1994* (Washington, D.C.: ICMA, 1994), 33.

8 Elaine Morley, "Local Government Use of Alternative Service Delivery Approaches," in *The Municipal Year Book 1999* (Washington, D.C.: ICMA, 1999), 37.

9 Ibid., 40.

10 Ibid.

11 Ibid., 40–41.

12 Mildred Warner and Amir Hefetz, "Pragmatism over Politics: Alternative Service Delivery in Local Government, 1992–2002," in *The Municipal Year Book 2004* (Washington, D.C.: ICMA, 2004), 12.

13 Mildred E. Warner and Amir Hefetz, "Cooperative Competition: Alternative Service Delivery, 2002–2007," in *The Municipal Year Book 2009* (Washington, D.C.: ICMA Press, 2009), 16.

14 Ibid., 15.

15 Ibid., 16.

16 The 2007 survey was conducted on paper because the survey is complex, and ICMA researchers have found that public managers benefit from a paper copy that can be filled out over time, after respondents have had an opportunity to check with the relevant departments.

17 See Warner and Hefetz, "Cooperative Competition," 12.

18 For the analyses whose results are shown in Tables 7–3 through 7–7, we created a "dummy" (yes/no) variable to indicate volunteer use in each service area. If a locality used volunteers to provide any service in a given area, we coded the dummy variable for the service area as yes; if no volunteers were used to provide any services in a given area, we coded the dummy variable no. To preserve the overall sample size when we constructed the aggregate volunteering variables for the seven service delivery areas, we coded all localities that did not use volunteers as no (instead of coding them as missing). Thus, with the exception of Table 7–2, all tables show the percentage of responding local governments that used volunteers, rather than the percentage of local governments that (1) indicated a service delivery method and (2) used volunteers. Because not all local governments provided every service or indicated a method of service delivery for each service, the percentages of local governments using volunteers in Tables 7–3 through 7–7 are lower than those in Table 7–2, as well as those found in the articles on local government volunteer use that we cited earlier.

19 The *p* value is the probability value—that is, the risk of error in rejecting the "null hypothesis," under which there is no difference or no relationship between two variables. The lower the *p* value, the more confident we can be in inferring that the two variables being tested are related. For example, because the *p* values are so small for the relationship between population size and the percentage of localities using volunteers in the areas of public works/transportation ($p < .05$), public safety ($p < .001$), health and human services ($p < .001$), and cultural and arts programs ($p < .05$), we can be very confident that a relationship exists between population size and volunteer use in those service areas. In this article, *p* values above .10 have been omitted.

20 See Mark A. Hager, *Volunteer Management Capacity in America's Charities and Congregations: A Briefing Report* (Washington, D.C.: Urban Institute Press, 2004), urban.org/publications/410963.html; and Mark A. Hager and Jeffrey L. Brudney, *Volunteer Management Practices and Retention of Volunteers* (Washington, D.C.: Urban Institute Press, 2004), urban.org/publications/411005.html.

Recurrent Themes in Local Government Innovation

Karen Thoreson
Alliance for Innovation

James H. Svara
Center for Urban Innovation, Arizona State University

Local governments can be seedbeds of new ideas and practices. Some look to other governments for ideas, others consider what is new in the nonprofit or for-profit sectors, and still others come up with their own approaches to innovation. Each year, hundreds of local governments take the time to document their journeys and submit their findings, either to be considered for awards or to have the honor of presenting their experiences to colleagues.

Sharing information about creative problem solving and innovative solutions is an important service that any jurisdiction can provide to the entire local government community. To support that effort, the Alliance for Innovation (AFI)—a partnership of ICMA, Arizona State University, and the former Innovation Groups—is dedicated to promoting a "community of practice" among innovative local governments and others, including academics who teach and conduct research related to local government. Among the professional development opportunities provided by AFI is the Transforming Local Government (TLG) conference, at which awards are presented to the most inspiring new programs.

Awards programs are among the most important ways that information about innovation can be shared. For each of the past five years, we have reviewed more than 1,000 award-winning programs, selecting

SELECTED FINDINGS

To move into the top tier among its competitor cities in educational attainment, Louisville, Kentucky, created 55,000 Degrees—a public-private partnership designed to add 40,000 bachelor's degrees and 15,000 associate's degrees to the city's population by 2020.

Baltimore's Virtual Supermarket Program, which is designed to give low-income residents of "food deserts" access to healthy and affordable food, allows participants to place weekly orders from libraries, elementary schools, or any Internet-enabled electronic device and pick up the groceries in their own neighborhoods.

In 2010, Boulder, Colorado, became the first locality in the United States to adopt ordinances requiring rental housing to meet specific energy-efficiency standards. To help landlords meet the requirements, the city has partnered with EnergySmart, which provides guidance on upgrades and financing, and helps clients obtain the many rebates available through state, local, and federal programs.

about 25 each year to include in our article about local government innovation. We then group the featured programs into categories that attempt to capture the current areas of emphasis among leading innovative practices. While some of the topic areas have varied from year to year, they generally cluster around six primary themes: community and economic development, citizen engagement, sustainability, service content or delivery, public safety, and organizational development. For localities, these themes speak to the fundamental purpose of place-based governance and the ongoing need to revisit what residents want from their communities and how their wishes will be addressed. The themes also capture the recurring challenges that local governments face.

The continuity in themes does not imply that local government innovation is decreasing: specific actions taken within the broad categories continue to change, formerly distinct strategies become blended over time, and new approaches emerge. For example, one category—e-government and expanding uses of technology—appeared only in the first year; it then moved from being a category of its own to being integral to many other kinds of innovation. Similarly, although we identified new forms of relating to citizens in our first review, citizen engagement crystallized as a theme starting in the second year. Since then, citizen engagement has been integrated into many other categories, including planning, budgeting, community revitalization, and service improvement. Just as technological change is rarely pursued for its own sake, citizen engagement is incorporated at all levels of local government endeavors.

The programs we have selected this year fall into five major categories: the economic environment, sustainability, infrastructure, citizen engagement, and organizational development. The closing section of the article reflects on the featured programs and explores what can be learned from them.

Improving the Economic Environment

Many communities make job creation a top priority, but communities vary widely in how they go about achieving their job-creation goals.

One Block at a Time

Independence, Missouri (pop. 117,213)[1]
2011 National League of Cities' City Showcase participant

The goal of the One Block at a Time program is to attract reinvestment and encourage families to return to the northwest quadrant of Independence. The pro-

---

Sources of Featured Programs

More than 200 submissions and 60 award winners were reviewed for this article. They included Innovation Case Studies and top-ranking award submissions from the Alliance for Innovation; recipients of ICMA honors; winners of the National Civic League's All-America City Award; participants in the National League of Cities' City Showcase; recipients of Innovations in American Government Awards, sponsored by the Ash Center for Democratic Governance and Innovation, Harvard University; and winners of the Local Innovations Awards Scheme, United Kingdom.

---

gram identifies a single block in a residential neighborhood (no more than one-quarter of a mile long) to serve as an anchor; it then brings together public and private partners to completely transform the environment—principally through economic development and the targeted construction of infrastructure and housing. Infrastructure may be repaired or replaced, and housing units and vacant lots are assessed and redeveloped. To date, three residential blocks have been targeted, and work on two is complete.

For more information, go to ci.independence.mo.us/ ComDev/OBAAT.aspx.

Virginia Green Destination

Virginia Beach, Virginia (pop. 442,707)
2011 National League of Cities' City Showcase participant

The Virginia Beach tourism and hospitality industry has made a commitment to increasing tourism while decreasing tourism's impact on the environment. The program's holistic approach is based on a partnership between the Virginia Beach Convention and Visitors Bureau (VBCC), which includes both the convention center and the visitor information center; the Virginia Beach hospitality industry; and the government of Virginia Beach. As a result of the program, the city was named the Commonwealth's first Virginia Green Destination.

Among the activities undertaken as a result of the program are the following:

- *Recycling:* The VBCC's single-stream recycling program captures plastic and glass bottles, steel and aluminum cans, paper, and cardboard.

- *Waste reduction:* China and linen are used for catering, and any disposables necessary for concessions are recyclable and/or made from bio-based materials.

- *Water efficiency:* The VBCC uses low-flow toilets, faucets with auto sensors, high-efficiency dishwashers, and microfiber mops.
- *Energy efficiency:* Compact, energy-efficient fluorescent lighting is used, and lighting, heating, ventilation, and air-conditioning are programmable.

For more information, go to visitvirginiabeach.com/ uploadedFiles/Content/Site/conventioncenter/pdfs/ VBCVB-GreenBrochure2011.pdf.

Norton Priory Museum

Halton Borough Council, United Kingdom (pop. 125,746)[2]
2010 Local Innovation Awards Scheme winner

The Country Garden Kitchen catering business operates the cafeteria at the Norton Priory Museum, a 12th-century monastery in Halton Borough Council. The cafeteria, which obtains fresh organic fruit and vegetables from the museum's market garden, provides work for 10 people with learning disabilities.

Priory Ales, a microbrewery on the grounds of the museum, is an extension of the catering business—and an added attraction that has increased both foot traffic and revenue for the museum. The brewery offers public viewing areas, and visitors may purchase the ales from the museum shop or from local commercial outlets. The brewery provides jobs for people on the autism spectrum, for young people leaving foster care, for people with mental health issues, and for people with learning disabilities.

Cup Cake Caterers, another business entity affiliated with the museum, provides homemade cakes and confections that are sold at the cafeteria and nearby cafés. Cup Cake Caterers is staffed by people with physical disabilities.

For more information, go to localinnovation.idea.gov .uk/idk/aio/15284791 and www3.halton.gov.uk/news/ newsroom/164932/.

Economic Gardening

Littleton, Colorado (pop. 42,639)
2011 Innovations in American Government Award, Ash Center

In 1987, Littleton took steps to revitalize employment opportunities by creating the Department of Business/Industry Affairs and partnering with a think tank, which recommended that the city shift its focus from "economic hunting" (recruiting out-of-state industries and using various enticements to persuade them to relocate) to "economic gardening" (focusing on local industrial growth). Over the course of more than two decades, through careful cultivation of its local entrepreneurial spirit and the application of new tools and technologies (including geographic information systems and database research), Littleton doubled its job base and tripled its sales tax revenues. The city has also received inquiries from 700 communities looking to revitalize their economies.

For more information, go to innovations.harvard.edu/ awards.html?id = 2377464.

55,000 Degrees

Louisville/Jefferson County, Kentucky (pop. 602,011)
2011 National League of Cities' City Showcase participant

55,000 Degrees (55K) is a new public-private partnership designed to create a "college-going culture" that will move Louisville into the top tier among its competitor cities in educational attainment. The intent is that by 2020, the number of bachelor's degrees held by city residents will increase by 40,000, and associate's degrees by 15,000. By galvanizing education, business, faith, civic, and community leaders and organizations in support of a common agenda, 55K hopes to create a world-class, seamless, and coordinated educational system that will swell the ranks of skilled workers while creating opportunities for creativity and critical thinking.

For more information, go to 55000degrees.org/about-55k/ our objectives/.

Sustainability Initiatives

Communities are constantly expanding the scope of their sustainability initiatives and finding more effective ways to meet their sustainability goals.

Virtual Supermarket Program

Baltimore, Maryland (pop. 619,493)
2011 National League of Cities' City Showcase participant

Baltimore's Virtual Supermarket Program (VSP) provides low-income residents with access to healthy food. Thanks to VSP, Baltimore residents can place weekly orders at VSP sites (or from any Internet-enabled electronic device) and pick up their groceries in their own neighborhoods: at the local libraries or elementary schools. Cash, credit, debit, or electronic benefit transfers are accepted, and there is no service fee. Volunteers, working under the supervision of city employees, provide some program administration.

For more information, go to baltimarket.org/?page_id = 149 and baltimorehealth.org/virtualsupermarket.html.

Alternative Fuel Vehicle Program

Kansas City, Missouri (pop. 463,202)
2011 National League of Cities' City Showcase participant

Kansas City's Alternative Fuel Vehicle Program uses hybrid electric vehicles, fuel blends, and idle reduction to improve the fuel economy of the city's fleet vehicles and mobile equipment. The city uses compressed natural gas to power 287 vehicles; an additional 2,796 vehicles are powered by biodiesel (1,060), 10% ethanol (1,700), battery electricity (31), and propane (5). Alternative fuels have replaced more than 500,000 gallons of conventional gasoline and diesel, representing 15% of the city's total annual fuel use.

For more information, go to nlc.org/Documents/Utility% 20Navigation/About%20NLC/Awards/City%20Showcase %202011/showcase-alternative-fuel-vehicle-kansas-city-mo-dec11.pdf.

EnergySmart

Boulder, Colorado (pop. 98,889)
2012 J. Robert Havlick Award for Innovation in Local Government, AFI

Recognizing that residential energy consumption was the primary source of greenhouse gas emissions in the city and that half the residences are rental units, Boulder became the first locality in the United States to adopt ordinances requiring rental housing to meet specific energy-efficiency standards. Adopted in 2010, the ordinances require rental housing to meet the standards by 2019. To assist landlords in meeting the requirements, the city has partnered with Energy-Smart, a comprehensive, multijurisdictional effort to help implement energy upgrades for owner-occupied units, rentals, and businesses. EnergySmart provides guidance on upgrades and financing, and helps clients obtain the many rebates available through state, local, and federal programs. Each customer is assigned an individual adviser, streamlining the normally arduous renovation process.

For more information, go to energysmartyes.com/files/ EnergySmart_Navigant_ProgressReport_2012_FINAL .pdf and bouldercounty.org/sustainability/programs/ pages/energysmart.aspx.

Building the Local Solar Market

Beaverton, Oregon (pop. 91,625)
Gainesville, Florida (pop. 125,326)
2011 TLG Case Study Presenter, AFI

Through a competitive selection process, Beaverton partnered with a local solar installation contractor to provide residents with bulk discounts of approximately 20% off the contractor's usual asking price for solar energy systems. The program, which also leveraged state incentives and state and local tax credits to further reduce residents' net costs for solar energy investments, has resulted in about 300 solar installations. In Gainesville, a "feed-in tariff" is available for both commercial and residential solar installations; through the tariff, residences and businesses sell back to the utility all or any excess power generated by their solar equipment.

For more information, go to thesolarfoundation.org/sites/ thesolarfoundation.org/files/TLG%20Conference%20 Slides%2004.20.12.pdf.

Innovative Infrastructure

Local governments are developing new approaches to achieving their long-term infrastructure goals.

Resiliency and Preparedness Study

Flagstaff, Arizona (pop. 65,914)
2012 Outstanding Achievement in Innovation Award, AFI

Flagstaff's *Resiliency and Preparedness Study*, published in 2012, assessed the vulnerability of critical government operations and the area's natural and built infrastructure to weather-related disasters. In light of the study's recommendation that future policies focus on protecting the government operations and assets, the city is assigning greater priority to disaster preparedness.

For more information, go to flagstaff.az.gov/ DocumentCenter/Home/View/38841.

The "Perks" of Innovation

Clearwater, Florida (pop. 107,784)
2012 Outstanding Achievement in Innovation Award, AFI

After a Clearwater code enforcement official discovered that an organic waste by-product could be an effective alternative to a costly, carbon-based means of removing nutrients from incoming wastewater, the city developed a method for integrating the by-product—which is derived from the flavorings used by a coffee beverage manufacturer—into its waste-water treatment. The city and the manufacturer are also collaborating to reduce manufacturing costs and thereby reduce subsequent costs to the city.

For more information, go to transformgov .org/en/knowledge_network/documents/kn/ Document/303662/The_Perks_of_Innovating.

Making the Most of Bricks and Mortar

San Antonio, Texas (pop. 1,359,758)
2012 TLG Case Study Presenter, AFI

With the goal of reducing its budget deficit, San Antonio thoroughly analyzed the operations of all city facilities, identifying more than 25 underused buildings. By disposing of underused space, improving its use of existing space, and co-locating services in community facilities, San Antonio achieved $1 million in annual savings.

For more information, go to prezi.com/qcmhmpb0jhj9/ making-the-most-out-of-bricks-and-mortar/?auth_key = 1ee4a7799693b492b757ed96ed01193510f0f844.

West Lethbridge Centre

Lethbridge, Alberta (pop. 83,517)[3]
2012 TLG Case Studies, AFI

Thanks to a collaborative effort on the part of the city of Lethbridge, the Lethbridge Public Library Board, and local public and private school boards, Lethbridge has a new neighborhood center that offers 45 acres of parkland and sports fields, two large gyms, a theater, a public library, and two high schools—and all the buildings are LEED (Leadership in Energy and Environmental Design) certified. The effort that led to the development of the West Lethbridge Centre is a prime example of the value that can be achieved when public entities collaborate.

For more information, go to transformgov.org/en/ knowledge_network/documents/kn/Document/303667/ P4_Enhanced_Public_Partnership_Practice_West_ Lethbridge_Centre_Projecttlgconference.org/Program/ Program_ISLethbridge.htm.

Engaging Citizens for Community Development

By finding new ways to broaden and deepen citizen engagement, local governments are transforming their image as vending machines that dispense one-size-fits-all services.

Bank On Brazos Valley

Bryan, Texas (pop. 77,321)
2011 National League of Cities' City Showcase participant

Bank On Brazos Valley is a public-private partnership designed to improve the financial stability of lower-income consumers by enabling them to stop relying on fringe financial services (such as payday lenders and check-cashing businesses) and to engage instead in mainstream financial practices, such as opening checking and/or savings accounts. Through the program, banks and credit unions in the Brazos Valley region offer affordable products and services to "underbanked" or "unbanked" customers—those who had previously used mainstream banking services very little or not at all.

For more information, go to bankonbrazosvalley.com/.

Health on a Shelf

Tupelo, Mississippi (pop. 35,059)
2011 National League of Cities' City Showcase participant

Through Health on a Shelf, a program developed by the Healthy Tupelo Task Force, participating local convenience stores set aside a special area to prominently display nutritious food and snacks. Each item has no more than 250 calories and no more than 5 grams of fat, and is designated with a sticker showing that it has been approved by the Healthy Tupelo Task Force. Participating retailers are permitted to display colorful signs designating them as Health on a Shelf stores.

For more information, go to tippah360.com/bookmark/ 12784964-'Health-on-a-Shelf'-begins-in-Tupelo.

Designed for Safety

Bayside, Wisconsin (pop. 4,411)
2012 TLG Case Study Presenter, AFI

In an initiative designed to foster the values of transparency, accountability, and citizen engagement, Bayside created a contest, inviting elementary school students to create attention-grabbing signs that would improve safety for pedestrians and bicyclists by encouraging motorists to slow down and stop at crosswalks in school zones. The winning designs were made into professionally produced signs and placed on village roadways.

For more information, go to transformgov.org/en/ knowledge_network/documents/kn/Document/ 303834/Citizen_Engagement_Right_Brain_and_the_ Emotional_Draw.

iMesa: Helping to Build a Better Mesa

Mesa, Arizona (pop. 446,518)
2011 National League of Cities' City Showcase participant

In 2011, at the annual mayor's breakfast, Mesa mayor Scott Smith launched iMesa, a grassroots investment and improvement effort designed to build a better Mesa. As part of the iMesa strategy, the city is using technology to engage residents, who are invited to submit, vote on, and comment on proposals for transformative community projects. After gathering community input for more than a year, the Mesa City Council agreed to forward a $70 million bond package of iMesa projects to voters, which passed on November 6, 2012.

For more information, go to mesaaz.gov/iMesa/.

Performance Measures Meet Community Engagement

Durham, North Carolina (pop. 233,252)
2012 TLG Case Studies, AFI

In 2008, as part of its strategic plan, the city of Durham created an online dashboard that allows citizens to track the city's progress on the five goals articulated in the plan. In addition, all 25 city departments are developing department-level strategic plans—and dashboards—that align with those of the city. Since August 2011, when the dashboard was implemented, Durham has increased transparency and improved both public participation and internal and external communication.

For more information, go to transformgov.org/en/ knowledge_network/documents/kn/Document/302703/ Strategic_Planning_Charting_Our_Course and durhamnc .gov/strategicplan/goals.

Golden Vision 2030

Golden, Colorado (pop. 19,035)
2012 TLG Case Study Presenter, AFI

Through Golden Vision 2030, a two-year community engagement effort, Golden sought to identify its values by telling, sharing, and retelling stories. By reaching out to all its citizens, including those whose voices had always been underrepresented, Golden has deepened community engagement, identified what defines quality of life in the city, and helped to ensure that decisions about the future are driven by shared community values.

For more information, go to transformgov.org/en/ knowledge_network/documents/kn/Document/303659/ From_Storytelling_to_Policy__Golden_Vision_2030.

Leveraging Technology to Promote Citizen Engagement

Olathe, Kansas (pop. 127,907)
2012 TLG Case Study Presenter, AFI

In 2011, to increase public participation during the budgeting process, Olathe used an e-town hall event, which allowed citizens to provide input using either social media or traditional means. Using the same approach, the city gathered input from one out of every 84 residents—an unprecedented level of involvement—during the update of its comprehensive plan.

For more information, go to transformgov .org/en/knowledge_network/documents/kn/ Document/303733/ETown_Hall.

Organizational Design

New processes and policies are fundamentally changing how local government work is undertaken.

Municipal Partnering Initiative

Glenview, Illinois (pop. 44,888)
2012 Outstanding Achievement in Innovation Award, AFI

In 2010, with the goal of reducing costs while preserving service quality, 18 Illinois municipalities created the Municipal Partnering Initiative (MPI). Through the MPI, members share workloads and best practices, and engage in bulk purchasing. To allow flexibility, a community can opt out of any proposed project.

For more information, go to icma.org/Documents/ Document/Document/304199.

Innovation and Efficiency Task Force

Phoenix, Arizona (pop. 1,469,471)
2012 Outstanding Achievement in Innovation Award, AFI

In 2010, Phoenix created the Innovation and Efficiency Task Force to develop and implement processes that would increase service efficiency. In Phase I alone, the task force, which is made up of city staff and Phoenix residents, found ways to save the city more than $25 million by, among other things, discontinuing paper paychecks for employees and retirees, redesigning the transport system used by seniors, consolidating trash and recycling pickups, requesting rebates from consultants doing business with the city, and restructuring the personnel system.

These and other changes are expected to save about $125 million by 2015.

For more information, go to phoenix.gov/citygovernment/ efficiency/index.html.

Improving Health by Increasing Accountability

Manatee County, Florida (pop. 327,142)
2012 TLG Case Study Presenter, AFI

By focusing on (1) an accountable benefit design tied to preventive care; (2) high financial incentives for successful outcomes (not just for participation); and (3) on-site, integrated health care management, including advocates to help employees improve their modifiable conditions and to encourage compliance with treatment protocols, Manatee County has transformed its health plan. In addition to being cost-effective, the program has yielded better outcomes.

For more information, go to transformgov.org/en/ knowledge_network/documents/kn/Document/303664/ Creating_a_Culture_of_Health_through_Accountable_ Wellness_and_Health_Management_Initiatives.

Think Forward: The New Employee Relations Model

Las Vegas, Nevada (pop. 589,317)
2012 TLG Case Study Presenter, AFI

To develop new ways of providing services while staying within budgetary limits, Las Vegas created Think Forward: The New Employee Relations Model. The city not only engaged employees in the process but also encouraged public participation as well. Implementation of the model led to three principal sources of savings: project and service reviews, restructured salaries and benefits, and staff reductions.

For more information, go to transformgov.org/en/ knowledge_network/documents/kn/Document/ 304439/Think_Forward_The_New_Employee_Relations _Model.

Arlington Challenge Grants

Arlington, Texas (pop. 373,698)
2012 TLG Case Study Presenter, AFI

In fiscal year 2011, Arlington faced a projected $10.3 million budget deficit. Using earmarked one-time gas revenues as funding, the city took a new approach to balancing the budget: each department was given the opportunity to compete for one-time "challenge grant" funds, which had to be used to provide services innovatively. In addition to allowing departments additional time to balance their fiscal year 2012 budgets, the approach allowed departments to compete to provide essential services.

For more information, go to transformgov.org/en/ knowledge_network/documents/kn/Document/303832/ City_of_Arlington_Challenge_Grant_Consider_the_ Possibilities.

The Power of Forecasts

Pinellas County, Florida (pop. 917,398)
2012 TLG Case Study Presenter, AFI

In the face of serious fiscal challenges, Pinellas County revamped its forecasting model: instead of looking backward, the new model looks forward. As part of its new approach, Pinellas's budgetary forecast (1) includes overviews of the national, state, and local economies over the next 10 years; (2) fully discloses all methods and assumptions used in the forecast; and (3) provides user-friendly analyses of the forecasts for each of the county's 10 major funds. The forecast document will strengthen the county's ability to prepare for and navigate the fiscal stresses of the coming years.

For more information, go to transformgov.org/en/ knowledge_network/documents/kn/Document/ 303738/Polishing_Your_Crystal_Ball_The_Power_of_ the_Forecast.

Lessons Learned

One purpose of an annual review of award-winning programs and practices is to deepen understanding of key attributes of the innovation process. The case studies are instructive not only because they offer new ways of addressing community problems, but also because they demonstrate that even when the difficulties being addressed are similar, there are widely differing means of achieving success. The cases featured in *The Municipal Year Book 2011* offered insight into innovative methods for responding to the fiscal crisis.[4] This year, the lessons focus on unique substantive contributions to five major categories of innovation.

Economic Development

Our five case studies in this area exemplify the various approaches that communities are using to bolster their economies. Independence, for example, is attracting new residents, businesses, and investment by redeveloping vulnerable neighborhoods one block at a time. Littleton, in contrast, began by building a broad vision of what kind of community it wanted to be, and then stayed the course for two decades, using new tools and technologies and building partnerships with a local community college, the chamber of commerce, think tanks, and other organizations to achieve its goals.

Virginia Beach, Halton Borough Council, and Louisville are pursuing branding-based economic strategies that are designed to distinguish them from other destinations. Importantly, each community's strategies reflect its values. Virginia Beach, where the economy depends heavily on tourism, has chosen to increase the sustainability of the hospitality industry. Louisville's 55K initiative focuses on increasing educational attainment as a means of setting the city apart from its competitors. Halton Borough began by capitalizing on a unique architectural feature and then used two strategies to strengthened its viability and reach: (1) the development of specialized food and drink and (2) the creation of opportunities to train and employ people with disabilities.

Sustainability

The theme of sustainability is woven throughout many of the award-winning solutions described in this article. Baltimore is unique in providing healthy, affordable food to vulnerable populations residing in urban food deserts—areas where vehicle ownership is limited, and where residents have little or no access to fresh foods and produce.

Kansas City, Gainesville, and Beaverton have approached their sustainability goals by focusing on alternative energy sources. Kansas City stands out for its commitment to improving the energy efficiency of its fleet and thereby reducing carbon emissions. Both Gainesville and Beaverton have implemented strategies designed to encourage broad adoption of solar technology. Beaverton's approach focuses on making solar more affordable through bulk purchasing and maximizing tax incentives. Gainesville facilitates residential and commercial investment in photovoltaics by guaranteeing that the local electric utility will purchase some or all of the energy produced by solar installations.

Boulder's energy-efficiency standards for rental housing, the first of their kind in the United States, were accompanied by a program to help landlords determine which improvements need to be made and how to finance the upgrades.

Infrastructure

Developing and maintaining a community's infrastructure is a primary role for local governments. In a challenging economy, our award winners found new ways to accomplish that goal. To develop a community center that would leverage all assets and ensure that the entire community would have a stake in the facility, Lethbridge collaborated with other public entities in a way that can serve as a model for similar initiatives. San Antonio, recognizing that many of its properties were underused, undertook an extensive evaluation of all community assets. The initiative enabled the city to consolidate operations and dispose of 25 properties.

Thanks to an ingenious idea proposed by a code enforcement officer, Clearwater improved its wastewater treatment operations and lowered their costs: the city now uses a by-product from the manufacturing process of a local company to remove nutrients from incoming wastewater. After undertaking a resiliency and preparedness study, Flagstaff is focusing on disaster preparedness to protect service delivery.

Community Development through Citizen Engagement

Local governments across North America are embracing the notion of engaging residents and businesses in policy development, neighborhood revitalization, and program delivery. Both Health on a Shelf and Bank On Brazos Valley are excellent examples of how governments can engage the private and nonprofit sectors to further community goals.

Bayside and Golden have succeeded in engaging residents through programs designed to highlight shared community values. In Bayside, elementary school students developed signs that would encourage motorists to slow down and stop near crosswalks in school zones. And in Golden, a unique visioning approach based on storytelling has yielded both a deeper level of community engagement and practical input that is providing long-term direction for the city.

Durham, Mesa, and Olathe are using technology to bring local government to the people. Durham has achieved this by developing a remarkable website that shows residents how the city is meeting its goals. Mesa invited residents to propose and respond to ideas for community transformation, some of which were ultimately incorporated into a successful bond issue. And Olathe engaged residents in the budgeting process through e-town hall meetings that yielded unprecedented levels of citizen participation.

Organizational Design

Faced with a challenging national economy, many organizations are rethinking what they do and how they do it. Arlington and Phoenix used very different approaches, but both were successful. Arlington earmarked one-time gas revenues for investment in innovative new programs. Phoenix established a task force, made up of both city staff and local residents, to review local government operations: the effort yielded more than $25 million in annual savings.

Manatee County and Las Vegas chose to improve their organizations by strengthening internal design. Manatee's new health plan, which focuses on preventive care, incentives for successful outcomes, and on-site health management, has led to healthier employees and lower costs. Las Vegas revised its approach to working with employees on performance, salary expectations, benefits, and responsibilities.

The city of Glenview and Pinellas County opted to revise specific practices. Glenview spearheaded an 18-member municipal partnership to save money on procurement and service delivery, and Pinellas dealt with fiscal challenges by developing a transparent, accessible, and broad-based budgetary forecasting model that focuses on the county's economic future rather than on its past.

Conclusion

Each of the programs highlighted in this article demonstrates that innovation—both incremental and profound—is alive and well in local government. The unifying threads are the inspiration and leadership to create, nurture, and bring innovation to fruition.

Local officials can learn from these examples and adapt the ideas to fit their own communities. The cases summarized here are particularly noteworthy, but there are many other examples of exciting innovations among all the award-winning programs we reviewed. We hope that readers will consider whether these or other cases offer workable approaches for achieving their goals or solving their problems; if not, we invite them to develop their own innovations and share them with other governments.

Notes

1 Unless otherwise noted, all populations are 2011 estimates from the U.S. Census Bureau.

2 Office of National Statistics, 2011 Census, United Kingdom.

3 Statistics Canada, "Census Profile: Lethbridge," 2011, statcan.gc.ca/start-debut-eng.html.

4. Karen Thoreson and James H. Svara, "How Local Government Are Navigating the Fiscal Crisis: Taking Stock and Looking Forward," in *The Municipal Year Book 2011* (Washington, D.C.: ICMA Press, 2011), 75–82.

9

CAO Salary and Compensation: Stability Is the Trend

Evelina R. Moulder
ICMA

Ron Carlee
ICMA

Compensation of public employees, whether related to pensions and benefits or to actual salaries, is often a topic of media coverage, and this is especially so when an outlier in benefits and compensation becomes a headline story. But what are the norms? What is typical in salary and benefits for a city or county manager or chief appointed official (CAO)?

"ICMA Guidelines for Compensation" state that the compensation of local government managers should be "fair, reasonable, transparent, and based on comparable public salaries nationally and regionally."[1] But what is fair and reasonable? CAOs are the chief appointed professional managers and administrators in cities, counties, towns, and villages. If the CAO is a city, county, or town manager, he or she serves as the chief executive officer (CEO) of a major enterprise, with more lines of business than most comparably sized private companies have. If the CAO works for a mayor or county executive, he or she serves as chief operating officer, again with substantial executive responsibilities for a highly complex organization. Additionally, the actual range of services for which the CAO is responsible varies widely.

While ICMA recommends that compensation benchmarks be established in accordance with comparable local government and/or public sector agencies, there is no consensus to date on what external

SELECTED FINDINGS

The overall median salary for chief appointed officials (CAOs) overall is $103,000. Base salary is generally related to population size of the local government; however, even within each population category and within the same geographic regions, the specifics are unique.

Thirty-eight percent of CAOs, as well as 55% of those in local governments with a population of 50,000 and over, reported that their base salaries are publically available on the local government website.

In 85% of cases overall, benefit packages for CAOs are calculated in the same manner as for other employees of the local government.

positions are appropriate for benchmarking CAO pay. ICMA guidelines are broad, stating that "compensation should be based on the position requirements, the complexity of the job reflected in the composition of the organization and community, the leadership needed, labor market conditions, cost of living in the community, and the organization's ability to pay."[2]

Examining new data from a 2012 national survey of local government executives, this article looks at compensation issues for city, county, and town managers and administrators in local governments with the council-manager plan, and at the equivalent appointed positions in local governments with the mayor-council, town meeting, or representative town meeting plan. Judging from the results of this survey, it would be inaccurate to provide an unqualified, relevant amount of pay for the "average" CAO; there *is* no average CAO any more than there is an average city, county, or town. Responses show that pay practices vary widely according to the size, location, and philosophy of each local government.

Survey Methodology

The 2012 *ICMA Compensation Survey for Local Government Chief Appointed Officials* was sent to all local governments in the ICMA database for which ICMA has a name in the CAO position. The survey was designed to collect information on compensation for CAOs that would reflect the norms around the country, and to examine practices in relation to the principles contained within the "ICMA Guidelines for Compensation."

The initial survey was mailed in April 2012, and a follow-up survey was later mailed to nonrespondents. It was clear from some of the responses that clerks or elected officials were reporting for themselves, in which case those records were excluded from the final analysis. With those records excluded, the survey response rate was 42%, with 2,974 surveys submitted from among 7,103 mailed (Table 9–1).

Base Salary

It is not possible to determine from the survey what the base salary benchmark should be for the CAO in any specific jurisdiction. In brief, the "ICMA Guidelines" recommend that the following factors be considered in establishing CAO pay:

- Scope of services provided
- Requirements of the job
- Experience needed to successfully perform
- Market pay for comparable public sector executives
- Local government's financial position
- The individual CAO's credentials, experience, and expertise.

Base salary is generally related to population size of the local government; however, even within each population category and within the same geographic regions, the specifics are unique. Arguably in smaller local governments the CAOs may have a breadth of hands-on responsibility uncommon in large communities,

Table 9-1 Survey Response

Classification	No. of municipalities surveyed[a] (A)	Respondents No.	Respondents % of (A)
Total respondents	7,103	2,974	42
Population group			
Over 1,000,000	35	14	40
500,000–1,000,000	65	21	32
250,000–499,999	121	53	44
100,000–249,999	344	152	44
50,000–99,999	586	243	42
25,000–49,999	916	388	42
10,000–24,999	1,636	689	42
5,000–9,999	1,327	567	43
2,500–4,999	1,167	461	40
Under 2,500	906	386	43
Geographic region			
Northeast	1,489	498	33
North-Central	1,997	943	47
South	2,343	899	38
West	1,274	634	50
Geographic division			
New England	593	247	42
Mid-Atlantic	896	251	28
East North-Central	1,155	513	44
West North-Central	845	431	51
South Atlantic	1,372	580	42
East South-Central	297	87	29
West South-Central	675	232	34
Mountain	446	236	53
Pacific Coast	824	397	48
Metro status			
Metropolitan Statistical Area	3,926	1,730	44
Micropolitan Statistical Area	1,112	457	41
New England City and Town Area	358	151	42
Undesignated	1,707	636	37
Form of government			
Mayor-council	1,984	722	36
Council-manager	3,561	1,731	49
Commission	75	26	35
Town meeting	256	107	42
Representative town meeting	41	11	27
County commission	350	68	19
Council-administrator (manager)	614	248	40
Council-elected executive	222	61	28

a For a definition of terms, please see "Inside the *Year Book*," xi–xiv.

The Principles

Compensation and personnel matters should be guided by the core principles of the ICMA Code of Ethics. ICMA affirms that the standard practice for establishing the compensation of local government managers be fair, reasonable, transparent, and based on comparable public salaries nationally and regionally. ICMA members should act with integrity in all personal and professional matters in order to merit the trust of elected officials, the public and employees. Local government managers have an ethical responsibility to be clear about what is being requested and to avoid excessive compensation.

Elected officials perform a critical governance role providing oversight of the management of the organization. To that end, they must be engaged in establishing the process for determining the compensation for all executives appointed by the governing body.

Compensation should be based on the position requirements, the complexity of the job reflected in the composition of the organization and community, the leadership needed, labor market conditions, cost of living in the community, and the organization's ability to pay.

Source: "ICMA Guidelines for Compensation" (2010), 1, icma.org/Documents/Document/Document/302085.

Table 9-2   Median Salaries, in Total and by Population

Population	Overall median salary ($)
Total	103,000
Over 1,000,000	235,099
500,000-1,000,000	190,409
250,000-499,999	181,865
100,000-249,999	162,651
50,000-99,999	148,365
25,000-49,999	130,000
10,000-24,999	115,000
5,000-9,999	92,000
2,500-4,999	76,000
Under 2,500	63,000

($101,000). By population groupings, the median amounts for 2012 are shown in Table 9–2.

As Figure 9–1 shows, the median salary increases steadily among the population groups. The median is used instead of the mean, or average, because it is not as influenced by outliers as the average salary can be; nonetheless, the variance is significant. Maximum salaries show more variation among the population groups and are influenced by many factors, such as manager experience and tenure; particular characteristics of the locality; cost of living; median income in the locality; services delivered; and breadth of responsibility, such as responsibility for schools, public hospitals, airports, and ports. Maximum salaries do not show a correlation to populations but rise and fall across the population categories. Appendix Tables 9–A1 and 9–A2 show the mean, median, minimum, and maximum salaries for cities and counties, respectively, within each state by population group.

When the median salaries of 2012 are compared with those reported in 2011,[3] the data show that the salaries overall have not increased (Figure 9–2). In fact, the actual median salaries have decreased slightly in all population categories since 2011.

Base Salary Documentation

Documentation of base salary is important for providing transparency to taxpayers and shielding CAOs from accusations of trying to hide their compensation. Asked whether their base salaries are documented in contracts or letter of agreements with the appointing authority, 71% of respondents overall responded in the affirmative (not shown).

The most notable variation occurs when the data are arrayed by form of government, with 78% of respondents serving in council-manager governments and 58% of those in mayor-council governments

and managers in large communities typically bring to their positions extensive experience acquired in smaller communities. A small community may have a strong financial capacity while a large city may have a weak financial position, or vice versa. This reality is reflected in the wide variation in base pay.

To ensure that respondents reported the same information, survey instructions defined base salary as follows:

This amount is not necessarily your taxable income. It is your salary before any pre-tax contributions are deducted to arrive at taxable income. For example, if your salary is $250,000 and you put $17,000 in pre-tax dollars into a retirement account, your base salary is $250,000.

Survey results show that the overall median salary is $103,000, which is slightly higher than the median shown in the 2011 ICMA salary survey data reporting base salary documentation. In the former case, the full council is normally responsible for setting compensation, while in the latter case, compensation may be negotiated between only the mayor and the CAO. But while 78% is a high percentage replying that base salary is documented, there are no obvious reasons in a council-manager form of government for the percentage to be less than 100%.

Figure 9-1   Base Salary by Population Group

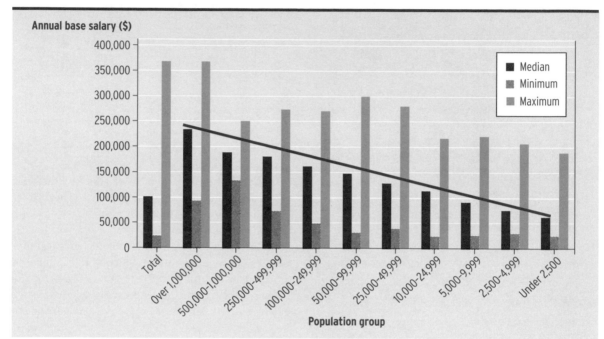

Figure 9-2   Comparison of Median CAO Salaries, 2011 and 2012

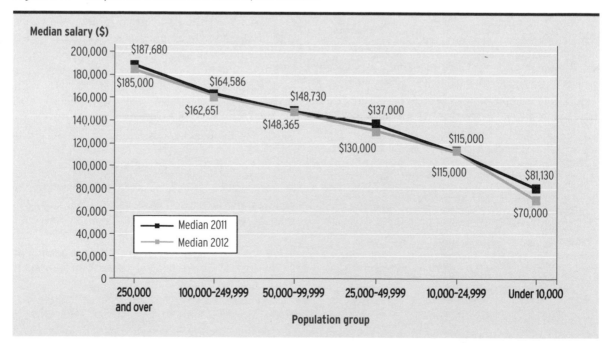

Base Salary Publically Accessible on Website

While salaries are a matter of public record, they are not always easy for the public to access. For maximum transparency, 38% of respondents overall, as well as a majority of CAOs in local governments with a population of 50,000 and greater, reported that their base salaries are publically available on the local government website (Figure 9–3).

Compensation beyond Base Salary

Beyond base pay, the only additional compensation that is common practice is car allowance. In local governments with populations of 10,000 and above, a majority of managers receive a car allowance (Figure 9–4). Other creative forms of compensation, such as health club benefits, are rare.

Salary and Performance Review

Annual performance evaluations of the manager/CAO can benefit both the manager and the governing body, identifying both successes and missed opportunities, as well as future goals and objectives. The review process offers an occasion for discussion among all parties and can help the governing body avoid some of the pitfalls of unclear direction. A majority of all respondents reported an annual performance evaluation (76%), regardless of whether compensation is considered during that process (Figure 9–5).

Transparency

1. Local government managers should provide their total compensation package to the governing body when requesting compensation changes so that the governing body has a comprehensive view of the compensation package.

2. In the interest of fairness and transparency, there should be full disclosure to the governing body, prior to formal consideration and approval, of the potential cost of any benefit changes negotiated during employment.

3. When the terms and conditions of employment are being renegotiated with the employer and at the end when the employment is being terminated, ICMA members have a duty to advise the elected officials to seek legal advice.

4. In the interests of transparency, the salary plan and salary ranges for local government positions, including that of the manager, should be publicly accessible on the agency's website.

Source: "ICMA Guidelines for Compensation" (2010), 3, icma.org/Documents/Document/Document/302085.

Figure 9-3 Base Salary Publically Available on Website

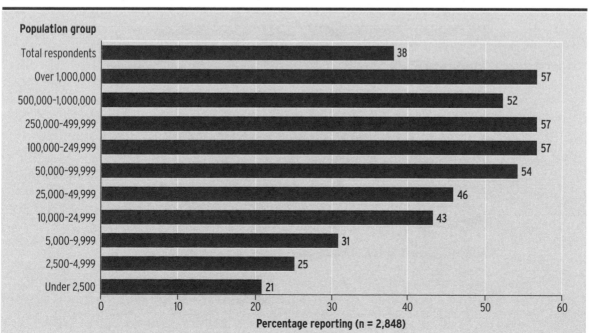

Population group / Percentage reporting (n = 2,848)

Population group	Percentage
Total respondents	38
Over 1,000,000	57
500,000–1,000,000	52
250,000–499,999	57
100,000–249,999	57
50,000–99,999	54
25,000–49,999	46
10,000–24,999	43
5,000–9,999	31
2,500–4,999	25
Under 2,500	21

Figure 9-4 Car Allowance

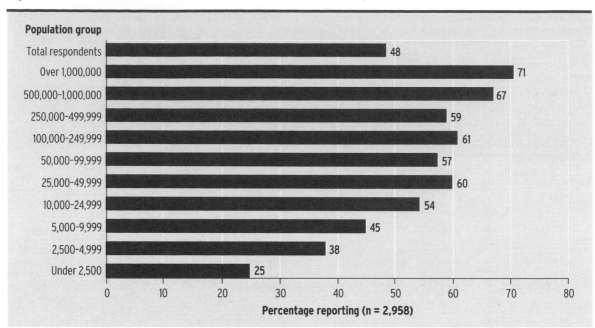

Population group

	Percentage reporting (n = 2,958)
Total respondents	48
Over 1,000,000	71
500,000–1,000,000	67
250,000–499,999	59
100,000–249,999	61
50,000–99,999	57
25,000–49,999	60
10,000–24,999	54
5,000–9,999	45
2,500–4,999	38
Under 2,500	25

Figure 9-5 Annual Performance and Salary Reviews

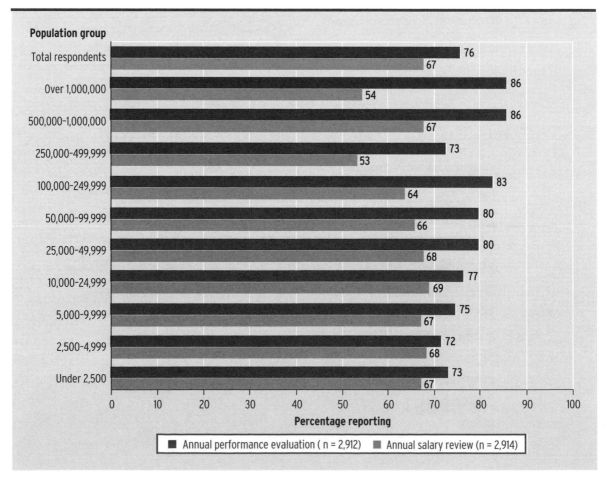

Population group

Population group	Annual performance evaluation (n = 2,912)	Annual salary review (n = 2,914)
Total respondents	76	67
Over 1,000,000	86	54
500,000–1,000,000	86	67
250,000–499,999	73	53
100,000–249,999	83	64
50,000–99,999	80	66
25,000–49,999	80	68
10,000–24,999	77	69
5,000–9,999	75	67
2,500–4,999	72	68
Under 2,500	73	67

Percentage reporting

■ Annual performance evaluation (n = 2,912)   ■ Annual salary review (n = 2,914)

While a majority of respondents also reported having annual salary reviews (67%) (Figure 9–5), the remaining 33% indicated other frequencies of salary review (Figure 9–6). Consistent with the "ICMA Guidelines" concerning transparency, 91% of respondents indicated that their total compensation package is available to all members of the governing body (not shown).

Figure 9-6 Frequency of Salary Review

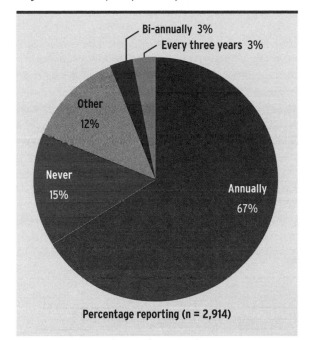

Percentage reporting (n = 2,914)

Pay Decreases and Furlough Days

Overall, 10% of respondents reported cuts in base pay since December 2007, and of note is the high percentage in Pacific Coast localities (23%) (not shown). California local governments in particular have suffered during the fiscal crisis: there have been media reports of California city managers taking pay cuts to help balance the budget or to provide raises for city staff.[4]

Furlough days were reported by 10% overall, but with noticeably higher percentages reported among the larger population groups (Figure 9–7). The median number of furlough days is six (not shown).

Benefits

The survey collected information on benefits provided to CAOs with attention to how those benefits are calculated—that is, whether they are calculated using the same process used to calculate the benefits for other employees. The following definition was provided to survey respondents:

> "The same" does not necessarily mean the same dollar amount; it means that the benefit is determined in the same manner, e.g., if health insurance premiums paid by the employee are based [on] type of coverage, is that how your premium contribution is calculated?

In every instance, a majority of respondents reported that their benefits are calculated in the same

Figure 9-7 Use of Furlough Days

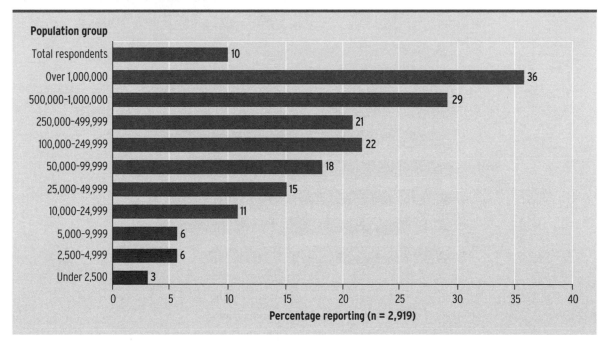

manner as the benefits are calculated for other employees (Figure 9–8).

Employment Contracts/Agreements

Eighty-one percent of CAOs reported having an employment agreement or contract (not shown), although there is noticeable variation between the percentages reported in mayor-council localities (69%) and those in council-manager (87%) localities. In 87% of the cases where an employment agreement or contract is in place, the agreement documents the CAO's full compensation. In addition, respondents reported that the agreement

- Was approved in a public session (95%)
- Is available to the public upon request (98%)
- Is posted on the local government website (13%). Among local governments with a population 50,000 and over, however, a majority reported that the agreement is available on the website.

The fact that the employment agreements are typically approved in a public session and are available to the public upon request reflects the value of transparency to the public.

Severance Benefits

Because CAOs serve at the pleasure of elected officials, their positions can be more vulnerable to political shifts than those of other professions. To financially buffer CAOs from the consequences of suddenly finding themselves without a job, severance benefits are particularly important. Overall, 78% of respondents reported that they are eligible to receive severance pay (Figure 9–9).

Among those who have an employment agreement, 85% reported that the severance pay is specified in their contracts (not shown). For the majority of respondents (56%) and for all population groups except the very smallest, the amount of severance pay reported is up to six months (Figure 9–10), although the ICMA model employment agreement recommends one year.

Summary

In summary, the following findings reflect the current situation:

- Base salaries are generally correlated to the size of the local government, but variations are extremely

Figure 9-8 Benefits Calculated in the Same Manner as for Other Employees

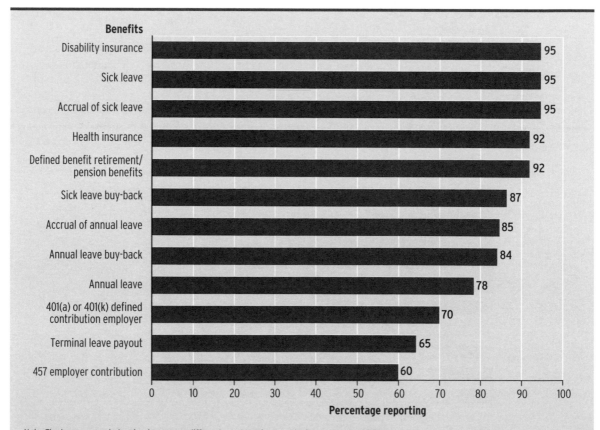

Note: The bases are not showing because a different number of respondents answered each item.

Figure 9-9 Eligible for Severance Pay

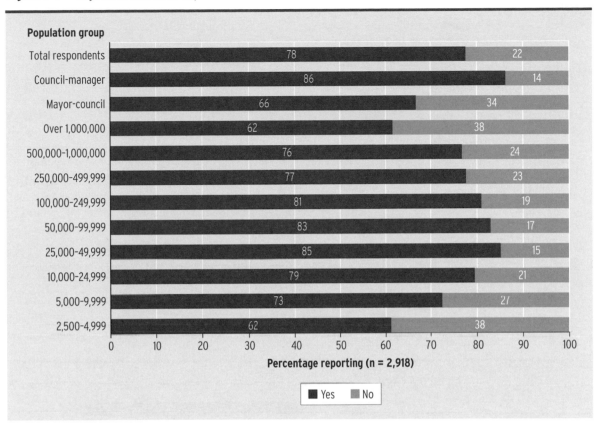

Population group

	Yes	No
Total respondents	78	22
Council-manager	86	14
Mayor-council	66	34
Over 1,000,000	62	38
500,000–1,000,000	76	24
250,000–499,999	77	23
100,000–249,999	81	19
50,000–99,999	83	17
25,000–49,999	85	15
10,000–24,999	79	21
5,000–9,999	73	27
2,500–4,999	62	38

Percentage reporting (n = 2,918)

■ Yes ■ No

Figure 9-10 Amount of Severance Pay for CAOs Eligible to Receive It

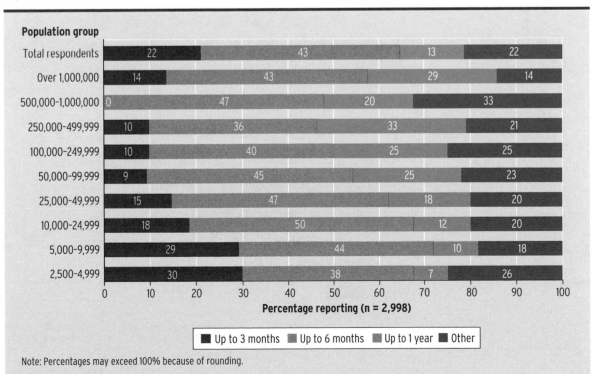

Population group

	Up to 3 months	Up to 6 months	Up to 1 year	Other
Total respondents	22	43	13	22
Over 1,000,000	14	43	29	14
500,000–1,000,000	0	47	20	33
250,000–499,999	10	36	33	21
100,000–249,999	10	40	25	25
50,000–99,999	9	45	25	23
25,000–49,999	15	47	18	20
10,000–24,999	18	50	12	20
5,000–9,999	29	44	10	18
2,500–4,999	30	38	7	26

Percentage reporting (n = 2,998)

■ Up to 3 months ■ Up to 6 months ■ Up to 1 year ■ Other

Note: Percentages may exceed 100% because of rounding.

broad, distorting the value of a calculated mean or average.

- The CAO base salary is documented, the total compensation package is available to all members of the governing body, and, in a majority of jurisdictions with populations of 50,000 or more, the base salary is posted on the local government's website.
- Most CAOs receive an annual salary review and an annual performance review.
- Most CAOs receive a car allowance.
- Typical benefit packages for CAOs, usually calculated for the CAO in the same manner as for other local government employees, include the following:
  - Health insurance
  - Disability insurance
  - Annual leave
  - Sick leave
  - Accrual of annual leave
  - Accrual of sick leave
  - Annual leave buy-back
  - Sick leave buy-back
  - Terminal leave payout
  - Defined benefit retirement/pension benefits
  - 401(a) or 401(k) defined contribution employer retirement contribution
  - 457 employer retirement contribution.
- CAOs have employment agreements or contracts that have been approved in a public session and are made available to the public upon request.
- CAOs are eligible to receive severance pay, which is specified in the employment agreement and, most commonly, amounts to either six months or one year of pay.

In addition to the prevalent practices, the survey revealed that a number of CAOs in larger jurisdictions have taken pay reductions and furlough days since December 2007.

Figure 9-11 Norms for Compensation Packages across Local Governments

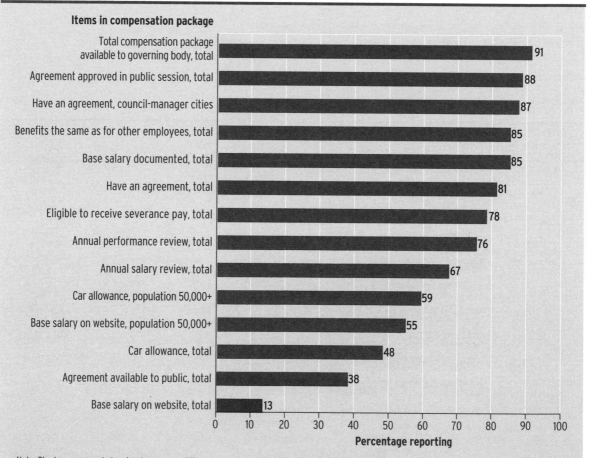

Note: The bases are not showing because a different number of respondents answered each item.

General Compensation Guidelines for all Employees

1. Each local government should establish benchmark agencies which are determined using set criteria, such as, but not limited to
   - Close geographic proximity
   - Similarity with regard to the nature of the services provided
   - Similarity in employer size/population size
   - Similarity in the socio-economic makeup of the population
   - Other similar employers in the immediate area

2. The local government should develop appropriate compensation levels that are in line with their labor market. Doing so will enable the organization to establish and maintain a reputation as a competitive, fair, and equitable employer as well as a good steward of public funds.

3. When considering any salary or benefit changes, the immediate and anticipated long-term financial resources of the organization always should be taken into account.

4. Appropriate financial practices should be followed to both disclose and properly fund any related future liability to the local government.

Source: "ICMA Guidelines for Compensation" (2010), 3, icma.org/ Documents/Document/Document/302085.

Results of the *2012 ICMA Compensation Survey for Local Government Chief Appointed Officials* serve several purposes. Survey data demonstrate the impossibility of establishing actual salary benchmarks outside of a specific market; however, survey data do establish the norms for compensation practices across local governments (see, e.g., Figure 9–11).

There will always be variations based on characteristics of the local government, its financial condition, its service provisions, and the characteristics of the CAO, such as tenure, experience, and education. Nonetheless, with data on what the majority of respondents report, norms can be established, providing a framework for elected officials in determining compensation packages in conjunction with the "General Compensation Guidelines for all Employees" (see the accompanying sidebar).

Notes

1 "ICMA Guidelines for Compensation" (2010), 1, icma .org/Documents/Document/Document/302085.

2 Ibid.

3 Ron Carlee, Martha Perego, and Evelina Moulder, "CAO Salary and Compensation: The Big Picture," in *The Municipal Year Book 2012* (Washington, D.C.: ICMA Press, 2012), 66.

4 Larry Conley, "City Manager Takes Pay Cut to Give Other Execs Raises," *American City and County*, December 7, 2012, americancityandcounty.com/finance/city-manager-takes-pay-cut-give-other-execs-raises (accessed January 16, 2013); Sally Ho, "Tigard City Manager to Take $10,000 Pay Cut," *Oregon Live*, June 5, 2012, oregonlive .com/tigard/index.ssf/2012/06/tigard_city_manager_ to_take_10.html. (accessed January 16, 2013).

Appendix Table 9–A1 City Salaries by Population Group within States

State	No. reporting	Annual base salary			
		Minimum ($)	Mean ($)	Median ($)	Maximum ($)
Alabama					
Total	20	38,000	105,465	108,000	168,000
250,000-499,999	1	130,000	130,000	130,000	130,000
100,000-249,999	1	152,000	152,000	152,000	152,000
50,000-99,999	4	64,000	121,750	129,000	165,000
25,000-49,999	3	40,000	112,333	129,000	168,000
10,000-24,999	6	79,500	112,199	108,000	147,692
5,000-9,999	2	66,186	104,398	104,398	142,610
2,500-4,999	1	43,316	43,316	43,316	43,316
Under 2,500	2	38,000	39,000	39,000	40,000
Alaska					
Total	14	95,600	120,798	120,000	165,000
250,000-499,999	1	119,891	119,891	119,891	119,891
50,000-99,999	1	165,000	165,000	165,000	165,000
10,000-24,999	1	123,000	123,000	123,000	123,000
5,000-9,999	3	109,000	128,000	120,000	155,000
2,500-4,999	5	97,000	115,800	120,000	132,000
Under 2,500	3	95,600	99,744	99,744	103,887
Arizona					
Total	46	45,000	133,221	130,025	227,198
Over 1,000,000	1	227,198	227,198	227,198	227,198
500,000-1,000,000	1	200,000	200,000	200,000	200,000
250,000-499,999	1	200,000	200,000	200,000	200,000
100,000-249,999	7	148,025	167,346	170,000	184,500
50,000-99,999	3	113,000	146,333	147,500	178,500
25,000-49,999	10	120,000	146,825	146,862	165,000
10,000-24,999	8	76,000	131,613	127,500	181,404
5,000-9,999	7	55,055	97,484	98,000	130,050
2,500-4,999	6	70,000	90,167	90,000	115,000
Under 2,500	2	45,000	73,000	73,000	101,000
Arkansas					
Total	5	26,647	83,814	81,793	149,500
50,000-99,999	1	149,500	149,500	149,500	149,500
10,000-24,999	3	50,000	80,975	81,793	111,132
5,000-9,999	1	26,647	26,647	26,647	26,647

| State | No. reporting | Annual base salary | | | |
		Minimum ($)	Mean ($)	Median ($)	Maximum ($)
California					
Total	211	49,000	182,934	190,000	338,458
Over 1,000,000	4	243,000	287,615	284,500	338,458
500,000-1,000,000	1	250,224	250,224	250,224	250,224
250,000-499,999	8	162,000	225,439	235,075	273,000
100,000-249,999	24	168,996	225,280	225,400	270,000
50,000-99,999	41	142,500	202,167	198,912	300,000
25,000-49,999	48	146,000	198,942	199,500	280,000
10,000-24,999	47	100,000	157,901	160,000	214,000
5,000-9,999	20	80,000	132,112	126,000	221,000
2,500-4,999	11	49,000	110,023	86,800	207,386
Under 2,500	7	82,000	128,575	100,700	189,000
Colorado					
Total	83	43,300	116,144	110,000	213,358
500,000-1,000,000	1	150,000	150,000	150,000	150,000
250,000-499,999	3	160,586	169,195	162,000	185,000
100,000-249,999	6	125,000	184,593	198,208	213,358
50,000-99,999	3	150,000	170,250	165,750	195,000
25,000-49,999	4	126,000	149,913	152,100	169,450
10,000-24,999	14	83,000	128,383	129,584	171,438
5,000-9,999	17	55,400	109,863	110,595	150,000
2,500-4,999	7	57,387	104,557	97,575	151,640
Under 2,500	28	43,300	84,030	79,000	142,800
Connecticut					
Total	24	65,668	121,044	125,000	155,000
100,000-249,999	1	111,733	111,733	111,733	111,733
50,000-99,999	1	155,000	155,000	155,000	155,000
25,000-49,999	11	70,000	127,326	130,000	154,175
10,000-24,999	8	84,589	126,846	130,000	152,543
5,000-9,999	1	78,412	78,412	78,412	78,412
2,500-4,999	2	65,668	75,179	75,179	84,689
Delaware					
Total	12	51,500	79,411	73,200	132,031
10,000-24,999	1	107,000	107,000	107,000	107,000
5,000-9,999	2	92,855	112,443	112,443	132,031
2,500-4,999	3	60,500	72,247	63,240	93,000
Under 2,500	6	51,500	67,383	70,700	82,400
Florida					
Total	163	31,072	131,156	130,957	290,000
Over 1,000,000	2	195,000	242,500	242,500	290,000
500,000-1,000,000	4	170,000	189,875	182,250	225,000
250,000-499,999	9	153,985	173,968	175,000	190,000
100,000-249,999	13	122,000	166,021	161,085	212,909
50,000-99,999	24	32,500	158,527	158,000	237,395
25,000-49,999	16	100,027	142,793	141,000	180,375
10,000-24,999	37	96,533	132,293	132,600	185,000
5,000-9,999	20	70,000	107,312	105,047	180,000
2,500-4,999	19	65,000	91,138	88,000	125,000
Under 2,500	19	31,072	74,459	73,625	116,500

State	No. reporting	Annual base salary			
		Minimum ($)	Mean ($)	Median ($)	Maximum ($)
Georgia					
Total	92	48,000	105,877	102,956	239,731
500,000-1,000,000	2	228,000	233,866	233,866	239,731
100,000-249,999	6	95,000	134,819	140,456	153,000
50,000-99,999	11	83,000	126,954	130,500	181,578
25,000-49,999	13	51,000	114,077	117,000	162,000
10,000-24,999	26	53,000	107,569	109,500	154,500
5,000-9,999	13	72,000	91,547	89,500	115,000
2,500-4,999	17	56,650	4,746	69,680	107,000
Under 2,500	4	48,000	62,600	60,500	81,400
Hawaii					
Total	1	126,732	126,732	126,732	126,732
250,000-499,999	1	126,732	126,732	126,732	126,732
Idaho					
Total	7	78,000	99,301	97,723	120,000
25,000-49,999	2	120,000	120,000	120,000	120,000
10,000-24,999	3	90,000	100,391	100,391	110,781
5,000-9,999	1	78,000	78,000	78,000	78,000
2,500-4,999	1	97,723	97,723	97,723	97,723
Illinois					
Total	130	53,550	125,994	121,183	231,817
500,000-1,000,000	1	228,062	228,062	228,062	228,062
100,000-249,999	5	105,000	126,306	121,000	166,260
50,000-99,999	14	54,632	153,725	175,802	231,817
25,000-49,999	26	76,916	150,263	154,000	225,000
10,000-24,999	36	78,937	126,832	118,000	217,000
5,000-9,999	24	65,000	118,220	113,654	192,800
2,500-4,999	18	54,300	85,353	75,850	136,500
Under 2,500	6	53,550	86,846	68,762	184,000
Indiana					
Total	14	47,500	70,660	69,610	120,967
50,000-99,999	3	47,500	57,060	50,495	73,184
10,000-24,999	4	73,000	92,335	87,687	120,967
5,000-9,999	3	55,000	66,833	66,000	79,500
2,500-4,999	3	59,000	66,073	67,219	72,000
Under 2,500	1	50,000	50,000	50,000	50,000
Iowa					
Total	86	25,264	94,908	87,243	231,750
100,000-249,999	2	204,617	218,184	218,184	231,750
50,000-99,999	4	155,000	182,213	172,333	229,188
25,000-49,999	8	88,382	134,309	132,572	170,000
10,000-24,999	13	25,264	105,303	110,150	156,510
5,000-9,999	25	62,500	92,869	91,600	120,959
2,500-4,999	18	56,000	75,124	70,750	117,000
Under 2,500	16	42,307	56,269	53,675	77,250

State	No. reporting	Annual base salary			
		Minimum ($)	Mean ($)	Median ($)	Maximum ($)
Kansas					
Total	75	38,600	94,066	87,986	190,409
500,000–1,000,000	1	190,409	190,409	190,409	190,409
250,000–499,999	1	178,000	178,000	178,000	178,000
100,000–249,999	2	175,000	175,000	175,000	175,000
50,000–99,999	3	119,724	125,128	125,661	130,000
25,000–49,999	10	88,272	111,932	110,297	133,300
10,000–24,999	11	85,000	108,263	110,000	133,000
5,000–9,999	13	76,080	94,479	93,000	127,000
2,500–4,999	18	49,700	80,356	80,033	115,000
Under 2,500	16	38,600	63,575	65,000	83,000
Kentucky					
Total	17	38,500	90,342	86,000	138,500
100,000–249,999	1	132,328	132,328	132,328	132,328
50,000–99,999	1	134,888	134,888	134,888	134,888
25,000–49,999	3	46,000	87,967	79,400	138,500
10,000–24,999	6	38,500	91,709	99,880	120,000
5,000–9,999	2	70,000	78,000	78,000	86,000
2,500–4,999	3	69,000	77,813	77,440	87,000
Under 2,500	1	65,000	65,000	65,000	65,000
Louisiana					
Total	5	108,000	120,993	116,542	150,000
100,000–249,999	4	108,000	120,886	112,771	150,000
50,000–99,999	1	121,422	121,422	121,422	121,422
Maine					
Total	83	32,000	70,514	66,000	123,050
250,000–499,999	1	105,165	105,165	105,165	105,165
25,000–49,999	4	55,500	77,790	69,250	117,160
10,000–24,999	8	82,000	101,006	103,543	110,038
5,000–9,999	19	58,000	80,884	78,000	123,050
2,500–4,999	23	44,500	64,884	63,000	102,000
Under 2,500	28	32,000	54,879	51,122	102,564
Maryland					
Total	35	41,600	105,445	100,000	202,944
100,000–249,999	5	114,735	138,107	131,000	180,000
50,000–99,999	3	105,000	150,981	145,000	202,944
25,000–49,999	4	95,599	118,100	115,000	146,800
10,000–24,999	4	84,157	113,814	114,000	143,100
5,000–9,999	6	72,500	93,128	86,656	126,485
2,500–4,999	8	63,000	79,897	80,000	100,000
Under 2,500	5	41,600	69,543	73,104	90,364

State	No. reporting	Annual base salary			
		Minimum ($)	Mean ($)	Median ($)	Maximum ($)
Massachusetts					
Total	71	38,470	121,775	125,000	169,000
100,000-249,999	1	150,000	150,000	150,000	150,000
25,000-49,999	7	140,400	153,423	150,000	169,000
10,000-24,999	37	65,000	128,717	131,000	168,000
5,000-9,999	20	76,168	107,027	109,000	153,000
2,500-4,999	4	52,612	95,526	108,746	112,000
Under 2,500	2	38,470	46,339	46,339	54,208
Michigan					
Total	153	28,080	85,969	83,595	178,113
Over 1,000,000	1	94,136	94,136	94,136	94,136
500,000-1,000,000	1	178,113	178,113	178,113	178,113
100,000-249,999	6	107,978	131,129	137,404	145,000
50,000-99,999	9	82,400	115,830	130,000	152,000
25,000-49,999	15	63,607	98,405	96,400	129,532
10,000-24,999	25	54,500	97,470	94,780	125,000
5,000-9,999	24	74,000	96,178	90,750	155,000
2,500-4,999	38	31,200	74,265	72,500	111,000
Under 2,500	34	28,080	58,904	60,000	78,000
Minnesota					
Total	130	40,000	102,843	100,155	167,000
Over 1,000,000	1	166,000	166,000	166,000	166,000
250,000-499,999	1	162,211	162,211	162,211	162,211
100,000-249,999	3	152,000	160,404	162,211	167,000
50,000-99,999	12	102,000	135,455	138,421	155,779
25,000-49,999	21	90,000	117,572	122,700	152,000
10,000-24,999	30	69,089	108,205	112,050	130,000
5,000-9,999	19	88,000	97,904	97,055	110,729
2,500-4,999	26	60,401	86,992	89,587	110,000
Under 2,500	17	40,000	63,362	62,395	80,545
Mississippi					
Total	11	38,733	94,316	92,000	136,154
100,000-249,999	2	100,000	106,000	106,000	112,000
50,000-99,999	1	86,785	86,785	86,785	86,785
25,000-49,999	3	79,500	97,543	83,130	130,000
10,000-24,999	4	38,733	88,514	89,585	136,154
5,000-9,999	1	92,000	92,000	92,000	92,000
Missouri					
Total	85	30,742	92,528	88,058	195,312
250,000-499,999	1	187,200	187,200	187,200	187,200
100,000-249,999	3	97,500	147,604	150,000	195,312
50,000-99,999	4	124,900	142,975	138,500	170,000
25,000-49,999	6	110,000	136,546	136,000	165,276
10,000-24,999	21	67,500	102,722	97,968	150,000
5,000-9,999	26	36,000	82,712	78,110	145,948
2,500-4,999	15	30,742	69,603	70,500	100,000
Under 2,500	9	41,000	54,379	50,000	74,000

State	No. reporting	Annual base salary			
		Minimum ($)	Mean ($)	Median ($)	Maximum ($)
Montana					
Total	11	69,500	96,892	103,081	117,630
50,000-99,999	4	95,000	104,698	103,081	117,630
25,000-49,999	1	116,136	116,136	116,136	116,136
10,000-24,999	1	105,000	105,000	105,000	105,000
5,000-9,999	4	69,525	86,498	79,969	110,000
2,500-4,999	1	69,500	69,500	69,500	69,500
Nebraska					
Total	35	34,000	85,810	85,790	129,409
250,000-499,999	1	129,409	129,409	129,409	129,409
100,000-249,999	1	119,350	119,350	119,350	119,350
50,000-99,999	1	122,500	122,500	122,500	122,500
25,000-49,999	2	106,000	111,425	111,425	116,850
10,000-24,999	7	100,000	116,373	120,000	128,710
5,000-9,999	5	74,090	88,517	92,881	97,000
2,500-4,999	6	54,080	81,228	82,550	101,500
Under 2,500	12	34,000	55,391	54,091	85,790
Nevada					
Total	10	117,416	172,195	182,469	225,000
Over 1,000,000	1	205,000	205,000	205,000	205,000
250,000-499,999	2	184,938	204,969	204,969	225,000
100,000-249,999	2	180,000	189,000	189,000	198,000
50,000-99,999	2	138,592	161,796	161,796	185,000
25,000-49,999	1	117,416	117,416	117,416	117,416
10,000-24,999	1	156,000	156,000	156,000	156,000
5,000-9,999	1	132,000	132,000	132,000	132,000
New Hampshire					
Total	39	48,577	88,452	86,250	143,168
50,000-99,999	2	100,152	101,576	101,576	103,000
25,000-49,999	1	143,168	143,168	143,168	143,168
10,000-24,999	10	93,730	114,245	115,500	132,000
5,000-9,999	12	63,500	82,007	80,500	112,200
2,500-4,999	9	50,000	69,575	69,000	86,500
Under 2,500	5	48,577	66,343	70,000	88,140
New Jersey					
Total	61	35,096	129,759	129,009	199,500
250,000-499,999	3	145,000	177,021	190,000	196,064
100,000-249,999	2	135,000	152,502	152,502	170,004
50,000-99,999	4	124,000	174,708	187,666	199,500
25,000-49,999	9	84,750	133,822	127,000	168,000
10,000-24,999	23	90,000	133,374	139,500	184,449
5,000-9,999	14	35,096	102,916	111,046	155,037
2,500-4,999	4	41,221	106,055	117,500	148,000
Under 2,500	2	105,328	113,664	113,664	122,000

State	No. reporting	Annual base salary			
		Minimum ($)	Mean ($)	Median ($)	Maximum ($)
New Mexico					
Total	23	52,000	101,674	95,428	163,000
500,000-1,000,000	2	145,600	146,800	146,800	148,000
100,000-249,999	1	155,000	155,000	155,000	155,000
50,000-99,999	2	130,000	146,500	146,500	163,000
25,000-49,999	3	110,598	115,666	114,000	122,401
10,000-24,999	7	56,343	85,404	91,000	108,331
5,000-9,999	5	70,000	83,080	75,400	100,000
2,500-4,999	1	52,000	52,000	52,000	52,000
Under 2,500	2	83,000	83,000	83,000	83,000
New York					
Total	34	49,000	119,274	112,000	192,207
100,000-249,999	2	114,000	121,239	121,239	128,477
50,000-99,999	7	96,306	121,323	120,000	182,158
25,000-49,999	6	86,592	126,040	115,300	174,450
10,000-24,999	5	99,358	137,510	112,000	192,207
5,000-9,999	7	77,845	127,535	155,000	174,500
2,500-4,999	6	49,000	90,340	3,040	153,400
Under 2,500	1	84,991	84,991	84,991	84,991
North Carolina					
Total	136	42,800	106,260	93,165	242,633
500,000-1,000,000	1	229,000	229,000	229,000	229,000
250,000-499,999	4	160,000	180,800	183,100	197,000
100,000-249,999	15	129,995	172,375	167,980	242,633
50,000-99,999	11	92,000	119,325	115,008	171,934
25,000-49,999	15	92,000	127,811	120,748	159,362
10,000-24,999	23	64,728	110,770	115,500	145,000
5,000-9,999	18	68,000	87,573	90,500	108,000
2,500-4,999	22	42,800	74,365	76,146	141,110
Under 2,500	27	43,775	70,123	65,000	112,438
North Dakota					
Total	4	76,560	112,640	110,500	153,000
100,000-249,999	1	153,000	153,000	153,000	153,000
25,000-49,999	1	115,000	115,000	115,000	115,000
10,000-24,999	1	106,000	106,000	106,000	106,000
5,000-9,999	1	76,560	76,560	76,560	76,560
Ohio					
Total	107	40,394	99,831	98,800	232,000
Over 1,000,000	1	156,500	156,500	156,500	156,500
500,000-1,000,000	1	175,000	175,000	175,000	175,000
250,000-499,999	1	232,000	232,000	232,000	232,000
100,000-249,999	3	95,000	108,000	114,000	115,000
50,000-99,999	8	60,000	119,424	124,453	160,000
25,000-49,999	17	55,000	105,531	111,811	180,000
10,000-24,999	27	51,000	104,562	109,000	140,400
5,000-9,999	30	57,500	95,198	93,226	146,642
2,500-4,999	15	56,000	77,352	75,096	108,325
Under 2,500	4	40,394	47,224	48,500	51,500

State	No. reporting	Annual base salary			
		Minimum ($)	Mean ($)	Median ($)	Maximum ($)
Oklahoma					
Total	42	30,900	93,146	89,000	215,184
500,000-1,000,000	1	215,184	215,184	215,184	215,184
50,000-99,999	2	147,725	148,863	148,863	150,000
25,000-49,999	4	112,000	122,501	124,001	130,000
10,000-24,999	10	103,750	114,621	113,000	126,000
5,000-9,999	9	78,000	90,822	85,000	115,000
2,500-4,999	11	51,000	66,667	62,750	92,500
Under 2,500	5	30,900	50,043	50,399	61,772
Oregon					
Total	115	26,000	94,114	93,592	205,000
250,000-499,999	3	147,900	156,098	154,000	166,394
100,000-249,999	3	139,056	168,352	161,000	205,000
50,000-99,999	7	128,000	142,978	143,555	154,548
25,000-49,999	7	70,404	122,999	126,000	164,000
10,000-24,999	20	96,132	120,239	120,612	137,000
5,000-9,999	20	72,000	94,418	95,000	112,787
2,500-4,999	14	61,200	78,197	76,812	99,000
Under 2,500	41	26,000	58,365	57,250	133,450
Pennsylvania					
Total	155	39,000	87,212	85,848	202,989
500,000-1,000,000	1	137,700	137,700	137,700	137,700
250,000-499,999	2	74,500	98,930	98,930	123,360
100,000-249,999	1	95,000	95,000	95,000	95,000
50,000-99,999	3	56,750	113,080	79,500	202,989
25,000-49,999	14	59,000	108,824	100,054	182,000
10,000-24,999	53	58,000	101,667	100,000	152,980
5,000-9,999	42	42,000	74,390	71,606	134,900
2,500-4,999	29	39,000	70,541	69,253	97,000
Under 2,500	10	43,500	63,757	60,220	93,158
Rhode Island					
Total	8	100,940	120,680	123,088	156,847
25,000-49,999	4	106,900	127,687	123,500	156,847
10,000-24,999	3	100,940	117,038	124,175	126,000
5,000-9,999	1	103,580	103,580	103,580	103,580
South Carolina					
Total	38	55,500	101,882	97,750	169,220
250,000-499,999	1	167,000	167,000	167,000	167,000
100,000-249,999	4	98,500	132,821	131,783	169,220
50,000-99,999	4	89,500	106,375	106,000	124,000
25,000-49,999	4	68,000	117,095	117,689	165,000
10,000-24,999	11	73,000	102,351	105,705	128,650
5,000-9,999	7	78,000	87,561	82,000	105,000
2,500-4,999	5	55,500	72,103	68,000	90,000
Under 2,500	2	83,060	90,030	90,030	97,000

State	No. reporting	Annual base salary			
		Minimum ($)	Mean ($)	Median ($)	Maximum ($)
South Dakota					
Total	12	56,250	81,498	72,500	128,466
25,000-49,999	1	128,466	128,466	128,466	128,466
10,000-24,999	3	69,755	99,910	103,920	126,054
5,000-9,999	1	85,000	85,000	85,000	85,000
2,500-4,999	2	60,000	66,500	66,500	73,000
Under 2,500	5	56,250	66,357	64,245	79,290
Tennessee					
Total	38	31,000	100,803	98,461	175,000
500,000-1,000,000	1	135,000	135,000	135,000	135,000
100,000-249,999	1	144,900	144,900	144,900	144,900
50,000-99,999	2	108,165	116,610	116,610	125,054
25,000-49,999	7	106,500	139,915	132,000	175,000
10,000-24,999	9	68,800	96,412	98,461	125,000
5,000-9,999	9	56,500	90,232	87,000	131,193
2,500-4,999	4	46,500	74,922	81,111	97,155
Under 2,500	5	31,000	43,667	49,000	51,000
Texas					
Total	178	30,000	121,751	116,880	355,000
Over 1,000,000	2	222,707	288,854	288,854	355,000
500,000-1,000,000	2	212,409	225,684	225,684	238,959
250,000-499,999	3	200,000	211,400	214,200	220,000
100,000-249,999	8	167,491	203,857	208,248	228,575
50,000-99,999	11	153,000	178,220	174,500	223,196
25,000-49,999	27	51,483	143,608	146,900	198,000
10,000-24,999	40	36,000	124,728	125,000	217,000
5,000-9,999	36	64,178	105,688	101,200	159,000
2,500-4,999	31	41,122	79,295	75,930	144,000
Under 2,500	18	30,000	66,912	62,500	117,009
Utah					
Total	47	45,000	102,514	101,500	141,000
100,000-249,999	4	50,000	111,588	130,675	135,000
50,000-99,999	5	125,000	132,625	132,250	141,000
25,000-49,999	9	103,000	122,690	124,335	138,800
10,000-24,999	11	97,500	106,062	102,500	127,504
5,000-9,999	12	45,000	84,672	86,112	110,316
2,500-4,999	1	70,000	70,000	70,000	70,000
Under 2,500	5	48,432	71,306	74,600	87,593
Vermont					
Total	20	55,000	80,943	81,775	117,500
10,000-24,999	4	89,519	99,881	96,254	117,500
5,000-9,999	7	65,000	86,355	89,900	100,020
2,500-4,999	6	55,000	68,697	70,591	76,000
Under 2,500	3	56,000	67,558	58,275	88,400

State	No. reporting	Annual base salary			
		Minimum ($)	Mean ($)	Median ($)	Maximum ($)
Virginia					
Total	92	41,000	125,685	125,000	368,282
Over 1,000,000	1	368,282	368,282	368,282	368,282
250,000-499,999	4	206,000	230,435	224,190	267,361
100,000-249,999	5	157,000	200,969	200,938	245,000
50,000-99,999	11	126,000	161,761	162,000	220,000
25,000-49,999	19	88,788	131,444	126,126	170,000
10,000-24,999	21	73,060	126,389	125,000	186,805
5,000-9,999	10	75,236	94,436	90,962	145,000
2,500-4,999	11	43,000	72,518	70,500	105,170
Under 2,500	10	41,000	67,612	71,084	85,238
Washington					
Total	55	73,020	124,513	125,820	210,148
250,000-499,999	1	175,000	175,000	175,000	175,000
100,000-249,999	2	167,500	188,824	188,824	210,148
50,000-99,999	4	124,016	145,254	150,500	156,000
25,000-49,999	4	140,000	144,078	144,156	148,000
10,000-24,999	18	88,000	130,672	131,036	155,470
5,000-9,999	13	97,000	119,871	121,644	146,016
2,500-4,999	8	73,020	98,514	97,518	136,000
Under 2,500	5	78,000	90,408	88,250	110,000
West Virginia					
Total	9	48,000	85,643	90,221	137,683
100,000-249,999	1	110,000	110,000	110,000	110,000
50,000-99,999	1	137,683	137,683	137,683	137,683
25,000-49,999	1	58,381	58,381	58,381	58,381
10,000-24,999	1	90,221	90,221	90,221	90,221
5,000-9,999	2	82,500	90,250	90,250	98,000
2,500-4,999	3	48,000	64,667	50,000	96,000
Wisconsin					
Total	105	36,500	88,449	85,225	165,000
100,000-249,999	2	117,456	141,228	141,228	165,000
50,000-99,999	5	98,000	116,611	120,000	135,000
25,000-49,999	10	92,742	108,133	105,000	130,370
10,000-24,999	21	81,973	102,407	101,000	122,500
5,000-9,999	29	68,000	84,324	84,316	107,584
2,500-4,999	22	36,500	73,392	75,250	85,700
Under 2,500	16	52,000	69,455	66,500	101,000
Wyoming					
Total	7	95,000	122,393	115,000	170,000
50,000-99,999	1	170,000	170,000	170,000	170,000
25,000-49,999	1	132,000	132,000	132,000	132,000
10,000-24,999	3	95,000	107,333	112,000	115,000
5,000-9,999	2	95,950	116,375	116,375	136,800

Appendix Table 9-A2 County Salaries by Population Group within States

State	No. reporting	Annual base salary			
		Minimum ($)	Mean ($)	Median ($)	Maximum ($)
Alabama					
Total	7	40,000	98,643	95,000	152,000
250,000-499,999	1	130,000	130,000	130,000	130,000
100,000-249,999	1	152,000	152,000	152,000	152,000
50,000-99,999	2	64,000	79,500	79,500	95,000
25,000-49,999	1	40,000	40,000	40,000	40,000
10,000-24,999	2	79,500	104,750	104,750	130,000
Alaska					
Total	2	123,000	144,000	144,000	165,000
50,000-99,999	1	165,000	165,000	165,000	165,000
10,000-24,999	1	123,000	123,000	123,000	123,000
Arizona					
Total	7	55,055	138,968	148,025	227,198
Over 1,000,000	1	227,198	227,198	227,198	227,198
100,000-249,999	3	148,025	152,508	149,500	160,000
50,000-99,999	1	113,000	113,000	113,000	113,000
25,000-49,999	1	120,000	120,000	120,000	120,000
5,000-9,999	1	55,055	55,055	55,055	55,055
California					
Total	16	103,000	199,420	172,000	338,458
Over 1,000,000	3	243,000	295,486	305,000	338,458
500,000-1,000,000	1	250,224	250,224	250,224	250,224
250,000-499,999	4	162,000	210,692	235,000	235,075
100,000-249,999	2	168,996	195,148	195,148	221,300
50,000-99,999	2	142,500	146,250	146,250	149,999
25,000-49,999	1	146,000	146,000	146,000	146,000
10,000-24,999	3	103,000	131,249	118,746	172,000
Colorado					
Total	14	55,400	111,568	112,500	162,000
500,000-1,000,000	1	150,000	150,000	150,000	150,000
250,000-499,999	2	160,586	161,293	161,293	162,000
100,000-249,999	1	125,000	125,000	125,000	125,000
50,000-99,999	1	150,000	150,000	150,000	150,000
10,000-24,999	4	83,000	100,395	93,457	131,668
5,000-9,999	4	55,400	88,850	90,000	120,000
2,500-4,999	1	57,387	57,387	57,387	57,387
Florida					
Total	28	32,500	156,481	161,000	290,000
Over 1,000,000	2	195,000	242,500	242,500	290,000
500,000-1,000,000	4	170,000	189,875	182,250	225,000
250,000-499,999	9	153,985	173,968	175,000	190,000
100,000-249,999	5	122,000	140,728	140,000	170,000
50,000-99,999	5	32,500	112,209	125,000	142,043
25,000-49,999	2	100,027	105,014	105,014	110,000
10,000-24,999	1	96,533	96,533	96,533	96,533

| State | No. reporting | Annual base salary | | | |
		Minimum ($)	Mean ($)	Median ($)	Maximum ($)
Georgia					
Total	25	51,000	110,637	99,835	239,731
500,000-1,000,000	2	228,000	233,866	233,866	239,731
100,000-249,999	4	95,000	130,000	137,500	150,000
50,000-99,999	7	83,000	114,378	106,000	140,000
25,000-49,999	5	51,000	90,509	92,951	123,400
10,000-24,999	7	53,000	75,000	75,000	95,000
Illinois					
Total	10	54,632	103,923	92,000	228,062
500,000-1,000,000	1	228,062	228,062	228,062	228,062
100,000-249,999	3	105,000	114,756	110,518	128,750
50,000-99,999	3	54,632	77,349	71,750	105,664
25,000-49,999	2	76,916	77,958	77,958	79,000
10,000-24,999	1	78,937	78,937	78,937	78,937
Indiana					
Total	3	47,500	57,060	50,495	73,184
50,000-99,999	3	47,500	57,060	50,495	73,184
Iowa					
Total	3	25,264	54,549	50,000	88,382
25,000-49,999	1	88,382	88,382	88,382	88,382
10,000-24,999	2	25,264	37,632	37,632	50,000
Kansas					
Total	10	76,080	117,431	107,100	190,409
500,000-1,000,000	1	190,409	190,409	190,409	190,409
250,000-499,999	1	178,000	178,000	178,000	178,000
50,000-99,999	1	119,724	119,724	119,724	119,724
25,000-49,999	6	88,272	98,534	97,000	110,297
5,000-9,999	1	76,080	76,080	76,080	76,080
Kentucky					
Total	3	38,500	72,276	46,000	132,328
100,000-249,999	1	132,328	132,328	132,328	132,328
25,000-49,999	1	46,000	46,000	46,000	46,000
10,000-24,999	1	38,500	38,500	38,500	38,500
Louisiana					
Total	4	108,000	122,105	115,211	150,000
100,000-249,999	3	108,000	122,333	109,000	150,000
50,000-99,999	1	121,422	121,422	121,422	121,422
Maine					
Total	4	55,500	74,791	69,250	105,165
250,000-499,999	1	105,165	105,165	105,165	105,165
25,000-49,999	3	55,500	64,667	65,500	73,000
Maryland					
Total	9	100,000	130,059	130,000	180,000
100,000-249,999	5	114,735	138,107	131,000	180,000
50,000-99,999	2	105,000	125,000	125,000	145,000
25,000-49,999	2	100,000	115,000	115,000	130,000

| State | No. reporting | Annual base salary | | | |
		Minimum ($)	Mean ($)	Median ($)	Maximum ($)
Michigan					
Total	18	54,500	95,204	86,750	178,113
Over 1,000,000	1	94,136	94,136	94,136	94,136
500,000-1,000,000	1	178,113	178,113	178,113	178,113
100,000-249,999	3	107,978	120,156	115,000	137,491
50,000-99,999	4	82,400	88,617	87,755	96,560
25,000-49,999	7	63,607	83,260	83,800	100,473
10,000-24,999	2	54,500	65,860	65,860	77,220
Minnesota					
Total	22	60,401	110,358	100,750	167,000
Over 1,000,000	1	166,000	166,000	166,000	166,000
250,000-499,999	1	162,211	162,211	162,211	162,211
100,000-249,999	2	152,000	159,500	159,500	167,000
50,000-99,999	4	102,000	120,413	120,025	139,600
25,000-49,999	8	90,000	104,388	99,363	124,375
10,000-24,999	5	69,089	80,704	83,658	90,000
2,500-4,999	1	60,401	60,401	60,401	60,401
Mississippi					
Total	6	38,733	95,195	93,393	136,154
100,000-249,999	1	100,000	100,000	100,000	100,000
50,000-99,999	1	86,785	86,785	86,785	86,785
25,000-49,999	2	79,500	104,750	104,750	130,000
10,000-24,999	2	38,733	87,444	87,444	136,154
Missouri					
Total	2	36,000	66,750	66,750	97,500
100,000-249,999	1	97,500	97,500	97,500	97,500
5,000-9,999	1	36,000	36,000	36,000	36,000
Montana					
Total	2	95,000	100,000	100,000	105,000
50,000-99,999	2	95,000	100,000	100,000	105,000
Nebraska					
Total	2	119,350	124,380	124,380	129,409
250,000-499,999	1	129,409	129,409	129,409	129,409
100,000-249,999	1	119,350	119,350	119,350	119,350
Nevada					
Total	3	117,416	169,118	184,938	205,000
Over 1,000,000	1	205,000	205,000	205,000	205,000
250,000-499,999	1	184,938	184,938	184,938	184,938
25,000-49,999	1	117,416	117,416	117,416	117,416
New Hampshire					
Total	2	100,152	101,576	101,576	103,000
50,000-99,999	2	100,152	101,576	101,576	103,000
New Jersey					
Total	4	145,000	175,267	180,002	196,064
250,000-499,999	3	145,000	177,021	190,000	196,064
100,000-249,999	1	170,004	170,004	170,004	170,004

State	No. reporting	Annual base salary			
		Minimum ($)	Mean ($)	Median ($)	Maximum ($)
New Mexico					
Total	7	56,343	104,349	93,700	155,000
500,000-1,000,000	1	148,000	148,000	148,000	148,000
100,000-249,999	1	155,000	155,000	155,000	155,000
50,000-99,999	1	130,000	130,000	130,000	130,000
10,000-24,999	3	56,343	74,014	72,000	93,700
5,000-9,999	1	75,400	75,400	75,400	75,400
New York					
Total	10	86,592	110,077	109,300	130,000
100,000-249,999	2	114,000	121,239	121,239	128,477
50,000-99,999	6	96,306	111,184	111,500	130,000
25,000-49,999	2	86,592	95,596	95,596	104,600
North Carolina					
Total	36	64,728	134,294	127,498	242,633
500,000-1,000,000	1	229,000	229,000	229,000	229,000
250,000-499,999	4	160,000	180,800	183,100	197,000
100,000-249,999	9	129,995	167,457	162,651	242,633
50,000-99,999	10	92,000	112,749	112,504	134,100
25,000-49,999	6	92,000	108,545	112,200	120,748
10,000-24,999	5	64,728	77,093	77,974	87,696
5,000-9,999	1	85,000	85,000	85,000	85,000
Ohio					
Total	10	55,000	97,600	91,000	175,000
Over 1,000,000	1	156,500	156,500	156,500	156,500
500,000 1,000,000	1	175,000	175,000	175,000	175,000
100,000-249,999	3	95,000	108,000	114,000	115,000
50,000-99,999	2	60,000	73,500	73,500	87,000
25,000-49,999	3	55,000	57,833	57,500	61,000
Oregon					
Total	10	70,404	137,409	137,634	205,000
250,000-499,999	3	147,900	156,098	154,000	166,394
100,000-249,999	2	139,056	172,028	172,028	205,000
50,000-99,999	1	136,212	136,212	136,212	136,212
25,000-49,999	2	70,404	98,916	98,916	127,428
10,000-24,999	2	104,000	113,849	113,849	123,698
Pennsylvania					
Total	7	56,750	86,642	75,682	137,700
500,000-1,000,000	1	137,700	137,700	137,700	137,700
250,000-499,999	2	74,500	98,930	98,930	123,360
50,000-99,999	2	56,750	68,125	68,125	79,500
25,000-49,999	2	59,000	67,341	67,341	75,682
South Carolina					
Total	13	68,000	111,205	101,000	169,220
250,000-499,999	1	167,000	167,000	167,000	167,000
100,000-249,999	4	98,500	132,821	131,783	169,220
50,000-99,999	4	89,500	106,375	106,000	124,000
25,000-49,999	2	68,000	74,000	74,000	80,000
10,000-24,999	2	73,000	86,940	86,940	100,880

State	No. reporting	Annual base salary			
		Minimum ($)	Mean ($)	Median ($)	Maximum ($)
South Dakota					
Total	1	69,755	69,755	69,755	69,755
10,000-24,999	1	69,755	69,755	69,755	69,755
Tennessee					
Total	2	68,800	101,900	101,900	135,000
500,000-1,000,000	1	135,000	135,000	135,000	135,000
10,000-24,999	1	68,800	68,800	68,800	68,800
Texas					
Total	5	36,000	117,920	67,000	222,707
Over 1,000,000	1	222,707	222,707	222,707	222,707
500,000-1,000,000	1	212,409	212,409	212,409	212,409
25,000-49,999	1	51,483	51,483	51,483	51,483
10,000-24,999	2	36,000	51,500	51,500	67,000
Utah					
Total	1	134,000	134,000	134,000	134,000
25,000-49,999	1	134,000	134,000	134,000	134,000
Virginia					
Total	41	73,060	145,161	126,714	368,282
Over 1,000,000	1	368,282	368,282	368,282	368,282
250,000-499,999	3	206,000	232,063	222,829	267,361
100,000-249,999	3	157,000	186,292	161,000	240,875
50,000-99,999	9	126,000	161,941	162,000	220,000
25,000-49,999	13	88,788	121,247	125,000	165,375
10,000-24,999	10	73,060	106,717	99,163	145,000
5,000-9,999	2	82,400	113,700	113,700	145,000
Washington					
Total	3	88,000	129,005	124,016	175,000
250,000-499,999	1	175,000	175,000	175,000	175,000
50,000-99,999	1	124,016	124,016	124,016	124,016
10,000-24,999	1	88,000	88,000	88,000	88,000
West Virginia					
Total	2	58,381	84,191	84,191	110,000
100,000-249,999	1	110,000	110,000	110,000	110,000
25,000-49,999	1	58,381	58,381	58,381	58,381
Wisconsin					
Total	15	72,650	108,236	102,556	165,000
100,000-249,999	2	117,456	141,228	141,228	165,000
50,000-99,999	4	98,000	113,889	111,278	135,000
25,000-49,999	6	92,742	104,230	103,169	119,500
10,000-24,999	2	86,500	93,750	93,750	101,000
5,000-9,999	1	72,650	72,650	72,650	72,650
Wyoming					
Total	1	115,000	115,000	115,000	115,000
10,000-24,999	1	115,000	115,000	115,000	115,000

10

Police and Fire Personnel, Salaries, and Expenditures for 2012

Evelina R. Moulder
ICMA

Continuing the trend identified in 2010 when police and fire departments, like other local government departments, saw their budgets reduced, police and fire expenditures in 2012 continue to be a concern in some communities. There is hope that as the housing market continues to strengthen, property tax revenues may slowly increase. The national median existing-home price for all housing types was $183,900 in September, up 11.3% from a year ago.[1] This increase in revenue for municipal budgets may eventually bring a halt to staffing reductions, whether such reductions are due to a lack of hiring for vacant positions or to layoffs.

The statistics in this annual article are not intended to be used for benchmarking, which requires that many factors be considered to identify localities of similar characteristics, such as population density, vulnerability to natural disasters, and the like. Rather, these statistics are meant to provide a general picture of police and fire personnel and expenditures for each year.

Methodology

The data in this research were collected from responses to ICMA's annual *Police and Fire Personnel, Salaries, and Expenditures* survey, which was mailed in February 2012 to 3,310 municipalities with populations of 10,000 or more (Table 10–1). A second survey was sent to those local governments that did not respond to the first. Respondents had a choice of completing and submitting the survey on the web or by mail. A total of 1,095 jurisdictions submitted surveys for an overall response rate of 33%—which is slightly lower than last year's response rate (35%)—with a smaller percentage of municipalities under 50,000 in population responding in 2012.

The survey response patterns are presented in Table 10–1 by population group, geographic region, and geographic division. The response pattern varies by population size, with a high of 42% in cities with

SELECTED FINDINGS

The average entrance salaries are $44,996 for police and $40,689 for fire personnel. The average maximum salaries for police and fire personnel are $64,018 and $56,404, respectively.

The average maximum salary including longevity pay for police officers is $69,696; for fire personnel, it is $61,306. These salaries vary significantly by geographic division: East South-Central cities show the lowest average maximums while Mid-Atlantic and Pacific Coast cities show the highest.

Per capita average overtime expenditures were $10.48 for police and $8.22 for fire departments.

The average per capita total departmental expenditures in 2012 were $251.71 for police and $156.43 for fire departments.

Table 10-1 Survey Response

Classification	No. of municipalities[a] surveyed (A)	Respondents No.	% of (A)
Total	3,310	1,095	33
Population group			
Over 1,000,000	9	3	33
500,000-1,000,000	23	8	35
250,000-499,999	36	15	42
100,000-249,999	180	66	37
50,000-99,999	422	138	33
25,000-49,999	791	244	31
10,000-24,999	1,849	620	34
Geographic region			
Northeast	901	184	20
North-Central	933	336	36
South	847	327	39
West	629	248	39
Geographic division			
New England	352	72	21
Mid-Atlantic	549	112	20
East North-Central	685	234	34
West North-Central	249	102	41
South Atlantic	387	173	45
East South-Central	169	44	26
West South-Central	290	110	38
Mountain	163	70	43
Pacific Coast	466	178	38

a For a definition of terms, please see "Inside the *Year Book*," xi-xiv.

Cities Reporting a Public Safety Department (Consolidated Police and Fire)

Sunnyvale, CA	Maryville, MO
Eustis, FL	Sikeston, MO
Greenacres, FL	Columbus, OH
East Grand Rapids, MI	North Augusta, SC
Farmington, MI	Mitchell, SD
Grand Haven, MI	South Ogden, UT
Gross Pointe Park, MI	Ashwaubenon, WI
Holland, MI	

---

a population of 250,000–499,999. By geographic division, the pattern reveals that New England and Mid-Atlantic jurisdictions were the least likely to complete the questionnaire (both showing about 20%), while South Atlantic, Mountain, and West North-Central jurisdictions were the most likely to do so (45%, 43%, and 41%, respectively).

Administration

Respondents were asked several questions about service provision and delivery. Virtually all the jurisdictions responding to the 2012 survey (96%) indicated that they provide police services, and 84% reported that they provide fire services (not shown)—figures that have remained almost identical for several years. Fifteen jurisdictions reported having a public safety department. To be counted among these respondents, a city had to report "public safety department" as the type of service for both police and fire (see the accompanying sidebar).

These data on cities that provide police and fire services do not necessarily mean that all these cities actually deliver each service. Five percent of jurisdictions reported contracting with another government for police service delivery (Figure 10–1); the highest percentage of cities reporting this arrangement is in the Pacific Coast division (19%) (not shown). Among the 42 cities that do not provide police services, 40 answered the question about how the services *are* provided, and of those cities, a majority (24)—all of which are under 250,000 in population—reported that the county provides the service (not shown). Four cities reported a regional police service; two reported a special district.

Of the cities that provide fire protection services, a majority (67%) reported having a full-time paid or a full-time and part-time paid fire department, 16% reported a combination of paid and volunteer fire personnel, 10% reported an all-volunteer fire department, and the remaining cities said they contract out for such services or provide them in some other way (Figure 10–1). Among the 171 cities that do not provide fire services, 160 provided information on how the services *are* provided, and of those, 51% reported that the services are provided by a special district, and 30% indicated that the county provides the services (not shown). Regional fire services were reported by 11%.

Personnel

As Figure 10–2 shows, for the 316 municipalities that responded to the survey each year from 2008 to 2012, the average number of sworn police officers was comparatively high in 2009, decreasing gradually but consistently each year after that. The gradual decrease reflects the attempts of local governments to retain

Figure 10-1 Type of Service, 2012

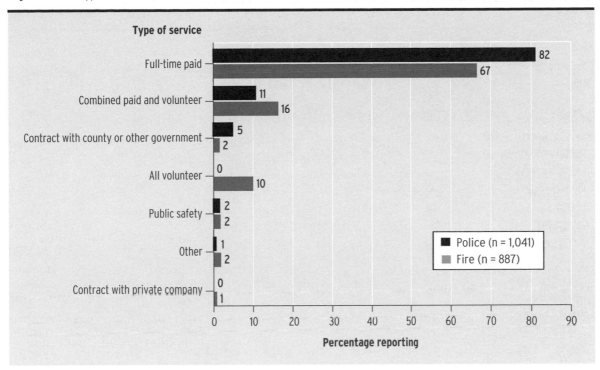

Figure 10-2 Average Numbers of Sworn Police and Firefighters, 2008-2012

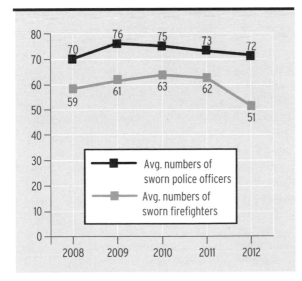

responded to each survey and provided fire personnel data from 2008 through 2012.

The average size of the full-time paid workforce for both police and fire departments in 2012 is shown in Table 10-2. The data include both uniformed and civilian, or nonuniformed, personnel. The average number of total police department employees reported, 135, represents an increase over the average number reported in 2011, which was 117. Using the average number of personnel per capita normalizes the data, however, and when the per capita per 1,000 population is calculated, the average drops slightly for police (from 2.69 in 2011 to 2.38 in 2012) even though the overall average is higher. As for fire personnel, the average number reported is 77, compared with 80 in 2011; and the average number of full-time paid personnel per capita per 1,000 population is 1.51, down from 1.70 in 2011.

As with all averages in this article, these fluctuate depending on which cities report information each year. One difference this year is that the District of Columbia responded to the survey. Because the District is home to federal buildings, including the White House and Congress, where protests, parades, and other activities occur, it requires higher levels of staffing than other municipalities in the population group 500,000–1,000,000. These different needs skew the staffing and expenditure data for the small number of cities (8) reporting from that group.

pre-recession levels of staffing for police officers to the extent allowed by the fiscal crisis. Interestingly, for fire services, a notable reduction in the average number of staff is not seen until 2012. It may be that the staffing necessary for fire equipment made reductions difficult until the fiscal crisis made such staffing untenable. For fire services, 124 municipalities

Table 10-2   Full-Time Paid Personnel, 2012

Classification	Police			Fire		
	No. of cities reporting	Mean	Per capita per 1,000 population	No. of cities reporting	Mean	Per capita per 1,000 population
Total	888	135	2.38	467	77	1.51
Population group						
Over 1,000,000	3	3,784	2.87	1	1,902	1.32
500,000–1,000,000	6	2,646	4.70	4	1,284	2.01
250,000–499,999	14	1,073	2.76	6	503	1.24
100,000–249,999	52	388	2.20	26	240	1.21
50,000–99,999	108	167	2.18	64	98	1.32
25,000–49,999	192	88	2.18	95	62	1.54
10,000–24,999	512	44	2.47	271	28	1.58
Geographic division						
New England	65	54	2.09	40	40	1.47
Mid-Atlantic	91	54	2.03	33	46	1.35
East North-Central	184	68	2.17	107	37	1.31
West North-Central	87	115	2.12	39	32	1.03
South Atlantic	141	203	3.28	78	154	2.23
East South-Central	37	192	3.11	29	85	2.43
West South-Central	102	203	2.56	55	71	1.52
Mountain	59	253	2.29	31	162	1.31
Pacific Coast	122	147	1.94	55	80	1.00

The average numbers of full-time police personnel in the other population categories in 2012 have decreased somewhat from the 2011 figures. The average for cities over 1,000,000 in 2012 is almost identical to the 2011 average. For cities below 250,000, there has been a decline.

The patterns for fire departments are somewhat different from those for police departments (Table 10–2). The two largest population groups and cities of 100,000–249,999 show higher average numbers of full-time personnel than in 2011. The remaining groups tend to show similar or lower average numbers of full-time personel.

As with full-time paid police personnel, per capita figures per 1,000 population in all but the 500,000–1,000,000 population group show slightly lower numbers of full-time paid fire personnel in 2012 than in 2011. The cities under 50,000 population show higher numbers of fire personnel per capita per 1,000 population than the larger cities show.

The cross-sectional pattern by geographic division indicates that municipalities in the Mountain division have the highest average number of full-time police

employees (253) and that those in the Mid-Atlantic and New England divisions have the lowest (54 each) (Table 10–2). Regarding full-time paid fire employees, the highest average number is also in the Mountain division (162), followed by the South Atlantic division (154), and the lowest average number is in the West North-Central division (32).

For police departments, the South Atlantic division shows the highest average number of full-time paid personnel per 1,000 population (3.28), while the lowest is in the Pacific Coast division (1.94). For fire, the highest average number of full-time paid personnel per 1,000 population is in the East South-Central division (2.43), followed by the South Atlantic division (2.23), while the lowest is in the Pacific Coast division (1.00), followed closely by the West North-Central division (1.03).

Figure 10–3 shows the changes over ten years in the average numbers of full-time employees per 1,000 population for both services.

Table 10–3 presents the average numbers of full-time uniformed, or sworn, personnel in police and fire departments as of January 1, 2012. Among reporting cities, these numbers are 106 for police departments

Figure 10-3 Police and Fire Trends in Employees per 1,000 Population, 2002-2012

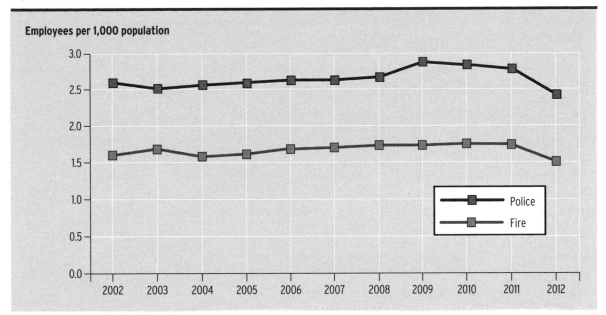

Table 10-3 Uniformed Sworn Personnel, 2012

	Police			Fire		
Classification	No. of cities reporting	Mean	Per capita per 1,000 population	No. of cities reporting	Mean	Per capita per 1,000 population
Total	878	106	1.88	445	76	1.48
Population group						
Over 1,000,000	3	3,117	2.37	1	1,586	1.10
500,000-1,000,000	6	2,186	3.88	4	1,223	1.92
250,000-499,999	14	769	1.94	6	478	1.18
100,000-249,999	53	288	1.61	26	228	1.15
50,000-99,999	108	127	1.65	63	95	1.29
25,000-49,999	195	69	1.70	93	59	1.47
10,000-24,999	498	36	1.99	252	28	1.57
Geographic division						
New England	60	46	1.74	35	47	1.64
Mid-Atlantic	83	49	1.78	26	54	1.46
East North-Central	184	51	1.70	100	38	1.31
West North-Central	86	89	1.71	38	31	1.00
South Atlantic	143	165	2.65	78	146	2.11
East South-Central	39	144	2.37	30	81	2.34
West South-Central	102	160	1.90	52	70	1.44
Mountain	59	189	1.70	32	142	1.20
Pacific Coast	122	105	1.40	54	72	0.89

and 76 for fire departments, higher than the 2011 average for police and lower by two for fire. For the three cities reporting with over 1,000,000 in population, the average number of sworn police personnel reported in 2012 is 3,117. Predictably, the remaining averages are consistently correlated with the population size of the responding jurisdictions, although the police department average for cities of 500,000–1,000,000 is 2,186, which is noticeably higher than the average in 2011. This is because of the number of sworn police officers for the District of Columbia, as noted above. The District has the highest number of sworn police officers (3,814) for all reporting cities (not shown). The next highest is Baltimore, Maryland, with 2,854, and the lowest number reported in that population group is Oklahoma City with 992. The figures per capita per 1,000 population show a high of 3.88 for the 500,000–1,000,000 population group and a low of 1.61 for cities of 100,000–249,999.

It is important to recognize that fluctuations in averages within population groups from year to year depend on the population size of the responding jurisdictions. If, in a given year, most of the respondents have populations at the high end of the range—that is, closer to 249,999 than to 100,000—that will usually result in a higher average number of personnel.

The Mountain division shows the highest average number of full-time sworn police personnel (189), while the Mid-Atlantic and New England divisions show the lowest (49 and 46, respectively) (Table 10–3). When per capita per 1,000 population figures are reviewed, the South Atlantic (2.65) and East South-Central (2.37) divisions are the highest, and the Pacific Coast division is the lowest (1.40), which was also the case in 2010 and 2011. For fire personnel, South Atlantic and Mountain divisions show the highest average numbers of full-time sworn personnel (146 and 142, respectively), while the West North-Central division shows the lowest (31). As for per capita per 1,000 population figures, the East South-Central division shows the highest average number of uniformed personnel (2.34), followed by the South Atlantic division (2.11), while the Pacific Coast and West North-Central divisions show the lowest (0.89 and 1.00, respectively).

Staffing Requirements for Fire Personnel

All three reporting jurisdictions with a population of 1,000,000 and over reported minimum staffing requirements, as did 79% of reporting jurisdictions overall (not shown). The responses by geographic division indicate that the majority of jurisdictions in all areas of the country except the Mid-Atlantic division have a minimum requirement, and that more than 90% of cities in the South Atlantic and East South-Central divisions have requirements or policies advising minimum staffing per shift.

The average minimum staffing for apparatus—pumpers, ladders, and other equipment—is shown in Table 10–4. For pumpers, ladders, and rescue units, the average minimum crew is generally higher among larger cities.

Hours Worked per Shift

Several questions were asked regarding the average number of hours worked per week and per shift for both services. The results, which are not displayed, are as expected. Approximately 73% of jurisdictions reported that their police department employees work 40 hours a week, and 16% reported a 42-hour workweek. The remainder show other workweek hours. Fire departments had more varied responses to the workweek question: 37% indicated that their workweek is 56 hours, and only 6% reported a 40-hour workweek. Twenty-four percent reported a 50- to 54-hour workweek in 2012.

The average number of hours worked per shift also varies between the services. Thirty-three percent of the cities indicated that their police officers work 8-hour shifts, and 54% reported 10- or 12-hour shifts (not shown). Fire departments, on the other hand, are most likely to have 24-hour shifts (78%), virtually unchanged from 2011.

Salary and Longevity Pay

Tables 10–5 through 10–8 present various salary and longevity pay data for full-time police officers and firefighters.

Minimum and Maximum Salaries

Tables 10–5 and 10–6 present detailed entrance and maximum salary data for police officers and firefighters, respectively, as well as the average number of years required for each to reach the maximum. In addition to the measures of central tendency (mean and median) for the salary data, the first and third quartiles are included to indicate the degree of dispersion. The annual base salaries are the entrance salaries paid to sworn police officers or firefighters within their first 12 months of employment. Each reported amount excludes uniform allowances, holiday pay, hazardous duty pay, and any other form of additional compensation. The maximum is the highest annual base salary paid to uniformed personnel who do not hold any promotional rank.

The median entrance salary for police personnel in 2012 is $43,816 and the mean is $44,996 (Table 10–5). The median maximum salary for police is $62,254 and

Table 10-4   Minimum Crew per Fire Apparatus, 2012

	Pumpers		Ladders		Rescue units	
Classification	No. of cities reporting	Average minimum crew	No. of cities reporting	Average minimum crew	No. of cities reporting	Average minimum crew
Total	515	3.1	489	3.0	413	2.5
Population group						
Over 1,000,000	3	4.0	3	4.0	2	2.0
500,000–1,000,000	7	4.0	7	4.0	6	3.0
250,000–499,999	12	3.4	12	3.3	12	3.3
100,000–249,999	41	3.3	41	3.4	36	2.3
50,000–99,999	83	3.2	83	3.1	64	2.4
25,000–49,999	121	3.0	115	3.0	90	2.2
10,000–24,999	248	3.1	228	2.9	203	2.5
Geographic division						
New England	21	2.9	19	2.4	17	2.2
Mid-Atlantic	36	3.6	33	3.6	29	3.4
East North-Central	95	3.0	90	2.9	83	2.4
West North-Central	48	3.3	47	3.0	39	2.9
South Atlantic	105	3.1	100	2.9	81	2.3
East South-Central	33	3.2	34	3.0	29	2.3
West South-Central	69	3.2	63	3.0	50	2.4
Mountain	36	3.3	36	3.4	27	2.3
Pacific Coast	72	2.9	67	3.1	58	2.3

Table 10-5   Police Officers' Annual Base Salary, January 1, 2012

	Entrance salary				Maximum salary				No. of years to reach maximum	
Classification	No. of cities reporting	Mean ($)	First quartile ($)	Median ($)	Third quartile ($)	No. of cities reporting	Mean ($)	First quartile ($)	Median ($)	Third quartile ($)	No. of cities reporting	Mean
Total	896	44,996	36,610	43,816	50,856	883	64,018	52,618	62,254	72,002	710	8
Population group												
Over 1,000,000	3	44,151	40,746	41,209	46,084	3	67,322	65,134	67,101	69,400	3	14
500,000–1,000,000	6	51,849	45,070	49,132	52,338	6	70,662	59,974	70,932	75,521	6	14
250,000–499,999	13	49,774	41,520	46,236	52,994	13	68,933	62,784	66,994	76,176	11	10
100,000–249,999	54	50,554	39,798	50,232	57,358	54	72,421	63,006	69,104	80,446	47	10
50,000–99,999	107	48,706	40,432	47,724	56,082	107	68,369	59,054	68,836	76,302	88	9
25,000–49,999	197	46,693	37,794	45,594	51,660	195	64,785	54,672	61,693	71,549	156	7
10,000–24,999	515	42,821	35,404	42,557	48,287	504	61,703	49,584	59,584	70,030	399	8
Geographic division												
New England	64	45,481	40,617	45,976	49,431	63	58,919	52,954	58,592	64,545	63	9
Mid-Atlantic	91	48,427	40,403	45,900	52,768	90	84,657	69,354	83,556	99,384	93	7
East North-Central	190	47,327	42,402	47,146	51,866	187	64,855	56,341	63,898	73,950	179	7
West North-Central	87	40,854	35,548	41,520	45,167	86	56,981	49,181	58,693	65,598	62	7
South Atlantic	145	36,457	32,100	35,118	40,178	142	57,297	48,055	55,248	65,440	62	14
East South-Central	39	31,805	27,230	31,616	34,082	37	46,300	41,184	45,656	51,268	28	14
West South-Central	102	40,464	35,200	40,504	45,424	100	54,600	46,606	55,394	64,718	71	10
Mountain	58	44,655	38,655	43,616	49,933	58	62,604	55,990	62,150	70,681	41	10
Pacific Coast	120	60,066	51,620	59,448	66,831	120	76,904	66,804	76,452	85,618	111	6

Table 10-6 Firefighters' Annual Base Salary, January 1, 2012

Classification	Entrance salary					Maximum salary					No. of years to reach maximum	
	No. of cities reporting	Mean ($)	First quartile ($)	Median ($)	Third quartile ($)	No. of cities reporting	Mean ($)	First quartile ($)	Median ($)	Third quartile ($)	No. of cities reporting	Mean
Total	450	40,689	33,008	40,024	47,240	593	56,404	47,476	55,520	64,557	458	8
Population group												
Over 1,000,000	1	46,149	46,149	46,149	46,149	2	61,361	59,390	61,361	63,332	1	8
500,000–1,000,000	4	48,484	42,446	45,548	51,587	6	65,635	58,907	61,244	73,292	5	17
250,000–499,999	7	46,579	40,452	43,681	51,490	8	61,112	55,378	56,634	71,346	6	14
100,000–249,999	27	47,100	37,930	46,044	52,837	40	61,858	55,257	61,660	67,292	36	8
50,000–99,999	62	47,112	38,572	44,953	53,922	87	62,995	54,063	64,281	71,256	72	8
25,000–49,999	93	41,309	33,774	40,530	47,590	134	57,993	49,809	56,750	63,712	102	8
10,000–24,999	256	37,928	31,147	37,885	44,078	315	52,913	43,651	52,024	61,021	236	8
Geographic division												
New England	39	41,776	37,694	42,536	45,286	44	52,323	47,418	52,528	56,959	41	7
Mid-Atlantic	29	39,848	36,674	40,437	42,662	32	63,152	53,462	58,796	71,276	29	8
East North-Central	104	43,573	39,598	43,968	48,490	132	60,683	53,060	61,138	67,693	127	7
West North-Central	35	39,120	32,387	37,556	42,024	55	53,880	48,108	53,202	59,124	37	9
South Atlantic	76	32,162	28,013	31,656	35,260	107	51,270	42,410	50,021	57,148	43	14
East South-Central	31	30,113	26,788	31,296	33,490	36	44,084	37,683	44,908	49,130	27	15
West South-Central	50	37,750	32,262	37,500	43,352	81	51,512	43,848	51,489	59,420	59	8
Mountain	33	40,864	34,356	39,792	46,797	39	56,767	50,642	58,633	61,456	28	10
Pacific Coast	53	56,804	49,738	55,592	61,812	67	70,026	64,020	68,317	76,380	67	5

the mean is $64,018. The entrance salaries for firefighters tend to be lower than those for police, with a median of $40,024 and a mean of $40,689 (Table 10–6). The maximum fire salary median and mean are $55,520 and $56,404, respectively. For both police and fire personnel, the mean is higher than the median for both entrance and maximum salaries. This indicates that some higher salaries are positively skewing the mean.

The highest average entrance salaries for both police and fire personnel are found in the Pacific Coast division. The highest average maximum salary for police personnel is found in the Mid-Atlantic division, followed by the Pacific Coast division. For fire personnel, the highest average maximum salary is in the Pacific Coast division. The lowest average entrance and maximum salaries for both police personnel and firefighters are found in the East South-Central division. For both services, the difference between the highest and lowest average entrance salaries among the geographic divisions is substantial: $28,261 for police and $26,691 for fire. The difference between the highest and lowest average maximum salaries

among the geographic divisions for police is $38,357, compared with $25,942 for firefighters.

For both police and fire services, an average of eight years of service is required to reach the maximum salary—identical to 2011.

Longevity Pay

Longevity pay is defined as compensation beyond the regular maximum salary based on number of years of service. Longevity serves as an economic incentive to decrease employee turnover and reward those employees who have already achieved the maximum salary and now have limited opportunities for promotion. Longevity pay can be administered in several ways: a flat dollar amount, a percentage of the base salary, a percentage of the maximum pay, or a step increase in the basic salary plan.

Tables 10–7 and 10–8 show a range of longevity pay data for police and firefighter personnel, respectively. The tables cover whether personnel can receive longevity pay, the maximum salary they can receive including longevity pay, and the average number of

Table 10-7   Longevity Pay for Police Officers, January 1, 2012

Classification	No. of cities reporting (A)	Personnel can receive longevity pay Yes No.	Personnel can receive longevity pay Yes % of (A)	Personnel can receive longevity pay No No.	Personnel can receive longevity pay No % of (A)	Maximum salary including longevity pay No. of cities reporting	Maximum salary including longevity pay Mean ($)	Maximum salary including longevity pay First quartile ($)	Maximum salary including longevity pay Median ($)	Maximum salary including longevity pay Third quartile ($)	No. of years of service to receive longevity pay No. of cities reporting	No. of years of service to receive longevity pay Mean
Total	917	584	64	333	36	456	69,696	56,332	66,787	78,988	534	6
Population group												
Over 1,000,000	3	3	100	0	0	3	73,587	72,000	75,698	76,230	3	3
500,000-1,000,000	6	3	50	3	50	2	58,633	55,554	58,633	61,712	3	14
250,000-499,999	14	6	43	8	57	6	68,390	65,844	67,284	70,332	6	6
100,000-249,999	55	33	60	22	40	27	77,005	67,062	71,471	91,080	32	8
50,000-99,999	113	72	64	41	36	57	76,177	63,954	70,759	85,329	66	7
25,000-49,999	200	134	67	66	33	110	71,828	57,101	66,944	82,080	120	7
10,000-24,999	525	333	63	192	37	251	66,577	54,051	63,740	74,030	304	6
Geographic division												
New England	66	48	73	18	27	42	63,913	55,764	63,070	68,809	44	7
Mid-Atlantic	91	81	89	10	11	71	91,647	71,362	85,616	102,308	76	6
East North-Central	199	145	73	54	27	115	65,625	56,659	65,500	73,220	140	6
West North-Central	89	48	54	41	46	41	63,013	55,152	65,055	71,471	46	8
South Atlantic	147	63	43	84	57	41	61,255	51,874	56,337	69,575	51	6
East South-Central	38	18	47	20	53	6	49,065	44,405	50,264	51,933	17	8
West South-Central	103	98	95	5	5	70	57,999	49,154	57,490	65,920	87	2
Mountain	60	21	35	39	65	15	62,267	56,492	62,774	69,927	18	6
Pacific Coast	124	62	50	62	50	55	84,728	74,406	82,507	95,240	55	10

years of service that is required for them to receive longevity pay.

Sixty-four percent of all police departments reporting have a system that awards longevity pay to their personnel (Table 10–7). The West South-Central and Mid-Atlantic divisions show the highest percentages of cities with longevity pay for police personnel (95% and 89%, respectively).

The average maximum salary including longevity pay for police officers is $69,696. The figures range from a low of $58,633 for cities with populations of 500,000–1,000,000 to a high of $77,005 for cities with a population of 100,000–249,999. Geographic divisions show a clear disparity in this regard. Once again, cities in the East South-Central division show the lowest average maximum at $49,065, while the highest average maximums are $91,647 for Mid-Atlantic and $84,728 for Pacific Coast jurisdictions. Cost of living is certainly a factor to consider. The median home prices in the central United States are much lower than they are on the East and West Coasts.

The longevity pay patterns for firefighters (Table 10–8) show that 58% of jurisdictions overall reported longevity pay for fire personnel, including 94% of jurisdictions in the West South-Central division (the high) and 42% of those in the Mountain, Mid-Atlantic, and South Atlantic divisions (the low).

The average maximum salary with longevity pay for firefighters is $61,306. Among population groups, the 22 cities reporting with populations 100,000–249,999 show the highest average maximum salary with longevity pay ($72,256). Geographically, Pacific Coast jurisdictions show the highest average maximum salary with longevity pay ($79,719), and East South-Central communities again show the lowest ($46,972).

Overall, the length of service required for both police and firefighters to receive longevity pay is six years, which is almost identical to the numbers reported every year since 2006. However, the number of years varies somewhat within the classification categories. In the Pacific Coast division, for example,

Table 10-8 Longevity Pay for Firefighters, January 1, 2012

Classification	No. of cities reporting (A)	Personnel can receive longevity pay — Yes No.	Yes % of (A)	No No.	No % of (A)	No. of cities reporting	Maximum salary including longevity pay Mean ($)	First quartile ($)	Median ($)	Third quartile ($)	No. of cities reporting	No. of years of service to receive longevity pay Mean
Total	668	389	58	279	42	292	61,306	51,132	60,179	69,345	368	6
Population group												
Over 1,000,000	2	2	100	0	0	2	68,529	68,142	68,529	68,916	2	4
500,000-1,000,000	6	5	83	1	17	4	65,560	58,532	63,849	70,877	5	7
250,000-499,999	8	4	50	4	50	4	68,320	58,148	62,136	72,307	4	6
100,000-249,999	42	27	64	15	36	22	72,256	60,871	66,548	79,209	26	6
50,000-99,999	92	59	64	33	36	49	67,318	57,708	66,356	78,469	51	5
25,000-49,999	145	90	62	55	38	68	63,711	53,476	60,621	73,289	87	7
10,000-24,999	372	202	54	170	46	143	56,001	45,982	54,467	63,412	193	5
Geographic division												
New England	51	35	69	16	31	28	56,802	51,048	54,598	61,518	33	8
Mid-Atlantic	52	22	42	30	58	22	68,105	55,672	61,708	82,048	21	6
East North-Central	151	105	70	46	31	86	62,462	54,613	63,099	70,514	104	7
West North-Central	64	29	45	35	55	22	56,025	51,632	53,532	57,871	27	7
South Atlantic	115	48	42	67	58	29	55,319	43,298	49,762	69,277	44	6
East South-Central	35	18	51	17	49	6	46,972	40,752	46,114	50,320	16	7
West South-Central	86	81	94	5	6	58	56,465	47,264	55,104	63,720	77	2
Mountain	43	18	42	25	58	11	59,606	50,191	60,758	65,902	15	6
Pacific Coast	71	33	47	38	54	30	79,719	70,727	76,815	86,216	31	11

both groups of personnel serve a well-above-average number of years (10 for police and 11 for fire) to qualify for longevity pay.

Expenditures

Respondents were asked to provide expenditure (not budget) figures for their police and fire departments' most recently completed fiscal year. The items include salaries and wages for all department personnel, contributions for employee benefits, capital outlays, and all other departmental expenditures. Average expenditures are presented in Tables 10–9 through 10–16. Per capita expenditures are shown in addition to average expenditures. Again, per capita presentations are useful because they normalize the information.

Salaries and Wages

Part of ICMA's process of reviewing survey results is to design logic checks that will identify problematic values. One logic check is that total expenditures for salaries and wages must be greater than the minimum salary for police (or fire) sworn personnel multiplied by the number of sworn personnel reported. For those jurisdictions reporting total expenditures for salaries and wages below that amount, the total amount of salary and wage expenditures was removed.

Table 10–9 shows the average per capita expenditure for civilian and uniformed police personnel in 2012 to be $155.04, a decrease from the 2011 average of $170.14. As population decreases, average per capita expenditures also generally decrease. The exception here is for cities with a population of 500,000–1,000,000, where the average per capita of $363.44 is more than twice the overall average per capita. This is because the District of Columbia and the City and County of Honolulu (which also did not report last year) have much higher per capita expenditures for salaries and wages. Average salary and wage expenditures for police decrease from $259,687,067 for the three cities with populations over 1,000,000 to $2,834,883 for reporting cities of 10,000–24,999 in population.

Table 10-9 Expenditures for Salaries and Wages (Civilian and Uniformed), 2012

	Police			Fire		
Classification	No. of cities reporting	Mean ($)	Per capita ($)	No. of cities reporting	Mean ($)	Per capita ($)
Total	829	9,468,806	155.04	598	6,174,734	99.11
Population group						
Over 1,000,000	3	259,687,067	196.13	2	143,009,761	103.10
500,000-1,000,000	6	207,471,652	363.44	6	100,056,994	181.99
250,000-499,999	13	76,885,438	198.29	8	50,076,023	124.34
100,000-249,999	51	24,858,205	147.57	38	16,829,383	95.02
50,000-99,999	104	11,194,054	147.08	86	7,895,496	104.71
25,000-49,999	177	5,916,519	145.55	129	4,052,833	100.58
10,000-24,999	474	2,834,883	156.68	328	1,713,409	95.04
Geographic division						
New England	60	4,008,552	150.72	50	2,954,419	101.82
Mid-Atlantic	81	4,966,924	192.45	36	3,287,236	92.20
East North-Central	168	5,333,683	151.91	129	3,412,928	96.32
West North-Central	84	6,900,274	119.79	61	4,689,442	65.24
South Atlantic	134	12,189,472	173.96	107	8,186,967	121.71
East South-Central	33	10,142,119	135.16	32	7,906,180	109.03
West South-Central	96	13,384,232	147.18	82	8,370,300	91.45
Mountain	56	17,263,786	138.37	40	10,403,829	82.10
Pacific Coast	117	12,917,836	159.50	61	7,681,715	117.41

Overall, the spread of average per capita salary and wage expenditures is much greater for police departments than for fire departments ($217.89 vs. $86.97). The average per capita police expenditures show a low of $145.55 in cities of 25,000–49,999 in population and a high of $363.44 in cities of 500,000–1,000,000 in population (Table 10–9). For firefighters, the average per capita expenditures range from a low of $95.02 in cities with populations of 100,000–249,999 and $95.04 in cities 10,000–24,999 to a high of $181.99 in cities with populations of 500,000–1,000,000.

Geographically, Mid-Atlantic jurisdictions show the highest average per capita salary and wage expenditures for police personnel ($192.45), and South Atlantic jurisdictions show the highest for firefighters ($121.71). Cities in the West North-Central division show the lowest for both police ($119.79) and fire ($65.24) personnel.

Social Security and Retirement Benefits

The average expenditures for municipal contributions to federal Social Security and other employee retirement programs are reported in Table 10–10. These expenditures are for both uniformed and civilian personnel. The table shows combined retirement and Social Security contributions because some states opt out of Social Security programs for local government employees, relying instead on employee-sponsored retirement programs. Zeros have been removed from the calculations because although zero is a legitimate answer, it skews the averages. There is always extensive variation in these reported amounts, which often do not seem realistic in relation to the number of employees.

The average per capita expenditure for employee Social Security and retirement benefits for police departments in 2012 ($33.87) is down from the 2011 amount ($36.39). Among the population groups, the highest average police per capita expenditure for Social Security and retirement ($52.74) is for the 500,000–1,000,000 population group. Geographically, the highest average police department per capita expenditure for these benefits is found in the Pacific Coast division ($42.97); the lowest is in the West North-Central division ($21.57).

Table 10-10 Total Municipal Contributions to Social Security and State/City-Administered Employee Retirement Systems, 2012

Classification	Police No. of cities reporting	Police Mean ($)	Police Per capita ($)	Fire No. of cities reporting	Fire Mean ($)	Fire Per capita ($)
Total	793	2,007,669	33.87	570	1,321,380	22.24
Population group						
Over 1,000,000	3	62,573,221	47.58	2	30,094,632	21.73
500,000-1,000,000	4	28,903,128	52.74	4	10,598,722	23.51
250,000-499,999	13	16,632,985	42.67	7	14,152,701	34.87
100,000-249,999	48	6,534,336	37.56	38	4,139,312	23.57
50,000-99,999	96	2,775,212	36.95	82	2,062,435	28.37
25,000-49,999	168	1,285,615	31.07	120	910,752	22.40
10,000-24,999	460	599,753	33.32	316	365,366	20.09
Geographic division						
New England	45	817,486	30.52	35	567,674	17.39
Mid-Atlantic	75	930,266	40.81	33	576,601	23.50
East North-Central	160	1,227,159	34.70	121	883,638	23.42
West North-Central	87	1,378,002	21.57	63	1,247,868	13.92
South Atlantic	134	1,905,897	39.13	106	1,572,961	29.01
East South-Central	35	1,308,288	26.60	33	893,146	20.86
West South-Central	91	2,935,402	27.40	78	1,654,355	17.94
Mountain	55	3,932,042	28.36	40	2,270,147	16.82
Pacific Coast	111	3,466,030	42.97	61	1,847,559	28.61

The average per capita expenditure for employee Social Security and retirement benefits reported for fire departments in 2012 is $22.24 (Table 10–10), compared with $23.09 in 2011. The per capita amounts fluctuate among the population groups. Among the geographic divisions, the highest average fire department per capita expenditure for Social Security and retirement benefits is in the South Atlantic division ($29.01), followed closely by the Pacific Coast division ($28.61), and the lowest is again in the West North-Central division ($13.92).

Health, Hospitalization, Disability, and Life Insurance

Table 10–11 shows the average total municipal contributions for health, hospitalization, disability, and life insurance programs. The mean per capita expenditures for 2012 how a slight decrease since 2011—from $30.82 to $28.45 for police and from $19.42 to $17.84 for fire. However, the amounts reported for the District of Columbia increased the per capita averages for police and fire in the 500,000–1,000,000 population range.

Total Personnel Expenditures

Table 10–12 shows the total personnel expenditures for civilian and uniformed employees for both police and fire services. These data represent total salaries and wages; contributions for federal Social Security and other retirement programs; and contributions to health, hospitalization, disability, and life insurance programs. To be included in this table, the jurisdiction had to provide each of these expenditures. Those that reported an amount of zero were excluded from the table. Again, although zero is a legitimate amount, it negatively skews the average.

For fire services in particular, the workforce composition affects personnel expenditures. Departments that rely heavily on volunteers have significantly lower personnel expenditures than those that use paid staff. The amounts reported are for all departments, regardless of whether they rely on volunteers.

The mean per capita personnel expenditures are $209.83 for police and $120.70 for fire. For police departments, the amounts fluctuate among population groups, although the per capita figures are lower

Table 10-11   Total Municipal Contributions for Health, Hospitalization, Disability, and Life Insurance Programs, 2012

	Police			Fire		
Classification	No. of cities reporting	Mean ($)	Per capita ($)	No. of cities reporting	Mean ($)	Per capita ($)
Total	763	1,668,099	28.45	615	1,097,072	17.84
Population group						
Over 1,000,000	3	40,932,052	30.39	3	18,062,918	13.43
500,000-1,000,000	5	30,075,683	56.85	6	14,626,746	26.33
250,000-499,999	13	12,471,185	32.65	11	7,288,421	18.75
100,000-249,999	48	4,968,546	29.35	44	2,786,206	15.65
50,000-99,999	92	2,142,324	27.65	87	1,430,672	18.60
25,000-49,999	165	1,081,498	26.46	132	780,291	19.56
10,000-24,999	436	510,470	28.69	331	308,147	17.01
Geographic division						
New England	39	864,014	33.04	31	703,603	23.86
Mid-Atlantic	66	950,584	40.73	32	443,662	20.82
East North-Central	153	1,087,351	29.88	132	781,600	19.18
West North-Central	87	1,223,926	21.63	70	797,042	11.85
South Atlantic	133	1,515,838	26.61	113	1,119,832	19.69
East South-Central	32	1,630,954	22.63	31	1,140,184	17.85
West South-Central	90	2,043,316	20.36	87	1,238,503	13.33
Mountain	54	2,944,930	24.29	44	1,865,155	14.84
Pacific Coast	109	2,814,283	35.52	75	1,706,975	21.53

among the smaller population groups. Again, in the population group 500,000–1,000,000, the respondents with high expenditures affected the average. Among the geographic divisions, the high for police is in the Mid-Atlantic division ($260.21) and the low is in the West North-Central division ($158.86).

For fire departments, the mean per capita personnel expenditures also vary among population groups. Geographically, the average per capita high is seen in the South Atlantic division ($157.96), followed by the East South-Central division ($139.13), and the low is again seen in the West North-Central ($81.23) division.

Overtime Expenditures

At the request of some local governments, a new survey question was added in the 2010 survey to address overtime expenditures (Table 10–13). The reported 2012 per capita average overtime expenditures are $10.48 for police departments and $8.22 for fire departments. Overtime expenditures for fire personnel show more variation than those for police among

population groups, and both services show noticeable variation among the geographic divisions.

As with all police and fire expenditures, it is important to consider population density and other factors before making definitive comparisons. A community with high manufacturing activity may pose a higher risk for fire, resulting in more overtime, and high levels of gang activity may influence the need for police overtime. In addition, for some communities, paying overtime is less costly than hiring additional personnel.

Capital Outlays

Table 10–14 (see page 140) shows departmental expenditures for capital outlays. These outlays include the purchase and replacement of equipment, the purchase of land and existing structures, and construction. The amounts include the capital expenditures within individual departmental budgets as well as those expenditures included in citywide capital budgets designated for departmental programs or equipment.

Total capital outlay expenditures may fluctuate dramatically from one year to the next for both police

Table 10-12 Total Personnel Expenditures, 2012

Classification	Police			Fire		
	No. of cities reporting	Mean ($)	Per capita ($)	No. of cities reporting	Mean ($)	Per capita ($)
Total	844	12,694,884	209.83	687	7,453,241	120.70
Population group						
Over 1,000,000	3	363,192,340	274.10	3	133,465,847	96.66
500,000-1,000,000	6	251,803,474	445.97	7	104,356,761	191.99
250,000-499,999	14	98,418,922	254.07	12	48,320,810	120.43
100,000-249,999	51	35,684,447	210.53	44	20,895,533	118.07
50,000-99,999	104	15,650,921	205.65	98	9,924,498	132.13
25,000-49,999	178	8,099,182	198.58	144	5,104,890	126.69
10,000-24,999	487	3,782,723	209.66	378	2,062,038	114.16
Geographic division						
New England	60	5,183,276	195.09	55	3,443,659	117.07
Mid-Atlantic	82	6,522,310	260.21	46	3,294,902	103.49
East North-Central	173	7,276,120	206.04	147	4,424,212	121.02
West North-Central	87	9,264,261	158.86	70	6,006,637	81.23
South Atlantic	137	15,258,292	234.27	116	10,080,004	157.96
East South-Central	35	12,362,015	174.73	34	9,347,567	139.13
West South-Central	96	18,082,357	192.24	93	9,926,387	108.15
Mountain	56	23,965,367	189.65	46	12,804,910	100.21
Pacific Coast	118	18,668,416	231.38	80	8,866,361	131.53

and fire departments. This is because the cost of individual capital projects varies widely among communities as well as within the same community over time. Whereas the number of employees, which relates to population size, determines personnel expenditures, fire equipment such as pumpers will cost the same regardless of the size of the community. Thus, the per capita cost for the pumpers will necessarily be higher among cities with fewer people.

The 2012 average municipal expenditures for capital outlays per capita are $7.62 for police, a decrease from the $10.56 shown in 2011, and $7.93 for fire, which is below the 2011 figure of $12.02. For police and fire services, the highest average capital outlays per capita ($11.65 and $10.33, respectively) are in the population group 500,000–1,000,000. Geographically, the highest average capital outlays per capita for police services are in the Mountain and East South-Central divisions ($15.59 and $11.88, respectively); for fire services, they are in the New England and Mid-Atlantic divisions ($10.52 and $10.34, respectively). For police services, the lowest

average capital outlay per capita is in the Mid-Atlantic division ($3.77); for fire, it is in the Pacific Coast division ($5.43).

Other Expenditures

Table 10–15 (see page 141) presents the data for all other departmental expenditures not accounted for in the previous tables. These include ongoing maintenance, utilities, fuel, supplies, and other miscellaneous items. The average per capita expenditures reported for 2012 are $34.29 for police, a decrease from the $39.75 reported in 2011, and $20.33 for fire, also a decrease from the 2011 average ($23.69).

Total Department Expenditures

Table 10–16 (see page 142) shows the combined personnel, capital outlay, and all other departmental expenditures. The average per capita figures for 2012 are $251.71 for police and $156.43 and fire—decreases for both services from totals reported in 2011.

Total expenditures are not included for those localities in which the sum of expenditures reported

Table 10-13   Total Overtime Expenditures, 2012

	Police			Fire		
Classification	No. of cities reporting	Mean ($)	Per capita ($)	No. of cities reporting	Mean ($)	Per capita ($)
Total	816	635,654	10.48	561	500,863	8.22
Population group						
Over 1,000,000	3	8,720,510	6.46	2	11,611,368	8.66
500,000-1,000,000	5	16,827,260	32.99	5	7,466,070	14.92
250,000-499,999	14	5,293,068	13.81	8	4,129,793	10.81
100,000-249,999	49	2,063,482	13.21	38	1,204,830	6.74
50,000-99,999	102	811,398	10.78	88	645,956	8.94
25,000-49,999	174	371,126	9.19	123	338,542	8.74
10,000-24,999	468	183,356	10.31	296	145,648	7.81
Geographic division						
New England	58	416,298	16.13	44	492,636	17.78
Mid-Atlantic	78	381,012	11.45	28	565,857	7.64
East North-Central	161	386,636	10.79	116	261,551	7.40
West North-Central	87	385,494	6.72	57	246,838	3.82
South Atlantic	135	631,744	8.60	106	382,159	6.52
East South-Central	34	675,620	11.22	31	388,167	6.61
West South-Central	95	659,789	6.84	78	693,247	5.90
Mountain	55	984,303	8.96	37	902,135	7.14
Pacific Coast	113	1,274,068	15.19	64	922,817	14.32

(salaries and wages, employee benefit contributions, capital outlays, and other expenses) differs from the amount reported for total expenditures by more than $100. Most of the variations were by thousands of dollars. This same logic has been applied each year for the analysis.

Not all cities include the same expenditures in their budgets. Of the 639 jurisdictions providing information about services included in the fire department budget, 52% cited ambulance personnel and 53% cited ambulance equipment (not shown). Emergency medical technicians (EMTs) were included by 89%, and EMT equipment was included by 92%. This does not necessarily mean, however, that these are the only jurisdictions that provide EMT and ambulance services; these are just the cities that reported having these services in the fire department budget.

Notes

1 RealEstateABC.com, "Existing Home Sales–November Report" (last updated October 26, 2012), realestateabc.com/outlook.htm (accessed November 18, 2012).

Conclusion

This report has examined the cross-sectional and longitudinal patterns found in the responses to ICMA's annual *Police and Fire Personnel, Salaries, and Expenditures* survey. Most of the changes over time in police and fire employment and expenditures have been small, incremental shifts. It is not uncommon for one year to show increases and the next to show decreases in average expenditures.

Although using per capita figures instead of absolute numbers reduces the skew of the data, any analysis of the reported changes must control for population size of the responding jurisdictions. Another influential factor is a significant difference in the number reporting in any population group. Any major increase or decrease in that number can affect the average.

Table 10-14   Municipal Expenditures for Capital Outlays, 2012

Classification	Police			Fire		
	No. of cities reporting	Mean ($)	Per capita ($)	No. of cities reporting	Mean ($)	Per capita ($)
Total	682	405,280	7.62	517	397,770	7.93
Population group						
Over 1,000,000	3	7,238,565	5.18	3	7,143,353	5.58
500,000–1,000,000	4	6,026,507	11.65	6	4,999,220	10.33
250,000–499,999	13	3,492,578	7.89	10	2,357,477	6.37
100,000–249,999	38	1,037,388	4.76	34	296,043	1.74
50,000–99,999	85	411,443	5.31	76	438,312	5.84
25,000–49,999	140	388,486	9.33	111	382,923	9.06
10,000–24,999	398	140,398	7.65	276	160,968	8.75
Geographic division						
New England	45	128,370	5.63	37	262,656	10.52
Mid-Atlantic	58	100,245	3.77	32	168,304	10.34
East North-Central	133	150,736	5.33	116	243,250	6.89
West North-Central	78	284,971	6.96	57	298,339	7.32
South Atlantic	121	330,277	7.71	87	450,619	8.03
East South-Central	30	427,121	11.88	27	295,026	8.04
West South-Central	80	464,637	6.76	70	702,760	9.79
Mountain	52	1,648,526	15.59	35	513,479	7.31
Pacific Coast	85	551,326	9.79	56	553,324	5.43

Table 10-15   All Other Department Expenditures, 2012

Classification	Police			Fire		
	No. of cities reporting	Mean ($)	Per capita ($)	No. of cities reporting	Mean ($)	Per capita ($)
Total	786	2,075,012	34.29	646	1,202,470	20.33
Population group						
Over 1,000,000	3	56,389,928	42.14	3	26,276,533	19.87
500,000-1,000,000	5	31,105,599	59.33	6	16,971,927	30.70
250,000-499,999	14	16,722,710	43.70	11	6,729,120	17.99
100,000-249,999	48	5,661,407	32.99	43	2,938,261	17.00
50,000-99,999	96	3,074,418	41.14	89	1,714,774	23.49
25,000-49,999	166	1,394,958	33.21	135	788,921	18.62
10,000-24,999	453	601,888	32.60	358	381,145	20.50
Geographic division						
New England	54	433,965	18.70	50	392,185	16.56
Mid-Atlantic	74	396,275	16.64	46	308,930	16.10
East North-Central	157	1,288,676	30.22	134	847,397	20.13
West North-Central	86	1,416,224	27.42	68	774,375	17.65
South Atlantic	133	2,248,440	47.25	111	1,206,028	23.54
East South-Central	33	1,839,171	35.53	31	1,272,855	20.24
West South-Central	87	2,772,465	27.58	85	1,650,951	17.87
Mountain	56	4,195,891	37.41	46	2,536,376	22.27
Pacific Coast	106	3,945,036	53.37	75	1,952,472	25.14

Table 10-16   Total Departmental Expenditures, 2012

Classification	Police			Fire		
	No. of cities reporting	Mean ($)	Per capita ($)	No. of cities reporting	Mean ($)	Per capita ($)
Total	485	18,033,331	251.71	476	10,939,665	156.43
Population group						
Over 1,000,000	2	476,803,906	359.02	1	224,420,918	187.36
500,000–1,000,000	6	303,058,279	537.41	5	137,778,194	247.54
250,000–499,999	11	120,904,255	307.28	9	147,086,533	430.01
100,000–249,999	29	45,158,572	269.00	31	26,600,538	148.50
50,000–99,999	59	19,763,580	255.80	64	12,557,073	167.57
25,000–49,999	100	9,392,361	231.26	96	6,788,944	169.11
10,000–24,999	278	4,422,214	247.25	270	2,556,230	139.26
Geographic division						
New England	45	5,855,500	213.37	44	5,285,981	187.18
Mid-Atlantic	50	6,870,456	272.36	46	2,973,078	95.56
East North-Central	113	9,618,793	236.89	101	6,984,009	159.98
West North-Central	43	10,021,524	192.84	42	23,608,667	145.77
South Atlantic	67	25,406,824	294.61	69	9,971,009	178.69
East South-Central	20	19,213,348	243.58	18	5,959,316	168.81
West South-Central	39	28,827,938	226.54	57	13,748,873	134.59
Mountain	33	38,576,075	225.53	33	14,187,789	129.73
Pacific Coast	75	28,499,625	305.45	66	16,573,288	185.23

Directories

1 Directory Tables

2 Professional, Special Assistance, and Educational Organizations Serving Local and State Governments

1

Directory Tables

Directory 1 in this section of the Year Book provides the names and websites of U.S. state municipal leagues; provincial and territorial associations and unions in Canada; state agencies for community affairs; provincial and territorial agencies for local affairs in Canada; U.S. municipal management associations; international municipal management associations; state associations of counties; and U.S. councils of governments recognized by ICMA. In all cases, where there is no website available, we have provided the name of the president/permanent officer/executive director and all contact information for that individual.

U.S. State Municipal Leagues

Directory Table 1 – 1 shows 49 state leagues of municipalities serving 49 states. (Hawaii does not have a league.) Information, which was obtained from the National League of Cities (nlc.org), includes league address and website. State municipal leagues provide a wide range of research, consulting, training, publications, and legislative representation services for their clients.

Provincial and Territorial Associations and Unions in Canada

Directory 1 – 2 shows the websites of the 16 associations and unions serving the 12 provinces and territories of Canada. Information was obtained from the Federation of Canadian Municipalities (fcm.org).

State Agencies for Community Affairs

Directory 1 – 3 shows the addresses and websites of agencies for community affairs in 47 states. Information was obtained from the Council of State Community Development Agencies (coscda.org). These agencies of state governments offer a variety of research,

financial information, and coordination services for cities and other local governments.

Provincial and Territorial Agencies for Local Affairs in Canada

Directory 1 – 4 shows the addresses, phone numbers, fax numbers, and websites of the agencies for local affairs serving the 12 provinces and territories of Canada. Information was obtained from the Ontario Ministry of Municipal Affairs and Housing (mah.gov.on.ca).

U.S. Municipal Management Associations

Directory 1 – 5, with information obtained from ICMA files, shows the websites of municipal management associations serving 47 of the United States. (The states of Wyoming, Idaho, Montana, North Dakota, and South Dakota are served by the Great Open Spaces City Management Association; Idaho and South Dakota are also served by their own associations; and neither Hawaii nor Louisiana has an association.)

International Municipal Management Associations

Directory 1 – 6, with information obtained from ICMA files, shows the websites (where available) or contact information of municipal management associations in Canada and 22 other countries.

U.S. State Associations of Counties

Directory 1 – 7 shows the websites for 53 county associations serving 47 states, as obtained from the National Association of Counties (naco.org). (Two associations serve the states of Arizona, South Dakota, Washington, and West Virginia; three associations serve the state of Illinois; and three states—Connecticut, Rhode Island, and Vermont—do not have associations.) Like their municipal league counterparts, these associations provide a wide range of research, training, consulting, publications, and legislative representation services.

U.S. Councils of Governments Recognized by ICMA

Directory 1 – 8, with information obtained from ICMA files, gives the websites for 96 councils of governments recognized by ICMA.

Other Local Government Directories

The names of municipal officials not reported in the *Year Book* are available in many states through directories published by state municipal leagues, state municipal management associations, and state associations of counties. Names and websites of these leagues and associations are shown in Directories 1 – 1, 1 – 5, and 1 – 7. In some states, the secretary of state, the state agency for community affairs (Directory 1 – 3), or another state agency publishes a directory that includes municipal and county officials. In addition, several directories with national coverage are published for health officers, welfare workers, housing and urban renewal officials, and other professional groups.

Directory 1-1 U.S. State Municipal Leagues

Shown below are the state municipal leagues of municipalities serving 49 states. For each league, the directory provides the address and website so that readers can go directly to the site to find additional information.

Alabama
Alabama League of Municipalities
P.O. Box 1270
Montgomery 36102
alalm.org

Alaska
Alaska Municipal League
217 Second Street, Suite 200
Juneau 99801
akml.org

Arizona
League of Arizona Cities and Towns
1820 West Washington Street
Phoenix 85007
azleague.org

Arkansas
Arkansas Municipal League
301 West Second Street
Box 38
North Little Rock 72115
arml.org

California
League of California Cities
1400 K Street, Suite 400
Sacramento 95814
cacities.org

Colorado
Colorado Municipal League
1144 Sherman Street
Denver 80203
cml.org

Connecticut
Connecticut Conference of Municipalities
900 Chapel Street, 9th Floor
New Haven 06510-2807
ccm-ct.org

Delaware
Delaware League of Local Governments
P.O. Box 484
Dover 19903-0484
ipa.udel.edu/localgovt/dllg

Florida
Florida League of Cities
301 South Bronough Street, Suite 300
Tallahassee 32301
floridaleagueofcities.com

Georgia
Georgia Municipal Association
201 Pryor Street, S.W.
Atlanta 30303
gmanet.com/home

Idaho
Association of Idaho Cities
3100 South Vista Avenue, Suite 310
Boise 83705
idahocities.org

Illinois
Illinois Municipal League
500 East Capitol Avenue
Springfield 62701
iml.org

Indiana
Indiana Association of Cities and Towns
200 South Meridian Street, Suite 340
Indianapolis 46225
citiesandtowns.org

Iowa
Iowa League of Cities
317 Sixth Avenue, Suite 800
Des Moines 50309-4111
iowaleague.org

Kansas
League of Kansas Municipalities
300 S.W. Eighth Avenue
Topeka 66603
lkm.org

Kentucky

Kentucky League of Cities
100 East Vine Street, Suite 800
Lexington 40507
klc.org

Louisiana

Louisiana Municipal Association
700 North 10th Street
Baton Rouge 70802
lamunis.org

Maine

Maine Municipal Association
60 Community Drive
Augusta 04330
memun.org

Maryland

Maryland Municipal League
1212 West Street
Annapolis 21401
mdmunicipal.org

Massachusetts

Massachusetts Municipal Association
One Winthrop Square
Boston 02110
mma.org

Michigan

Michigan Municipal League
1675 Green Road
Ann Arbor 48105
mml.org

Minnesota

League of Minnesota Cities
145 University Avenue West
St. Paul 55103-2044
lmnc.org

Mississippi

Mississippi Municipal League
600 East Amite Street, Suite 104
Jackson 39201
mmlonline.com

Missouri

Missouri Municipal League
1727 Southridge Drive
Jefferson City 65109
mocities.com

Montana

Montana League of Cities and Towns
208 North Montana Avenue, Suite 106
Helena 59601
mlct.org

Nebraska

League of Nebraska Municipalities
1335 L Street
Lincoln 68508
lonm.org

Nevada

Nevada League of Cities and Municipalities
310 South Curry Street
Carson City 89703
nvleague.org

New Hampshire

New Hampshire Local Government Center
25 Triangle Park Drive
Concord 03301
nhlgc.org

New Jersey

New Jersey State League of Municipalities
222 West State Street
Trenton 08608
njslom.com

New Mexico

New Mexico Municipal League
1229 Paseo de Peralta
Santa Fe 87501
nmml.org

New York

New York State Conference of Mayors and Municipal Officials
119 Washington Avenue
Albany 12210
nycom.org

North Carolina

North Carolina League of Municipalities
215 North Dawson Street
Raleigh 27603
nclm.org

North Dakota

North Dakota League of Cities
410 East Front Avenue
Bismarck 58504
ndlc.org

Ohio

Ohio Municipal League
175 South Third Street, Suite 510
Columbus 43215
omlohio.org

Oklahoma

Oklahoma Municipal League
201 N.E. 23rd Street
Oklahoma City 73105
oml.org

Oregon

League of Oregon Cities
1201 Court Street, N.E., Suite 200
Salem 97301
orcities.org

Pennsylvania

Pennsylvania League of Cities and Municipalities
414 North Second Street
Harrisburg 17101
plcm.org

Rhode Island

Rhode Island League of Cities and Towns
One State Street, Suite 502
Providence 02908
rileague.org

South Carolina

Municipal Association of South Carolina
1411 Gervais Street
Columbia 29211
masc.sc

South Dakota

South Dakota Municipal League
208 Island Drive
Fort Pierre 57532
sdmunicipalleague.org

Tennessee

Tennessee Municipal League
226 Capitol Boulevard, Suite 710
Nashville 37219
tml1.org

Texas

Texas Municipal League
1821 Rutherford Lane, Suite 400
Austin 78754
tml.org

Utah

Utah League of Cities and Towns
50 South 600 East, Suite 150
Salt Lake City 84102
ulct.org

Vermont

Vermont League of Cities and Towns
89 Main Street, Suite 4
Montpelier 05602-2948
vlct.org

Virginia

Virginia Municipal League
13 East Franklin Street
Richmond 23219
vml.org

Washington

Association of Washington Cities
1076 Franklin Street, S.E.
Olympia 98501
awcnet.org

West Virginia

West Virginia Municipal League
2020 Kanawha Boulevard
Charleston 25311
wvml.org

Wisconsin

League of Wisconsin Municipalities
122 West Washington Avenue, Suite 300
Madison 53703-2715
lwm-info.org

Wyoming

Wyoming Association of Municipalities
315 West 27th Street
Cheyenne 82001
wyomuni.org

Directory 1-2 Provincial and Territorial Associations and Unions in Canada

Shown below are the 16 associations and unions serving the provinces and territories of Canada. For each association, the directory provides the website so that readers can go directly to the site to find additional information. Where there is no website available, we have provided the names of the president and permanent officer, along with all contact information for the latter.

Alberta

Alberta Association of Municipal Districts and Counties
aamdc.com

Alberta Urban Municipalities Association
munilink.net/live/

British Columbia

Union of British Columbia Municipalities
ubcm.ca

Manitoba

Association of Manitoba Municipalities
amm.mb.ca

New Brunswick

Association Francophone des Municipalités du Nouveau-Brunswick
afmnb.org

Cities of New Brunswick Association
President: Joel Richardson
Executive Director: Sandra Mark
P.O. Box 1421, Station A
Fredericton E3B 5E3
506 693-0008 (phone)
506 693-0009 (fax)
cities@rogers.com

Newfoundland and Labrador

Municipalities Newfoundland and Labrador
municipalitiesnl.ca

Northwest Territories

Northwest Territories Association of Communities
nwtac.com

Nova Scotia

Union of Nova Scotia Municipalities
unsm.ca

Ontario

Association of Municipalities of Ontario
amo.on.ca

Federation of Canadian Municipalities
fcm.ca

Prince Edward Island

Federation of Prince Edward Island Municipalities
fpeim.ca

Québec

Union des Municipalités du Québec
umq.qc.ca

Saskatchewan

Saskatchewan Association of Rural Municipalities
sarm.ca

Saskatchewan Urban Municipalities Association
suma.org

Yukon

Association of Yukon Communities
ayc-yk.ca

Directory 1-3 State Agencies for Community Affairs

Shown below are the agencies for community affairs for 47 states. For each agency, the directory provides the name, address, and website so that readers can go directly to the site to find additional information.

Alabama
Department of Economic and Community Affairs
401 Adams Avenue
Montgomery 36104
adeca.state.al.us

Alaska
Housing Finance Corporation
4300 Boniface Parkway
P.O. Box 101020
Anchorage 99510-1020
ahfc.state.ak.us

Arizona
Department of Housing
1110 West Washington Street, Suite 310
Phoenix 85007
azhousing.gov

Arkansas
Department of Human Services
Division of County Operations–
Community Services
P.O. Box 1437, Slot S330
Little Rock 72204-1437
state.ar.us/dhs/ctyops

Development Finance Authority
900 West Capitol Avenue, Suite 310
Little Rock 72201
state.ar.us/adfa

Economic Development Commission
900 West Capitol Avenue
Little Rock 72201
arkansasedc.com

Natural Resources Commission
101 East Capitol Avenue, Suite 350
Little Rock 72201
anrc.arkansas.gov

California
Department of Housing and Community Development
1800 Third Street
Sacramento 95811-6942
hcd.ca.gov

Colorado
Department of Local Affairs
1313 Sherman Street, Suite 518
Denver 80203
dola.state.co.us

Connecticut
Department of Economic and Community Development
505 Hudson Street
Hartford 06106-7106
ct.gov/ecd/site/default.asp

Delaware
State Housing Authority
18 The Green
Dover 19901 destatehousing.com/

Florida
Department of Economic Opportunity
107 East Madison Street
Caldwell Building
Tallahassee 32399-4120
dca.state.fl.us

Georgia
Department of Community Affairs
60 Executive Park South, N.E.
Atlanta 30329
dca.state.ga.us

Idaho
Department of Commerce
700 West State Street
Boise 83720-0093
commerce.idaho.gov

Illinois
Department of Commerce and Economic Opportunity
500 East Monroe
Springfield 62701
commerce.state.il.us/dceo

Indiana
Housing and Community Development Authority
30 South Meridian Street, Suite 1000
Indianapolis 46204
in.gov/ihfa

Office of Community and Rural Affairs
One North Capitol, Suite 600
Indianapolis 46204
ocra.in.gov

Iowa
Economic Development Authority
200 East Grand Avenue
Des Moines 50309
iowalifechanging.com

Kansas
Department of Commerce
Division of Community Development
1000 S.W. Jackson Street, Suite 100
Topeka 66612
kansascommerce.com

Kentucky
Department for Local Government
1024 Capital Center Drive, Suite 340
Frankfort 40601
dlg.ky.gov

Louisiana
Housing Finance Agency
2415 Quail Drive
Baton Rouge 70808
lhfa.state.la.us/

Office of Community Development
Division of Administration
1201 North Third Street, Suite 7-270
Baton Rouge 70802
doa.louisiana.gov

Maine
Department of Economic and Community Development
59 State House Station
Augusta 04333-0059
econdevmaine.com

Maryland

Department of Housing and Community Development
100 Community Place
Crownsville 21032
dhcd.state.md.us

Massachusetts

Department of Housing and Community Development
100 Cambridge Street, Suite 300
Boston 02114
state.ma.us/dhcd/dhcd.htm

Michigan

Economic Development Corporation
300 North Washington Square
Lansing 48913
medc.michigan.org

State Housing Development Authority
735 East. Michigan Avenue
P.O. Box 30044
Lansing 48909
michigan.gov/mshda

Minnesota

Minnesota Housing Finance Agency
400 Sibley Street, Suite 300
St. Paul 55101
mnhousing.gov

Mississippi

Mississippi Development Authority
501 North West Street
Jackson 39201
Mississippi.org

Missouri

Department of Economic Development
301 West High Street
P.O. Box 1157
Jefferson City 65102
ded.mo.gov

Montana

Department of Commerce
Local Government Assistance Division
301 South Park
P.O. Box 200501
Helena 59620-0501
commerce.mt.gov

Nebraska

Department of Economic Development
301 Centennial Mall South
P.O. Box 94666
Lincoln 68509-4666
neded.org

New Hampshire

Community Development Finance Authority
14 Dixon Avenue, Suite 102
Concord 03301
nhcdfa.org

Department of Health and Human Services
Bureau of Homeless and Housing Services
105 Pleasant Street
Concord 03301
state.nh.us/dhhs/ofs/ofs_ind.htm

Housing Finance Authority
P.O. Box 5087
Manchester 03108
nhhfa.org

New Jersey

Department of Community Affairs
101 South Broad Street
P.O. Box 800
Trenton 08625-0800
state.nj.us/dca

Housing and Mortgage Finance Agency
637 South Clinton Avenue
Trenton 08650-2085
njhousing.gov

New Mexico

Department of Finance and Administration
Local Government Division
407 Galisteo Street
Santa Fe, 87501
local.nmdfa.state.nm.us

New York

New York State Homes and Community Renewal
38-40 State Street, 8th Floor
Albany 12207
nysdhcr.gov

North Carolina

Department of Commerce
301 North Wilmington Street
Raleigh 27601-1058
nccommerce.com/en

North Dakota

Department of Commerce, Division of Community Services
1600 East Century Avenue, Suite 2
P.O. Box 2057
Bismarck 58503-2057
state.nd.us

Ohio

Department of Development
77 South High Street
Columbus 43216-1001
odod.state.oh.us

Housing Finance Agency
57 East Main Street
Columbus 43215
ohiohome.org

Oklahoma

Department of Commerce
900 North Stiles Avenue
Oklahoma City 73104
okcommerce.gov

Oregon

Economic and Community Development
775 Summer Street, N.E., Suite 200
Salem 97301-1280
econ.state.or.us

Pennsylvania

Department of Community and Economic Development
Commonwealth Keystone Building
400 North Street, 4th Floor
Harrisburg 17120-0225
newpa.com

Housing Finance Agency
Housing Finance Agency
211 North Front Street
Harrisburg 17101
phfa.org

Rhode Island

Office of Housing and Community Development
One Capitol Hill, 3rd Floor
Providence 02908-5873
muni-info.state.ri.us

South Carolina

Governor's Office of Economic Opportunity
1205 Pendleton Street
Columbia 29201
govoepp.state.sc.us/oeo

South Dakota

Governor's Office of Economic Development
711 East Wells Avenue
Pierre 57501-3369
state.sd.us/goed

Housing Development Authority
P.O. Box 1237
3060 East Elizabeth Street
Pierre 57501-1237
sdhda.org/

Tennessee

Housing Development Agency
404 James Robertson Parkway, Suite 1200
Nashville 37243-0900
state.tn.us/thda

Texas

CDM-Smith
3050 Post Oak Boulevard # 300
Houston 77056-6527
cdmsmith.com/

Utah

Department of Workforce Services
140 East 300 South
Salt Lake City 84111
community.utah.gov

Vermont

Agency of Commerce and Community Development
Department of Economic, Housing and Community Development
National Life Building, Drawer 20
Montpelier 05620-0501
state.vt.us/dca/housing

Virginia

Department of Housing and Community Development
Main Street Centre
600 East Main Street, Suite 300
Richmond 23219
dhcd.virginia.gov

West Virginia

Development Office
Capitol Complex, Building 6, Room 553
Charleston, West Virginia 25305-0311
wvdo.org

Wisconsin

Wisconsin Department of Administration, Division of Housing
P. O. Box 7970
Madison 53707-7970
housing.wi.gov

Wyoming

Wyoming Business Council
214 West 15th Street
Cheyenne 82001-0240
wyomingbusiness.org

Directory 1-4   Provincial and Territorial Agencies for Local Affairs in Canada

Shown below are the agencies for local affairs serving the provinces and territories of Canada. For each agency the directory provides the address and website for the ministry so that readers can go directly to the site to find additional information.

Alberta

Alberta Municipal Affairs
Communications Branch
Commerce Place, 18th Floor
10155-102 Street
Edmonton T5J 4L4
municipalaffairs.gov.ab.ca

British Columbia

Ministry of Community, Sport and Cultural Development
P.O. Box 9490
Station Provincial Government
Victoria V8W 9N7
gov.bc.ca/cserv/index.html

Manitoba

Manitoba Aboriginal and Northern Affairs
344-450 Broadway
Winnipeg R3C 0V8
gov.mb.ca/ana

New Brunswick

Aboriginal Affairs Secretariat
Kings Place
P.O. Box 6000
Fredericton E3B 5H1
gov.pe.ca/aboriginalaffairs

Newfoundland and Labrador

Department of Municipal Affairs
Confederation Building, 4th Floor (West Block)
P.O. Box 8700
St. John's A1B 4J6
ma.gov.nl.ca/ma

Northwest Territories

Department of Education, Culture and Employment
P.O. Box 1320
Yellowknife X1A 2L9
ece.gov.nt.ca

Nova Scotia

Service Nova Scotia and Municipal Relations
Mail Room, 8 South, Maritime Centre
1505 Barrington Street
Halifax B3J 3K5
gov.ns.ca/snsmr/

Ontario

Ministry of Municipal Affairs and Housing
777 Bay Street, 17th Floor
Toronto M5G 2E5
mah.gov.on.ca

Prince Edward Island

Department of Finance, Energy, and Municipal Affairs
Shaw Building, Second Floor South
95 Rochford Street
P.O. Box 2000
Charlottetown C1A 7N8
gov.pe.ca/finance

Québec

Affaires Municipales, Régions et Occupation du territoire
(Ministry of Municipal Affairs, Regions and Land Occupancy)
10, rue Pierre-Olivier-Chauveau
Québec G1R 4J3
mamrot.gouv.qc.ca/

Saskatchewan

Public Service Commission
2350 Albert Street
Regina S4P 4A6
psc.gov.sk.ca

Yukon

Department of Community Services
Government of Yukon
Box 2703
Whitehorse Y1A 2C6
community.gov.yk.ca/

Directory 1-5   U.S. Municipal Management Associations

Shown below are the names of the 47 municipal management associations in the United States. For each association, the directory provides the website so that readers can go directly to the site to find additional information. Where there is no website available, we have provided the name, address, and all contact information for the association president (current as of January 19, 2013).

Alabama

Alabama City/County Management Association
accma-online.org/

Alaska

Alaska Municipal Management Association
alaskamanagers.org/

Arizona

Arizona City/County Management
Association azmanagement.org/

Arkansas

Arkansas City/County Management Association
Raymond W. Gosack (as of May 2012)
City Administrator
City of Fort Smith
P.O. Box 1908
Fort Smith 72902-1908
rgosack@fortrsmithar.gov

Arkansas Municipal League
arml.org/resources.html

California

City Manager's Department, League of California Cities
cacities.org

Cal-ICMA
icma.org/en/ca/home

Colorado

Colorado City and County Management Association
coloradoccma.org

Connecticut

Connecticut Town and City Management Association
cttcma.govoffice3.com

Delaware

City Management Association of Delaware
Cathryn C. Thomas
City Administrator
City of New Castle
220 Delaware Street
New Castle 19720-4816
cathrynthomas@newcastlecity.org

Florida

Florida City and County Management Association
fccma.org/

Georgia

Georgia City-County Management Association
gccma.com

Idaho

Idaho City/County Management Association
See Wyoming

Illinois

Illinois City/County Management Association
ilcma.org/

Indiana

Indiana Association of Cities and Towns
citiesandtowns.org

Iowa

Iowa City/County Management Association
iacma.net

Kansas

Kansas Association of City/County Management
kacm.us

Kentucky

Kentucky City/County Management Association
kccma.org

Maine

Maine Town and City Management Association
mtcma.org

Maryland

Maryland City County Management Association
icma.org/en/md/home

Massachusetts

Massachusetts Municipal Management Association
massmanagers.org

Michigan

Michigan Local Government Management Association
mlgma.org

Minnesota

Minnesota City/County Management Association
mncma.org

Missouri

Missouri City/County Management Association
momanagers.org

Montana

See Wyoming

Nebraska

Nebraska City/County Management Association
nebraskacma.org

Nevada

Local Government Managers Association of Nevada
nevadalogman.org

New Hampshire

New Hampshire Municipal Management Association
nhmunicipal.org

New Jersey

New Jersey Municipal Management Association
njmma.org

New Mexico

New Mexico City Management Association
Ferron M. Lucero Sr.
City Manager
Town of Clayton
1 Chestnut Street
Clayton 88415-3523
flucerotoc@plateautel.net

New York

New York State City/County Management Association
nyscma.govoffice.com

North Carolina

North Carolina City and County Management Association
ncmanagers.org

North Dakota

See Wyoming

Ohio

Ohio City/County Management Association
ocmaohio.org

Oklahoma

City Management Association of Oklahoma
cmao-ok.org/

Oregon

Oregon City/County Management Association
occma.org

Pennsylvania

Association for Pennsylvania Municipal Management
apmm.net

Rhode Island

Rhode Island City and Town Management Association
William Sequino Jr.
Town Manager
Town of East Greenwich
P.O. Box 111
East Greenwich 02818-0111
wsequino@eastgreenwichri.com

South Carolina

South Carolina City and County Management Association
icma.org/en/sc/home

South Dakota

South Dakota City Management Association
sdmunicipalleague.org (Go to "Affiliate Organizations" and then to "City Management")

Tennessee

Tennessee City Management Association
tncma.org

Texas

Texas City Management Association
tcma.org

Utah

Utah City Management Association
ucma-utah.org

Vermont

Vermont Town and City Management Association
Dominic Dean Cloud
City Manager
City of St. Albans
100 North Main Street
Saint Albans 05478
d.cloud@stalbansvt.com

Virginia

Virginia Local Government Management Association
vlgma.org

Washington

Washington City/County Management Association
wccma.org

West Virginia

West Virginia City Management Association
wvmanagers.org

Wisconsin

Wisconsin City/County Management Association
wcma-wi.org

Wyoming, Idaho, Montana, North Dakota, and South Dakota

Great Open Spaces City Management Association
icma.org/en/go/home

Directory 1-6   International Municipal Management Associations

Shown below are the names of 25 international municipal management associations. For each association the directory provides the website so that readers can go directly to the site to find additional information. Where there is no website available, we have provided the name, address, and all contact information for the president of the association (current as of January 19, 2013).

Australia

Local Government Managers Australia (LGMA)
lgma.org.au

Canada

Canadian Association of Municipal Administrators (CAMA)
camacam.ca

Denmark

National Association of Chief Executives in Danish Municipalities (KOMDIR)
komdir.dk

Georgia

Municipal Service Providers' Association (Georgia)
mspa.ge

Hungary

Partnership of Hungarian Local Government Associations
kisvarosok.hu

India

City Managers' Association, Gujarat
cmag-india.com

City Managers' Association, Karnataka (CMAK)
cmakarnataka.com

City Managers' Association, Orissa
cmao.nic.in

Indonesia

All-Indonesia Association of City Government (APEKSI)
apeksi.or.id

Ireland

County and City Managers' Association
Anne O'Keeffe
Director
Office for Local Authority Management
Floor 2 Cumberland House
Dublin 2
353-94-9 (phone)

Israel

Union of Local Authorities in Israel (ULAI)
masham.orq.il/Enqlish

Mexico

ICMA Latinoamérica
icma.org/en/international/Page/100260/ICMA_Latinoamrica

Nepal

Municipal Association of Nepal (MuAN)
muannepal.org.np

Netherlands

Dutch City Managers Association
gemeentesecretaris.nl

New Zealand

New Zealand Society of Local Government Managers
solgm.org.nz

Norway

Norwegian Forum of Municipal Executives
Oystein Sivertsen
Executive Director
Norwegian Forum of Municipal Executives
477-785-0100

Russia

Russian National Congress of Municipalities
www.rncm.ru (no English version)

Slovakia

Slovak City Managers' Association
apums.sk

South Africa

Institute for Local Government Management of South Africa
ilgm.co.za

South Korea

Korean Urban Management Association
knuma.org

Spain

L'Union des Dirigeants Territoriaux de l'Europe (U.Di.T.E.)
udite.eu

Sri Lanka

Federation of Sri Lankan Local Government Authorities (FSLGA)
fslga.lk

Sweden

Association of Swedish City Managers
Anna Sandborgh
Chair
Karlstads kommun
Kommunledningskontoret
651 84 Karlstad
anna.sandborgh@karlstad.se
46-5-429-5102

United Kingdom

Society of Local Authority Chief Executives (SOLACE)
solace.org.uk

Viet Nam

Association of Cities of Viet Nam
acvn.vn

Directory 1-7 U.S. State Associations of Counties

Shown below are the names of the 53 state associations of counties in the United States. For each association the directory provides the address and website so that readers can go directly to the site to find additional information. Where there is no website available, we have provided the name and phone number for the executive director (current as of January 19, 2013).

Alabama

Association of County Commissions of Alabama
100 North Jackson Street
Montgomery 36104
acca-online.org

Alaska

Alaska Municipal League
217 Second Street, Suite 200
Juneau 99801
akml.org

Arizona

Arizona Association of Counties
1910 West Jefferson, Suite 1
Phoenix 85009
azcounties.org

County Supervisors Association of Arizona
1905 West Washington Street, Suite 100
Phoenix 85009
countysupervisors.org

Arkansas

Association of Arkansas Counties
1415 West Third Street
Little Rock 72201
arcounties.org

California

California State Association of Counties
1100 K Street, Suite 101
Sacramento 95814
csac.counties.org

Colorado

Colorado Counties, Inc.
800 Grant Street, Suite 500
Denver 80203
ccionline.org

Delaware

Delaware Association of Counties
Richard Cecil
Executive Director
12 North Washington Avenue
Lewes 19958-1806
302-645-0432 (phone)
302-645-2232 (fax)
dick_cecil@yahoo.com

Florida

Florida Association of Counties
100 South Monroe Street
Tallahassee 32301
fl-counties.com

Georgia

Association County Commissioners of Georgia
50 Hurt Plaza, Suite 1000
Atlanta 30303
accg.org

Hawaii

Hawaii State Association of Counties
4396 Rice Street, Suite 206
Lihue 96766
808-270-7760 (phone)
808-270-7639 (fax)

Idaho

Idaho Association of Counties
700 West Washington
P.O. Box 1623
Boise 83701
idcounties.org

Illinois

Illinois Association of County Board Members
413 West Monroe Street, 2nd Floor
Springfield 62704
ilcounty.org

Metro Counties of Illinois
Dwight Magalis
Executive Director
1303 Brandywine Road
Libertyville 60048-3000
847-816-0889 (phone)
847-247-9915 (fax)
magalisike@msn.com

United Counties Council of Illinois
W. Michael McCreery
Executive Director
217 East Monroe, Suite 101
Springfield 62701-1743
217-544-5585 (phone)
217-544-5571 (fax)
mike@mmccreery.com

Indiana

Association of Indiana Counties
101 West Ohio Street, Suite 1575
Indianapolis 46204
indianacounties.org

Iowa

Iowa State Association of Counties
5500 Westown Parkway, Suite 190
West Des Moines 50266
iowacounties.org

Kansas

Kansas Association of Counties
300 S.W. Eighth Street, 3rd Floor
Topeka 66603
kansascounties.org

Kentucky

Kentucky Association of Counties
400 Englewood Drive
Frankfort 40601
kaco.org

Louisiana

Police Jury Association of Louisiana
707 North Seventh Street
Baton Rouge 70802
lpgov.org

Maine

Maine County Commissioners Association
4 Gabriel Drive
Augusta 04330
mainecounties.org

Maryland

Maryland Association of Counties
169 Conduit Street
Annapolis 21401
mdcounties.org

Massachusetts

Massachusetts Association of County Commissioners
William P. O'Donnell
Executive Director
614 High Street
Dedham 02027-0310
781-461-6105 (phone)
781-326-6480 (fax)

Michigan

Michigan Association of Counties
935 North Washington Avenue
Lansing 48906
micounties.org

Minnesota

Association of Minnesota Counties
125 Charles Avenue
St. Paul 55103-2108
mncounties.org

Mississippi

Mississippi Association of Supervisors
793 North President Street
Jackson 39202
masnetwork.org

Missouri

Missouri Association of Counties
516 East Capitol Avenue
P.O. Box 234
Jefferson City 65102-0234
mocounties.com

Montana

Montana Association of Counties
2715 Skyway Drive
Helena 59602-1213
maco.cog.mt.us

Nebraska

Nebraska Association of County Officials
625 South 14th Street
Lincoln 68508
nacone.org

Nevada

Nevada Association of Counties
304 South Minnesota Street
Carson City 89703
nvnaco.org

New Hampshire

New Hampshire Association of Counties
Bow Brook Place
46 Donovan Street, Suite 2
Concord 03301-2624
nhcounties.org

New Jersey

New Jersey Association of Counties
150 West State Street
Trenton 08608
njac.org

New Mexico

New Mexico Association of Counties
613 Old Santa Fe Trail
Santa Fe 87505
nmcounties.org

New York

New York State Association of Counties
540 Broadway, 5th Floor
Albany 12207
nysac.org

North Carolina

North Carolina Association of County Commissioners
215 North Dawson Street
Raleigh 27603
ncacc.org

North Dakota

North Dakota Association of Counties
1661 Capitol Way
P.O. Box 877
Bismarck 58502-0877
ndaco.org

Ohio

County Commissioners Association of Ohio
209 East State Street
Columbus 43215-4309
ccao.org

Oklahoma

Association of County Commissioners of Oklahoma City
429 N.E. 50th Street
Oklahoma City 73105
okacco.com

Oregon

Association of Oregon Counties
1201 Court Street N.E., Suite 300
Salem 97301
aocweb.org

Pennsylvania

County Commissioners Association of Pennsylvania
P.O. Box 60769
Harrisburg 17106-0769
pacounties.org

South Carolina

South Carolina Association of Counties
1919 Thurmond Mall
Columbia 29201
sccounties.org

South Dakota

South Dakota Association of County Officials
211 East Prospect Avenue
Pierre 57501
sdcounties.org

South Dakota Association of County Commissioners
211 East Prospect Avenue
Pierre 57501
sdcc.govoffice2.com

Tennessee

Tennessee County Services Association
226 Capitol Boulevard, Suite 700
Nashville 37219-1896
tncounties.org

Texas

Texas Association of Counties
1210 San Antonio Street
Austin 78701
county.org

Utah

Utah Association of Counties
5397 South Vine Street
Salt Lake City 84107
uacnet.org

Virginia

Virginia Association of Counties
1207 East Main Street, Suite 300
Richmond 23219-3627
vaco.org

Washington

Washington Association of County Officials
206 Tenth Avenue, S.E.
Olympia 98501
wacounties.org/waco

Washington State Association of Counties
206 Tenth Avenue, S.E.
Olympia 98501
wacounties.org/wsac

West Virginia

County Commissioners' Association of West Virginia
2309 Washington Street, East
Charleston 25311
polsci.wvu.edu/wv

West Virginia Association of Counties
2211 Washington Street East
Charleston 25311-2118
wvcounties.org

Wisconsin

Wisconsin Counties Association
22 East Mifflin Street, Suite 900
Madison 53703
wicounties.org

Wyoming

Wyoming County Commissioners Association
P.O. Box 86
Cheyenne 82003
wyo-wcca.org

Directory 1-8   U.S. Councils of Governments Recognized by ICMA

Shown below are the names and websites of the 96 U.S. councils of government recognized by ICMA state associations of counties in the United States. Where there is no website available, we have provided the phone number for the council office.

ALABAMA–4

Central Alabama Regional Planning and Development Commission
carpdc.com

East Alabama Regional Planning and Development Commission
earpdc.org

Regional Planning Commission of Greater Birmingham
rpcgb.org

South Central Alabama Development Commission
scadc.net

ARIZONA–2

Maricopa Association of Governments
azmag.gov

Pima Association of Governments
pagnet.org

ARKANSAS–3

Metroplan
metroplan.org

Northwest Arkansas Regional Planning Commission
nwarpc.org

White River Planning & Development District
wrpdd.org

CALIFORNIA–9

Association of Bay Area Governments
abag.ca.gov

Fresno Council of Governments
fresnocog.org

Sacramento Area Council of Governments
sacog.org

San Bernardino Associated Governments
sanbag.ca.gov

San Diego Association of Governments
sandag.org

Santa Barbara County Association of Governments
sbcag.org

Southern California Association of Governments
scag.ca.gov

Stanislaus Council of Governments
stancog.org

Western Riverside Council of Governments
wrcog.cog.ca.us

COLORADO-1

Denver Regional Council of Governments
drcog.org

DISTRICT OF COLUMBIA-1

Metropolitan Washington Council of Governments
mwcog.org

FLORIDA-2

Solid Waste Authority of Palm Beach County
swa.org

Tampa Bay Regional Planning Council
tbrpc.org

GEORGIA-3

Atlanta Regional Commission
atlantaregional.com

Middle Georgia Regional Commission
middlegeorgiarc.org

Southern Georgia Regional Commission
sgrdc.com

IDAHO-1

Panhandle Area Council
pacni.org

ILLINOIS-9

Bi-State Regional Commission
bistateonline.org

Champaign County Regional Planning Commission
ccrpc.org

DuPage Mayors and Managers Conference
dmmc-cog.org

Lake County Municipal League
lakecountyleague.org

North Central Illinois Council of Governments
ncicg.org

Northwest Municipal Conference
nwmc-cog.org

South Central Illinois Regional Planning and Development Commission
scirpdc.com

Southwestern Illinois Metropolitan and Regional Planning Commission
618 344-4250

Tri-County Regional Planning Commission
tricountyrpc.org

IOWA-1

Midas Council of Governments
midascog.net

KENTUCKY-4

Barren River Area Development District
bradd.org

Big Sandy Area Development District
bigsandy.org

Lincoln Trail Area Development District
ltadd.org

Northern Kentucky Area Development District
nkadd.org

MARYLAND-2

Baltimore Metropolitan Council
baltometro.org

Tri-County Council For Southern Maryland
tccsmd.org

MICHIGAN-1

Southeast Michigan Council of Governments
semcog.org

MISSISSIPPI-1

Central Mississippi Planning & Development District
cmpdd.org

MISSOURI-3

East-West Gateway Council of Governments
ewgateway.org

Mid-America Regional Council
marc.org

South Central Ozark Council of Governments
scocog.org

NEW MEXICO-2

Mid-Region Council of Governments
mrcog-nm.gov

Southwest New Mexico Council of Governments
swnmcog.org

NEW YORK-1

Capital District Regional Planning Commission
cdrpc.org

NORTH CAROLINA-5

Centralina Council of Governments
centralina.org

Eastern Carolina Council of Governments
eccog.org

Lumber River Council of Governments
lumberrivercog.org

Piedmont Triad Council of Governments
ptcog.org

Upper Coastal Plain Council of Governments
ucpcog.org

OHIO-4

Miami Valley Regional Planning Commission
mvrpc.org

Ohio-Kentucky-Indiana Regional Council of Governments
oki.org

Ohio Mid-Eastern Governments Association
omegadistrict.org

Toledo Metropolitan Area Council of Governments
tmacog.org

OKLAHOMA-2

Association of Central Oklahoma Governments
acogok.org

Central Oklahoma Economic Development District
coedd.org

OREGON-4

Lane Council of Governments
lcog.org

Mid-Columbia Economic Development District
mcedd.org

Mid-Willamette Valley Council of Governments
mwvcog.org

Oregon Cascades West Council of Governments
ocwcog.org

SOUTH CAROLINA-3

Central Midlands Council of Governments
centralmidlands.org

South Carolina Appalachian Council of Governments
scacog.org

Upper Savannah Council of Governments
uppersavannah.com

SOUTH DAKOTA-2

Northeast Council of Governments
necog.org

Planning and Development District III
districtiii.org

TEXAS-15

Alamo Area Council of Governments
aacog.dst.tx.us

Ark-Tex Council of Governments
atcog.org

Capital Area Planning Council of Governments
capcog.org

Central Texas Council of Governments
ctcog.org

Coastal Bend Council of Governments
cbcog98.org

Concho Valley Council of Governments
cvcog.org

Deep East Texas Council of Governments
detcog.org

Heart of Texas Council of Governments
hotcog.org

Houston-Galveston Area Council
h-gac.com

Nortex Regional Planning Commission
nortexrpc.org

North Central Texas Council of Governments
nctcog.org

Panhandle Regional Planning Commission
theprpc.org

South Plains Association of Governments
spag.org

Texoma Council of Governments
texoma.cog.tx.us

West Central Texas Council of Governments
wctcog.org

UTAH-1

Five County Association of Governments
fcaog.state.ut.us

VIRGINIA-5

Crater Planning District Commission
craterpdc.org

Hampton Roads Planning District Commission
hrpdc.org

Northern Neck Planning District Commission
nnpdc.org

Northern Virginia Planning District Commission
novaregion.org

West Piedmont Planning District Commission
wppdc.org

WASHINGTON-1

Benton-Franklin Regional Council of Governments
bfcog.us

WEST VIRGINIA-3

Belomar Regional Council
belomar.org

Mid-Ohio Valley Regional Council
movrc.org

Region One Planning & Development Council
regiononepdc.org

WISCONSIN-1

East Central Wisconsin Regional Planning Commission
eastcentralrpc.org

2

Professional, Special Assistance, and Educational Organizations Serving Local and State Governments

This article briefly describes 79 organizations that provide services of particular importance to cities, counties, and other local and state governments. Most of the organizations are membership groups for school administrators, health officers, city planners, city managers, public works directors, city attorneys, and other administrators who are appointed rather than elected. Several are general service and representational organizations for states, cities, counties, and administrators and citizens. Some organizations provide distinctive research, technological, consulting, and educational programs on a cost-of-service basis and have been established to meet specific needs of state and local governments. The others support educational activities and conduct research in urban affairs or government administration, thereby indirectly strengthening professionalism in government administration.

The assistance available through the secretariats of these national organizations provides an excellent method of obtaining expert advice and actual information on specific problems. The information secured in this way enables local and state officials to improve administrative practices, organization, and methods and thus improve the quality of services rendered. Many of these organizations also are active in raising the professional standards of their members through

in-service training, special conferences and seminars, and other kinds of professional development.

Research on current problems is a continuing activity of many of these groups, and all issue a variety of publications ranging from newsletters and occasional bulletins to diversified books, monographs, research papers, conference proceedings, and regular and special reports.

These organizations provide many of the services that in other countries would be the responsibility of the national government. They arrange annual conferences, answer inquiries, provide in-service training and other kinds of professional development, provide placement services for members, and develop service and cost standards for various activities. Most of the organizations listed have individual memberships, and several also have agency or institutional memberships. Some of these organizations have service memberships that may be based on the population of the jurisdiction, the annual revenue of the jurisdiction or agency, or other criteria that roughly measure the costs of providing service. In addition to these kinds of membership fees, some of the organizations provide specialized consulting, training, and information services both by annual subscription and by charges for specific projects.

Listing of Organizations

Airports Council International–North America (201)

1615 L Street, N.W., Suite 300
Washington, D.C. 20006
202-293-8500; fax: 202-331-1362

Website: aci-na.org

President: Greg Principato

Major publications: *Airport Highlights;* studies, surveys, reports

Purpose: To advocate policies and provide services that strengthen the ability of airports to serve their passengers, customers, and communities. ACI is recognized as the authoritative voice of airports worldwide. ACI-NA presents the unique views and recommendations of airport management to federal, state, provincial, and local governments; industry; the media; and the general public. As "the Voice of Airports," ACI-NA (1) promotes cooperation with all elements of the commercial civil aviation industry; (2) exchanges ideas, information, and experiences on common airport issues; (3) identifies, interprets, and disseminates information to its members on current industry trends and practices; and (4) creates forums of common interest, builds professional relationships, and interprets key airport policy and business issues to the ACI-NA membership. Established 1948.

American Association of Airport Executives (AAAE)

601 Madison Street, Suite 400
Alexandria, Virginia 22314
703-824-0500; fax: 703-820-1395

Website: aaae.org

President: Charles M. Barclay

Major publications: *Airport Report; Airport Magazine; Airport Report Express*

Purpose: To assist airport managers in performing their complex and diverse responsibilities through an airport management reference library; a consulting service; publications containing technical, administrative, legal, and operational information; an electronic bulletin board system; and Aviation News and Training Network, a private satellite broadcast network for airport employee training and news. AAAE is the world's largest professional organization for airport executives, representing thousands of airport management personnel at public-use commercial and general aviation airports. Its members represent some 850 airports and hundreds of companies and organizations that support airports. AAAE serves its membership through results-oriented representation in Washington, D.C., and delivers a wide range of industry services and professional development opportunities, including training, meetings and conferences, and a highly respected accreditation program. Established 1928.

American Association of Port Authorities (AAPA)

1010 Duke Street
Alexandria, Virginia 22314-3589
703-684-5700; fax: 703-684-6321

E-mail: info@aapa-ports.org

Website: aapa-ports.org

President: Kurt J. Nagle

Major publications: *Alert Newsletter; AAPA Directory–Seaports of the Americas; Seaport Magazine*

Purpose: To promote the common interests of the port community and provide leadership on trade, transportation, environmental, and other issues related to port development and operations. As the alliance of ports of the Western Hemisphere, AAPA furthers public understanding of the essential role fulfilled by ports within the global transportation system. It also serves as a resource to help members accomplish their professional responsibilities. Established 1912.

American Association of School Administrators (AASA)

1615 Duke Street
Alexandria, Virginia 22314
703-528-0700; fax: 703-841-1543

Website: aasa.org

Executive director: Daniel A. Domenech

Major publications: *The School Administrator;* Critical Issues Series

Purpose: To develop qualified educational leaders and support excellence in educational administration; to initiate and support laws, policies, research, and practices that will improve education; to promote programs and activities that focus on leadership for learning and excellence in education; and to cultivate a climate in which quality education can thrive. Established 1865.

American College of Healthcare Executives (ACHE)

One North Franklin Street, Suite 1700
Chicago, Illinois 60606-3529
312-424-2800; fax: 312-424-0023

Website: ache.org

President/CEO: Thomas C. Dolan, PhD, FACHE, CAE

Major publications: *Journal of Healthcare Management; Healthcare Executive; Frontiers of Health Services Management;* miscellaneous studies and task force, committee, and seminar reports

Purpose: To be the premier professional society for health care executives who are dedicated to improving health care delivery and to advancing health care management excellence. Established 1933.

American Institute of Architects (AIA)

1735 New York Avenue, N.W.
Washington, D.C. 20006
202-626-7300; fax: 202-626-7547
800-242-3837

Website: aia.org

President: Jeffery Potter, FAIA

Major publication: *AIArchitect*

Purpose: To organize and unite in fellowship the members of the architectural profession; to promote the aesthetic, scientific, and practical efficiency of the profession; to advance the science and art of planning and building by advancing the standards of architectural education, training, and practice; to coordinate the efforts of the building industry and the profession of architecture to ensure the advancement of living standards for people through improved environment; and to make the profession of architecture one of ever-increasing service to society. Established 1857.

American Library Association (ALA)

50 East Huron Street
Chicago, Illinois 60611
312-944-6780; fax: 312-440-9374
800-545-2433
Also at 1615 New Hampshire Avenue, N.W.
Washington, D.C. 20009-2520
202-628-8410; fax: 202-628-8419
800-941-8478

Website: www.ala.org

Executive director: Keith Michael Fiels

Major publications: *American Libraries; Booklist; Book Links Magazine; Smart Libraries Newsletter; Library Technology Reports;* Guide to Reference (a subscription database); and the websites ALA TechSource and RDA [Research Description and Access] Toolkit.

Purpose: To assist libraries and librarians in promoting and improving library service and librarianship. Established 1876.

American Planning Association (APA), and its professional institute, the American Institute of Certified Planners (AICP)

1030 15th Street, N.W., Suite 750 West
Washington, D.C. 20005-1503
202-872-0611; fax: 202-872-0643
Also at 205 North Michigan Avenue, Suite 1200
Chicago, Illinois 60601
312-431-9100; fax: 312-786-6700

Website: planning.org

Executive director/CEO: W. Paul Farmer, FAICP

Major publications: *Journal of the APA; Planning; Planning and Environmental Law; Zoning Practice; The Commissioner; Practicing Planner; Interact; APA Advocate;* Planning Advisory Service (PAS) Reports

Purpose: To encourage planning that will meet the needs of people and society more effectively. APA is a nonprofit public interest and research organization representing 43,000 practicing planners, officials, and citizens involved with urban and rural planning issues. Sixty-five percent of its members work for state and local government agencies and are involved daily in formulating planning policies and preparing land use regulations. AICP is APA's professional institute, providing recognized leadership nationwide in the certification of professional planners, ethics, professional development, planning education, and the standards of planning practice. APA resulted from a consolidation of the American Institute of Planners, founded in 1917, and the American Society of Planning Officials, established in 1934.

American Public Gas Association (APGA)

201 Massachusetts Avenue, N.E., Suite C-4
Washington, D.C. 20002
202-464-2742; fax: 202-464-0246

E-mail: bkalisch@apga.org

Website: apga.org

President/CEO: Bert Kalisch

Major publications: *Public Gas News* (bi-weekly newsletter); *Publicly Owned Natural Gas System Directory* (annual); *The Source* (quarterly magazine)

Purpose: To be an advocate for publicly owned natural gas distribution systems, and effectively educate and communicate with members to promote safety, awareness, performance, and competitiveness. Established 1961.

American Public Health Association (APHA)

800-I Street, N.W.
Washington, D.C. 20001-3710
202-777-2742; fax: 202-777-2534

Website: apha.org

Executive director: Georges Benjamin, MD

Major publications: *American Journal of Public Health; The Nation's Health*

Purpose: To protect the health of the public through the maintenance of standards for scientific procedures, legislative education, and practical application of innovative health programs. Established 1872.

American Public Human Services Association (APHSA)

1133 19th Street, N.W., Suite 400
Washington, D.C. 20036
202-682-0100; fax: 202-289-6555

Website: aphsa.org

Executive director: Tracy Wareing

Major publications: *Policy and Practice* magazine; *Public Human Services Directory; This Week in Health; This Week in Washington; W-Memo; Working for Tomorrow*

Purpose: To develop and promote policies and practices that improve the health and well-being of families, children, and adults. Established 1930.

American Public Power Association (APPA)

1875 Connecticut Avenue, N.W., Suite 1200
Washington, D.C. 20009
202-467-2900; fax: 202-467-2910

Website: publicpower.org

President/CEO: Mark Crisson

Major publications: *Public Power* (magazine); *Public Power Weekly* (newsletter); *Public Power Daily*

Purpose: To promote the efficiency and benefits of publicly owned electric systems; to achieve cooperation among public systems; to protect the interests of publicly owned utilities; and to provide service in the fields of management and operation, energy conservation, consumer services, public relations, engineering, design, construction, research, and accounting practice. APPA represents more than 2,000 community-owned electric utilities and provides services in the areas of government relations, engineering and operations, accounting and finance, energy research and development, management, customer relations, and public communications. The association represents public power interests before Congress, federal agencies, and the courts; provides educational programs and energy planning services in technical and management areas; and collects, analyzes, and disseminates information on public power and the electric utility industry. APPA publishes a weekly newsletter, a magazine, and many specialized publications; funds energy research and development projects; recognizes utilities and individuals for excellence in management and operations; and serves as a resource for federal, state, and local policy makers and officials, news reporters, public interest and other organizations, and the general public on public power and energy issues. Established 1940.

American Public Transportation Association (APTA)

1666 K Street, N.W., Suite 1100
Washington, D.C. 20006
202-496-4800; fax: 202-496-4324

Website: apta.com

President: Gary C. Thomas

Major publications: *Passenger Transport; Public Transportation Fact Book*

Purpose: To represent the operators of and suppliers to public transit; to provide a medium for discussion, exchange of experiences, and comparative study of industry affairs; and to research and investigate methods to improve public transit. The association also assists public transit entities with special issues, and collects and makes available public transit-related data and information. Established 1882.

American Public Works Association (APWA)

2345 Grand Boulevard, Suite 700
Kansas City, Missouri 64108-2625
816-472-6100; fax: 816-472-1610
Also at 1275 K Street, N.W., Suite 750
Washington, D.C. 20005-4083
202-408-9541; fax: 202-408-9542

Website: apwa.net

Executive director: Peter B. King

Major publications: *APWA Reporter* (12 issues), research reports, technical publications and manuals

Purpose: To develop and support the people, agencies, and organizations that plan, build, maintain, and improve our communities. Established 1894.

American Society for Public Administration (ASPA)

1301 Pennsylvania Avenue, N.W., Suite 700
Washington, D.C. 20004
202-393-7878; fax: 202-638-4952

Website: aspanet.org

Executive director: Antoinette A. Samuel

Major publications: *Public Administration Review; PA Times*

Purpose: To improve the management of public service at all levels of government; to advocate on behalf of public service; to advance the science, processes, and art of public administration; and to disseminate information and facilitate the exchange of knowledge among persons interested in the practice or teaching of public administration. Established 1939.

American Water Works Association (AWWA)

6666 West Quincy Avenue
Denver, Colorado 80235
303-794-7711; fax: 303-347-0804

Website: awwa.org

Executive director: David B. LaFrance

Major publications: *AWWA Journal; MainStream; OpFlow; WaterWeek*

Purpose: To promote public health and welfare in the provision of drinking water of unquestionable and sufficient quality. Founded 1881.

Association of Public-Safety Communications Officials–International, Inc.

351 North Williamson Boulevard
Daytona Beach, Florida 32114-1112
386-322-2500; fax: 386-322-2501
Also at 1426 Prince Street
Alexandria, Virginia 22314-2815
571-312-4400; fax: 386-322-2501

Website: apcointl.org

Interim executive director: Derek Poarch

Major publications: *APCO BULLETIN; The Journal of Public Safety Communications; Public Safety Operating Procedures Manual;* APCO training courses

Purpose: To promote the development and progress of public safety telecommunications through research, planning, and training; to promote cooperation among public safety agencies; to perform frequency coordination for radio services administered by the Federal Communications Commission; and to act as a liaison with federal regulatory bodies. Established 1935.

Association of Public Treasurers of the United States and Canada (APTUSC)

2851 South Parker Road, Suite 560
Aurora, Colorado 80014
720-248-2771; fax: 303-755-7363

Website: aptusc.org

Executive director: Lindsey Dively

Major publications: *Cash Flow Forecasting Guide; Cash Handling Training Manual; Debt Policy Handbook; Disaster Preparedness Guide; Guide to Internal Controls; Revenue Collections Manual; Stop That Fraud Handbook*

Purpose: To enhance local treasury management by providing educational training, technical assistance, legislative services, and a forum for treasurers to exchange ideas and develop policy papers and positions. Established 1965.

Canadian Association of Municipal Administrators (CAMA)

P.O. Box 128, Station A
Fredericton, New Brunswick E3B 4Y2
866-771-2262; fax: 506-460-2134

Website: camacam.ca

Executive director: Ron Shaw

Purpose: To achieve greater communication and cooperation among municipal managers across Canada, and to focus the talents of its members on the preservation and advancement of municipal government by enhancing the quality of municipal management in Canada. Established 1972.

Center for State and Local Government Excellence (SLGE)

777 North Capitol Street, N.E., Suite 500
Washington, D.C. 20002-4201
202-682-6100; fax: 202-962-3604

Website: slge.org

President and CEO: Elizabeth Kellar

Recent research reports: *The Funding of State and Local Pensions: 2011-2015; The Evolving Role of Defined Contribution Plans in the Public Sector; State and Local Pensions: An Overview of Funding Issues and Challenges; The Business Case for Wellness Programs in Public Employee Health Plans; State and Local Government Workforce: 2012 Trends;* and case studies on public sector pensions and retiree health, wellness and chronic care management programs, and other health care reform issues.

Purpose: To help state and local governments become knowledgeable and competitive employers so that they can attract and retain talented, committed, and well-prepared individuals to public service. Research areas include workforce analyses and implications of changing demographics, competitive employment practices, compensation analyses, state and local government retirement plans, postemployment and retiree health care benefits, and financial wellness and retirement planning. Public Plans Database, developed in partnership with the Center for Retirement Research at Boston College, provides comprehensive financial, governance, and plan design information for more than 120 state and local defined benefit plans. Established 2006.

Council of State Community Development Agencies (COSCDA)

1825 K Street, Suite 515
Washington, D.C. 20006
202-293-5820; fax: 202-293-2820

Website: coscda.org

Executive director: Dianne Taylor

Major publications: *The National Line; StateLine; Member Update; Annual Report*

Purpose: To promote the value and importance of state involvement in community development, economic development, affordable housing, and homelessness programs. For over 30 years, COSCDA has positioned itself as the premier national association charged with advocating and enhancing the leadership role of states in these issue areas, which it accomplishes through information sharing and a variety of technical assistance programs. COSCDA seeks to support, facilitate, and communicate states' priorities to its membership, as well as to elected and appointed officials and to state and federal policy makers. Its Training Academy offers basic and advanced courses on community development block grants and an introductory course on housing programs. COSCDA also holds an annual training conference in the fall and a program managers' conference in the spring. Established 1974.

Council of State Governments (CSG)

2760 Research Park Drive
Lexington, Kentucky 40578
859-244-8000; fax: 859-244-8001

Website: csg.org

Executive director/CEO: David Adkins

Major publications: *Book of the States; Capitol Ideas* magazine; *CSG State Directories*

Purpose: To prepare states for the future by interpreting changing national and international trends and conditions; to promote the sovereignty of the states and their role in the American federal system; to advocate multistate problem solving and partnerships; and to build leadership skills to improve decision making. CSG is a multibranch and regionally focused association of the states, U.S. territories, and commonwealths. Established 1933.

Federation of Canadian Municipalities (FCM)

24 Clarence Street
Ottawa, Ontario K1N 5P3
613-241-5221; fax: 613-241-7440

E-mail: ceo@fcm.ca

Website: fcm.ca

CEO: Brock Carlton

Resources: Case studies; multimedia; presentations; reports, guides, and templates for legal documents

Purpose: To represent the interests of all municipalities on policy and program matters within federal jurisdictions. Policy and program priorities are determined by FCM's board of directors, standing committees, and task forces. Issues include payments in lieu of taxes, goods and service taxes, economic development, municipal infrastructure, environment, transportation, community safety and crime prevention, quality-of-life social indicators, housing, race relations, and international trade and aid. Members include Canada's largest cities, small urban and rural communities, and the 18 major provincial and territorial municipal associations, which together represent more than 20 million Canadians. Established 1937.

Government Finance Officers Association (GFOA)

203 North LaSalle Street, Suite 2700
Chicago, Illinois 60601-1210
312-977-9700; fax: 312-977-4806
Also at 1301 Pennsylvania Avenue, N.W., Suite 309
Washington, D.C. 20004
202-393-8020; fax: 202-393-0780

Website: gfoa.org

Executive director/CEO: Jeffrey L. Esser

Major publications: GFOA *Newsletter; Government Finance Review Magazine; Public Investor; GAAFR Review; Pension & Benefits Update; Governmental Accounting, Auditing, and Financial Reporting; Investing Public Funds; Elected Official's Series*

Purpose: To enhance and promote the professional management of governmental financial resources by identifying, developing, and advancing fiscal strategies, policies, and practices for the public benefit. Established 1906.

GMIS International (GMIS)

P.O. Box 27923
Austin, Texas 78755
877-963-4647; fax: 512-857-7711

Website: gmis.org

GMIS listserv: Headquarters@GMIS.org

Executive director: Johnny A. Walton

Purpose: To provide a forum for the exchange of ideas, information, and techniques; and to foster enhancements in hardware, software, and communication developments as they relate to government activities. State and local government agencies are members represented by their top computer or information technology professionals. The GMIS Annual Educational Conference promotes the sharing of ideas and the latest technology. GMIS sponsors an annual "Professional of the Year" program and publishes a newsletter. It also provides organizational support to 19 state chapters, which enable member agencies within a geographical area to develop close relationships and to foster the spirit and intent of GMIS through cooperation, assistance, and mutual support. GMIS is affiliated with KommITS, a sister organization of local governments in Sweden; SOCITM in the United Kingdom; ALGIM in New Zealand; VIAG in The Netherlands; MISA/ASIM in Ontario, Canada; LOLA-International (Linked Organisation of Local Authority ICT Societies); and V-ICT-OR in Belgium. Established 1971.

Governmental Accounting Standards Board (GASB)

401 Merritt 7
P.O. Box 5116
Norwalk, Connecticut 06856-5116
203-847-0700; fax: 203-849-9714

Website: gasb.org

Chairman: Robert Attmore

Major publications: Governmental Accounting Standards Series; Codification of Standards; implementation guides; Suggested Guidelines for Voluntary Reporting; exposure drafts; Preliminary Views documents; *The GASB Report* (monthly newsletter); plain-language user guides

Purpose: To establish and improve standards of financial accounting and reporting for state and local governmental entities. GASB standards guide the preparation of those entities' external financial reports so that users of the reports can obtain the state and local government financial information needed to make economic, social, and political decisions. Interested parties are encouraged to read and comment on discussion documents of proposed standards, which can be downloaded for free from the GASB website. Final standards, guides to implementing standards and using government financial reports, and subscriptions to the GASB's publications can be ordered through the website as well. GASB's website also provides up-to-date information about current projects, forms for submitting technical questions and signing up for e-mail news alerts, a section devoted to financial report users, and a link to its Performance Measurement for Government website. The GASB is overseen by the Financial Accounting Foundation's Board of Trustees. Established 1984.

Governmental Research Association (GRA)

P.O. Box 292300
402 Samford Hall
Samford University
Birmingham, Alabama 35229
585-327-7054

Website: graonline.org

President: Kent Garder

Major publications: *Directory of Organizations and Individuals Professionally Engaged in Governmental Research and Related Activities* (annual); *GRA Reporter* (quarterly)

Purpose: To promote and coordinate the activities of governmental research agencies; to encourage the development of effective organization and methods for the administration and operation of government; to encourage the development of common standards for the appraisal of results; to facilitate the exchange of ideas and experiences; and to serve as a clearinghouse. Established 1914.

ICMA

777 North Capitol Street, N.E., Suite 500
Washington, D.C. 20002-4201
202-289-4262; fax: 202-962-3500

Website: icma.org

Executive director: Robert J. O'Neill Jr.

Major publications: "Green" Books: *Management Policies in Local Government Finance* (6th ed.), *Managing Fire and Rescue Services, Local Planning: Contemporary Principles and Practice, Emergency Management: Principles and Practice for Local Government* (2nd ed.); *Statistics for Public Administration: Practical Uses for Better Decision Making; Economic Development: Strategies for State and Local Practice* (2nd ed.); *Capital Budgeting and Finance: A Guide for Local Governments* (2nd ed.); *Homeland Security: Best Practices for Local Government; Human Resource Management in Local Government: An Essential Guide* (3rd ed.); *Managing Local Government: Cases in Effectiveness; Effective Supervisory Practices* (4th ed.); *Budgeting: A Guide for Local Governments; A Revenue Guide for Local Government; The Municipal Year Book, Public Management (PM)* magazine, *InFocus* (formerly *IQ Reports*), *ICMA Newsletter;* self-study courses, training packages

Purpose: To create excellence in local governance by developing and advocating professional management of local government worldwide. ICMA provides member support; publications, data, and information; peer and results-oriented assistance; and training and professional development to more than 9,000 city, town, and county experts and other individuals throughout the world. The management decisions made by ICMA's members affect 185 million individuals living in thousands of communities, from small villages and towns to large metropolitan areas. Established 1914.

ICMA Retirement Corporation (ICMA-RC)

777 North Capitol Street, N.E., Suite 600
Washington, D.C. 20002
202-962-4600; fax: 202-962-4601
800-669-7400

Website: icmarc.org

President/CEO: Joan McCallen

Purpose: To provide retirement plans and related services for more than 920,000 public employees in over 9,000 retirement plans. An independent financial services corporation focused on the retirement savings needs of the public sector, ICMA-RC is dedicated to helping build retirement security for public employees by providing investment tools, financial education, and other retirement-related services. The corporation also works to ease the administrative responsibility of local, city, and state governments that offer these benefits to their employees. Established 1972.

Institute of Internal Auditors, Inc. (The IIA)

247 Maitland Avenue
Altamonte Springs, Florida 32701-4201
407-937-1111; fax: 407-937-1101

Website: theiia.org

Chairman of the Board: Philip D. Tarling

Major publications: *International Professional Practices Framework; The Marketing Strategy: A Risk and Governance Guide to Building a Brand; Auditing Outsourced Functions: Risk Management in an Outsourced World; The Practitioner's Blueprint to Construction Auditing; Combined Assurance: Case Studies on a Holistic Approach to Organizational Governance; Sawyer's Guide for Internal Auditors* (6th ed.); *Internal Auditor Magazine*

Purpose: To provide comprehensive professional development and standards for the practice of internal auditing; and to research, disseminate, and promote education in internal auditing and internal control. The IIA offers the Certified Government Auditing Professional (CGAP) to distinguish leaders in public sector auditing. In addition to providing quality assessment services, the IIA performs custom on-site seminars for government auditors and offers educational products that address issues pertaining to government auditing. An international professional association with global headquarters in Altamonte Springs, Florida, The IIA has more than 140,000 members in internal auditing, governance, internal control, information technology audit, education, and security. With representation from more than 165 countries, The IIA is the internal audit profession's global voice, recognized authority, acknowledged leader, chief advocate, and principal educator worldwide. Established 1941.

Institute for Public Administration (IPA)

180 Graham Hall
University of Delaware
Newark, Delaware 19716-7380
302-831-8971; fax: 302-831-3488

Website: ipa.udel.edu

Director: Jerome R. Lewis

Major publications: IPA Reports, available at dspace.udel.edu:8080/dspace/handle/19716/7

Purpose: To address the policy, planning, and management needs of its partners through the integration of applied research, professional development, and the education of tomorrow's leaders. IPA provides direct staff assistance, research, policy analysis, training, and forums while contributing to the scholarly body of knowledge in public administration. Established 1973.

Institute of Transportation Engineers (ITE)

1627 Eye Street, N.W., Suite 600
Washington, D.C. 20006
202-785-0060; fax: 202-785-0609

Website: ite.org

Executive director: Thomas W. Brahms

Major publications: *Trip Generation, Parking Generation; Innovative Bicycle Treatments; Transportation and Land Use Development; Traffic Engineering Handbook; Transportation Planning Handbook; Manual of Transportation Engineering Studies; Designing Walkable Urban Thoroughfares; Urban Street Geometric Design Handbook; Traffic Safety Toolbox, A Primer on Traffic Safety; Manual of Uniform Traffic Control Devices, 2009; Traffic Control Devices Handbook; ITE Journal*

Purpose: To promote professional development in the field through education, research, development of public awareness, and exchange of information. Established 1930.

International Association of Assessing Officers (IAAO)

314 West 10th Street
Kansas City, Missouri 64105
816-701-8100; fax: 816-701-8149

Website: iaao.org

Executive director: Lisa J. Daniels

Major publications: *Property Assessment Valuation* (3rd ed.); *Fundamentals of Tax Policy; Fundamentals of Industrial Valuation; Fundamentals of Mass Appraisal; GIS Guidelines for Assessors* (2nd ed., with URISA); *Journal of Property Tax Assessment & Administration* (quarterly journal); *Fair & Equitable* (monthly magazine); Technical Standards (iaao.org/sitePages.cfm?Page=219)

Purpose: To promote innovation and excellence in property appraisal, assessment administration, and property tax policy through professional development, education, research, and technical assistance. A nonprofit, educational and research association, the IAAO is a professional membership organization of government assessment officials and others interested in the administration of the property tax. IAAO members—more than 7,300 members worldwide from governmental, business, and academic communities—subscribe to a Code of Ethics and Standards of Professional Conduct and to the Uniform Standards of Professional Appraisal Practice. Established 1934.

International Association of Chiefs of Police (IACP)

515 North Washington Street
Alexandria, Virginia 22314-2357
703-836-6767; fax: 703-836-4543
800-THE IACP

Website: theiacp.org

Executive director: Bart Johnson

Major publications: *Police Chief; Training Keys*

Purpose: To advance the art of police science through the development and dissemination of improved administrative, technical, and operational practices, and to promote the use of such practices in police work. Fosters police cooperation through the exchange of information among police administrators, and encourages all police officers to adhere to high standards of performance and conduct. Established 1893.

International Association of Fire Chiefs (IAFC)

4025 Fair Ridge Drive, Suite 300
Fairfax, Virginia 22033-2868
703-273-0911; fax: 703-273-9363

Website: iafc.org

Executive director/CEO: Mark Light, CAE

Major publication: *On Scene* (twice-monthly newsletter)

Purpose: To lead, educate, and serve the fire service; to enhance the professionalism and capabilities of career and volunteer fire chiefs, chief fire officers, company officers, and managers of emergency service organizations throughout the international community through vision, services, information, education, and representation. Established 1873.

International Association of Venue Managers (IAVM)

635 Fritz Drive, Suite 100
Coppell, Texas 75019-4442
972-906-7441; fax: 972-906-7418

Website: iavm.org

President/CEO: Vicki Hawarden, CMP

Major publications: *Facility Manager; IAVM Guide to Members and Services; IAVM E-Newsletter*

Purpose: To educate, advocate for, and inspire public assembly venue professionals worldwide. Established 1925.

International Code Council

500 New Jersey Avenue, N.W., 6th Floor
Washington, D.C. 20001-2070
888-422-7233; fax: 202-783-2348

Website: iccsafe.org

CEO: Dominic Sims

Major publication: *The International Codes*

Purpose: To build safety and fire prevention by developing the codes used to construct residential and commercial buildings, including homes and schools. Most U.S. cities, counties, and states that adopt codes choose the international codes developed by the ICC, a membership association. Established 1994.

International Economic Development Council (IEDC)

734 15th Street, N.W., Suite 900
Washington, D.C. 20005
202-223-7800; fax: 202-223-4745

Website: iedconline.org

President/CEO: Jeffrey A. Finkle, CEcD

Major publications: *Economic Development Journal; Economic Development Now; Economic Development America; Federal Directory; Federal Review; Budget Overview*

Purpose: To help economic development professionals improve the quality of life in their communities. With more than 4,000 members, IEDC represents all levels of government, academia, and private industry, providing a broad range of member services that includes research, advisory services, conferences, professional certification, professional development, publications, and legislative tracking. Established 2001.

International Institute of Municipal Clerks (IIMC)

8331 Utica Avenue, Suite 200
Rancho Cucamonga, California 91730
909-944-4162; fax: 909-944-8545
800-251-1639

Website: iimc.com

Executive director: Chris Shalby

Major publications: *IIMC News Digest; The Language of Local Government; Meeting Administration Handbook; Parliamentary Procedures in Local Government; Role Call: Strategy for a Professional Clerk;* "Partners in Democracy" video, case study packets, technical bulletins

Purpose: To promote continuing education and certification through university and college-based institutes, and provide networking solutions, services, and benefits to its members worldwide. Established 1947.

International Municipal Lawyers Association (IMLA)

7910 Woodmont Avenue, Suite 1440
Bethesda, Maryland 20814
202-466-5424; fax: 202-785-0152

E-mail: info@imla.org

Website: imla.org

General counsel/executive director: Chuck Thompson

Major publications: *The IMLA Model Ordinance Service; Municipal Lawyer*

Purpose: To provide continuing legal education events, publications, research, legal advocacy assistance, and excellent networking opportunities for the local government legal community. IMLA is a membership organization of U.S. and Canadian city and county attorneys. Established 1935.

International Public Management Association for Human Resources (IPMA-HR)

1617 Duke Street
Alexandria, Virginia 22314
703-549-7100; fax: 703-684-0948

Website: ipma-hr.org

Executive director: Neil E. Reichenberg

Major publications: *Public Personnel Management; HR Bulletin; IPMA-HR News*

Purpose: To improve service to the public by promoting quality human resource management in the public sector. Established 1906.

League of Women Voters of the United States (LWVUS)

1730 M Street, N.W., Suite 1000
Washington, D.C. 20036-4508
202-429-1965; fax: 202-429-0854

Website: lwv.org

Executive director: Nancy Tate

Major publications: *High School Voter Registration Training Manual; Debate Watching 101;* "From Theory to Practice: A Grassroots Education Campaign" *Shares Lessons Learned by Leagues in Kansas and South Carolina;* voters' reference guides and brochures in English and Spanish

Purpose: To encourage informed and active participation in government and to influence public policy through education and advocacy. The league's current advocacy priorities are health care reform, climate change, election reform, a fair judiciary, immigration, openness in government, redistricting reform, campaign finance, lobbying, and election reform. The League of Women Voters Education Fund, a separate but complementary organization, provides research and public education services to the public to encourage and enable citizen participation in government. Current public education programs include voter outreach and education, the Vote 411.org website, election reform, judicial independence, and international forms and exchange activities. The league is a nonpartisan political organization. Established 1920.

National Animal Control Association (NACA)

101 North Church Street
Olathe, KS 66051
913-768-1319; fax: 913-768-1378

Website: nacanet.org

President: Todd Stosuy

Major publications: *The NACA News; The NACA Training Guide*

Purpose: To provide training for animal control personnel; consultation and guidance for local governments on animal control ordinances, animal shelter design, budget and program planning, and staff training; and public education. Established 1978.

National Association of Counties (NACo)

25 Massachusetts Avenue, N.W., Suite 500
Washington, D.C. 20001-1431
202-393-6226; fax: 202-393-2630

Website: naco.org

Executive director: Matthew D. Chase

Major publications: *County News; NACo e-News*

Purpose: To provide essential services to the nation's 2,341 counties. The only national organization that represents county governments in the United States, NACo advances issues with a unified voice before the federal government; improves the public's understanding of county government, assists counties in finding and sharing innovative solutions through education and research, and provides value-added services to save counties and taxpayers money. Established 1935.

National Association of County and City Health Officials (NACCHO)

1100 17th Street, N.W., 7th Floor
Washington, D.C. 20036
202-783-5550; fax: 202-783-1583

Website: naccho.org

Executive director: Robert M. Pestronk, MPH

Major publications: *National Profile of Local Health Departments* (annual); *Public Health Dispatch* (newsletter); *NACCHO Exchange* (quarterly); research briefs and videos

Purpose: To support efforts that protect and improve the health of all people and all communities by promoting national policy, developing resources and programs, seeking health equity, and supporting effective local public health practice and systems. Established 1960s.

National Association for County Community and Economic Development (NACCED)

2025 M Street, N.W., Suite 800
Washington, D.C. 20036-3309
202-367-1149; fax: 202-367-2149

Website: nacced.org

Executive director: John Murphy

Purpose: To help develop the technical capacity of county agencies in administering community development, economic development, and affordable housing programs. Created as an affiliate of the National Association of Counties (NACo), NACCED is a nonprofit national organization that also serves as a voice within NACo to articulate the needs, concerns, and interests of county agencies. Established 1978.

National Association of Development Organizations (NADO)

400 North Capitol Street, N.W., Suite 390
Washington, D.C. 20001
202-624-7806; fax: 202-624-8813

Website: nado.org

Executive director: Joe McKinney

Major publications: *EDFS Reporter; NADO News; Regional Development Digest*

Purpose: To provide training, information, and representation for regional development organizations serving small metropolitan and rural America. Building on nearly four decades of experience, the association offers its members exclusive access to a variety of services and benefits—all of which are crafted to enhance the activities, programs, and prospects of regional development organizations. Established 1970s.

National Association of Housing and Redevelopment Officials (NAHRO)

630 Eye Street, N.W.
Washington, D.C. 20001
202-289-3500; fax: 202-289-8181
877-866-2476

Website: nahro.org

CEO: Saul N. Ramirez

Major publications: *Journal of Housing and Community Development; NAHRO Monitor; Directory of Local Agencies; The NAHRO Public Relations Handbook; Commissioners Handbook*

Purpose: To help create a nation in which all people, especially those of low and moderate income, have decent, safe, affordable housing and economic opportunity in viable, sustainable communities. To this end, NAHRO (1) ensures that housing and community development professionals have the leadership skills, education, information, and tools to serve communities in a rapidly changing environment; (2) advocates for appropriate laws, adequate funding levels, and responsible public policies that address the needs of the people served, are financially and programmatically viable, are flexible, reduce regulatory burdens, and promote local decision making; and (3) fosters the highest standards of ethical behavior, service, and accountability. A professional membership organization of about 23,000 housing and community development agencies and officials throughout the United States who administer a variety of affordable housing and community development programs at the local level, NAHRO enhances the effectiveness of its members and the industry through its comprehensive professional development curriculum, including certifications, conferences, and publications. Established 1933.

National Association of Regional Councils (NARC)

777 North Capitol Street, N.E., Suite 305
Washington, D.C. 20002
202-986-1032; fax: 202-986-1038

Website: narc.org

Executive director: Fred Abousleman

Purpose: To promote regional approaches and collaboration in addressing diverse development challenges. A nonprofit membership organization, NARC has represented the interests of its members and has advanced regional cooperation through effective interaction and advocacy with Congress, federal officials, and other related agencies and interest groups for more than 40 years. Its member organizations are composed of multiple local government units, such as regional councils and metropolitan planning organizations, that work together to serve American communities, large and small, urban and rural. Among the issues it addresses are transportation, homeland security and regional preparedness, economic and community development, the environment, and a variety of community concerns of interest to member organizations. NARC provides its members with valuable information and research on key national policy issues, federal policy developments, and best practices; in addition, it conducts enriching training sessions, conferences, and workshops. Established 1967.

National Association of Schools of Public Affairs and Administration (NASPAA)

1029 Vermont Avenue, N.W., Suite 1100
Washington, D.C. 20005
202-628-8965; fax: 202-626-4978

E-mail: naspaa@naspaa.org

Websites: naspaa.org; globalmpa.org; publicservicecareers.org

Executive director: Laurel McFarland

Major publications: *Journal of Public Affairs Education (J-PAE); Newsletter; MPA Accreditation Standards; MPA/MPP Brochure;* peer review and accreditation documents

Purpose: To serve as a national and international center for information about programs and developments in the area of public affairs and administration; to foster goals and standards of educational excellence; to represent members' concerns and interests in the formulation and support of national, state, and local policies for public affairs education and research; and to serve as a specialized accrediting agency for MPA/MPP degrees. Established 1970.

National Association of State Chief Information Officers (NASCIO)

c/o AMR Management Services
201 East Main Street, Suite 1405
Lexington, Kentucky 40507
859-514-9156; fax: 859-514-9166

Website: nascio.org

Executive director: Doug Robinson

Major publications: *State CIO Top Ten Policy and Technology Priorities for 2012; 2011 Best Practices in the Use of Information Technology in State Government; The 2011 State CIO Survey; State Cyber Security Resource Guide: Awareness, Education, and Training Initiatives; Capitals in the Clouds—The Case for Cloud Computing in State Government, Parts I-III; CIO Leadership for State Governments: Emerging Trends and Practices; On the Fence: IT Implications of the Health Benefit Exchanges; State IT Workforce: Under Pressure; State Governments at Risk: A Call to Secure Citizen Data and Inspire Public Trust; Friends, Followers, and Feeds: A National Survey of Social Media Use in State Government; The Heart of the Matter: A Core Services Taxonomy for State IT Security Programs; NASCIO Connections* (newsletter)

Purpose: To be the premier network and resource for state chief information officers (CIOs) and a leading advocate for information technology (IT) policy at all levels of government. NASCIO represents CIOs and IT executives from the states, territories, and the District of Columbia. Its primary state government members are senior officials with executive-level and statewide responsibility for IT leadership. State officials who are involved in agency-level IT management may participate as state members; representatives from other public sector and nonprofit organizations may participate as associate members. Private sector firms may join as corporate members and participate in the Corporate Leadership Council. Established 1969.

National Association of Towns and Townships (NATaT)

1130 Connecticut Avenue, N.W., Suite 300
Washington, D.C. 20036
202-454-3950; fax: 202-331-1598

Website: natat.org

Federal director: Jennifer Imo

Major publication: *Washington Report*

Purpose: To strengthen the effectiveness of town and township government by educating lawmakers and public policy officials about how small-town governments operate, and by advocating policies on their behalf in Washington, D.C. Established 1976.

National Career Development Association (NCDA)

305 North Beech Circle
Broken Arrow, Oklahoma 74012 918-663-7060; fax: 918-663-7058

Website: ncda.org

Executive director: Deneen Pennington

Major publications: *A Counselor's Guide to Career Assessments; The Internet: A Tool for Career Planning; Career Developments* magazine

Purpose: To promote career development of all people throughout the lifespan. A division of the American Counseling Association, NCDA provides services to the public and to professionals involved with or interested in career development; services include professional development activities, publications, research, public information, professional standards, advocacy, and recognition for achievement and service. Established 1913.

National Civic League (NCL)

1889 York Street
Denver, Colorado 80206
303-571-4343; fax: 888-314-6053

E-mail: ncl@ncl.org

Website: ncl.org

Blog: allamericacityaward.com

President: Gloria Rubio-Cortés

Major publications: *The Community Visioning and Strategic Planning Handbook; Model County Charter; National Civic Review; 8th Edition of the Model City Charter; New Civic Index; The Guide for Charter Commission*

Purpose: To strengthen democracy by increasing the capacity of our nation's people to fully participate in and build healthy and prosperous communities across America. NCL facilitates community-wide strategic planning in fiscal sustainability and comprehensive plans. Good at the science of local government and the art of public engagement, NCL leads and celebrates the progress that can be achieved when people work together. NCL is the home of the All-America City Award, now in its 63rd year. The year 2011 was the *National Civic Review*'s 100th year of publishing; the yearlong theme was "What's Working in American Communities." Established 1894.

National Community Development Association (NCDA)

522 21st Street, N.W., #120
Washington, D.C. 20006
202-293-7587; fax: 202-887-5546

Website: ncdaonline.org

Executive director: Cardell Cooper

Purpose: To serve as a national clearinghouse of ideas for local government officials and federal policy makers on pertinent national issues affecting America's communities. NCDA is a national nonprofit organization comprising more than 550 local governments across the country that administer federally supported community and economic development, housing, and human service programs, including those of the U.S. Department of Housing and Urban Development, the Community Development Block Grant program, and HOME Investment Partnerships. NCDA provides timely, direct information and technical support to its members in their efforts to secure effective and responsive housing and community development programs. Established 1968.

National Conference of State Legislatures (NCSL)

7700 East First Place
Denver, Colorado 80230
303-364-7700; fax: 303-364-7800
Also at 444 North Capitol Street, N.W., Suite 515
Washington, D.C. 20001-1201
202-624-5400; fax: 202-737-1069

Website: ncsl.org

Executive director: William T. Pound

Major publications: *All Access, StateConnect, Mason's Manual, Federal Update, State Legislatures*

Purpose: To improve the quality and effectiveness of state legislatures; to ensure that states have a strong, cohesive voice in the federal decision-making process; and to foster interstate communication and cooperation. A bipartisan organization that serves the legislators and staffs of the nation's states, commonwealths, and territories, NCSL provides research, technical assistance, and opportunities for policy makers to exchange ideas on the most pressing state issues. Established 1975.

National Environmental Health Association (NEHA)

720 South Colorado Boulevard, Suite 1000-N
Denver, Colorado 80246
303-756-9090; fax: 303-691-9490

E-mail: staff@neha.org

Website: neha.org

Executive director: Nelson E. Fabian

Major publications: *2009 H1N1 Pandemic Influenza Planning Manual; Microbial Safety of Fresh Produce; Planet Water: Investing in the World's Most Valuable Resource; Environmental Toxicants: Human Exposures and Their Health Effects; Resolving Messy Policy Problems; Journal of Environmental Health*

Purpose: To advance the professional in the environmental field through education, professional meetings, and the dissemination of information. NEHA also publishes information relating to environmental health and protection and promotes professionalism in the field. Established 1937.

National Fire Protection Association (NFPA)

One Batterymarch Park
Quincy, Massachusetts 02169-7471
617-770-3000; fax: 617-770-0700

Website: nfpa.org

President/CEO: James M. Shannon

Major publications: *Fire Protection Handbook; Fire Technology; NFPA Journal; National Electrical Code®; National Fire Codes®; Life Safety Code®; Risk Watch™; Learn Not to Burn® Curriculum;* and textbooks, manuals, training packages, detailed analyses of important fires, and fire officers guides

Purpose: To reduce the worldwide burden of fire and other hazards on the quality of life by providing and advocating scientifically based consensus codes and standards, research, training, and education. Established 1896.

National Governors Association (NGA)

Hall of the States
444 North Capitol Street, Suite 267
Washington, D.C. 20001-1512
202-624-5300; fax: 202-624-5313

Website: nga.org

Executive director: Dan Crippen

Major publications: *The Fiscal Survey of States; Policy Positions;* reports on a wide range of state issues

Purpose: To act as a liaison between the states and the federal government, and to serve as a clearinghouse for information and ideas on state and national issues. Established 1908.

National Housing Conference (NHC)

1900 M Street, N.W., Suite 200
Washington, D.C. 20036
202-466-2121; fax: 202-466-2122

Website: nhc.org

Interim president/CEO: Chris Estes

Major publications: *Losing Ground: The Struggle of Moderate-Income Households to Afford the Rising Costs of Housing and Transportation; NHC at Work; NHC Affordable Housing Policy Review; Washington Wire*

Purpose: To promote better communities and affordable housing for Americans through education and advocacy. Established 1931.

National League of Cities (NLC)

1301 Pennsylvania Avenue, N.W., Suite 550
Washington, D.C. 20004-1763
202-626-3000; fax: 202-626-3043

Website: nlc.org

Executive director: Clarence Anthony

Major publications: *Nation's Cities Weekly*, guide books, directories, and research reports

Purpose: To strengthen and promote cities as centers of opportunity, leadership, and governance; to serve as an advocate for its members in Washington in the legislative, administrative, and judicial processes that affect them; to offer training, technical assistance, and information to local government and state league officials to help them improve the quality of local government; and to research and analyze policy issues of importance to cities and towns in America. Established 1924.

National Public Employer Labor Relations Association (NPELRA)

1012 South Coast Highway, Suite M
Oceanside, California 92054
760-433-1686; fax: 760-433-1687

E-mail: info@npelra.org

Website: npelra.org

Executive director: Michael T. Kolb

Purpose: To provide its members with high-quality, progressive labor relations professional development that balances the needs of management, employees, and the public. The premier organization for public sector labor relations and human resource professionals, NPELRA is a network of state and regional affiliates. Its more than 3,000 members around the country represent public employers in a wide range of areas, from employee-management contract negotiations to arbitration under grievance and arbitration procedures. NPELRA also works to promote the interests of public sector management in the judicial and legislative arenas, and to provide opportunities for networking among members by establishing state and regional organizations throughout the country. The governmental agencies represented in NPELRA employ more than 4 million workers in federal, state, and local government.

National Recreation and Park Association (NRPA)

22377 Belmont Ridge Road
Ashburn, Virginia 20148
800-626-6772; fax: 703-858-0794

Website: nrpa.org

CEO: Barbara Tulipane

Major publication: *Parks & Recreation Magazine*

Purpose: To advance parks, recreation, and environmental conservation efforts that enhance the quality of life for all people. Established 1965.

National School Boards Association (NSBA)

1680 Duke Street
Alexandria, Virginia 22314-3493
703-838-6722; fax: 703-683-7590

Website: nsba.org

Executive director: Thomas Gentzel

Major publications: *American School Board Journal;* ASBK.com; *Inquiry and Analysis; Leadership Insider*

Purpose: To work with and through all our state associations to advocate for excellence and equity in public education through school board leadership. Established 1940.

NIGP: The Institute for Public Procurement

151 Spring Street
Herndon, Virginia 20170-5223
703-736-8900; fax: 703-736-2818
800-FOR NIGP (800-367-6447)

Website: nigp.org

CEO: Rick Grimm, CPPO, CPPB

Major publications: *GoPro: Government Procurement* magazine, a bimonthly publication distributed to NIGP members and procurement professionals; NIGP *Sector Spotlight* edition of *BuyWeekly*, published electronically each month for NIGP members and offering procurement-related news briefs; NIGP's *BuyWeekly*, an electronic newsletter offering a quick overview of current highlights in the profession

Purpose: To develop, support, and promote the public procurement profession through premier educational and research programs, professional support, technical services, and advocacy initiatives; to secure recognition and esteem for the government procurement profession and its dedicated practitioners. With over 20,000 professionals from more than 2,500 local, state, provincial, and federal government contracting agencies across the United States, Canada, and countries outside of North America, NIGP is international in its reach. NIGP led the way in developing values and guiding principles of public procurement. Its Learning Central offers traditional face-to-face courses, independent and interactive online courses, and webinars that address current industry issues and trends affecting how governments do business. All NIGP education experiences qualify toward achieving certification from the Universal Public Procurement Certification Council (UPPCC). NIGP hosts an annual Forum and Products Exposition, the largest gathering of public procurement officials in North America. Spikes Cavell and NIGP bring a proven spend analysis solution to the U.S. public sector. The NIGP Observatory is a spend-

and-supplier management solution that delivers the data, tools, and intelligence that enable procurement to reduce cost, realize cooperative opportunities, improve contract compliance, and drive continuous improvements. NIGP's technology partner, Periscope Holdings, supports the ongoing development of the NIGP Code and the agencies that already use it, a universal taxonomy for identifying commodities and services in their procurement systems. NIGP is a cofounding sponsor of U.S. Communities and its affiliate, Canadian Communities, demonstrating its support for the practice of cooperative purchasing for the efficiencies it achieves for public entities and the tremendous savings it realizes for taxpayers. NIGP is also a cofounding supporter of the UPPCC and its two-level certification program for public procurement personnel. Established 1944.

Police Executive Research Forum (PERF)

1120 Connecticut Avenue, N.W., Suite 930
Washington, D.C. 20036
202-466-7820; fax: 202-466-7826

Website: policeforum.org

Executive director: Chuck Wexler

Major publication: *Subject to Debate* (bimonthly newsletter)

Purpose: To improve policing and advance professionalism through research and involvement in public policy debate. PERF is a national membership organization of progressive police executives from the largest city, county, and state law enforcement agencies. It conducts research and convenes national meetings of police executives and other stakeholders to identify best practices and policies on issues such as police use of force, crime reduction strategies, community and problem-oriented policing, and racial bias, as well as on organizational issues in policing. Incorporated 1977.

Police Foundation

1201 Connecticut Avenue, N.W.
Washington, D.C. 20036-2636
202-833-1460; fax: 202-659-9149

E-mail: pfinfo@policefoundation.org

Website: policefoundation.org

President: Jim Bueermann

Major publications: *Ideas in American Policing* series; research and technical reports on a wide range of law enforcement and public safety issues

Purpose: To improve policing through research, evaluation, field experimentation, training, technical assistance, technology, and information. Objective, nonpartisan, and nonprofit, the Police Foundation helps national, state, and local governments, both in the United States and abroad, improve performance, service delivery, accountability, and community satisfaction with police services. The foundation offers a wide range of services and specializations, including research, evaluation, surveys, management and operational reviews, climate and culture assessment, training and technical assistance, early-warning and intervention systems, community police collaboration, accountability and ethics, community policing strategies, performance management, racial profiling/biased policing, professional and leadership development. Motivating all its efforts is the goal of efficient, effective, humane policing that operates within the framework of democratic principles. Established in 1970.

Public Risk Management Association (PRIMA)

700 South Washington Street, Suite 218
Alexandria, Virginia 22314-1516
703-528-7701; fax: 703-739-0200

E-mail: info@primacentral.org

Website: primacentral.org

Executive director: Marshall W. Davies, PhD

Major publications: *Public Risk Magazine*

Purpose: To promote effective risk management in the public interest as an essential component of public administration. Established 1978.

Public Technology Institute (PTI)

1426 Prince Street, Suite 200
Alexandria, Virginia 22314
202-626-2400; fax: 202-626-2498

E-mail: dbowen@pti.org

Website: pti.org

Executive director: Alan R. Shark

Major publications: *CIO Leadership for Cities & Counties; Local Energy Assurance Planning Guide; Beyond e-Government & e-Democracy: A Global Perspective; Measuring Up 2.0; Performance Is the Best Politics; Roads Less Traveled: ITS for Sustainable Communities; Sustainable Building Technical Manual; Mission Possible: Strong Governance Structures for the Integration of Justice Information Systems; E-Government: Factors Affecting ROI; E-Government: A Strategic Planning Guide for Local Officials; Why Not Do It Ourselves? A Resource Guide for Local Government Officials and Citizens Regarding Public Ownership of Utility Systems; Online* magazine (www.prismonline.org); *Winning Solutions* (annual); numerous case studies on energy and environmental technology development and sustainable management

Purpose: To identify and test technologies and management approaches that help all local governments provide the best possible services to citizens and businesses. With ICMA, NLC, and NACo, PTI works with progressive member cities and counties to (1) make communities "well-connected" by advancing communication capabilities; (2) develop tools and processes for wise decision making; and (3) promote sustainable approaches that ensure a balance between economic development and a clean, quality environment. PTI's member program engages cities and counties as laboratories for research, development, and public enterprise to advance technology applications in telecommunications, energy, the environment, transportation, and public safety. To disseminate research findings, PTI provides print and electronic resources, peer consultation, and networking. Through partnerships with private vendors, PTI offers several technology products and services that help local governments save money by bypassing rigorist RFP requirements as the products and services are competitively bid and chosen for superior quality and competitive pricing. PTI's research and development division continues to examine information and Internet technology, public safety, geographic information systems (GIS), energy-conserving technologies, sustainable management, and intelligent transportation systems. Established 1971.

Sister Cities International (SCI)

915 15th Street, N.W., 4th Floor
Washington DC 20005
202-347-8630; fax 202-393-6524

E-mail: info@sister-cities.org

Website: sister-cities.org

President and CEO: Mary Kane

Major publication: Sister Cities International Membership Directory

Purpose: To build global cooperation at the municipal level, promote cultural understanding, and stimulate economic development. SCI is a nonprofit citizen diplomacy network that creates and strengthens partnerships between U.S. and international communities. With its international headquarters in Washington, D.C., SCI promotes global economic development, youth involvement, cultural understanding, and humanitarian assistance. As an international membership organization, SCI officially certifies, represents, and supports partnerships between U.S. cities, counties, and states and similar jurisdictions in other countries to ensure their continued commitment and success to peace and prosperity. The SCI network represents nearly 2,000 partnerships in 136 countries. Established 1956.

Solid Waste Association of North America (SWANA)

1100 Wayne Avenue, Suite 700
Silver Spring, Maryland 20910
800-467-9262; fax: 301-589-7068

E-mail: info@swana.org

Website: swana.org

Executive director: John H. Skinner, PhD

Purpose: To advance the practice of environmentally and economically sound municipal solid-waste management in North America. Established 1961.

Special Libraries Association (SLA)

331 South Patrick Street
Alexandria, Virginia 22314-3501
703-647-4900; fax: 703-647-4901

E-mail: sla@sla.org

Website: sla.org

CEO: Janice R. Lachance

Major publication: *Information Outlook*

Purpose: To further the professional growth and success of its membership. Representing the interests of thousands of information professionals in 84 countries, SLA offers a variety of programs and services designed to help its members serve their customers more effectively and succeed in an increasingly challenging global information arena. Established 1909.

State and Local Legal Center

Hall of States
444 North Capitol Street, N.W., Suite 515
Washington, D.C. 20001
202-434-4845; fax: 202-737-1069

Website: statelocallc.org

Chief consult: Lisa Sorenson

Publication list: Available on request

Purpose: The State and Local Legal Center files amicus briefs in the U.S. Supreme Court in support of states and local governments, conducts moot courts for attorneys arguing in the Supreme Court, and provides other assistance to states and local governments in connection with Supreme Court litigation.

Universal Public Procurement Certification Council (UPPCC)

151 Spring Street
Herndon, Virginia 20170
800-884-6073; fax: 703-796-9611

E-mail: certification@uppcc.org

Website: uppcc.org

Director: Ann Peshoff, CAE, CMP

Purpose: To identify and establish a standard of competency for the public procurement profession; establish and monitor eligibility requirements of those interested in achieving certification; and further the cause of certification in the public sector. The UPPCC certification programs have been established to meet the requirements of all public procurement personnel in federal, state, and local governments. Certification, which reflects established standards and competencies for those engaged in governmental procurement and attests to the purchaser's ability to obtain maximum value for the taxpayer's dollar, is applicable to all public and governmental organizations, regardless of size. The council offers two credentials: the Certified Professional Public Buyer (CPPB), which applies to individuals who have demonstrated prescribed levels of professional competency as buyers in governmental procurement, and the Certified Public Procurement Officer (CPPO), which applies to similar individuals who also assume managerial functions within their jurisdictions or agencies. As the trend in governmental procurement is for mandatory certification of procurement professionals, these credentials communicate to the taxpayer that the public employee who manages tax dollars has reached a level of education and practical experience within government procurement to be recognized by the UPPCC. Established 1978.

Urban Affairs Association (UAA)

University of Wisconsin–Milwaukee
P.O. Box 413
Milwaukee, Wisconsin 53201-0413
414-229-3025

Website: urbanaffairsassociation.org

Executive director: Dr. Margaret Wilder

Major publications: *Journal of Urban Affairs; Urban Affairs* (a newsletter)

Purpose: To encourage the dissemination of information and research findings about urbanism and urbanization; to support the development of university education, research, and service programs in urban affairs; and to foster the development of urban affairs as a professional and academic field. Established 1969.

Urban Institute (UI)

2100 M Street, N.W.
Washington, D.C. 20037
202-833-7200

Website: urban.org

President: Sarah Rosen Wartell

Publications: Research papers, policy briefs, events, podcasts, web modules, and books on social and economic issues, including health care, welfare reform, immigration policy, tax reform, prisoner reentry, housing policy, retirement, charitable giving, school accountability, economic development, and community revitalization; all publications available online except books

Purpose: To respond to needs for objective analyses and basic information on the social and economic challenges confronting the nation, and for nonpartisan evaluation of the government policies and programs designed to alleviate such problems. Established 1968.

Urban and Regional Information Systems Association (URISA)

701 Lee Street, Suite 680
Des Plaines, Illinois 60016
847-824-6300; fax: 847-824-6363

Website: urisa.org

Executive director: Wendy Nelson

Major publications: *URISA Journal; The GIS Professional;* Quick Studies, books and compendiums, salary surveys, conference proceedings, videos

Purpose: To promote the effective and ethical use of spatial information and information technologies for the understanding and management of urban and regional systems. URISA is a nonprofit professional, educational, and multidisciplinary association where professionals from all parts of the spatial data community can come together and share concerns and ideas. It is the professional home of choice for public sector GIS and information technology executives throughout the United States, Canada, and other countries worldwide. Established 1963.

U.S. Conference of Mayors (USCM)

1620 Eye Street, N.W.
Washington, D.C. 20006
202-293-7330; fax: 202-293-2352

E-mail: info@usmayors.org

Website: usmayors.org

Executive director/CEO: Tom Cochran

Major publications: *U.S. Mayor; Mayors of America's Principal Cities*

Purpose: To act as the official nonpartisan organization of cities with populations of 30,000 or more; to aid the development of effective national urban policy; to ensure that federal policy meets urban needs; and to provide mayors with leadership and management tools. Each city is represented in the conference by its mayor. Established 1932.

Water Environment Federation (WEF)

601 Wythe Street
Alexandria, Virginia 22314-1994
703-684-2430; fax: 703-684-2492
800-666-0206

Websites: wef.org, weftec.org

Executive director: Jeff Eger

Major publications: *Water Environment Research; Water Environment and Technology; Water Environment Regulation Watch; The Stormwater Report;* series of Manuals of Practice

Purpose: To provide bold leadership, champion innovation, connect water professionals, and leverage knowledge to support clean and safe water worldwide. The WEF is a not-for-profit technical and educational organization of 36,000 individual members and 75 affiliated member associations representing water-quality professionals around the world. Established 1928.

Authors and Contributors

Authors and Contributors

Jennifer Claire Auer, a PhD candidate in the School of Public Affairs at Arizona State University, has studied urban development in a variety of local and federal policy organizations. Her recent projects include an assessment of the diversity goals laid out in the general plans of Arizona's local governments. She is completing her dissertation research on regional resilience and entrepreneurship.

Jeffrey L. Brudney is the inaugural holder of the Betty and Dan Cameron Family Distinguished Professorship of Innovation in the Nonprofit Sector at the University of North Carolina at Wilmington. Editor in chief of *Nonprofit and Voluntary Sector Quarterly,* the premier academic journal in nonprofit sector studies worldwide, Dr. Brudney is the author of numerous publications relating to volunteerism; his book *Fostering Volunteer Programs in the Public Sector: Planning, Initiating, and Managing Voluntary Activities* won the John Grenzebach Award for Outstanding Research in Philanthropy for Education. He also received the Harriet Naylor Distinguished Member Service Award from the Association for Volunteer Administration for "outstanding contribution to the Association through advocacy, research, publication, and/or program development and management." Dr. Brudney served on the technical advisory board of the United Nations Volunteers Programme's *State of the World's Volunteerism Report,* and President George W. Bush invited him to the White House to hear his "Remarks on Volunteering." He received his BA from the University of California at Berkeley, and his MA and PhD at the University of Michigan at Ann Arbor.

Ron Carlee was ICMA's chief operating officer (and an adjunct professor at the George Washington University's Trachtenberg School of Public Policy and Public Administration) until April 1 of this year, when he began service as city manager of Charlotte, North Carolina. Prior to joining ICMA in 2009, he had held several positions in Arlington, Virginia, including county manager, director of health and human services, director of parks and recreation, and director of information services. Before that, he was assistant to the mayor in Birmingham, Alabama. Dr. Carlee is a Fellow in the National Academy for Public Administration. He holds a bachelor's degree from the University of Montevallo, a master's degree from the University of Alabama at Birmingham, and a doctorate in public administration from George Mason University.

Catherine M. Gerard is director of the Program for the Advancement of Research on Conflict and Collaboration (PARCC) at Syracuse University's Maxwell School of Citizenship and Public Affairs, where she oversees an internationally known center for theory building and practice in conflict analysis and resolution, collaborative governance, and advocacy and activism. Her research focus is on the education and practice of managers and students in the skills of collaborative leadership and change. Her graduate courses in leadership, group conflict, and conflict fundamentals are targeted to midcareer managers from public and nonprofit organizations in the United States and abroad. She also conducts leadership training for government officials, and consults with public and nonprofit organizations in the areas of strategic planning, leadership/management, organizational change, team building, and conflict resolution. Ms. Gerard received her MA from the University of Toronto and her MPA from the State University of New York at Albany.

Laura Goddeeris is a specialist with the Michigan State University (MSU) Center for Regional Food Systems. She coordinates outreach that engages national organizations in improving food systems and community environments, linking ground-level efforts and national stakeholders to inform policy and systems change. With a broad background in research, community activism, and program administration, she has recently been exploring opportunities for local governments to support regional food systems. She holds a bachelor's degree in interdisciplinary studies in social science from MSU and a master's degree in urban planning and policy from the University of Illinois at Chicago.

Michael W. Hamm is the C. S. Mott Professor of Sustainable Agriculture at Michigan State University (MSU). He is director of MSU's Center for Regional Food Systems, which engages the people of Michigan, the United States, and the world in applied research, education, and outreach to develop regionally integrated, sustainable food systems. Community, regional, and sustainable food systems are his active research areas. Prior to coming to MSU, Dr. Hamm was dean of academic and student programs for Cook College, Rutgers University. He was co-founder and director of the New Jersey Urban Ecology Program and founding director of the Cook Student Organic Farm. Dr. Hamm is a member of the governor-appointed Michigan Food Policy Council. He has a BA in biology from Northwestern University and a PhD in human nutrition from the University of Minnesota.

Lydia J. Morken is a planner working as a research/extension specialist at Cornell University in Ithaca, New York. Her current work focuses on planning for the aging population across the urban–rural spectrum and on the potential of school–city collaboration to share services and facilities. Originally from Minnesota, Ms. Morken previously spent seven years in Chicago working in community and economic development, sustainability, philanthropy, and communications. She holds a master of regional planning degree from Cornell.

Evelina R. Moulder, director of ICMA's survey research, is responsible for the development of survey instruments, design of the sample, design of logic checks, quality control, and analysis of survey results. Among the surveys conducted by ICMA under her supervision are economic development, financing infrastructure, e-government, homeland security, labor-management relations, parks and recreation, police and fire personnel and expenditures, service delivery, technology, and sustainability. She has also directed several survey projects funded by other organizations. With more than 20 years of experience in local government survey research, Ms. Moulder has collaborated extensively with government agencies, professors, the private sector, and other researchers in survey development, and she has played a key role in ICMA's homeland security and emergency response initiatives, including concept and proposal development.

Rebecca Nesbit is an assistant professor of nonprofit management at the University of Kansas, where she teaches in the Master of Public Administration program. Her research explores issues of philanthropy and volunteerism, public policy, and management in the nonprofit sector. In particular, she studies volunteer programs, volunteers' characteristics and motivations, and volunteer management in public and nonprofit organizations. Her work has appeared in *Nonprofit and Voluntary Sector Quarterly, Nonprofit Management and Leadership, Public Administration Review, Journal of Public Administration Research and Theory,* and *Administration & Society.* Dr. Nesbit received her MPA from Brigham Young University and her PhD in public affairs with a specialization in nonprofit management from the School of Public and Environmental Affairs at Indiana University.

Donald F. Norris is professor and chair of the Department of Public Policy, and director of the Maryland Institute for Policy Analysis and Research at the University of Maryland, Baltimore County. He is a specialist in public management; urban politics; and the application, uses, and impacts of information technology (including e-government) on public organizations. He holds a BS in history from the University of Memphis and both an MA and a PhD in government from the University of Virginia.

Rosemary O'Leary is the Edwin O. Stene Distinguished Professor of Public Administration at the University of Kansas, with expertise in the areas of public management, collaboration, conflict resolution, environmental and natural resources management, and public law. Previously she was on the faculties of the Maxwell School of Syracuse University and the School of Public and Environmental Affairs at Indiana University in Bloomington. She is the author or editor of 11 books and more than 100 articles and book chapters on public management. The winner of 10 national research awards and 9 teaching awards, Dr. O'Leary is the only person to win three National Association of Schools of Public Affairs and Administration awards: Best Dissertation (1989), Excellence in Teaching (1996), and Distinguished Research (2004). She is an elected member of the National Academy of Public Administration. She received her JD from the University of Kansas and her PhD from Syracuse University.

Christopher G. Reddick is a professor and chair of the Department of Public Administration at the University of Texas in San Antonio. His research and teaching interests are in information technology and public sector organizations. Some of his publications can be found in *Government Information Quarterly, Electronic Government,* and the *International Journal of Electronic Government Research.* Dr. Reddick recently edited the two-volume *Handbook of Research on Strategies for Local E-Government Adoption and Implementation: Comparative Studies.* He is also author of *Homeland Security Preparedness and Information Systems,* which deals with the impact of information technology on homeland security preparedness. Dr. Reddick received his BA, MA, and MBA at the University of Guelph in Ontario, Canada, and his PhD at the University of Sheffield in the United Kingdom.

James H. Svara is a professor of public affairs at Arizona State University and the director of the Center for Urban Innovation. He specializes in local government leadership, innovation, and management. He is a Fellow of the National Academy of Public Admin-

istration, a member of the board of the Alliance for Innovation, and an honorary member of ICMA, and he has served on the ICMA Strategic Planning Committee. He is currently involved in research projects on sustainability in local government and codes of ethics in associations of public professionals.

Karen Thoreson is president/chief operating officer of the Alliance for Innovation. Prior to working for the Alliance, she was economic development director for the city of Glendale, Arizona. She also served as assistant city manager of Tucson and as director of the community services department. Ms. Thoreson began her career in local government in Boulder, Colorado; since then, she has been a trainer and a speaker on public-private partnerships, community revitalization, innovation, and strategic planning. She has a bachelor's degree from the University of Minnesota and a master's degree in public administration from the University of Northern Colorado.

Mildred E. Warner is a professor in the City and Regional Planning Department at Cornell University, where her work focuses on the role of local government in community development. Her research addresses trends facing local government, such as devolution, fiscal stress, and privatization. She gives special attention to the local government response as regards economic development strategy, service delivery design, and planning across generations. She publishes widely in the public administration, planning, and economic development literature. Dr. Warner received her BA from Oberlin College and her MA and PhD from Cornell.

Cumulative Index, 2009–2013

Cumulative Index, 2009-2013

The cumulative index comprises the years 2009 through 2013 of *The Municipal Year Book*. Entries prior to 2009 are found in earlier editions.

How to Use This Index. Entries run in chronological order, starting with 2009. The **year** is in **boldface** numerals, followed by a colon (e.g., **09:**); the relevant page numbers follow. Years are separated by semicolons.

Academy for State and Local Government, **09:** 310; **10:** 309; **11:** 120

Accountability
of CAO in mayor-council cities, **13:** 22, 33
as economic development strategy, **10:** 5-6; **11:** 33, 41
health care plans and, **13:** 95
system for evaluating social programs, **11:** 61-68

Administrative/political dichotomy, **12:** 7

Advertising, as business incentive, **10:** 4, 5; **11:** 37

Affordable housing, **09:** 43-44; **13:** 14, 51

Afghanistan, **12:** 3-4

Age Discrimination in Employment Act, **09:** 76-77; **10:** 69-70

Aging. *See* Older adults

Air pollution. *See* Environmental protection

Airport Improvement Program (AIP), **09:** 69; **10:** 59, 63

Airports Council International—North America, **09:** 310; **10:** 309; **11:** 120; **12:** 148; **13:** 162

Alabama
agency for community affairs, **09:** 175; **10:** 169; **11:** 107; **12:** 135; **13:** 149
association of counties, **09:** 184; **10:** 178; **11:** 113; **12:** 141; **13:** 156
councils of governments, **09:** 186; **10:** 180; **11:** 116; **12:** 143; **13:** 158
home rule, **09:** 54; **10:** 48
Jefferson County, bond defaults in, **12:** 5
municipal league, **09:** 172; **10:** 166; **11:** 104; **12:** 132; **13:** 146
municipal management association, **09:** 177; **10:** 171; **11:** 110; **12:** 138; **13:** 153
sustainability initiatives in, **11:** 50

Alachua County, Fla., conservation strategies in, **10:** 41-42; **11:** 81

Alaska
agency for community affairs, **09:** 175; **10:** 169; **11:** 107; **12:** 135; **13:** 149
association of counties, **09:** 184; **10:** 178; **11:** 113; **12:** 141; **13:** 156
gun control, **09:** 56
home rule, **09:** 53; **10:** 47
mandates, **09:** 55; **10:** 49
municipal league, **09:** 172; **10:** 166; **11:** 104; **12:** 132; **13:** 146
municipal management association, **09:** 177; **10:** 171; **11:** 110; **12:** 138; **13:** 153
pension and retirement costs, **09:** 55; **10:** 49
recession of 2007-2009 in, **12:** 106
revenue sharing, **09:** 62
state assumption of financial responsibility, **09:** 63

Alliance for Innovation
awards for best practices, **09:** 42, 49; **10:** 37; **12:** 96; **13:** 90
BIG IDEAS event, **12:** 95-96
budget crisis research, **11:** 76, 78, 79, 81
professional development promotion, **13:** 89
sustainability indicators and, **11:** 44

Alternative energy/fuel, **11:** 6; **13:** 92, 96

Alternative financing, **11:** 6-7

Alternative Fuel Vehicle Program (Kansas City, Mo.), **13:** 92

Alternative minimum tax, **09:** 70; **10:** 59

Alternative service delivery. *See also* Services, local government; Volunteers/volunteering

background, **09:** 11
  factors related to choice of, **09:** 16–19; **10:** 19–27
  local government provisions, **09:** 12–16
  surveys, **09:** 11–20; **10:** 19–27; **13:** 79–87
  use of volunteers in, **13:** 79–88
Alternative work schedules
  background, **09:** 28
  benefits and drawbacks, **09:** 30–32
  compressed workweeks, **09:** 28, 31–32
  factors influencing adoption, **09:** 29–30; **10:** 35
  types, **09:** 28, 31–32
  younger workforce and, **11:** 6
Ambulance Safety Initiative (Winter Park, Fla.), **09:** 45
American Association of Airport Executives, **09:** 310; **10:** 309; **11:** 120; **12:** 148; **13:** 162
American Association of Port Authorities, **09:** 310–311; **10:** 309–310; **11:** 120; **12:** 148; **13:** 162
American Association of Retired Persons (AARP), **09:** 37–38; **13:** 52
American Association of School Administrators, **09:** 311; **10:** 310; **11:** 120; **12:** 148; **13:** 162
American College of Healthcare Executives, **09:** 311; **10:** 310; **11:** 120; **12:** 148; **13:** 162
American Institute of Architects, **09:** 311; **10:** 310; **11:** 121; **12:** 149; **13:** 163
American Institute of Certified Planners. *See* American Planning Association
American Library Association, **09:** 311; **10:** 310; **11:** 121; **12:** 149; **13:** 163
American Planning Association (APA), **09:** 311; **10:** 310; **11:** 121; **12:** 149; **13:** 50–51, 52, 163
American Public Gas Association, **09:** 311; **10:** 310; **11:** 121; **12:** 149; **13:** 163
American Public Health Association, **09:** 311; **10:** 310; **11:** 121; **12:** 149; **13:** 163
American Public Human Services Association, **09:** 311; **10:** 310; **11:** 121; **12:** 149; **13:** 163
American Public Power Association, **09:** 311–312; **10:** 310–311; **11:** 122; **12:** 150; **13:** 164
American Public Transportation Association, **09:** 312; **10:** 311; **11:** 122; **12:** 150; **13:** 164
American Public Works Association, **09:** 312; **10:** 311; **11:** 122; **12:** 150; **13:** 164
American Recovery and Reinvestment Act (ARRA), **10:** 58–60, 63, 64; **11:** 37; **12:** 101, 105, 106
American Society for Public Administration, **09:** 312; **10:** 311; **11:** 122; **12:** 150; **13:** 164
American Water Works Association, **09:** 312; **10:** 311; **11:** 122; **12:** 150; **13:** 164
Americans with Disabilities Act Amendments, **09:** 67–68
Americans for Limited Government, **09:** 59; **10:** 53
Americans for Tax Reform, **09:** 59; **10:** 53
AmeriCorps, **10:** 60
Ammons, David N., **09:** 4; **10:** 59
Amtrak appropriations, **09:** 68–69; **10:** 59, 63
Anacortes, Wash., sustainability policies, **12:** 60
Anderson, Sam (Knoxville, Tenn.), **12:** 18
Ann Arbor, Mich., public-private partnership with, **11:** 79
Anti-mandate laws, **09:** 55–56; **10:** 50. *See also* Mandates
Antismoking regulations. *See* Tobacco issues

Antiterrorism measures, **10:** 64. *See also* Department of Homeland Security (DHS); Homeland security; Terrorism
Apple, **11:** 9; **12:** 5
Arab Spring, **12:** 5, 6
Ariely, Dan, **13:** 4
Arizona
  agency for community affairs, **09:** 175; **10:** 169; **11:** 107; **12:** 135; **13:** 149
  associations of counties, **09:** 184; **10:** 178; **11:** 113; **12:** 141; **13:** 156
  councils of governments, **09:** 186; **10:** 180; **11:** 116; **12:** 143; **13:** 158
  development impact fees, **12:** 32, 34
  eminent domain, **09:** 57
  highway-user revenue, **10:** 55
  illegal immigrants, **10:** 52; **11:** 7, 25–26, 28, 30
  locally raised revenues, **10:** 54
  municipal league, **09:** 172; **10:** 166; **11:** 104; **12:** 132; **13:** 146
  municipal management association, **09:** 177; **10:** 171; **11:** 110; **12:** 138; **13:** 153
  preemptive legislation, **10:** 53
  revenue sharing, **10:** 55
  sales tax, **09:** 61
  service consolidation, **10:** 55
  state assistance to localities, **10:** 55
  urban revenue-sharing program, **09:** 61–62
Arkansas
  agencies for community affairs, **09:** 175; **10:** 169; **11:** 107; **12:** 135; **13:** 149
  association of counties, **09:** 184; **10:** 178; **11:** 113; **12:** 141; **13:** 156
  councils of governments, **09:** 186; **10:** 180; **11:** 116; **12:** 143; **13:** 158
  home rule, **09:** 53; **10:** 47
  municipal league, **09:** 172; **10:** 166; **11:** 104; **12:** 132; **13:** 146
  municipal management associations, **09:** 177; **10:** 171; **11:** 110; **12:** 138; **13:** 153
  residency requirements, **10:** 52
Arlington, Tex.
  Arlington Urban Design Center (AUDC), **12:** 96–97
  challenge grants, **13:** 95, 97
  Neighborhood Strength Index, **09:** 43
Arlington County, Va., affordable housing in, **13:** 14
Army Corps of Engineers, **10:** 60
Arrest
  probable cause to, **09:** 73–74; **10:** 66
  searches incident to, **09:** 73–74; **10:** 66, 67
Arvada, Colo., e-government in, **09:** 47
Ask Arvada: Information and Service 24/7 (Arvada, Colo.), **09:** 47
Asset management system (Sarasota County, Fla.), **09:** 49
Association of Public-Safety Communications Officials—International, Inc., **09:** 312; **10:** 311; **11:** 123; **12:** 151; **13:** 165
Association of Public Treasurers, **09:** 312; **10:** 311; **11:** 123; **12:** 151; **13:** 165
Asthma, as an employee health concern, **12:** 42

At-risk pregnancy, as an employee health concern, **12:** 41–42

At-will employment, **09:** 76

Australia, municipal management association, **09:** 182; **10:** 176; **11:** 112; **12:** 140; **13:** 155

Ballard, Greg (mayor, Indianapolis), **12:** 12, 13

Baltimore, Md.
    CitiStat, **12:** 12, 16, 17
    Virtual Supermarket Program, **13:** 91–92, 96

Banfield, Edward, **09:** 7–8

Bank On Brazos Valley (Bryan, Tex.), **13:** 93, 96

Bankruptcy legislation, **10:** 60

Bauman, Gus, **12:** 26

Bayside, Wis., traffic safety design in, **13:** 93, 96

Beaverton, Ore., solar energy program in, **13:** 92, 96

Behn, Robert, **09:** 8

Bell, Calif., corruption in, **11:** 4; **12:** 63, 70

Belleville, Ill., citizen involvement in, **12:** 99

Benefits. *See* Health care plans; Retirement plans

Berkeley, Calif., and climate change, **09:** 46

Bernanke, Ben, **09:** 34

Bill and Melinda Gates Foundation, **11:** 9; **12:** 6

Biosolids treatment, **09:** 45–46

Bipartisan Campaign Finance Reform Act of 2002, **09:** 76

Birmingham, Ala., alternative work schedules in, **09:** 28

Block grants
    Child Care and Development, **10:** 59
    Community Development, **09:** 68; **10:** 59, 63
    Energy Efficiency and Conservation, **10:** 59; **12:** 100
    substance abuse treatment, **10:** 63
    Temporary Assistance to Needy Families (TANF), **10:** 59; **11:** 14

Bloomberg, Michael (mayor, New York City), **12:** 98

Bollens, John, **09:** 4, 6

Bonds, municipal, **12:** 4–5

Bosse, Matthew J., **09:** 4

Boulder, Colo.
    EnergySmart, **13:** 92, 96
    health care plan, **12:** 51

Bozeman, Mont., health care plan, **12:** 52

BP Deepwater Horizon oil spill, **11:** 9

Brenton, Theirry, **12:** 5

Brookings Institution, **09:** 61; **10:** 33

Brownfields Grants (EPA), **13:** 43, 44

Brushy Creek Regional Utility Authority (Tex.), **12:** 97

Bryan, Tex., Bank On Brazos Valley, **13:** 93, 96

Budgeting for Outcomes (Fort Collins, Colo.), **09:** 48–49

Budgeting for Outcomes to Managing for Results (Polk County, Fla.), **10:** 43; **11:** 79

Budgeting for Priorities (Jefferson County, Colo.), **11:** 78

Building Officials and Code Administrators International. *See* International Code Council

Burge, Gregory, **12:** 29, 30, 31

Business attraction strategies, **10:** 4, 6; **11:** 36–37

Business retention, as economic development policy, **10:** 4–5; **11:** 33, 37

Buy Belleville First (Belleville, Ill.), **12:** 99

Byrne Justice Assistance Grants, **10:** 64

Cabarrus County, N.C., food policy council in, **13:** 39

Cable franchising, **09:** 57–58

California
    agency for community affairs, **09:** 175; **10:** 169; **11:** 107; **12:** 135; **13:** 149
    association of counties, **09:** 184; **10:** 178; **11:** 113; **12:** 141; **13:** 156
    councils of governments, **09:** 186; **10:** 180; **11:** 116; **12:** 143; **13:** 158
    eminent domain, **09:** 57
    executive salaries, **12:** 66
    home rule charters, **09:** 21
    mandates, **09:** 55, 61; **10:** 50, 55
    mortgage foreclosures, **10:** 52
    municipal league, **09:** 172; **10:** 166; **11:** 104; **12:** 108, 132; **13:** 146
    municipal management associations, **09:** 177; **10:** 172; **11:** 110; **12:** 138; **13:** 153
    property tax, **09:** 61; **10:** 53, 54
    public-private partnerships in, **13:** 61–62
    retirement plans, **09:** 36; **12:** 108
    state assistance to localities, **09:** 62
    sustainability initiatives in, **11:** 49, 50
    telecommunications, **09:** 58

California Public Employees' Retirement System (CalPERS), **09:** 36

Campaign finance reform, **09:** 76

Canada
    municipal management association, **09:** 182; **10:** 176; **11:** 112; **12:** 140; **13:** 155
    provincial and territorial agencies for local affairs directory, **09:** 176–177; **10:** 171; **11:** 109–110; **12:** 137; **13:** 152
    provincial and territorial associations and unions directory, **09:** 173–174; **10:** 168–169; **11:** 106–107; **12:** 134; **13:** 148

Canadian Association of Municipal Administrators, **09:** 312; **10:** 311; **11:** 123; **12:** 151; **13:** 165

Cancer
    as an employee health concern, **12:** 43
    presumption laws, firefighters, **10:** 49

Cape Coral, Fla., lean government in, **10:** 43–44

Capital punishment, Supreme Court case, **09:** 74

Cardiac Cath Lab Field Activation Program (North Richland Hills, Tex.), **10:** 42

Caring for the Kenai (Kenai, Alas.), **12:** 98

Carlsbad, Calif., improving organizational performance in, **09:** 48

Casa Grande, Ariz., high-tech library in, **11:** 80–81

Center for American Progress, **11:** 7

Center for State and Local Government Excellence, **09:** 312; **10:** 311; **11:** 123; **12:** 151; **13:** 165

Center for the Study and Prevention of Violence, **11:** 63

Center for Substance Abuse Treatment, **10:** 63

Challenges, Solutions, and Innovations Alliance (CSI Alliance) (Sarasota County, Fla.), **12:** 98–99

Charlotte, N.C., citizens symposium, **10:** 30

Charlotte-Mecklenburg, N.C., collaborative planning in, **13:** 52

Charlottesville, Va., electricity savings in, **10:** 43

Chattanooga, Tenn., 311 system in, **12:** 12

Chesapeake, Va., quality-of-life study, **09:** 42–43

Chesterfield, Mo., health care plan, **12:** 52

Chicago, Ill., 311 system in, **12:** 12

Chief administrative officers (CAOs). *See also* City managers; Councils of governments; Municipal administration; Salaries

  community power structure facing, **09:** 5-6

  in county government, **09:** 21, 24-25

  management styles of, **09:** 6-7, 7-8

  position, **13:** 21-22

  retention/turnover rates, **09:** 3-5, 8-9

  salary and compensation, **12:** 63-81; **13:** 99-124

  trends, **13:** 17

Chief elected officials (CEOs)

  in county government, **09:** 22-23

  position, **13:** 22, 24-27

Child care, community development and, **10:** 5; **11:** 38, 39

Child Care and Development Block Grant, **10:** 59

Children. *See* Child/youth programs; Juveniles; Multigenerational planning

Children and family services

  economic development strategies focusing on, **13:** 50-51

  innovative programs in, **09:** 44

Children's Health Insurance Program Reauthorization Act (CHIPRA), **09:** 68; **10:** 61

Children's Mental Health, **10:** 63

Children's Services Council (Palm Beach, Fla.), **11:** 64-67

Child/youth programs. *See also* Juveniles

  innovative programs for at-risk youth/juvenile offenders, **09:** 44; **12:** 97-98, 101

  SCHIP health insurance, **09:** 68; **10:** 61

Cigarettes. *See* Tobacco issues

Cities for Climate Protection (ICLEI), **11:** 49

CitiStat (Baltimore), **10:** 32; **12:** 12, 16, 17

Citizen advisory boards, **10:** 7, 30; **13:** 26, 27, 29-30

Citizen Corps, **10:** 64

Citizen engagement. *See also* E-democracy; E-government

  in economic development, **10:** 7

  information access, **10:** 30-32

  opportunities for, **10:** 29-30; **12:** 96, 97-98

  professional managers and, **12:** 7-8

  in service delivery, **10:** 20, 23, 26

  social media and, **11:** 9-10; **12:** 5-6, 87

  sustainable communities and, **10:** 30; **11:** 4-5, 10, 47-49

  in visioning and strategic planning, **10:** 28-29; **11:** 4-5

Citizen surveys, **10:** 31; **11:** 70-74

City councils. *See* City managers; Council-manager government; Municipal government

City Fiscal Conditions in 2010 (NLC), **11:** 76

City government structure. *See also* Municipal government

  chief appointed official position, **13:** 21-23

  chief elected official, **13:** 22, 24-27

  committees and citizen boards, **13:** 29-30

  election and terms of council members, **13:** 27-29

  forms, **13:** 18-21

  initiative, referenda, and recall provisions, **13:** 30-32

  legal basis, **13:** 21

  survey, **13:** 17-33

  trends, **13:** 32-33

City managers. *See also* Chief administrative officers (CAOs); Council-manager government; Local government; Municipal administration; Municipal government

  decision making and prioritization, **10:** 13-14

  demographic characteristics of, **13:** 11

  general characteristics, **10:** 11-13

  historical background, **10:** 10; **11:** 4

  income disparity and, **13:** 11-12

  international municipal management associations directory, **09:** 182-184; **10:** 176-177; **11:** 112-113; **12:** 140; **13:** 155

  management styles and community power structures, **09:** 5-8

  municipal officials directory, **09:** 188-277; **10:** 182-276

  politics and, **12:** 3-9

  power structures facing, **09:** 5-6

  professionalism of, **11:** 4-5; **12:** 4, 6-9

  recession and, **10:** 35-36

  retention/turnover rates, **09:** 3-5, 8-9

  roles, **10:** 10, 16-17

  salaries, **09:** 81-102; **10:** 75-96; **12:** 72-78; **13:** 110-124

  second-order devolution and, **11:** 14-23

  tenure, **10:** 11

  time management, **10:** 14-16

  trends, **10:** 17-18

Citywide Performance Measurement Program (San Francisco), **12:** 15

Civic enfranchisement, **13:** 13

Civil Rights Act of 1964, Title VII, **09:** 76-77; **10:** 68-69

Classical pluralism, as community power structure, **09:** 6, 8

Clean Energy Act of 2007, **09:** 66

Clean Energy Bonds, **10:** 59

Clean Energy Corps, **10:** 60

Clean Water State Revolving Fund, **10:** 60

Clearwater, Fla., wastewater treatment innovation in, **13:** 92-93, 96

Climate change

  food issues and, **13:** 40, 41

  local government initiatives, **09:** 46-47; **11:** 49-50

  as local government priority, **11:** 6, 47

Cloud computing, **12:** 87-88

Coastal zone management. *See* Environmental protection

Code of Ethics (ICMA), **09:** 6; **10:** 17; **11:** 7, 8; **12:** 64, 68; **13:** 12, 101

Collaborative governance

  challenges, **13:** 65, 66

  consequences of, **13:** 63-65

  experiences with, **13:** 60-62

  factors contributing to positive experiences, **13:** 62-63

  as a management strategy, **13:** 58-60

  skills for successful, **13:** 65-69

  survey, **13:** 57-58, 69

Collective bargaining, **10:** 64

Colleges and universities. *See* Education

Colorado

  agency for community affairs, **09:** 175; **10:** 169; **11:** 107; **12:** 135; **13:** 149

  association of counties, **09:** 184; **10:** 178; **11:** 113; **12:** 141; **13:** 156

council of governments, **09:** 186; **10:** 180; **11:** 116; **12:** 144; **13:** 159

development impact fees, **12:** 26, 27, 30

eminent domain, **09:** 57; **10:** 52

highway-user revenue, **10:** 55

jurisdictional collaboration in, **13:** 61

local finances, **09:** 59; **10:** 53

municipal league, **09:** 172; **10:** 166; **11:** 104; **12:** 132; **13:** 146

municipal management association, **09:** 177; **10:** 172; **11:** 110; **12:** 138; **13:** 153

Commerce clause, Supreme Court cases, **09:** 77; **10:** 71

Commission government, **09:** 22; **13:** 18-21

Communities of intent, **11:** 4, 10. *See also* Sustainable communities

Community Challenge Planning Grants, **10:** 63

Community development. *See also* Housing; Land use

child care and, **10:** 5; **11:** 38, 39

community gardens, **10:** 41; **13:** 35, 37, 38, 39, 40, 91

economic programs, **10:** 5; **11:** 33, 37-39

innovative programs, **09:** 42-44, 45; **10:** 37-39; **12:** 100-101; **13:** 93-94

Community Development Block Grant (CDBG) program, **09:** 68; **10:** 59, 63; **13:** 43, 44

Community gardens, **10:** 41; **13:** 35, 37, 38, 39, 40, 91. *See also* Food system development

Community Oriented Policing Services, **10:** 64

Community Partnerships to End Homelessness Act, **09:** 68

Community power structures, city managers and, **09:** 3-9

Community service, volunteer opportunities for, **09:** 48. *See also* Volunteers/volunteering

Community Transportation Plan (Decatur, Ga.), **09:** 45

ComNET (Durham, N.C.), **10:** 37-38

Compensation. *See* Employee benefits; Salaries

Competing elites, as community power structure, **09:** 5, 7

Competition

cost savings through, **10:** 25-26

interlocal economic development and, **10:** 8, 9; **11:** 39-40

in service delivery, **10:** 20, 23-27

Compressed workweeks. *See* Alternative work schedules

Congress, U.S. *See also specific legislation by name*

actions affecting local government, **09:** 66-71; **10:** 58-65

annual appropriations, **09:** 69-70; **10:** 58, 60, 62-64

bankruptcy legislation, **10:** 60

crime control and prevention, **09:** 66-67; **10:** 63-64

economy, **09:** 70-71; **10:** 58-60, 65

education, **09:** 70; **10:** 59, 60, 63; **11:** 18

energy, **09:** 66; **10:** 58, 59, 60, 63, 64-65

environment and land use, **09:** 66; **10:** 64-65

equal pay, **10:** 65

farm bill reauthorization, **09:** 67

federal land ownership and PILT, **09:** 70

gay rights, **11:** 7

health care, **11:** 5

health and human services, **09:** 67-68; **10:** 60-63

homeland security and emergency preparedness, **10:** 64

housing and homelessness, **09:** 68; **10:** 59-60, 63

illegal aliens and immigration reform, **11:** 7, 25-26, 27-28

SCHIP reauthorization, **09:** 68; **10:** 61

social services, **09:** 67-68

telecommunications, **10:** 59

transportation, **09:** 68-69; **10:** 59, 60, 63, 65

unemployment benefits, **10:** 58, 59, 60

unresolved issues and stalled legislation, **09:** 71; **10:** 61

Connecticut

agency for community affairs, **09:** 175; **10:** 169; **11:** 107; **12:** 135; **13:** 149

eminent domain, **10:** 51-52

mandates, **09:** 56; **10:** 50

municipal league, **09:** 172; **10:** 166; **11:** 104; **12:** 132; **13:** 146

municipal management association, **09:** 178; **10:** 172; **11:** 110; **12:** 138; **13:** 153

open-records laws, **09:** 55

publication of legal notices, **10:** 49

Conservation. *See* Energy; Environmental protection; Land use

Consolidated Appropriations Act of 2008, **09:** 66, 69-70

Consolidated Appropriations Act of 2009, **10:** 62-63

Consolidated Omnibus Budget Reconciliation Act (COBRA), **09:** 37, 39; **10:** 59

Constitutional amendments. *See* specific amendments

Contract management, **10:** 19-21, 25

Contract negotiations/agreements for CAOs, **12:** 67-70. *See also* Employee benefits; Retirement plans; Salaries

Contracting

as a budget reduction measure, **10:** 35

competition and, **09:** 11-20

determinants for, **10:** 19-27

Corporation for National and Community Service, **10:** 60

Corrections, local government authority over, **11:** 15-16, 18

Corruption, in local government, **11:** 4; **12:** 5, 63

Council-manager government. *See also* City managers; County government; Municipal government

in counties, **09:** 22, 23, 25-26

definition, **13:** 18

historical background, **10:** 10

sustainability approaches in, **11:** 49-50

trends, **13:** 17, 19-21

Council members, election and terms, **13:** 27-29

Council of State Community Development Agencies, **09:** 312; **10:** 312; **11:** 123; **12:** 151; **13:** 165

Council of State Governments, **09:** 312-313; **10:** 312; **11:** 28, 123; **12:** 152; **13:** 166

Council of University Institutes for Urban Affairs. *See* Urban Affairs Association

Councils of governments recognized by ICMA, directory, **09:** 186-187; **10:** 180-181; **11:** 116-118; **12:** 143-145; **13:** 158-160

County government. *See also* Council-manager government; Local government

constitutional officers, **09:** 22-24

forms, **09:** 22-25

governing boards, **09:** 25

home rule charters, **09:** 21-22

political reform, **09:** 25-27

professional administrators, **09:** 24-25

sustainability actions taken by, **11:** 44–46

County officials
  directory, **09:** 278–309; **10:** 277–308
  salaries, **09:** 103–120; **10:** 97–114; **12:** 79–81; **13:** 120–124
  sheriffs, **09:** 24

Coursey, David, **12:** 85

Courts. *See* Legal cases; Supreme Court cases

Crime. *See also* Law enforcement; Police; Public safety
  DNA collection, **10:** 42
  hate, **10:** 63
  income disparity and, **13:** 8–9
  innovations to reduce, **09:** 42–43, 44
  legislation, **09:** 66–67; **10:** 63
  undocumented immigrants, **11:** 28

Cultural diversity, **11:** 26–27

Dade County, Fla., development impact fees, **12:** 30

Daley, Richard M. (mayor, Chicago), **09:** 7–8

Davenport, Iowa, Green City Initiative, **09:** 44

Death penalty. *See* Supreme Court cases, capital punishment

Decatur, Ga., Community Transportation Plan, **09:** 45

Decision making
  citizen engagement, **10:** 29–30
  city managers, **10:** 13–14

Defined benefit plans, **09:** 35–36, 40; **11:** 5; **12:** 105, 106,
    107–108, 109n1. *See also* Retirement plans

Defined contribution plans, **09:** 35–36, 40; **11:** 5; **12:** 107,
    109n1. *See also* Retirement plans

DeHoog, Ruth, **09:** 4

Delaware
  agency for community affairs, **09:** 175; **10:** 169; **11:** 107;
    12: 135; **13:** 149
  association of counties, **09:** 184; **10:** 178; **11:** 113; **12:** 141;
    13: 156
  municipal league, **09:** 172; **10:** 166; **11:** 104; **12:** 132; **13:**
    146
  municipal management association, **09:** 178; **10:** 172; **11:**
    110; **12:** 138; **13:** 153
  recession of 2007–2009 in, **12:** 106

Delray Beach Community Land Trust (Delray Beach, Fla.),
    09: 43–44

Denmark, municipal management association, **09:** 182; **10:**
    176; **11:** 112; **12:** 140; **13:** 155

Denver, Colo., 311/CRM citizen satisfaction survey in, **12:** 20,
    21, 22

Department of Agriculture (USDA), **10:** 59; **13:** 36, 39, 43–44

Department of Health and Human Services, **10:** 61, 62–63;
    13: 43

Department of Homeland Security (DHS), **09:** 69; **10:** 63;
    11: 8. *See also* Antiterrorism measures; Emergency
    preparedness; Homeland security; Terrorism

Department of Housing and Urban Development (HUD), **09:**
    68; **10:** 63; **13:** 43

Department of Justice, **10:** 63

Department of Transportation, **10:** 63; **13:** 43

Depression, as an employee health concern, **12:** 43

DeSantis, Victor, **09:** 4

Development impact fees
  assessment and payment, **12:** 27

authority to impose, **12:** 27–29
  background and definitions, **12:** 26–27
  for child- and age-friendly communities, **13:** 51–52
  policy considerations, **12:** 31
  research review, **12:** 25–26, 29–31
  survey methodology and findings, **12:** 31–34
  trends, **09:** 61; **10:** 54

*Development Impact Fees: Policy Rationale, Practice, Theory,
    and Issues* (Frank and Downing), **12:** 25

Devolution of responsibility, from state to local government,
    10: 47; **11:** 13–23

Diabetes, as an employee health concern, **12:** 42–43

Diesel Engine Recovery Act, **10:** 65

Digital technology. *See* Technology

Dillon's Rule, **09:** 53; **10:** 47

Directories
  Canadian provincial and territorial agencies for local affairs,
    09: 176–177; **10:** 171; **11:** 109–110; **12:** 137; **13:** 152
  Canadian provincial and territorial associations and
    unions, **09:** 173–174; **10:** 168–169; **11:** 106–107; **12:**
    134; **13:** 148
  councils of governments recognized by ICMA, **09:** 186–187;
    10: 180–181; **11:** 116–118; **12:** 143–145; **13:** 158–160
  county officials, **09:** 278–309; **10:** 277–308
  international municipal management associations, **09:**
    182–184; **10:** 176–177; **11:** 112–113; **12:** 140; **13:** 155
  municipal officials, **09:** 188–277; **10:** 182–276
  state agencies for community affairs, **09:** 175–176; **10:**
    169–170; **11:** 107–109; **12:** 135–137; **13:** 149–151
  state associations of counties, **09:** 184–185; **10:** 178–179;
    11: 113–115; **12:** 141–143; **13:** 156–158
  state municipal leagues, **09:** 172–173; **10:** 166–167; **11:**
    104–106; **12:** 132–134; **13:** 146–148
  state municipal management associations, **09:** 177–182;
    10: 171–175; **11:** 110–112; **12:** 138–139; **13:** 153–154

Disabilities. *See* Individuals with disabilities

Disasters, **12:** 3, 4. *See also* Department of Homeland Security
    (DHS); Emergency preparedness; Federal Emergency
    Management Agency (FEMA); Homeland security;
    Hurricane Katrina

Discrimination
  age, **09:** 76–77; **10:** 69–70
  in employment, **09:** 76–77; **10:** 68–69
  gay rights and, **11:** 7
  in public schools, **10:** 70–71
  religious, **11:** 7–8
  in retaliation, **10:** 69
  right of action under Education Amendments Title IX, **10:**
    70–71
  in service allocation, **13:** 12–13

Disease management/prevention programs, **12:** 41

Disparate-impact claims, **09:** 76–77; **10:** 69

Disparity. *See* Economic disparity; Income disparity

District of Columbia
  council of governments, **09:** 186; **10:** 180; **11:** 116; **12:**
    144; **13:** 159
  firearms regulation, **09:** 72

Diversity. *See* Cultural diversity

Divisiveness, in politics, **12:** 4, 6–8; **13:** 9–11

DNA collection, **10:** 42

Don't Ask, Don't Tell, **11:** 7

Downers Grove, Ill., budget prioritization system, **11:** 79–80

Downing, Paul B., **12:** 25–26

DPWStat (San Francisco), **12:** 16

DRIVE (Prince William County, Va.), **10:** 43

Dublin, Ohio
    DubLink, **09:** 47–48
    Healthy by Choice, **10:** 39

DubLink (Dublin, Ohio), **09:** 47–48

Due process, Supreme Court cases, **09:** 77; **10:** 71

Duncan Associates, **12:** 27, 28, 34

Durham, N.C.
    antigang initiative, **09:** 8
    citizen participation in community redesign, **13:** 52
    ComNET, **10:** 37–38
    "Durham First," **11:** 80
    performance measures and community engagement, **13:** 94, 96

eCitizen interest, in service delivery, **10:** 20, 23, 24

Economic development. *See also* Community development; Finances
    accountability, **10:** 5–6; **11:** 33, 41
    affordable housing, **11:** 38
    barriers, **10:** 7–9; **11:** 39–40
    base trends, **11:** 34–36
    business attraction and incentives, **10:** 4; **11:** 36–37
    business retention, **10:** 4–5; **11:** 33, 37
    community development strategies, **10:** 5; **11:** 33, 37–39; **12:** 96–97
    downtown redevelopment, **11:** 38
    eminent domain, **09:** 57; **10:** 48, 51–52
    infrastructure investments, **10:** 4; **11:** 37, 38, 81
    innovative programs, **09:** 42–43, 44, 45; **10:** 37–39; **11:** 79, 80, 81; **12:** 96–97, 99–101; **13:** 90–91, 93–96
    interlocal competition, **10:** 8, 9; **11:** 39–40
    job-creation initiatives, **13:** 90–91
    manufacturing, **11:** 34
    planning for, **10:** 6, 7; **11:** 37–38
    public-private collaboration/partnerships, **10:** 4, 5, 7, 8; **11:** 37, 38, 39, 79, 80–81; **12:** 97–98, 99–100, 101; **13:** 39, 42–43, 90, 91, 93, 96, 97
    recession and, **10:** 35; **11:** 33–42, 79, 80, 81
    residential sector, **10:** 6; **11:** 34
    retail/service sector, **11:** 34
    small-business development, **10:** 5; **11:** 33, 37–39
    strategies, **10:** 3–9; **11:** 33–42; **13:** 48–51
    surveys, **10:** 3–9; **11:** 33–42
    tax base and, **11:** 34–36
    technology/telecommunications, **10:** 4, 6–7; **11:** 34, 35, 78, 79, 81
    tourism, **10:** 7
    vacant property, **10:** 38

Economic disparity, **11:** 8; **12:** 4–6. *See also* Income disparity

E-democracy. *See also* E-government
    barriers to, **13:** 77–78
    e-participation activities, **13:** 73–75
    impact, **13:** 75–77
    management, **13:** 75
    planning, **13:** 75
    survey, **13:** 72–73

E-democracy.org, **10:** 32

Education. *See also* Schools; Teachers
    children with disabilities, **10:** 70
    finance and control, **09:** 62, 63
    innovative programs, **09:** 43
    local government authority over, **11:** 15–16, 17–18
    No Child Left Behind Act, **11:** 18
    Secure Rural Schools legislation, **09:** 70
    state assistance to localities, **09:** 62, 63

Education Amendments of 1972, **10:** 70–71

Education Corps, **10:** 60

Edward Byrne Memorial Justice Assistance Grant (JAG) Program, **09:** 66; **10:** 64

Edward M. Kennedy Serve America Act, **10:** 60

E-government. *See also* CitiStat; E-democracy; Technology; 311/CRM systems
    background, **13:** 71
    barriers to, **12:** 88–89
    changes resulting from, **12:** 89–90
    citizen engagement, **09:** 47, 49, 55; **10:** 30, 32, 40; **11:** 9–10; **12:** 5–6
    financing, **12:** 92
    functionality, **12:** 85–88
    innovations in, **09:** 47–48, 49; **10:** 37–38, 40; **12:** 83–94
    management, **12:** 90–92
    online health care provisions, **12:** 46–47
    reasons for adopting, **12:** 84
    survey, **12:** 83–94
    transparency, **09:** 55

Eighth Amendment, **09:** 74

Elderly individuals. *See* Older adults

Elections
    chief elected officials, **13:** 32, 34
    council members, **13:** 27–29
    county constitutional officers, **09:** 22–24
    county governing boards, **09:** 25
    legislation affecting, **09:** 75
    limits on campaign spending and contributions, **09:** 76
    minority election districts, **10:** 68

Electricity, expenditure reduction, **10:** 43

Electronic government. *See* E-government

Eli Lilly and Company, **12:** 13

Elite politics, as community power structure, **09:** 5, 7

Emergency Economic Stabilization Act of 2008, **09:** 70–71; **10:** 65

Emergency food provision, **13:** 35; 39

Emergency preparedness. *See also* Antiterrorism measures; Department of Homeland Security (DHS); Federal Emergency Management Agency (FEMA); Homeland security
    disaster funding, **09:** 69
    Resiliency and Preparedness Study (Flagstaff, Ariz.), **13:** 92
    sustainability and, **11:** 9

Emergency services, ambulance safety and, **09:** 45

Emeryville, Calif., multigenerational approach to planning in, **13:** 52

Eminent domain
economic development, **09:** 57; **10:** 48, 51–52
local authority, **09:** 57; **10:** 48, 51–52
Supreme Court cases, **09:** 57; **10:** 51–52
Employee benefits. *See also* Health care plans; Retirement
plans; Salaries; Workers' compensation, firefighters
executive compensation beyond base pay, **12:** 69–70; **13:**
105–108
innovative programs, **09:** 44–45; **10:** 39
mandates, **09:** 55; **10:** 49
Employees. *See* Public employees
Employment
at-will, **09:** 76
discrimination in, **09:** 76–77; **10:** 68–70
Employment contracts, chief administrative officers, **13:** 106
Employment discrimination, Supreme Court cases, **09:**
76–77; **10:** 69–70
Energy
energy-efficiency policies, **11:** 6–7
energy-efficient programs, **09:** 46–47; **10:** 41–42, 43, 44;
12: 99–100; **13:** 92, 96
legislation, **09:** 66, 70–71; **10:** 58, 59, 60, 63, 64–65
renewable energy programs, **09:** 46; **10:** 59, 64; **11:** 6; **13:**
92, 96
Energy Conservation Strategies Commission (Alachua
County, Fla.), **10:** 41–42
Energy Efficiency and Conservation Block Grant (EECBG)
program, **10:** 59; **12:** 100
Energy Efficiency and Solar Project (Oro Valley, Ariz.), **12:** 100
Energy Improvement and Extension Act, **09:** 70–71
Energy Loan Tax Assessment Program (ELTAP), **11:** 6–7
Energy Performance Contracting, **12:** 100
Energy Star certification, **11:** 53
EnergySmart (Boulder, Colo.), **13:** 92
England. *See* United Kingdom
Environmental protection. *See also* Land use; Solid waste;
Sustainability
innovative programs, **09:** 45–47; **10:** 40–42; **12:** 97, 98,
99–100
legislation, **09:** 66; **10:** 64–65
Environmental Protection Agency (EPA)
food system development programs, **13:** 43
Sustainable Communities Initiative, **10:** 63
E-participation. *See* E-democracy
Equal pay, **10:** 65
Equal protection clause, **09:** 76; **10:** 70–71
Establishment clause, **10:** 67
Ethics, in local government, **11:** 4, 7, 8
Ethier, William, **12:** 26
Eulau, Heinz, **09:** 6
Evidence-based programs (EBPs), **11:** 63–67
Exactions, **12:** 26
Exclusionary rule, Supreme Court cases, **10:** 66

Facebook
in local government, **10:** 31; **11:** 9; **12:** 87
popularity of, **12:** 5, 87
Fairfax County, Va.
Fairfax County Restoration Project (FCRP), **12:** 97

Magnet Housing Program, **09:** 43
Family services, innovative programs for, **10:** 39
Family Smoking Prevention and Tobacco Control Act,
10: 62
Fannie Mae, **09:** 68, 70
Farm bill reauthorization, **09:** 67
Farm Security and Rural Investment Act of 2002, **09:** 67
Farmers' markets, **10:** 41; **11:** 51, 52, 53; **13:** 35, 38–40. S*ee
also* Food system development
Federal Emergency Management Agency (FEMA). *See also*
Department of Homeland Security (DHS); Emergency
preparedness; Homeland security
disaster declarations in 2011, **12:** 3
Disaster Relief Fund, **09:** 69
Federal government. *See also* Congress, U.S.; Finance;
specific agencies/departments
economic intervention, **09:** 41
immigration reform, **11:** 7, 25–26, 27–28
local food system development support, **13:** 43–44
Federalism in the United States, **11:** 13–14
Federation of Canadian Municipalities, **09:** 313; **10:** 312; **11:**
124; **12:** 152; **13:** 166
Feiock, Richard, **09:** 5
55,000 Degrees (Louisville/Jefferson County, Ky.), **13:** 91
Finances. *See also* Federal government; Salaries; Taxes
municipal bonds, **12:** 4–5
state-local relations, **09:** 59–63; **10:** 53–55; **11:** 15–17, 18,
19–20
Firearms. *See* Gun control; Guns
Firefighters
contract disputes, **10:** 50
exemption from public disclosure requirements, **10:** 49
pension funds, **09:** 55; **10:** 49
residency requirements, **09:** 58; **10:** 48
salaries and expenditures, **09:** 55, 121–129, 149–167;
10: 115–124, 144–162; **11:** 83–100; **12:** 111–128; **13:**
125–141
workers' compensation, **10:** 49
written test for promotion, **10:** 69
Fire Rescue Adaptive Response Program (Oakland Park,
Fla.), **10:** 42
Fireworks, **10:** 53
First Amendment
establishment clause, **10:** 67
free speech, **10:** 67, 68
monuments in public parks, **10:** 67
state employee-payroll deductions, **10:** 67–68
Fiscal Survey of the States: Fall 2011, **12:** 106
Fitness, as an employee health concern, **12:** 43
Flagstaff, Ariz., *Resiliency and Preparedness Study*, **13:** 92, 96
Flextime, **09:** 28. *See also* Alternative work schedules
Flickr, in local government, **12:** 87
Florida
agency for community affairs, **09:** 175; **10:** 169; **11:** 107;
12: 135; **13:** 149
association of counties, **09:** 184; **10:** 178; **11:** 114; **12:**
141; **13:** 156
councils of governments, **09:** 186; **10:** 180; **11:** 116; **12:**
144; **13:** 159

development impact fees, **12:** 26, 30, 32
home rule, **10:** 51
land use regulation, **10:** 52
mandates, **09:** 56; **10:** 49, 50
municipal league, **09:** 172; **10:** 166; **11:** 104; **12:** 132; **13:** 146
municipal management association, **09:** 178; **10:** 172; **11:** 110; **12:** 138; **13:** 153
police and firefighter pension funds, **10:** 49
property tax, **09:** 60
red-light cameras, **10:** 52
tax issues, **09:** 60; **10:** 53, 54
Florida, Richard, **10:** 5; **11:** 38; **13:** 49, 50
Food, Conservation, and Energy Act of 2008, **09:** 67
Food policy councils, **13:** 41–43
Food system development
background, **13:** 35–36
community projects and programs, **13:** 38–40
federal support, **13:** 43–44
food access and production, **13:** 37–38
local government support, **13:** 44–45
plan types, **13:** 40–41
responsibility for, **13:** 41–43
survey, **13:** 36–45
Foreclosure Prevention Partnership Program (Las Vegas, Nev.), **12:** 101
Foreclosures. *See* Housing; Recession of 2007–2009
For-profit contracting, **09:** 11, 12, 15–20; **10:** 20, 25, 26
Fort Collins, Colo., Budgeting for Outcomes, **09:** 48–49
Fort Worth, Tex., youth involvement in community issues, **12:** 101
Fostering Connections to Success and Increasing Adoptions Act of 2008, **09:** 68
Fostering Volunteer Programs in the Public Sector, **13:** 79
Fourteenth Amendment, **09:** 76; **10:** 70
Fourth Amendment
probable cause to arrest, **09:** 73–74; **10:** 66
search and seizure, **09:** 73–74; **10:** 66–67, 71
Frank, James E., **12:** 25–26
Freddie Mac, **09:** 68, 70
Free speech, Supreme Court cases, **10:** 67, 68
French, Edward, **09:** 5
Fusion centers, **11:** 8

Gainesville, Fla.
anti-Muslim sentiment in, **11:** 8, 9
solar energy program in, **13:** 92, 96
Gated communities, regulation of, **13:** 13
Gays/lesbians
hate crimes, **10:** 63
social equity for, **11:** 7
Generations Invigorating Volunteerism and Education (GIVE) Act, **10:** 60
Georgia
agency for community affairs, **09:** 175; **10:** 169; **11:** 107; **12:** 135; **13:** 149
association of counties, **09:** 184; **10:** 178; **11:** 114; **12:** 141; **13:** 156

councils of governments, **09:** 186; **10:** 180; **11:** 116; **12:** 144; **13:** 159
illegal immigrants, **10:** 52
municipal league, **09:** 172; **10:** 166; **11:** 104; **12:** 132; **13:** 146
municipal management association, **09:** 178; **10:** 172; **11:** 110; **12:** 138; **13:** 153
public disclosure requirements, **10:** 49
Georgia, Republic of, municipal management association, **11:** 112; **12:** 140; **13:** 155
Gilligan, James, **13:** 8
Gini index, **13:** 4, 6, 7
Glenview, Ill., Municipal Partnering Initiative (MPI), **13:** 94, 97
Global Institute on Sustainability, **11:** 44
GMIS International, **09:** 313; **10:** 312; **11:** 124; **12:** 152; **13:** 166
Golden, Colo., Golden Vision 2030, **13:** 94, 96
Goodwill Industries, **10:** 39; **11:** 79, 80
Google, **12:** 5
Gould, Roy (city manager, Santa Monica, Calif.), **12:** 108
Government Barometer, **12:** 12, 15, 16, 17, 19
Government Finance Officers Association (GFOA), **09:** 313; **10:** 312; **11:** 124; **12:** 152; **13:** 166
Government forms. *See* Council-manager government; County government; Local government; Mayor-council government; Municipal government; State government
Government Management Information Sciences Users Group. *See* GMIS International
Governmental Accounting Standards Board (GASB), **09:** 39, 313; **10:** 312; **11:** 5, 124; **12:** 106, 109n7, 152; **13:** 166
Governmental Research Association, **09:** 313–314; **10:** 312; **11:** 124; **12:** 153; **13:** 167
Grants. *See* Block grants; Community development; *specific programs*
Great Britain. *See* United Kingdom
"Great Recession." *See* Recession of 2007–2009
Great Society programs, **10:** 10
Green Building Council (GBC), **11:** 6, 7
Green City Initiative (Davenport, Iowa), **09:** 44
Green roofs, **13:** 37
Green Vision (San José, Calif.), **10:** 40
Greenhouse gases, local government efforts to control, **11:** 49, 53, 54; **13:** 92
Greening Lakewood Business Partnership (Lakewood, Colo.), **12:** 99–100
Gulf Coast, disasters in, **11:** 9. *See also* Hurricane Katrina
Gun control, as a state-local issue, **09:** 56–57; **10:** 51
Guns
preemptions, **09:** 56–57; **10:** 51
Supreme Court case, **09:** 72
Gwinnett County, Ga., pension plans in, **12:** 107–108

Halton Borough Council, United Kingdom, **13:** 91, 96
Hampton, Va.
"I Value" Campaign, **12:** 99
Intensive Care Coordination Project, **10:** 39
Hanbury, George, **09:** 5
Handguns. *See* Gun control; Guns

Harvard Business Review, **11:** 76

Haslam, Bill (mayor, Knoxville, Tenn.), **12:** 12

Hassett, Wendy, **09:** 4

Hate crimes, **10:** 63

Hawaii, association of counties, **09:** 184; **10:** 178; **11:** 114; **12:** 141; **13:** 156

Health care

employee health concerns, **12:** 38–43

legislation, **10:** 60–63; **11:** 5; **12:** 50

local government authority over, **11:** 15–16, 17, 18

obstacles to, **12:** 47–48

options for the future, **12:** 46–47

programs promoting, **09:** 44–45; **10:** 39; **12:** 38–43, 51–52; **13:** 95

recession and, **10:** 34

State Children's Health Insurance Program (SCHIP), **09:** 68; **10:** 61

Health care plans

benefits survey, **12:** 44–46

costs of, **09:** 40–41; **12:** 38, 45–46, 48–50

coverage, **12:** 44–45

decision-making authority, **12:** 51

funding, **12:** 51

GASB regulations, **09:** 39; **11:** 5

insurance programs survey, **12:** 37–52

Medicare, **09:** 37, 39; **10:** 62; **12:** 45

mental illness and, **09:** 67

purchasing options, **12:** 51

recession and, **09:** 37, 39–41

for retirees, **09:** 37, 39–41; **12:** 44–45, 46

selection of provider, **12:** 50–51

Health reimbursement arrangement/account (HRA), **12:** 44, 45, 46

Health savings account (HSA), **12:** 44, 45, 46

Health on a Shelf (Tupelo, Miss.), **13:** 93, 96

Healthy by Choice program (Dublin, Ohio), **10:** 39

Healthy Futures Corps, **10:** 60

Heart disease, as an employee health concern, **12:** 43

Helping Families Save Their Homes Act, **10:** 59–60

Hickory, N.C.

approaches to budget retrenchment, **11:** 76, 77, 78

Operation No Vacancy, **10:** 38

High Springs (Fla.) Farmer's Market and Community Gardens, **10:** 41

Highways. *See* Transportation

Hispanics

growing population of, **11:** 31; **13:** 48

income disparity and, **13:** 5, 9

HOME Investment Partnerships Program, **10:** 59, 63

Home rule. *See also* Local government; Municipal government

county government, **09:** 21–22

local authority issues, **09:** 53–54; **10:** 47–48, 56; **11:** 16–17

Homeland security. *See also* Antiterrorism measures; Department of Homeland Security (DHS); Emergency preparedness

funding, **09:** 69; **11:** 8

legislation, **09:** 69; **10:** 64

local government measures in, **11:** 8–9

Homelessness, legislation addressing, **09:** 68; **10:** 59–60, 63

Homosexuals. *See* Gays/lesbians

Hospitals, local government authority over, **11:** 15–16, 17, 18

Housing. *See also* Community development

affordable, **09:** 43–44; **11:** 38, 71–72; **13:** 14, 50–51

decline in value, **09:** 38–39; **11:** 35

federal programs, **10:** 63

high cost of, **10:** 8; **11:** 39

legislation, **09:** 68; **10:** 59–60, 63

mortgage foreclosures, **09:** 34, 38, 68; **10:** 33–34, 52, 59–60, 63; **11:** 34; **12:** 4, 32, 101

segregation in, **13:** 9

Housing and Economic Recovery Act of 2008, **09:** 68; **12:** 101

Houston, Tex.

pension system, **12:** 108

311 citizen satisfaction survey in, **12:** 19–20, 22

Houston Municipal Employees Pension System (HMEPS), **12:** 108

Hungary, municipal management association, **10:** 176; **11:** 112; **13:** 155

Hurricane Irene, **12:** 3

Hurricane Katrina, **09:** 57

Hyperpluralism, as community power structure, **09:** 6, 8

"I Value" Campaign (Hampton, Va.), **12:** 99

ICLEI—Local Governments for Sustainability, **11:** 7, 49–50; **12:** 56

ICMA

alternative service delivery surveys, **09:** 11–20; **10:** 19–27; **13:** 79–87

Center for Performance Measurement consortium, **10:** 43

city manager continuity and change survey, **10:** 11–18

city manager retention/turnover rate survey, **09:** 3–4

Code of Ethics, **09:** 6; **10:** 17; **11:** 7, 8; **12:** 64, 68; **13:** 12, 101

compensation surveys, **12:** 63–81; **13:** 99–124

county form of government survey, **09:** 21–27

description, **09:** 313–314; **10:** 313; **11:** 125; **12:** 153; **13:** 167

development impact fee survey, **12:** 26

economic development survey, **10:** 3–9; **11:** 33–42

e-government survey, **12:** 83–94

guide for elected officials, **09:** 9

"Guidelines for Compensation," **12:** 63, 64, 67, 68–69; **13:** 99, 100, 101, 103, 105, 109

health care benefits survey, **12:** 37–52

historical background, **10:** 10; **11:** 4

immigration survey, **11:** 28–30

membership data for, **13:** 11

Model Employment Agreement, **12:** 64, 67–68, 69, 70; **13:** 106

municipal form of government survey, **13:** 17–33

project on workforce mobility, **09:** 28

service delivery surveys, **09:** 11–20; **10:** 19–27; **13:** 79–87

state of the profession survey, **10:** 28–32, 33–36; **11:** 76

sustainability policies, **12:** 56

sustainability survey, **11:** 43–60; **12:** 54, 57, 60

ICMA Retirement Corporation, **09:** 314; **10:** 313; **11:** 125; **12:** 153; **13:** 167

Idaho
   agency for community affairs, **09:** 175; **10:** 169; **11:** 107; **12:** 135; **13:** 149
   association of counties, **09:** 184; **10:** 178; **11:** 114; **12:** 141; **13:** 156
   council of governments, **09:** 186; **10:** 180; **11:** 116; **12:** 144; **13:** 159
   eminent domain, **09:** 57
   jurisdictional collaboration in, **13:** 61
   municipal league, **09:** 172; **10:** 166; **11:** 104; **12:** 132; **13:** 146
   municipal management association, **09:** 178; **10:** 172, 175; **11:** 110, 112; **12:** 138, 139; **13:** 153, 154
   open-meetings law, **10:** 49
   property rights, **09:** 57
Ihlanfeldt, Keith, **12:** 29-30, 31
Illegal immigrants. *See also* Immigration
   legislation, **11:** 7, 25-26, 27-28, 30
   local authority, **09:** 58; **10:** 52
   in the workforce, **11:** 7
Illinois
   access to information law, **10:** 49
   agency for community affairs, **09:** 175; **10:** 169; **11:** 107; **12:** 135; **13:** 149
   associations of counties, **09:** 184; **10:** 178; **11:** 114; **12:** 141; **13:** 156
   councils of governments, **09:** 186; **10:** 180; **11:** 116; **12:** 144; **13:** 159
   jurisdictional collaboration in, **13:** 61
   mandates, **10:** 49
   municipal league, **09:** 172; **10:** 166; **11:** 104; **12:** 132; **13:** 146
   municipal management association, **09:** 178; **10:** 172; **11:** 110; **12:** 138; **13:** 153
   pension plan funding, **12:** 107
Illinois Enterprise Zone 52, **13:** 61
Illinois Municipal Retirement Fund (IMRF), **12:** 107
iMesa (Mesa, Ariz.), **13:** 94
Immigration. *See also* Illegal immigrants
   legislation, **11:** 7, 25-26
   local government policies, **11:** 25-32
   national response to, **11:** 25-26, 27-28; **13:** 11
   rates of, **11:** 26, 27; **13:** 48
   reform, **11:** 7
   settlement patterns, **11:** 27
Immigration and Customs Enforcement (ICE), **11:** 28, 30
Impact fees. *See* Development impact fees
Impact Fees and Housing Affordability: A Guide for Practitioners (HUD), **12:** 28
Income disparity. *See also* Economic disparity
   assessments of, **13:** 4-7
   challenge for local government managers, **13:** 11-12
   consequences of, **13:** 7-9
   international comparisons of, **13:** 6, 7
   middle class and, **13:** 6-7
   national calculations of, **13:** 5-6
   perceptions of, **13:** 4
   political polarization as a barrier to addressing, **13:** 9-11
   tools for addressing, **13:** 12-14

An Inconvenient Truth, **11:** 6
Indemnity plans. *See* Health care plans
Independence, Miss., One Block at a Time, **13:** 90, 96
India, municipal management associations, **09:** 182-183; **10:** 176; **11:** 112; **12:** 140; **13:** 155
Indiana
   agencies for community affairs, **09:** 175; **10:** 169; **11:** 107; **12:** 135; **13:** 149
   association of counties, **09:** 184; **10:** 178; **11:** 114; **12:** 141; **13:** 156
   mandates, **10:** 49
   municipal league, **09:** 172; **10:** 166; **11:** 105; **12:** 132; **13:** 146
   municipal management association, **09:** 178; **10:** 172; **11:** 110; **12:** 138; **13:** 153
   pension costs, **09:** 55
   property tax, **09:** 60; **10:** 53-54
   red-light cameras, **09:** 58
Indianapolis–Marion County, Ind., centralized customer service system in, **12:** 12, 13-15, 19, 22
Individuals with disabilities, Supreme Court case, **10:** 70
Individuals with Disabilities Education Act (IDEA), **10:** 70
Indonesia, municipal management association, **09:** 183; **10:** 176; **11:** 112; **12:** 140; **13:** 155
IndyStat (Indianapolis, Ind.), **12:** 12, 13, 15, 19
Information access, citizen engagement, **10:** 30-32
Information Center (South Jordan, Utah), **10:** 40
Information technology. *See* E-government; Internet; Telecommunications
Infrastructure
   business incentives to improve, **10:** 4; **11:** 37, 38
   local government initiatives, **13:** 92-93, 96
   service decisions based on, **10:** 19-20
Initiative, local government provisions for, **13:** 30, 31, 32
Innovation and Efficiency Task Force (Phoenix, Ariz.), **13:** 94-95
Innovations. *See* Local government innovations
Institute of Internal Auditors, Inc., **09:** 314; **10:** 313; **11:** 125; **12:** 153; **13:** 167
Institute of Museum and Library Services, **12:** 6
Institute of Public Administration, **09:** 314; **10:** 313; **11:** 125; **12:** 153; **13:** 168
Institute of Transportation Engineers, **09:** 314; **10:** 313; **11:** 125; **12:** 154; **13:** 168
Intensive Care Coordination Project (Hampton, Va.), **10:** 39
Intergenerational planning. *See* Multigenerational planning
Intergovernmental contracting, trends, **09:** 11-20; **10:** 19-27
Intergovernmental relations. *See* Federal government; Local government; Mandates; State government; State-local relations
International Association of Assembly Managers. *See* International Association of Venue Managers
International Association of Assessing Officers, **09:** 314; **10:** 313; **11:** 125; **12:** 154; **13:** 168
International Association of Chiefs of Police, **09:** 314; **10:** 313-314; **11:** 126; **12:** 154; **13:** 168
International Association of Fire Chiefs, **09:** 314; **10:** 314; **11:** 126; **12:** 154; **13:** 168
International Association of Venue Managers, **09:** 314; **10:** 313; **11:** 126; **12:** 154; **13:** 168

International City/County Management Association. *See* ICMA

International Code Council, **09:** 314; **10:** 314; **11:** 126; **12:** 154; **13:** 168

International Conference of Building Officials. *See* International Code Council

International Council for Local Environmental Initiatives. *See* ICLEI—Local Governments for Sustainability

International Economic Development Council, **09:** 315; **10:** 314; **11:** 126; **12:** 154; **13:** 169

International Institute of Municipal Clerks, **09:** 315; **10:** 314; **11:** 126; **12:** 155; **13:** 169

International Municipal Lawyers Association, **09:** 315; **10:** 314; **11:** 126; **12:** 155; **13:** 169

International Public Management Association for Human Resources, **09:** 315; **10:** 314; **11:** 127; **12:** 155; **13:** 169

Internet. *See also* E-government; Social media; Telecommunications
   cloud computing, **12:** 87–88
   e-government and citizen interaction, **09:** 47, 49, 55; **10:** 30, 32, 40; **11:** 9–10; **12:** 5–6; **13:** 71–78
   legislation expanding broadband coverage, **10:** 59
   public access to, **11:** 9; **12:** 6

Iowa
   agency for community affairs, **09:** 175; **10:** 169; **11:** 107; **12:** 135; **13:** 149
   association of counties, **09:** 184; **10:** 178; **11:** 114; **12:** 141; **13:** 156
   bargaining-rights laws, **09:** 55
   cancer presumption laws for firefighters, **10:** 49
   council of governments, **09:** 186; **10:** 180; **11:** 116; **12:** 144; **13:** 159
   municipal league, **09:** 172; **10:** 166; **11:** 105; **12:** 132; **13:** 146
   municipal management association, **09:** 178; **10:** 173; **11:** 111; **12:** 138; **13:** 153
   recession of 2007–2009 in, **12:** 106
   traffic-control cameras, **10:** 52

Iraq war, **12:** 3–4

Ireland, municipal management association, **09:** 183; **10:** 176; **11:** 112; **12:** 140; **13:** 155

Israel, municipal management association, **09:** 183; **10:** 176; **11:** 112; **12:** 140; **13:** 155

Jefferson County, Ala., municipal bond defaults, **12:** 5

Jefferson County, Colo., approaches to budget retrenchment, **11:** 76, 77, 78, 79

Jersey City, N.J., gun control, **10:** 51

Job sharing, **09:** 28. *See also* Alternative work schedules

Job skills training, **09:** 43

Johnson City, Tenn., economic development in, **11:** 80

"Just compensation" legislation, **10:** 51

Juveniles. *See also* Child/youth programs
   child rape, **09:** 74
   with disabilities, **10:** 70
   health insurance legislation, **10:** 61
   intensive care coordination for, **10:** 39
   mental health programs, **10:** 63

Kaatz, James, **09:** 5

Kalamazoo, Mich., pension plan funding, **12:** 107

Kammerer, Gladys, **09:** 4

Kannapolis, N.C., bioscience research campus, **09:** 44

Kansas
   agency for community affairs, **09:** 175; **10:** 169; **11:** 107; **12:** 135; **13:** 149
   association of counties, **09:** 184; **10:** 178; **11:** 114; **12:** 141; **13:** 156
   municipal league, **09:** 172; **10:** 166; **11:** 105; **12:** 132; **13:** 146
   municipal management association, **09:** 178; **10:** 173; **11:** 111; **12:** 138; **13:** 153

Kansas City, Mo.
   Alternative Fuel Vehicle Program, **13:** 92, 96
   311 system, **12:** 12, 20, 21, 22–23

Kansas State University—Olathe Innovations Campus and Bioscience Park, **10:** 38

Keating, Larry, **09:** 6

Kellogg Foundation, **10:** 41

Kenai, Alas., environmental awareness in, **12:** 98

Kentucky
   agency for community affairs, **09:** 175; **10:** 169; **11:** 107; **12:** 135, 149
   association of counties, **09:** 185; **10:** 178; **11:** 114; **12:** 141; **13:** 156
   councils of governments, **09:** 186; **10:** 180; **11:** 117; **12:** 144; **13:** 159
   municipal league, **09:** 172; **10:** 166; **11:** 105; **12:** 133; **13:** 147
   municipal management association, **09:** 179; **10:** 173; **11:** 111; **12:** 138; **13:** 153
   pension costs, **09:** 55; **10:** 49
   sales tax, **09:** 59

Know Your Farmer, Know Your Food (KYF2), **13:** 43–44

Knoxville, Tenn., 311 system in, **12:** 12, 17–19

Labor, and economic development, **10:** 7, 8; **11:** 39

LaGrange, Ga., health care plan, **12:** 52

Lakewood, Colo., public-private partnership in, **12:** 99–100

Land availability and economic development, **10:** 7, 8; **11:** 39

Landfills. *See* Solid waste

Land use. *See also* Community development; Environmental protection
   local government authority over, **11:** 15–16, 18
   neighborhood creation and, **13:** 13
   state-local issues, **10:** 51–52

Larimer County, Colo., health care plan, **12:** 51

Las Vegas, Nev.
   approaches to budget retrenchment, **11:** 76, 77, 78, 79, 81
   Foreclosure Prevention Partnership Program, **12:** 101
   organizational design initiative, **13:** 95, 97
   use of GIS, **10:** 40

Law enforcement. *See also* Crime; Police; Public safety
   legislation, **09:** 66; **10:** 63–64
   local government authority over, **11:** 15–16, 18
   probable cause to arrest, **09:** 73–74; **10:** 66
   search and seizure, **09:** 73–74; **10:** 66–67, 71

Leadership in Energy and Environmental Design (LEED), **11:** 6, 53, 54

Leadership skills, of local government managers, **11:** 3-11; **12:** 3-9; **13:** 66-68

League of Women Voters, **09:** 315; **10:** 314; **11:** 127; **12:** 155; **13:** 169

Lean Government (Cape Coral, Fla.), **10:** 43-44

Leesburg, Va., biosolid fertilizer, **09:** 45-46

Legal cases. *See also* Supreme Court cases

    Allied-Signal, Inc. v. Director, Div. of Taxation, **09:** 77

    Arizona v. Gant, **10:** 66, 67, 72

    Arizona v. Johnson, **10:** 67

    Atkins v. Virginia, **09:** 74

    Bartlett v. Strickland, **10:** 68, 72

    Baze v. Rees, **09:** 74, 78

    Brendlin v. California, **10:** 67

    Brewer v. Williams, **09:** 73

    Buckley v. Valeo, **09:** 76

    Burlington Northern R. Co. v. Oklahoma Tax Comm'n, **09:** 78

    California Democratic Party v. Jones, **09:** 75-76

    California v. Greenwood, **09:** 73

    CBOCS West Inc. v. Humphries, **09:** 77

    Chimel v. California, **10:** 66, 67

    Coker v. Georgia, **09:** 74

    Crawford v. Marion County Election Board, **09:** 75

    Crawford v. Metropolitan Government of Nashville and Davidson County, Tennessee, **10:** 69

    CSX Transportation, Inc. v. Georgia State Board of Equalization et al., **09:** 78

    Davis v. Federal Election Commission, **09:** 76

    District of Columbia v. Heller, **09:** 72, 78

    Engquist v. Oregon Department of Agriculture, **09:** 76, 78

    Fitzgerald v. Barnstable School Committee, **10:** 70-71

    Forest Grove School District v. T.A., **10:** 70

    Gerstein v. Pugh, **09:** 73

    Gross v. FBL Financial Services, Inc., **10:** 69-70, 72

    Herring v. United States, **10:** 66, 72

    Kelo v. City on New London, **09:** 57; **10:** 51-52

    Kennedy v. Louisiana, **09:** 74

    Kirby v. Illinois, **09:** 73

    Ledbetter v. Goodyear Tire & Rubber Co., **10:** 65

    Maryland v. Wilson, **10:** 67

    Meacham v. Knolls Atomic Power Laboratory, **09:** 77, 78

    MeadWestvaco Corp v. Illinois Department of Revenue, **09:** 77

    Michigan v. Jackson, **09:** 73

    New Jersey v. T.L.O., **10:** 71

    New York v. Belton, **10:** 66-67

    Northwest Austin Municipal Utility District Number One v. Holder, **10:** 68, 72

    Pleasant Grove City, Utah, et al. v. Summum, **10:** 67, 72

    Polar Tankers, Inc. v. City of Valdez, **10:** 71-72

    Ricci v. DeStefano, **10:** 69

    Riley v. Kennedy, **09:** 75

    Roper v. Simmons, **09:** 74

    Rothgery v. Gillespie County, **09:** 73, 78

    Safford Unified School District #1 v. Redding, **10:** 71

    Smith v. City of Jackson, **09:** 77

    Steamship Co. v. Portwardens, **10:** 72

    Terry v. Ohio, **10:** 67

    Thornton v. United States, **10:** 66-67

    United States v. Leon, **10:** 66

    United States v. Miller, **09:** 72

    United States v. Wade, **09:** 73

    Village of Willowbrook v. Olech, **09:** 76

    Virginia v. Moore, **09:** 73-74

    Washington State Grange v. Washington State Republican Party, **09:** 76

    Whren v. United States, **09:** 73

    Ysursa, Secretary of State of Idaho v. Pocatello Education Association, **10:** 68, 72

Legislation. *See* Congress, U.S.; *specific legislation*

Legislative recall, **09:** 26, 27; **13:** 31

Legislative referendum, **09:** 26; **13:** 30-31

Leisure. *See* Parks and recreation

Lending ordinances, **09:** 58; **10:** 52

Lesbians. *See* Gays/lesbians

Lethbridge, Alberta

    deconstruction initiative, **12:** 100

    infrastructure initiative, **13:** 93, 96

Lewistown, Me., health care management system, **09:** 45

Licenses, gun, **09:** 72

Lifelong Communities (Atlanta, Ga.), **13:** 52

Lilly Ledbetter Fair Pay Restoration Act, **10:** 65

Lillydahl, Jane, **12:** 30

Lineberry, Robert L., **13:** 11-12

Littleton, Colo., economic gardening, **13:** 91, 96

Local government. *See also* Councils of governments; E-government; Municipal administration; Municipal government; State-local relations

    administrative capacity, **11:** 16, 17

    alternative service delivery, **09:** 11-20; **10:** 19-27; **13:** 79-87

    autonomy in, **11:** 13-23

    climate change, **11:** 47, 49-50

    collaboration in, **13:** 57-70

    development impact fees, **09:** 61; **10:** 54; **12:** 25-35; **13:** 51-52

    economic development policy, **10:** 3-9; **11:** 33-42; **12:** 25-35; **13:** 48-51

    equity in basic functions of, **13:** 12-14

    ethics in, **11:** 4, 7, 8

    financial controls, **11:** 15-17, 18, 19-20

    general operating concerns, **12:** 38, 39

    health care concerns, **12:** 38-43

    health care plans, **09:** 37, 39-41; **12:** 37-52

    home rule, **09:** 21-22; **10:** 47-48

    immigration policies, **11:** 25-32

    impact of e-democracy, **13:** 75-78

    leadership and management, **10:** 42-43; **11:** 3-11; **12:** 3-9; **13:** 57-70

    locally collected revenues, **09:** 59-62; **10:** 53-55

    mandates, **09:** 55-56; **10:** 49-50; **11:** 15, 17-18, 19, 20

    organizational design, **11:** 80; **13:** 94-95

    partnerships, **09:** 4 3-48; **10:** 4, 5, 7, 8, 38, 39, 41, 43; **11:** 37, 38, 39, 80-81; **12:** 97, 98, 99-100, 101; **13:** 39, 42-43, 61-62, 90, 91, 93, 96, 97 politics in, **12:** 4–8; **13:** 9–11

public participation, **13:** 71

recession and, **09:** 34–41, 68, 70; **10:** 33–36, 58–60; **11:** 5–6, 33–42, 69–74, 75–82; **12:** 4–5

reform movement, **09:** 4, 25–27; **10:** 10; **11:** 4; **13:** 11

retirement plans, **09:** 34–41; **10:** 35; **11:** 5; **12:** 5, 105–110

service improvements in, **12:** 12–19

social media in, **10:** 31; **11:** 9–10; **12:** 87

state financial aid, **09:** 62–63; **10:** 55

state intrusion into, **11:** 14–23

stimulus legislation, **10:** 58–59, 60, 63, 64; **11:** 37; **12:** 101, 105, 106

sustainability initiatives, **11:** 43–60; **12:** 54, 55–56

311/CRM systems, **12:** 11–24

tools to address income disparity, **13:** 12–15

volunteer use, **13:** 79–88

Local government innovations

affordable housing, **09:** 43–44

at-risk youth and juvenile offenders, **09:** 44; **12:** 97–98, 101

characteristics and principles, **09:** 49–50; **10:** 44

children and family services, **09:** 44; **10:** 39

citizen engagement, **10:** 28–32, 40, 44; **11:** 4–5, 9–10; **12:** 96–99; **13:** 93–94, 96

criminal justice and public safety, **09:** 44; **10:** 42; **11:** 80; **12:** 101

economic and community development, **09:** 42–44, 45; **10:** 37–39; **12:** 100–101; **13:** 90–91, 93–96

education and training, **10:** 38

e-government, **09:** 47–48, 49; **10:** 37–38, 40; **11:** 9–10; **12:** 11–24, 83–94

environmental enhancement and sustainability, **09:** 44, 45–47; **10:** 40–42; **11:** 6–7; **12:** 60, 97, 98, 99–100, 101; **13:** 91–92, 96

health and social services, **09:** 44–45; **10:** 39, 42

infrastructure, **13:** 92–93, 96

management and governance, **09:** 48–49; **10:** 42–44; **11:** 78–80; **12:** 98–99

organizational design, **13:** 94–95

public-private partnerships, **09:** 43–48; **10:** 38, 39, 41, 43, 44; **11:** 37, 38, 39, 80–81; **12:** 97, 98, 99–100, 101; **13:** 90, 91, 93, 96, 97

transportation, infrastructure, and public works, **09:** 45, 49

Local government managers. *See also* City managers

collaboration skills, **13:** 65–69

leadership skills, **11:** 3–11; **12:** 3–9; **13:** 66–68

Local Law Enforcement Hate Crimes Prevention Act (LLEHCPA) of 2009, **10:** 63

Local-state relations. *See* State-local relations

LODIS, the Local DNA Index System (Palm Bay, Fla.), **10:** 42

Los Angeles Times, **11:** 4; **12:** 63

Louisiana

agencies for community affairs, **09:** 175; **10:** 169; **11:** 108; **12:** 135; **13:** 149

association of counties, **09:** 185; **10:** 178; **11:** 114; **12:** 142; **13:** 157

mortgage foreclosures, **10:** 52

municipal league, **09:** 172; **10:** 166; **11:** 105; **12:** 133; **13:** 147

telecommunications, **09:** 58

Louisville/Jefferson County, Ky., 55,000 Degrees, **13:** 91, 96

Loveland, Colo., development impact fees, **12:** 27, 30

Low back pain, as an employee health concern, **12:** 43

Low-Income Home Energy Assistance Program (LIHEAP), **09:** 69; **10:** 63

Magnet Housing Program (Fairfax County, Va.), **09:** 43

Maine

agency for community affairs, **09:** 175; **10:** 169; **11:** 108; **12:** 135; **13:** 149

association of counties, **09:** 185; **10:** 178; **11:** 114; **12:** 142; **13:** 157

cancer presumption laws for firefighters, **10:** 49

municipal league, **09:** 172; **10:** 166; **11:** 105; **12:** 133; **13:** 147

municipal management association, **09:** 179; **10:** 173; **11:** 111; **12:** 138; **13:** 153

preemptive legislation, **10:** 53

service consolidation, **10:** 55

Management systems

executive styles, **09:** 6–7

innovative programs in, **09:** 48–49; **10:** 42–44; **11:** 15, 17–20; **12:** 98–99

Manassas, Va., Week of Hope, **10:** 38

Manatee County, Fla., improved health care in, **13:** 95, 97

Mandates, state, **09:** 55–56; **10:** 50

Manufacturing, economic development and, **11:** 34

Maritime Municipal Training and Development Board, **09:** 315; **10:** 314; **11:** 127

Maryland

agency for community affairs, **09:** 175; **10:** 169; **11:** 108; **12:** 135; **13:** 150

association of counties, **09:** 185; **10:** 178; **11:** 114; **12:** 142; **13:** 157

councils of governments, **09:** 186; **10:** 180; **11:** 117; **12:** 144; **13:** 159

development impact fees, **12:** 28

highway-user revenue, **10:** 55

municipal league, **09:** 172; **10:** 166; **11:** 105; **12:** 133; **13:** 147

municipal management association, **09:** 179; **10:** 173; **11:** 111; **12:** 138; **13:** 153

revenue sharing, **09:** 62; **10:** 55

schools, **09:** 62

speed-enforcement cameras, **10:** 52

tax increment financing, **10:** 54–55

Massachusetts

agency for community affairs, **13:** 150

association of counties, **09:** 185; **10:** 178; **11:** 114; **12:** 142; **13:** 157

home rule, **09:** 54; **10:** 48

local sales tax, **10:** 54

mandates, **09:** 56; **10:** 50

municipal league, **09:** 172; **10:** 166; **11:** 105; **12:** 133; **13:** 147

municipal management association, **09:** 179; **10:** 173; **11:** 111; **12:** 138; **13:** 153

property taxes, **10:** 53

state assistance to localities, **09:** 62; **10:** 55

sustainability initiatives in, **11:** 50

Maturing of America survey, **13:** 51, 52, 53–54

Mayor-council government. *See also* Local government; Municipal government

definition, **13:** 18

sustainability approaches in, **11:** 49–50

trends, **13:** 19–21

Mayors. *See* City managers; Mayor-council government

Mayor's Action Center (MAC) (Indianapolis), **12:** 12, 13–15

Mayors Climate Protection Agreement, **11:** 49–50

McGonigal, Jane, **11:** 10

McKinney-Vento Homeless Assistance Act, **09:** 68

McKinsey Global Institute, **12:** 6

McMinnville, Tenn., health care plan, **12:** 52

Medicaid, **10:** 62; **12:** 106

Medical care. *See* Health care

Medical insurance. *See* Health care plans

Medicare, **09:** 37, 39; **10:** 62; **12:** 45

Mental Health Parity and Addiction Equity Act of 2008, **09:** 67

Mentally ill individuals, coverage for, **09:** 67

Mentally Ill Offender Treatment and Crime Reduction Act, **09:** 67

Mesa, Ariz., iMesa project, **13:** 94, 96

Mesquite, Tex., health care plan, **12:** 52

Metro's Nature in Neighborhoods Initiative (Portland, Ore.), **10:** 41

Metro status

local government use of volunteers by, **13:** 87

multigenerational planning by, **13:** 51, 52, 53–55

service differences by, **10:** 24–26

Mexico, municipal management association, **09:** 183; **10:** 176; **11:** 112; **12:** 140; **13:** 155

Michigan

agencies for community affairs, **09:** 175; **10:** 169; **11:** 108; **12:** 135; **13:** 150

association of counties, **09:** 185; **10:** 178; **11:** 114; **12:** 142; **13:** 157

council of governments, **09:** 186; **10:** 180; **11:** 117; **12:** 144; **13:** 159

jurisdictional collaboration in, **13:** 61

mandates, **09:** 56; **10:** 49, 50

municipal league, **09:** 172; **10:** 166; **11:** 105; **12:** 133; **13:** 147

municipal management association, **09:** 179; **10:** 173; **11:** 111; **12:** 138; **13:** 153

residency requirements, **09:** 58

revenue sharing, **10:** 55

service consolidation, **10:** 55

state assistance to localities, **10:** 55

Michigan State University (MSU) Center for Regional Food Systems, **13:** 36

Middleton, Wis., food system development in, **13:** 39

Migrant workers, **11:** 7. *See also* Immigration

Migration Policy Institute, **11:** 27

Mihalic, Sharon, **11:** 64

Millionaire's Amendment (Bipartisan Campaign Finance Reform Act of 2002), **09:** 76

Minneapolis, Minn., 311 system in, **12:** 12, 20, 22

Minnesota

agency for community affairs, **09:** 175; **10:** 170; **11:** 108; **12:** 135; **13:** 150

association of counties, **09:** 185; **10:** 178; **11:** 114; **12:** 142; **13:** 157

municipal league, **09:** 172; **10:** 166; **11:** 105; **12:** 133; **13:** 147

municipal management association, **09:** 179; **10:** 173; **11:** 111; **12:** 138; **13:** 153

residency requirements, **09:** 58

state assistance to localities, **10:** 55

Minorities

birth rates, **13:** 48

election district lines, **10:** 68

employment discrimination, **10:** 68–69

Mississippi

agency for community affairs, **09:** 175; **10:** 170; **11:** 108; **12:** 136; **13:** 150

association of counties, **09:** 185; **10:** 178; **11:** 114; **12:** 142; **13:** 157

council of governments, **09:** 186; **10:** 180; **11:** 117; **12:** 144; **13:** 159

jurisdictional collaboration in, **13:** 61

local sales tax, **10:** 54

municipal league, **09:** 172; **10:** 166; **11:** 105; **12:** 133; **13:** 147

municipal management association, **09:** 179; **10:** 173; **11:** 111; **12:** 138

open-meeting laws, **09:** 55

red-light cameras, **10:** 52

sustainability initiatives in, **11:** 50

Missouri

agency for community affairs, **09:** 175; **10:** 170; **11:** 108; **12:** 136; **13:** 150

association of counties, **09:** 185; **10:** 178; **11:** 114; **12:** 142; **13:** 157

councils of governments, **09:** 186; **10:** 180; **11:** 117; **12:** 144; **13:** 159

eminent domain, **09:** 57; **10:** 52

illegal immigrants, **10:** 52

mandates, **10:** 50

municipal league, **09:** 172; **10:** 166; **11:** 105; **12:** 133; **13:** 147

municipal management association, **09:** 179; **10:** 173; **11:** 111; **12:** 138; **13:** 153

property tax, **09:** 60

red-light cameras, **09:** 58

transparency, **10:** 49

Mixed-income subsidy, **13:** 14

Mobile food vendors, **13:** 37

Montana

agency for community affairs, **09:** 175; **10:** 170; **11:** 108; **12:** 136; **13:** 150

association of counties, **09:** 185, **10:** 179; **11:** 114; **12:** 142; **13:** 157

municipal league, **09:** 172; **10:** 166; **11:** 105; **12:** 133; **13:** 147

municipal management association, **09:** 182; **10:** 175; **11:** 112; **12:** 139; **13:** 153, 154

red-light cameras, **10:** 52

Montgomery, Ohio, cross-team training in, **12:** 99

Monuments, in public parks, **10:** 67

Moody, Mitch, **12:** 26

Moore, Mark, **09:** 7

Morgan Hill, Calif., 22-Million-Pound Carbon Diet, **10:** 41

Mortgage Bankers Association, **09:** 38

Mortgages, recession of 2007–2009, **09:** 34, 38, 68; **10:** 33–34, 52; **11:** 34

Mullen, Clancy, **12:** 34

Mulrooney, Keith (past city manager, Claremont, Calif.), **09:** 8

Multigenerational planning. *See also* Older adults

　background, **13:** 51

　demographic and fiscal challenges, **13:** 53–55

　development strategies, **13:** 51–52

　metro status and, **13:** 51, 52, 53–55

　political coalitions, **13:** 52–53

　service integration, **13:** 52

Municipal administration. *See also* Canada; Chief
　　administrative officers (CAOs); City managers; Local
　　government; Municipal government; Salaries

　international municipal management associations
　　directory, **09:** 182–184; **10:** 176–177; **11:** 112–113; **12:**
　　140; **13:** 155

　municipal officials directory, **09:** 188–277; **10:** 182–276

　salaries, **09:** 81–102; **10:** 75–96; **12:** 72–78; **13:** 99–119

Municipal government. *See also* City government structure;
　　Council-manager government; Local government;
　　Municipal administration

　bonds, **12:** 4–5

　chief appointed official position, **13:** 21–23

　chief elected official, **13:** 22, 24–27

　committees and citizen boards, **10:** 29–30; **13:** 29–30

　council members election and terms, **13:** 27–29

　initiative, referenda, and recall provisions, **13:** 30–32

　legal basis, **13:** 21

　structural forms, **13:** 18–21

　structural trends, **13:** 32–33

　survey in 2011, **13:** 17–33

Municipal Partnering Initiative (MPI) (Glenview, Ill.), **13:** 94

Municipalities. *See* Directories; Finances; Local government;
　　Municipal administration; Municipal government

Muslims, religious discrimination against, **11:** 7–8

National Animal Control Association, **09:** 315; **10:** 314–315;
　　11: 127; **12:** 155; **13:** 169

National Association of Area Agencies on Aging, **13:** 51

National Association of Counties (NACo), **09:** 68, 70,
　　315–316; **10:** 62, 64, 315; **11:** 28, 127; **12:** 155; **13:** 170

National Association of County and City Health Officials, **09:**
　　316; **10:** 315; **11:** 127; **12:** 156; **13:** 170

National Association for County Community and Economic
　　Development, **09:** 316; **10:** 315; **11:** 128; **12:** 156; **13:**
　　170

National Association of Development Organizations, **09:** 316;
　　10: 315; **11:** 128; **12:** 156; **13:** 170

National Association of Housing and Redevelopment
　　Officials, **09:** 316; **10:** 315; **11:** 128; **12:** 156; **13:** 170

National Association of Regional Councils, **09:** 316; **10:** 315;
　　11: 128; **12:** 156; **13:** 171

National Association of Schools of Public Affairs and Admin-
　　istration, **09:** 316; **10:** 315; **11:** 128; **12:** 157; **13:** 171

National Association of State Chief Information Officers, **09:**
　　316; **10:** 315–316; **11:** 128–129; **12:** 157; **13:** 171

National Association of State Retirement Administrators, **09:**
　　36

National Association of Towns and Townships, **09:** 316; **10:**
　　316; **11:** 129; **12:** 157; **13:** 171

National Bureau of Economic Research, **09:** 34, 35

National Career Development Association, **09:** 317; **10:** 316;
　　11: 129; **12:** 157; **13:** 171

National Citizen Survey™, The, **11:** 70–74

National Civic League, **09:** 317; **10:** 316; **11:** 129; **12:** 157; **13:**
　　172

National Civilian Community Corps, **10:** 60

National Community Development Association, **09:** 317; **10:**
　　316; **11:** 129; **12:** 158; **13:** 172

National and Community Service Act of 1990, **10:** 60

National Conference of State Legislatures, **09:** 317; **10:** 316;
　　11: 28, 130; **12:** 106, 158; **13:** 172

National Defense Authorization Act for FY 2010, **10:** 63

National Environmental Health Association, **09:** 317; **10:** 316;
　　11: 130; **12:** 158; **13:** 172

National Fire Protection Association, **09:** 317; **10:** 316; **11:**
　　130; **12:** 158; **13:** 172

National Governors Association, **09:** 317; **10:** 316; **11:** 130; **12:**
　　158; **13:** 172

National Governors Conference. *See* National Governors
　　Association

National Housing Conference, **09:** 317; **10:** 316–317; **11:** 130;
　　12: 158; **13:** 173

National Housing Institute, **13:** 14

National Housing Trust Fund, **10:** 60

National Incident Management System (NIMS), **11:** 8

National Institute of Governmental Purchasing. *See* NIGP:
　　The Institute for Public Procurement

National League of Cities, **09:** 9, 318; **10:** 317; **11:** 76, 131; **12:**
　　4, 56, 158–159; **13:** 173

National Municipal League. *See* National Civic League

National Public Employer Labor Relations Association, **09:**
　　318; **10:** 317; **11:** 131; **12:** 159; **13:** 173

National Recreation and Park Association, **09:** 318; **10:** 317;
　　11: 131; **12:** 159; **13:** 173

National Research Center, **11:** 70–74

National Rifle Association, local gun control ordinances, **09:**
　　56–57; **10:** 51

National School Boards Association, **09:** 318; **10:** 317; **11:** 131;
　　12: 159; **13:** 173

National security. *See* Antiterrorism measures; Department of
　　Homeland Security (DHS)

National Service Trust, **10:** 60

National Telecommunications and Information
　　Administration (Department of Commerce), **10:** 59

Natural disasters. *See* Emergency preparedness; Federal
　　Emergency Management Agency (FEMA); Homeland
　　security; Hurricane Katrina

Natural resources, local government authority over, **11:**
　　15–16, 18

Navigating the Fiscal Crisis: Tested Strategies for Local Leaders, **11:** 76

Nebraska
    agency for community affairs, **09:** 175; **10:** 170; **11:** 108; **12:** 136; **13:** 150
    association of counties, **09:** 185; **10:** 179; **11:** 114; **12:** 142; **13:** 157
    municipal league, **09:** 172; **10:** 166; **11:** 105; **12:** 133; **13:** 147
    municipal management association, **09:** 179; **10:** 173; **11:** 111; **12:** 139; **13:** 153
    sustainability initiatives in, **11:** 50

Neighborhood Parks Council (San Francisco), **12:** 16–17
Neighborhood Quality of Life Study (Chesapeake, Va.), **09:** 42–43
Neighborhood Strength Index (Arlington, Tex.), **09:** 43
Nelson, Arthur, **12:** 26, 29
Nepal, municipal management association, **09:** 183; **10:** 176; **11:** 112; **12:** 140; **13:** 155
Netherlands, municipal management association, **09:** 183; **10:** 177; **11:** 113; **12:** 140; **13:** 155
Network governance, as community power structure, **09:** 6, 8
Networked Talent Model, **12:** 98–99

Nevada
    agency for community affairs, **09:** 175; **10:** 170; **11:** 108; **12:** 136
    association of counties, **09:** 185; **10:** 179; **11:** 114; **12:** 142; **13:** 157
    mortgage foreclosures, **10:** 52; **12:** 101
    municipal league, **09:** 172; **10:** 166; **11:** 105; **12:** 133; **13:** 147
    municipal management association, **09:** 180; **10:** 174; **11:** 111; **12:** 139; **13:** 154

"New federalism," **11:** 13–14
New Generations Initiative (Weston, Wis.), **12:** 60

New Hampshire
    agencies for community affairs, **09:** 175; **10:** 170; **11:** 108; **12:** 136; **13:** 150
    association of counties, **09:** 185; **10:** 179; **11:** 114; **12:** 142; **13:** 157
    benefits reductions, **09:** 55; **10:** 49
    home rule, **09:** 53
    mandates, **10:** 49, 50
    municipal league, **09:** 173; **10:** 167; **11:** 105; **12:** 133; **13:** 147
    municipal management association, **09:** 180; **10:** 174; **11:** 111; **12:** 139; **13:** 154
    revenue sharing, **10:** 55
    transparency, **09:** 55; **10:** 49

New Haven, Conn., fire department test for promotion, **10:** 69

New Jersey
    agencies for community affairs, **09:** 175; **10:** 170; **11:** 108; **12:** 136; **13:** 150
    association of counties, **09:** 185; **10:** 179; **11:** 114; **12:** 142; **13:** 157
    benefits reductions, **09:** 55
    eminent domain, **09:** 57; **10:** 52
    financial controls, **10:** 53
    gun control, **09:** 57; **10:** 51

    local finances, **09:** 59
    mandates, **09:** 56; **10:** 49–50
    municipal league, **09:** 173; **10:** 167; **11:** 105; **12:** 133; **13:** 147
    municipal management association, **09:** 180; **10:** 174; **11:** 111; **12:** 139; **13:** 154
    property taxes, **10:** 55
    service consolidation, **10:** 55
    state assistance to localities, **09:** 62, 63

New Mexico
    agency for community affairs, **09:** 175; **10:** 170; **11:** 108; **12:** 136; **13:** 150
    association of counties, **09:** 185; **10:** 179; **11:** 114; **12:** 142; **13:** 157
    cancer presumption laws for firefighters, **10:** 49
    councils of governments, **09:** 186; **10:** 180; **11:** 117; **12:** 144; **13:** 159
    mandates, **10:** 49
    municipal league, **09:** 173; **10:** 167; **11:** 105; **12:** 133; **13:** 147
    municipal management association, **09:** 180; **10:** 174; **11:** 111; **12:** 139; **13:** 154

New York City
    Islamic cultural center, **11:** 8
    NYC Service, **12:** 98
    311/CRM citizen satisfaction survey in, **12:** 19, 20

New York Daily News, **11:** 9

New York State
    agency for community affairs, **09:** 175; **10:** 170; **11:** 108; **12:** 136; **13:** 150
    association of counties, **09:** 185; **10:** 179; **11:** 115; **12:** 142; **13:** 157
    council of governments, **09:** 186; **10:** 180; **11:** 117; **12:** 144; **13:** 159
    jurisdictional collaboration in, **13:** 61
    mandates, **09:** 56; **10:** 49, 50
    municipal league, **09:** 173; **10:** 167; **11:** 105; **12:** 133; **13:** 147
    municipal management association, **09:** 180; **10:** 174; **11:** 111; **12:** 139; **13:** 154
    open-meetings law, **10:** 49
    service consolidation, **10:** 55, 56
    state assistance to localities, **09:** 62
    sustainability initiatives in, **11:** 50

New York State and Local Retirement Systems (NYSLRS), **09:** 38
New Zealand, municipal management association, **09:** 183; **10:** 177; **11:** 113; **12:** 140; **13:** 155
Newell, Charldean, **09:** 4
Newport News, Va., Open eGov, **09:** 47
Newport, Patrick, **12:** 4
Newsom, Gavin (mayor, San Francisco), **12:** 12, 19
Nielsen, François, **13:** 7
NIGP: The Institute for Public Procurement (formerly, National Institute of Government Purchasing), **09:** 317–318; **10:** 317; **11:** 130–131; **12:** 159–160; **13:** 173–174
No Child Left Behind Act, **11:** 18
Nonprofit contracting, **09:** 11, 12, 15–16

Norris, Donald, **12:** 85, 93
North Carolina
agency for community affairs, **09:** 175; **10:** 170; **11:** 108;
12: 136; **13:** 150
antismoking measures, **10:** 51
association of counties, **09:** 185; **10:** 179; **11:** 115; **12:** 142;
13: 157
councils of governments, **09:** 186; **10:** 181; **11:** 117; **12:**
144; **13:** 159
development impact fees, **12:** 28
home rule, **09:** 54; **10:** 48
local finances, **09:** 59
municipal league, **09:** 173; **10:** 167; **11:** 105; **12:** 133; **13:**
147
municipal management association, **09:** 180; **10:** 174; **11:**
111; **12:** 139; **13:** 154
sales tax, **10:** 54
state assistance to localities, **09:** 62
North Carolina Research Campus, **09:** 44
North Dakota
agency for community affairs, **09:** 175; **10:** 170; **11:** 108;
12: 136; **13:** 150
association of counties, **09:** 185; **10:** 179; **11:** 115; **12:** 142;
13: 157
municipal league, **09:** 173; **10:** 167; **11:** 105; **12:** 133; **13:**
147
municipal management association, **09:** 182; **10:** 175; **11:**
112; **12:** 139; **13:** 154
property tax, **09:** 60
recession of 2007–2009 in, **12:** 106
North Richland Hills, Tex., Cardiac Cath Lab, **10:** 42
Norton, Michael I., **13:** 4
Norton Priory Museum (Halton Borough Council), **13:** 91
Norway, municipal management association, **09:** 183; **10:**
177; **11:** 113; **12:** 140; **13:** 155
"Not in my back yard" (NIMBY) sentiment, **09:** 26; **13:** 52–53
Novi, Mich.
joint Public Safety Administration, **11:** 80
Novi Youth Council, **12:** 97–98
Nutrition, as an employee health concern, **12:** 41

Oakland Park, Fla., Fire Rescue Adaptive Response Program,
10: 42
Oasis: Citizens Online with Government (Seoul City, South
Korea), **10:** 40
Obesity, as an employee health concern, **12:** 40
Occupy movement, **12:** 4–6; **13:** 8
Ohio
agencies for community affairs, **09:** 176; **10:** 170; **11:** 108;
12: 136; **13:** 150
association of counties, **09:** 185; **10:** 179; **11:** 115; **12:** 142;
13: 157
councils of governments, **09:** 186; **10:** 181; **11:** 117; **12:**
144; **13:** 159
eminent domain, **10:** 48
gun control, **09:** 57; **10:** 51
home rule, **09:** 54, 58; **10:** 48
local finances, **09:** 59
local income tax, **09:** 61; **10:** 54

mandates, **10:** 49
municipal league, **09:** 173; **10:** 167; **11:** 105; **12:** 133; **13:**
147
municipal management association, **09:** 180; **10:** 174; **11:**
111; **12:** 139; **13:** 154
preemptive legislation, **10:** 53
residency requirements, **09:** 58; **10:** 52
telecommunications, **09:** 47–48
Oil spill (2010), **11:** 9
Oklahoma
agency for community affairs, **09:** 176; **10:** 170; **11:** 108;
12: 136; **13:** 150
association of counties, **09:** 185; **10:** 179; **11:** 115; **12:** 142;
13: 157
councils of governments, **09:** 186; **10:** 181; **11:** 117; **12:**
144; **13:** 159
illegal immigration policies, **09:** 58; **10:** 52
municipal league, **09:** 173; **10:** 167; **11:** 105; **12:** 133; **13:**
147
municipal management association, **09:** 180; **10:** 174; **11:**
111; **12:** 139; **13:** 154
sales tax exemptions, **09:** 56; **10:** 51
Olathe, Kan.
citizen engagement initiative, **13:** 94, 96
KSU—Olathe Innovations Campus and Bioscience Park,
10: 38
Older adults. *See also* Multigenerational planning;
Retirement; Retirement plans
age discrimination, **09:** 76–77; **10:** 69–70
economic development strategies focusing on, **13:** 48–49
government spending on, **13:** 48
health care, **09:** 37, 39–41
housing issues, **09:** 38–39; **13:** 51, 52
Maturing of America survey, **13:** 51, 52, 53, 54
recession of 2007–2009 and, **09:** 34–41
services for, **13:** 47, 51, 52, 53–55
in workforce, **09:** 39–40
O'Malley, Martin (mayor, Baltimore, Md.), **12:** 12
Omnibus Appropriations Act of 2009, **10:** 60
Omnibus Public Land Management Act, **10:** 65
One Block at a Time (Independence, Mo.), **13:** 90
O'Neill, Robert, Jr., **12:** 7; **13:** 11
O'Neill, Thomas ("Tip"), **11:** 31
Open City Hall™ (Peak Democracy), **10:** 31–32
Open eGov (Newport News, Va.), **09:** 47
Open-meeting/records laws, **09:** 55; **10:** 49
Operation No Vacancy (Hickory, N.C.), **10:** 38
Oregon
agency for community affairs, **09:** 176; **10:** 170; **11:** 108;
12: 136; **13:** 150
association of counties, **09:** 185; **10:** 179; **11:** 115; **12:** 142;
13: 157
cancer presumption laws for firefighters, **10:** 49
councils of governments, **09:** 186; **10:** 181; **11:** 117; **12:**
145; **13:** 160
development impact fees, **12:** 26
eminent domain, **09:** 57
municipal league, **09:** 173; **10:** 167; **11:** 105; **12:** 133; **13:** 147

municipal management association, **09:** 180; **10:** 174; **11:** 111; **12:** 139; **13:** 154

    sustainability initiatives in, **11:** 50

Organisation for Economic Co-operation and Development (OECD), **13:** 6

Organizational and Employment Development Program (Polk County, Fla.), **09:** 48

Organizational design initiatives, **13:** 94–95

Organized Retail Crime Act, **10:** 64

Oro Valley, Ariz., Energy Efficiency and Solar Project, **12:** 100

Other post-employment benefits (OPEBs), **11:** 5

Our Common Future, **11:** 43

Outsourcing. *See* Contracting

Overland Park, Kan., approaches to budget retrenchment, **11:** 76, 78

Palm Bay, Fla.

    LODIS, **10:** 42

    powered paragliders, **12:** 102

Palm Beach County, Fla., Children's Services Council, **11:** 64–67

Palm Beach Gardens, Fla., health care plan, **12:** 31

Palo Alto, Calif., and climate change, **09:** 46–47

Pammer, William, **09:** 9

Parks and recreation

    access for low-income individuals, **13:** 13

    local government authority over, **11:** 15–16, 17, 18

ParkScan (San Francisco), **12:** 16–17

Partnership regime, in community power structure, **09:** 5–8

Partnerships

    as economic development policy, **10:** 4–5; **11:** 37, 38, 39

    for food system development, **13:** 39, 42–43

    local government innovations, **09:** 43–48; **10:** 38, 39, 41, 43, 44; **11:** 37, 38, 39, 80–81; **12:** 97, 98, 99–100, 101; **13:** 90, 91, 93, 96, 97

Patient Protection and Affordable Care Act, **13:** 10

Pay-As-You-Throw program, **11:** 54

Payments in Lieu of Taxes (PILT) program, **09:** 70

Payroll deductions, First Amendment and state employee, **10:** 67–68

Peak Democracy, **10:** 31–32

Peak oil, **11:** 6

Pendleton Act of 1883, **10:** 10

Pennsylvania

    agencies for community affairs, **09:** 176; **10:** 170; **11:** 108; **12:** 136; **13:** 150

    antismoking measures, **09:** 56

    association of counties, **09:** 185; **10:** 179; **11:** 115; **12:** 142; **13:** 157

    gun ordinances, **10:** 51

    jurisdictional collaboration in, **13:** 61

    local income tax, **09:** 61; **10:** 54

    mandates, **10:** 49, 50

    mortgage foreclosures, **10:** 52

    municipal league, **09:** 173; **10:** 167; **11:** 105; **12:** 133; **13:** 147

    municipal management association, **09:** 181; **10:** 174; **11:** 111; **12:** 139; **13:** 154

    service consolidation, **10:** 55

Pension Benefit Guarantee Corporation, **09:** 35

Pension plans. *See* Retirement plans

Permit assistance, as business incentive, **10:** 4; **11:** 37

Personnel. *See* Public employees

Petersburg, Va., alternative programs for youth, **09:** 44

Pew Center

    report on climate change, **11:** 50

    surveys on income inequality, **12:** 4; **13:** 6–10

Philadelphia, Pa.

    public service areas, **11:** 80; **12:** 101

    residency requirements, **09:** 58

    revenue to meet pensions, **10:** 49

    311/CRM citizen satisfaction survey in, **12:** 20

Phoenix, Ariz.

    approaches to budget retrenchment, **11:** 76, 77, 78, 79–80

    form-based zoning code, **09:** 46

    Innovation and Efficiency Task Force, **13:** 94–95, 97

Photo identification, **09:** 75

Pickett, Kate, **13:** 9

Pinellas County, Fla.

    climate change, **09:** 47

    forecasting model, **13:** 95, 97

Pink, Daniel, **11:** 10

Pittsburgh, Pa., revenue to meet pensions, **10:** 49

Plano, Tex., development impact fees, **12:** 32–34

Plantation, Fla., health care plan, **12:** 51–52

Police. *See also* Crime; Law enforcement; Legal cases; Public safety

    DNA collection, **10:** 42

    local government authority over, **11:** 15–16, 18

    powers to impose impact fees, **12:** 27

    residency requirements, **09:** 58; **10:** 52

    salaries and expenditures, **09:** 55, 121–148; **10:** 115–143; **11:** 83–100; **12:** 111–128; **13:** 125–141

Police Executive Research Forum, **09:** 318; **10:** 317; **11:** 132; **12:** 160; **13:** 174

Police Foundation, **09:** 318; **10:** 317–318; **11:** 132; **12:** 160; **13:** 174

Political machine, as community power structure, **09:** 5, 7

Politics

    city power structures and, **09:** 3–9

    divisiveness in, **12:** 4, 6–8; **13:** 9–11

    health care reform, **10:** 61–62

    pension reform, **12:** 106, 107

    professional managers and, **12:** 4, 6–8

    social media in, **12:** 5–6

    stimulus legislation, **10:** 59

PolitiFact.com, **12:** 4

Polk County, Fla.

    approaches to budget retrenchment, **11:** 76, 77, 79, 80

    Budgeting for Outcomes, **10:** 43; **11:** 79

    Organization and Employment Development Program, **09:** 48

Pollution. *See* Environmental protection

Popular referendum, **09:** 26–27; **13:** 31–32

Portes, Alejandro, **11:** 27

Portland, Ore., Metro's Nature in Neighborhoods Initiative, **10:** 41

Powers, Rick (Indianapolis), **12:** 15

Predatory lending, **09:** 58; **10:** 52

Preemptions, state-local relations, **09:** 56–58; **10:** 51–53

Prentiss-Cooper, Hazel, **09:** 5

Presidential election of 2012, **13:** 9–11

Primary and Behavioral Health Care Integration, **10:** 63

Primary elections, **09:** 75–76

Prince William County, Va.

    approaches to budget retrenchment, **11:** 76, 77, 79

    DRIVE performance management system, **10:** 43

Privatization

    citizen opposition to, **09:** 18–19

    service delivery, **10:** 27

Prohibitions, state-local relations, **09:** 56–58; **10:** 51–53

Project for Public Spaces, **10:** 41

Projects for Assistance in Transition from Homelessness, **10:** 63

Property Assessed Clean Energy (PAE) program, **11:** 6–7

Property rights

    eminent domain, **09:** 57; **10:** 48, 51–52

    local authority, **10:** 51–52

Property tax

    alternatives to, **09:** 60

    economic development and, **11:** 35

    state-local issues, **09:** 59–60; **10:** 53–54

    on vessels, **10:** 71–72

Public employees. *See also* Health care plans; Retirement plans; Salaries

    alternative work schedules, **09:** 28–32; **10:** 35; **11:** 6

    local government responsibility for, **11:** 16–19

    recession and, **09:** 34–41; **10:** 34; **12:** 4, 5

    residency requirements for, **09:** 58; **10:** 52

    service delivery using, **09:** 12–15

Public Entity Risk Institute, **09:** 318–319; **10:** 318; **11:** 132

Public Housing Capital Fund, **10:** 60

Public parks, monuments in, **10:** 67

Public Plans Database, **12:** 105, 107

Public-private partnerships, **09:** 43–48; **10:** 38, 39, 41, 43, 44; **11:** 37–39, 79, 80–81; **12:** 97, 98, 99–100, 101; **13:** 39, 42–43, 61–62, 90, 91, 93, 96, 97

Public Risk Management Association, **09:** 319; **10:** 318; **11:** 132; **12:** 160; **13:** 174

Public safety. *See also* Crime; Law enforcement; Police

    appropriations, **10:** 63–64

    citizen engagement in, **13:** 93, 96

    innovative programs, **09:** 44–45; **10:** 42; **13:** 93

    legislation, **09:** 66–67; **10:** 63

Public Safety Employer-Employee Corporation Act, **10:** 64

Public schools. *See* Schools

Public Service Areas Model for Sustainable Change in High Crime Neighborhoods, **11:** 80; **12:** 101

Public Technology Institute, **09:** 319; **10:** 318; **11:** 132–133; **12:** 160; **13:** 174

Public welfare, local government authority over, **11:** 15–16, 18

Public works. *See* Electricity; Solid waste; Transportation

Puerto Rico, agency for community affairs, **09:** 176; **10:** 170; **11:** 108; **12:** 136

Quality of life

    Chesapeake, Va., study, **09:** 42–43

    as economic development strategy, **10:** 5; **11:** 33, 38, 39

    residents' assessment during recession, **11:** 72

Race

    economic segregation and, **13:** 9, 12–13

    election district lines, **10:** 68

    employment discrimination, **10:** 68–69

    income disparity and, **13:** 5, 9, 12

Rail Safety Improvement Act of 2008, **09:** 69

Railroad Revitalization and Regulatory Reform Act, **09:** 78

Rancho Cordova, Calif., approaches to budget retrenchment, **11:** 76, 79, 81

Rape, child, **09:** 74

Rating organizations for program accountability, **11:** 65–67

ReadyNation, **13:** 50

Reagan, Ronald, **11:** 13

Recession of 2007–2009

    defined, **09:** 35

    development impact fees, **12:** 32, 34

    economic environment and, **09:** 34–35, 68, 70; **10:** 58–60; **11:** 5–6, 33–42, 75–82; **12:** 4–5

    government benefits and, **09:** 37; **10:** 58–60

    government intervention, **09:** 41

    home mortgage foreclosures, **09:** 34, 38, 68; **10:** 33–34, 52, 59, 60, 63; **11:** 34; **12:** 4, 32, 101

    home values and, **09:** 38–39; **11:** 35; **12:** 4

    labor force participation and, **09:** 39–40; **12:** 4

    local job-generation stimulus programs, **12:** 100–101

    personal savings and, **09:** 37–38, 40

    residents' responses to local government services during, **11:** 69–74

    retiree health care and, **09:** 37, 39; **11:** 5

    retirement plans, **09:** 35–37, 40; **11:** 5; **12:** 5, 105–110

    stimulus legislation, **10:** 58–60

    unemployment, **10:** 33–34; **12:** 4

Recreation. *See* Parks and recreation

Recycling. *See* Solid waste

Recycling Investment Saves Energy bill, **10:** 65–66

Redistricting, Supreme Court cases, **10:** 68

Red-light and speed-enforcement cameras, **09:** 58; **10:** 52

Referenda, **09:** 26–27; **11:** 15; **13:** 30–32

Refuse collection and disposal. *See* Solid waste

Regional councils. *See* Councils of governments

Reiskin, Edward (San Francisco), **12:** 16

Religion

    discrimination based on, **11:** 7–8

    Supreme Court cases, **10:** 67

Renner, Tari, **09:** 4

Representative town meeting, **13:** 18, 19

"Republican Revolution" of 1994, **11:** 13–14

RequestIndy, **12:** 13

Residency requirements, state and local employees, **09:** 58; **10:** 52

Residential sector, economic development and, **10:** 6; **11:** 34

Resiliency and Preparedness Study (Flagstaff, Ariz.), **13:** 92

Resource Conservation and Recovery Act, **10:** 65

Retail/service sector, economic development and, **10:** 6; **11:** 34

Retention

    city manager survey, **09:** 3–5, 8–9

    strategy for business, **10:** 4–5; **11:** 33, 37

Retirement

    health care, **09:** 37, 39–41

recession of 2007–2009, **09:** 34–41
Retirement plans. *See also* Defined benefit plans; Defined
    contribution plans
    mandates for police and firefighters, **09:** 55
    market fluctuations, **09:** 36–37
    recession of 2007–2009, **09:** 34, 35, 40; **10:** 35; **11:** 5; **12:**
        5, 105–110
Retirement savings accounts, **09:** 37–38
Revenues
    locally collected, **09:** 59–62; **10:** 53–55
    recession of 2007–2009, **10:** 34–35
    regressive local government, **13:** 13–14
    state and local, **10:** 53–54
    state assistance to localities, **09:** 62; **10:** 55
    state raids on local, **11:** 15, 18, 19
Rhode Island
    agency for community affairs, **09:** 176; **10:** 170; **11:** 108;
        12: 136; **13:** 151
    mortgage foreclosures, **10:** 52
    municipal league, **09:** 173; **10:** 167; **11:** 106; **12:** 133; **13:**
        147
    municipal management association, **09:** 181; **10:** 174; **11:**
        111; **12:** 139; **13:** 154
    residency requirements, **09:** 58
    revenue sharing, **10:** 55
Rhynhart, Fred, **09:** 8
Ries, John, **09:** 4, 6
Right to counsel, Supreme Court case, **09:** 72–73
Rise of the Creative Class, The (Florida), **10:** 5; **11:** 38; **13:** 49, 50
Rizzo, Robert (Bell, Calif.), **12:** 63
Roads. *See* Transportation
Roanoke, Va., approach to sustainability, **10:** 41
Rockville, Md., approaches to budget retrenchment, **11:** 76,
    77–78, 79
Round Rock, Tex., regional utility partnership, **12:** 97
Rural Development Title, **09:** 67
Russia, municipal management association, **09:** 183; **10:** 177;
    11: 113; **12:** 140; **13:** 155

Safe, Accountable, Flexible, Efficient Transportation Equity
    Act (SAFETEA), **09:** 69
Safe Drinking Water State Revolving Fund, **10:** 60
Safety. *See* Public safety
Salaries. *See also* Employee benefits
    chief administrative officers, **13:** 99–124
    county officials, **09:** 103–120; **10:** 97–114; **12:** 63–81; **13:**
        120–124
    ICMA "Guidelines for Compensation," **12:** 63, 64, 67,
        68–69; **13:** 99–100, 101, 103, 105, 109
    municipal officials, **09:** 81–102; **10:** 75–96; **12:** 63–81; **13:**
        99–119
    pay decreases and furloughs, **13:** 105
    performance review and, **13:** 103–105
    police and fire personnel, **09:** 121–167; **10:** 115–162; **11:**
        83–100; **12:** 111–128; **13:** 125–141
    recession of 2007–2009 reductions, **10:** 34, 35
    variables affecting, **12:** 64–66
Sales tax
    economic development and, **11:** 35

exemptions, **09:** 56; **10:** 51
    locally imposed, **09:** 56; **10:** 54
San Antonio, Tex.
    approaches to budget retrenchment, **11:** 76, 77, 79, 80
    health services access program, **10:** 39
    infrastructure initiative, **13:** 93, 96
    311/CRM citizen satisfaction survey in, **12:** 20, 22
San Francisco, Calif., 311 system in, **12:** 12, 15–17, 19
San Gabriel, Calif., network management in, **09:** 8
San José, Calif., Green Vision program, **10:** 40
Sanctuary policies, **09:** 58; **10:** 52
Santa Rosa, Calif., and climate change, **09:** 46
Sapat, Alka, **09:** 5
Sarasota County, Fla.
    budgetary innovations, **09:** 49
    Challenges, Solutions, and Innovations Alliance (CSI
        Alliance), **12:** 98–99
    economic stimulus initiative, **10:** 38–39
Sawhill, Isabel V., **12:** 4
SB 1070 (Ariz.), **11:** 25–26, 28, 30
School districts, **09:** 62, 63; **10:** 55
Schools. *See also* Education
    children with disabilities, **10:** 70
    discrimination on basis of sex, **10:** 70–71
    rural, **09:** 70
    search of students, **10:** 71
Search and seizure, Supreme Court cases, **09:** 73–74; **10:**
    66–67, 71
Second Amendment, right to bear arms, **09:** 72
Second Chance Act, **09:** 67; **10:** 63–64
Second-order devolution
    degree of, since 2000, **11:** 14–23
    impact of state mandates on local governments, **11:** 17–18
    nature of state-local relations, **11:** 18–19
Section 8 Voucher Act (SEVRA), **09:** 68
Secure Rural Schools and Community Self-Determination
    Act, **09:** 70
Segregation, income inequality and, **13:** 9, 12–13, 14, 15
Senge, Peter, **09:** 8
Seoul City, South Korea, e-government in, **10:** 40
September 11 attack, **11:** 7–8. *See also* Antiterrorism
    measures; Terrorism
Serve America Act. *See* Edward M. Kennedy Serve America
    Act
Service integration, for child- and age-friendly communities,
    13: 52
Services, local government
    alternative delivery, **09:** 11–20; **10:** 19, 22; **13:** 79–87
    citizen interest, **10:** 20, 23, 26
    competition, **10:** 20, 23–27
    contract management, **10:** 19–21
    local government responsibility for, **11:** 16–18
    metro status differences, **10:** 24–26; **13:** 51, 52, 53–55
    residents' responses to during recession, **11:** 69–74
    shared, **10:** 35, 55–56
    surveys, **09:** 11–20; **10:** 19–27; **11:** 70–74; **12:** 19–23
    volunteer use, **13:** 79–88
Severance benefits, **13:** 106, 107
Sewerage. *See* Solid waste

Sex discrimination, Supreme Court case, **10:** 70–71

SFStat (San Francisco), **12:** 12, 16

Shaughnessy, Timothy, **12:** 29–30, 31

Shaw, Mississippi, **13:** 12

Singell, Larry, **12:** 30

Sister Cities International, **09:** 319; **10:** 318; **11:** 133; **12:** 161; **13:** 175

Six Sigma, approach to continuous improvement, **12:** 13

Sixth Amendment, right to counsel, **09:** 72–73

Slovakia, municipal management association, **09:** 183; **10:** 177; **11:** 113; **12:** 140; **13:** 155

Small-business development, **10:** 5; **11:** 33, 37–39

Small Communities Air Service Development Program, **09:** 69

Smart phones, **11:** 9

Smoking. *See* Tobacco issues

Snyder, Thomas, **12:** 25

Social equity, sustainability and, **11:** 7–8

Social justice, local government managers' view of, **13:** 3

Social media, **11:** 9–10; **12:** 5–6, 87. *See also* Internet; Telecommunications

Social programs, achieving accountability in, **11:** 61–68

Social Security, **09:** 37

as part of police and fire department expenditures, **09:** 126–127; **10:** 121–122; **11:** 94; **12:** 121; **13:** 135–136

for public employees, **09:** 37

Social services, innovative programs for, **09:** 44–45; **10:** 39, 42

Solar energy programs, **13:** 92, 96

Solid waste, innovative programs for, **09:** 45–46

Solid Waste Association of North America, **09:** 319; **10:** 318; **11:** 133; **12:** 161; **13:** 175

South Africa, municipal management association, **09:** 184; **10:** 177; **11:** 113; **12:** 140; **13:** 155

South Carolina

agency for community affairs, **09:** 176; **10:** 170; **11:** 109; **12:** 136; **13:** 151

antismoking measures, **09:** 56; **10:** 51

association of counties, **09:** 185; **10:** 179; **11:** 115; **12:** 142; **13:** 157

councils of governments, **09:** 186; **10:** 181; **11:** 117; **12:** 145; **13:** 160

home rule, **09:** 54; **10:** 48

illegal immigrants, **10:** 52

municipal league, **09:** 173; **10:** 167; **11:** 106; **12:** 133; **13:** 147

municipal management association, **09:** 181; **10:** 174; **11:** 111; **12:** 139; **13:** 154

traffic control, **09:** 61

South Dakota

access to government records, **10:** 49

agencies for community affairs, **09:** 176; **10:** 170; **11:** 109; **12:** 136; **13:** 151

associations of counties, **09:** 185; **10:** 179; **11:** 115; **12:** 142; **13:** 157

councils of governments, **09:** 186; **10:** 181; **11:** 117; **12:** 145; **13:** 160

municipal league, **09:** 173; **10:** 167; **11:** 106; **12:** 133; **13:** 147

municipal management association, **09:** 181, 182; **10:** 175; **11:** 111, 112; **12:** 139; **13:** 154

property tax, **09:** 60

sustainability initiatives in, **11:** 50

Southern Building Code Congress International, Inc. *See* International Code Council

South Jordan, Utah, e-government in, **10:** 40

South Korea, municipal management association, **09:** 184; **10:** 177; **11:** 113; **12:** 140; **13:** 155

Spain, municipal management association, **10:** 177; **11:** 113; **12:** 140; **13:** 155

Speak UP Winnipeg, **11:** 80

Special Libraries Association, **09:** 319–320; **10:** 318–319; **11:** 133; **12:** 161; **13:** 175

Speed enforcement, local authority over, **09:** 58; **10:** 52

Sri Lanka, municipal management association, **10:** 177; **11:** 113; **12:** 140; **13:** 155

St. James, Minn., citizen engagement in, **10:** 29

St. Lucie County, Fla., local job-stimulus program, **12:** 100–101

Standard City Planning Enabling Act (1934), **12:** 25

Standard & Poor's, **12:** 4

Standard State Zoning Enabling Act (1924), **12:** 25

Standing committees, **13:** 29

STAR Community Index, **11:** 7

State Children's Health Insurance Program (SCHIP), **09:** 68; **10:** 61

State enabling legislating, for impact fees, **09:** 61; **10:** 54; **12:** 25, 27–29, 32

State government

agencies for community affairs directory, **09:** 175–176; **10:** 169–170; **11:** 107–109; **12:** 135–137; **13:** 149–151

associations of counties directory, **09:** 184–185; **10:** 178–179; **11:** 113–115; **12:** 141–143; **13:** 156–158

financial aid for local government, **09:** 62–63; **10:** 55

municipal leagues directory, **09:** 172–173; **10:** 166–167; **11:** 104–106; **12:** 132–134; **13:** 146–148

municipal management associations directory, **09:** 177–182; **10:** 171–175; **11:** 110–112; **12:** 138–139; **13:** 153–154

State and Local Legal Center, **12:** 161

State-local relations

consolidation, dissolution, and cooperation, **09:** 63; **10:** 55–56

home rule, **09:** 53–54; **10:** 47–48, 56

income tax, **09:** 61

local authority, **09:** 53–58; **10:** 47–53, 56; **11:** 13–23

local finances/revenues, **09:** 59–63; **10:** 53–56; **11:** 15

mandates, **09:** 55–56; **10:** 49–50; **11:** 15; **11:** 17–18

prohibitions and preemptions, **09:** 56–58; **10:** 51–53

property tax, **09:** 60; **10:** 50, 51, 53–56

sales tax, **09:** 56, 60–61; **10:** 54

state assistance to localities, **10:** 55

state assumption of financial responsibility, **09:** 62–63

Stegman, Michael, **12:** 25

Story County, Iowa, food system development in, **13:** 39

Strategic Change Team (Carlsbad, Calif.), **09:** 48

Strategic planning

citizen engagement in, **10:** 28–29

recession of 2007–2009, **10:** 35

Stream, Christopher, **09:** 5

Streets. *See* Transportation

Stress management, as an employee health concern, **12:** 40–41

Subprime mortgage crisis, **09:** 68. *See also* Mortgages; Recession of 2007–2009

Substance Abuse and Mental Health Services Administration (SAMHSA) programs, **10:** 63

Sunnyvale, Calif., local job-stimulus program, **12:** 100–101

Supplemental Nutrition Assistance Program, **09:** 67

Support Our Law Enforcement and Safe Neighborhoods Act (SB 1070) (Ariz.), **11:** 25, 26, 28, 30

Supported Alternatives for Our Valued Youth (Petersburg, Va.), **09:** 44

Supreme Court cases. *See also* Legal cases
  age discrimination, **09:** 76–77; **10:** 69–70
  at-will employment, **09:** 76
  campaign finance, **09:** 76
  capital punishment, **09:** 74
  Civil Rights Act, Title VII, **10:** 68–69
  commerce clause, **09:** 77; **10:** 71
  constitutionality of lethal injection, **09:** 74
  cruel and unusual punishment, **09:** 74
  discrimination in public schools, **10:** 70–71
  discrimination in retaliation, **10:** 69
  disparate-impact claims, **09:** 76–77; **10:** 69
  due process, **09:** 77; **10:** 71
  Education Amendments Title IX, **10:** 70
  Eighth Amendment, **09:** 74
  eminent domain, **09:** 57; **10:** 51–52
  employee-payroll deductions, **10:** 67–68
  employment discrimination, **09:** 76–77; **10:** 68–70
  equal protection clause, **09:** 76; **10:** 70–71
  establishment clause, **10:** 67
  exclusionary rule, **10:** 66
  firearms regulation, **09:** 72
  First Amendment, **10:** 67–68
  Fourteenth Amendment, **09:** 76, 77; **10:** 70
  Fourth Amendment, **09:** 73–74; **10:** 66–67, 71
  free speech, **10:** 67, 68
  frisk of passengers during traffic stop, **10:** 67
  Individuals with Disabilities Education Act, **10:** 70
  local taxation on vessels, **10:** 71–72
  monuments in public parks, **10:** 67
  photo identification, **09:** 75
  primary elections, **09:** 75–76
  probable cause to arrest, **09:** 73–74; **10:** 66
  redistricting, **10:** 68
  right to counsel, **09:** 72–73
  search and seizure, **09:** 73–74; **10:** 66–67, 71
  sex discrimination, **10:** 70–71
  special education, **10:** 70
  taxation, **09:** 77, 78
  tonnage clause, **10:** 71–72
  Voting Rights Act, **10:** 68

Surface Transportation Board, **10:** 65

Sustainability. *See also* Environmental protection
  actions to promote, **09:** 45–47; **10:** 40–42; **11:** 43–60; **12:** 54, 55–56
  determinants of action, **11:** 47–52; **12:** 55–60
  economy, as a pillar of, **11:** 5–6
  environment, as a pillar of, **11:** 6–7
  factors influencing adoption, **12:** 55–59

innovative programs, **09:** 44, 45–47; **10:** 40–42; **12:** 99–100; **13:** 91–92, 96
  organizing actions for, **10:** 30; **11:** 47–50
  policy priorities, **11:** 46–47
  small communities and, **12:** 53–61
  social equity, as a pillar of, **11:** 7–8
  survey, **11:** 44–60; **12:** 54, 57; **12:** 60

Sustainable Cities Network, **11:** 44

Sustainable communities, **10:** 30; **11:** 4–5, 7

Sustainable Communities Initiative (federal), **10:** 63

Svara, James, **09:** 4, 7; **12:** 54

Sweden, municipal management association, **09:** 184; **10:** 177; **11:** 113; **12:** 140; **13:** 155

Systems Thinking, **11:** 62–63

Tax abatement, as business incentive, **10:** 4; **11:** 37

Taxes. *See also* specific types of taxes
  alternative minimum, **09:** 70
  from cell phone companies, **09:** 61
  exemptions, **09:** 56; **10:** 51
  local government authority to raise, **11:** 16, 20
  local revenue source, **09:** 59–61; **10:** 53–55
  multistate businesses, **09:** 77
  property, **09:** 60, 78, **10:** 53–54, 71–72
  sales, **09:** 56, 60–61; **10:** 51, 53, 54, 56
  state seizure of shared, **11:** 14, 15, 18
  Supreme Court cases, **09:** 77, 78

Tax expenditure limitations (TELs), **09:** 59

Tax Extenders and Alternative Minimum Tax Relief Act, **09:** 70

Taxpayer Bill of Rights (TABOR), **09:** 59; **10:** 53

Taylor, Sarah (Indianapolis), **12:** 13, 15

Teachers, residency requirements for, **09:** 58

Technology. *See also* E-government; Internet; Social media; Telecommunications
  cloud computing, **12:** 87–88
  digital, **12:** 5–6
  economic development and, **10:** 4, 6; **11:** 34
  local government trends in, **11:** 9–10; **12:** 5–6
  online services, **11:** 9–10; **12:** 6, 46–47, 85–86
  Y2K fears, **11:** 8

Telecommunications. *See also* Internet; Social media; Technology
  cable franchising, **09:** 57–58
  economic development and, **10:** 4, 6; **11:** 34
  legislation, **10:** 59
  state-local issues, **09:** 57–58

Telecommunications Act of 1996, **09:** 47

Telecommuting, **09:** 28. *See also* Alternative work schedules

Telluride Amendment (Colo.), **09:** 57; **10:** 52

Temporary Assistance to Needy Families (TANF), **10:** 59; **11:** 14

Tennessee
  agency for community affairs, **09:** 176; **10:** 170; **11:** 109; **12:** 136; **13:** 151
  association of counties, **09:** 185; **10:** 179; **11:** 115; **12:** 143; **13:** 158
  development impact fees, **12:** 28
  municipal league, **09:** 173; **10:** 167; **11:** 106; **12:** 134; **13:** 148

municipal management association, **09:** 181; **10:** 175; **11:** 111; **12:** 139; **13:** 154

open-records law, **09:** 55

sustainability initiatives in, **11:** 50

telecommunications, **09:** 58

Term limits

for chief elected officials, **13:** 24

for council members, **13:** 29

for county governing boards, **09:** 25

Terrorism, **11:** 8–9. *See also* Antiterrorism measures; Department of Homeland Security (DHS)

Terry, Larry, **09:** 8

Texas

agency for community affairs, **09:** 176; **10:** 170; **11:** 109; **12:** 136; **13:** 151

association of counties, **09:** 185; **10:** 179; **11:** 115; **12:** 143; **13:** 158

councils of governments, **09:** 186–187; **10:** 181; **11:** 117–118; **12:** 145; **13:** 160

development impact fees, **12:** 26, 27, 32–34

eminent domain, **10:** 52

municipal league, **09:** 173; **10:** 167; **11:** 106; **12:** 134; **13:** 148

municipal management association, **09:** 181; **10:** 175; **11:** 111; **12:** 139; **13:** 154

property tax, **09:** 60

telecommunications, **09:** 58

311/CRM systems

case studies of, **12:** 12–19

citizen satisfaction surveys, **12:** 19–23

popularity of, **12:** 20

Time management, city managers, **10:** 14–16

Tobacco issues

as an employee health concern, **12:** 41

legislation, **10:** 62

local restrictions, **09:** 56; **10:** 51

Tonnage clause, **10:** 71–71

Tourism sector, economic development and, **10:** 7

Town meeting, **13:** 18; 20

Traffic, local authority, **09:** 58, 61; **10:** 52

Traffic stops, frisk of passengers during, **10:** 67

Transforming Local Government (TLC) conference, **13:** 89

Transparency, in local government, **09:** 55; **10:** 49; **11:** 4

Transportation

federal funding, **10:** 63

highways and local government authority, **11:** 15–16, 18

innovative programs in, **09:** 45

legislation, **09:** 68–69

Transportation Security Administration, **11:** 8

Tupelo, Miss., Health on a Shelf, **13:** 93

2012 ICMA Compensation Survey for Local Government Chief Appointed Officials, **13:** 100, 109

22-Million-Pound Carbon Diet (Morgan Hill, Calif.), **10:** 41

Twitter

in local government, **10:** 31; **12:** 87

popularity of, **12:** 5, 87

Unemployment

jobs training programs, **10:** 63

during recession, **10:** 33–34; **12:** 4

Unfunded mandates. *See* Mandates

UNICEF, in food system development, **13:** 51, 52

Unigov (Indianapolis), **12:** 12, 13, 15

United Kingdom, municipal management association, **09:** 184; **10:** 177; **11:** 113; **12:** 140; **13:** 155

United States

demographic change, **13:** 47–49

income disparity, **13:** 3–16

presidential election of 2012, **13:** 9–11

Universal Public Procurement Certification Council, **09:** 319–320; **10:** 319; **11:** 133; **12:** 161; **13:** 175

Universities. *See* Education

Urban Affairs Association, **09:** 320; **10:** 319; **11:** 133–134; **12:** 162; **13:** 176

Urban Institute, **09:** 37, 320; **10:** 319; **11:** 134; **12:** 162; **13:** 176

Urban and Regional Information Systems Association, **09:** 320; **10:** 319; **11:** 134; **12:** 162; **13:** 176

U.S. Conference of Mayors, **09:** 320; **10:** 319; **11:** 28, 49, 134; **12:** 56, 162; **13:** 176

User fees, **10:** 54

Utah

agency for community affairs, **09:** 176; **10:** 170; **11:** 109; **12:** 136; **13:** 151

association of counties, **09:** 185; **10:** 179; **11:** 115; **12:** 143; **13:** 158

council of governments, **09:** 187; **10:** 181; **11:** 118; **12:** 145; **13:** 160

illegal immigrants, **10:** 52

municipal league, **09:** 173; **10:** 167; **11:** 106; **12:** 134; **13:** 148

municipal management association, **09:** 181; **10:** 175; **11:** 112; **12:** 139; **13:** 154

state involvement in local matters, **10:** 48

state statutes, **09:** 54–55

Utilities. *See* Electricity

Valdez, Alaska, local taxation on vessels, **10:** 71–72

Vermont

agency for community affairs, **09:** 176; **10:** 170; **11:** 109; **12:** 137; **13:** 151

home rule, **10:** 48

municipal league, **09:** 173; **10:** 167; **11:** 106; **12:** 134; **13:** 148

municipal management association, **09:** 181; **10:** 175; **11:** 112; **12:** 139; **13:** 154

state assumption of financial responsibility, **09:** 63

Vessels, property tax, **10:** 71–72

Veterans Service Corps, **10:** 60

Viet Nam, municipal management association, **10:** 177; **11:** 113; **12:** 140; **13:** 155

Villaraigosa, Antonio (mayor, Los Angeles, Calif.), **09:** 8

Violence, as consequence of income disparity, **13:** 9. *See also* Crime

Virginia

agency for community affairs, **09:** 176; **10:** 170; **11:** 109; **12:** 137; **13:** 151

association of counties, **09:** 185; **10:** 179; **11:** 115; **12:** 143; **13:** 158

councils of governments, **09:** 187; **10:** 181; **11:** 118; **12:** 145; **13:** 160

illegal immigrants, **10:** 52

mandates, **10:** 50

municipal league, **09:** 173; **10:** 167; **11:** 106; **12:** 134; **13:** 148

municipal management association, **09:** 182; **10:** 175; **11:** 112; **12:** 139; **13:** 154

schools, **09:** 62

state assistance to localities, **09:** 62; **10:** 55

Virginia Beach, Va., Virginia Green Destination, **13:** 90–91, 96

Virginia Tech shootings, **11:** 9

Virtual Supermarket Program (Baltimore), **13:** 91–92, 96

Visulia, Calif., citizen engagement in, **10:** 29

Volunteers/volunteering. *See also* Alternative service delivery

community, **09:** 48; **10:** 38; **12:** 98

local government service delivery, **13:** 79–88

strategic initiative, **09:** 48

survey, **13:** 79–87

Voting rights, Supreme Court cases, **09:** 75–76; **10:** 68

Voting Rights Act, **09:** 75; **10:** 68

Wages. *See* Salaries

Washington, Charles, **09:** 5

Washington, D.C. *See* District of Columbia

Washington State

agency for community affairs, **09:** 176; **10:** 170; **11:** 109; **12:** 137

associations of counties, **09:** 185; **10:** 179; **11:** 115; **12:** 143; **13:** 158

council of governments, **09:** 187; **10:** 181; **11:** 118; **12:** 145; **13:** 160

development impact fees, **12:** 26

local revenue, **10:** 55

municipal league, **09:** 173; **10:** 167; **11:** 106; **12:** 134; **13:** 148

municipal management association, **09:** 182; **10:** 175; **11:** 112; **12:** 139; **13:** 154

property tax, **09:** 60

record requests, **10:** 49

revenue sharing, **10:** 55

sustainability initiatives in, **11:** 50; **12:** 60

Washtenaw County, Mich., approaches to budget retrenchment, **11:** 76, 77, 79

Waste disposal. *See* Solid waste

Water Environment Federation, **09:** 320; **10:** 319; **11:** 134; **12:** 162; **13:** 176

Water pollution. *See* Environmental protection

Water Regional Utility Partnership (Round Rock, Tex.), **12:** 97

Watson, Douglas, **09:** 4

Weapons. *See* Gun control; Guns

We Are Legal (Fort Worth, Tex.), **12:** 101

Websites. *See* E-government; Internet

Week of Hope (Manassas, Va.), **10:** 38

Wellington, Fla., safe neighborhood initiative, **11:** 80

West Lethbridge Centre (Alberta), **13:** 93

West Vancouver, B.C., Community Centre, **12:** 98

West Virginia

agency for community affairs, **09:** 176; **10:** 170; **11:** 109; **12:** 137; **13:** 151

associations of counties, **09:** 185; **10:** 179; **11:** 115; **12:** 143; **13:** 158

councils of governments, **09:** 187; **10:** 181; **11:** 118; **12:** 145; **13:** 160

home rule, **09:** 54; **10:** 48

mandates, **10:** 49

municipal league, **09:** 173; **10:** 167; **11:** 106; **12:** 134; **13:** 148

municipal management association, **09:** 182; **10:** 175; **11:** 112; **12:** 139; **13:** 154

state assumption of financial responsibility, **09:** 63

Weston, Wis., sustainability policies, **12:** 60

Whitaker, Gordon, **09:** 4

Whitney, Meredith, **12:** 4

WikiLeaks, **11:** 10

Wilkinson, Richard, **13:** 9

Willis, Michael (general manager, Shellharbour City Council, NSW), **11:** 47

Windsor Heights, Iowa, citizen engagement in, **12:** 96

Winnipeg, Manitoba, community planning in, **11:** 80

Winter Park, Fla., Ambulance Safety Initiative, **09:** 45

Wisconsin

agency for community affairs, **09:** 176; **10:** 170; **11:** 109; **12:** 137; **13:** 151

antismoking measures, **10:** 51

association of counties, **09:** 185; **10:** 179; **11:** 115; **12:** 143; **13:** 158

council of governments, **09:** 187; **10:** 181; **11:** 118; **12:** 145; **13:** 160

gun control, **09:** 57

municipal league, **09:** 173; **10:** 167; **11:** 106; **12:** 134; **13:** 148

municipal management association, **09:** 182; **10:** 175; **11:** 112; **12:** 139; **13:** 154

pension plans, **12:** 5

service consolidation, **10:** 55

state assistance to localities, **09:** 63

telecommunications, **09:** 58

Workers' compensation, firefighters, **10:** 49

Workforce

immigrants in, **11:** 7

older adults in, **09:** 39–40

Work schedules. *See* Alternative work schedules

World Health Organization (WHO), in food system development, **13:** 51, 52

World Wide Web. *See* Internet

"World without Oil," **11:** 10

Wyoming

agency for community affairs, **13:** 151

association of counties, **09:** 185; **10:** 179; **11:** 115; **12:** 143; **13:** 158

municipal league, **09:** 173; **10:** 167; **11:** 106; **12:** 134; **13:** 148

municipal management association, **09:** 182; **10:** 175; **11:** 112; **12:** 139; **13:** 154

Yinger, John, **12:** 30
Y2K, **11:** 8
Youth programs. *See* Child/youth programs; Juveniles; Local
    government innovations
YouTube
    in local government, **10:** 31; **12:** 87
    popularity of, **12:** 5

Zoning. *See also* Land use
    as business incentive, **10:** 4; **11:** 37; **11:** 38
    for child- and age-friendly communities, **13:** 51
    neighborhood creation and, **13:** 13
    urban heat mitigation, **09:** 46
Zuccotti Park, **12:** 4